Community Justice

Table of Contents

1

❖

Criminal Justice
and the Community

Community justice is an emerging, innovative idea about the way criminal justice operations ought to be carried out in places where public safety is a significant problem and criminal justice is a significant fact of life. We call these locations high-impact areas because they are places where both crime and criminal justice responses to crime exist in concentrated levels. Community justice offers a way of rethinking how traditional criminal justice approaches to public safety can be reformulated to help make those high-impact locations better places to live and work.

Two assumptions are inherent within the idea of community justice. First, it is assumed that within existing jurisdictions, such as states or large cities, there are critically important differences from one community to another, and these differences suggest that criminal justice strategies need to be tailored to fit those differences. The same criminal law applies to everyone living in, say, California, but criminal justice strategies, if they are to be successful, will need to take different forms in locations as divergent as the crowded and impoverished Watts section of central Los Angeles and the pristine, wealthy neighborhoods of La Jolla. The second assumption is that formal systems of social control, such as the criminal justice system, are not the main mechanisms of public safety.

Rather, informal social controls—families, neighbors, social organizations, and friendship relations—form the most important foundation for public safety. Community justice, therefore, builds varying strategies of formal social control, depending on the particular problems facing the local area, and always has as one of its main aims strengthening the capacity of informal social control within that location.

High-impact areas are the logical targets of community justice initiatives because the formal and traditional methods of criminal justice have proven so inadequate in these locations. The criminal justice system identifies offenders, apprehends them, and imposes criminal sanction on them; but in high-impact areas, this focus on processing individual criminal cases through the justice system does not take into account the cumulative impact of these individual decisions when they disproportionately concentrate in specific places. In some high-impact areas, for example, more than 10 percent of the adult males are arrested, convicted, and incarcerated in any given year (Cadora & Swartz, 2000). However, the impact of removing these active offenders is blunted by the fact that an equivalent number of males re-enter this same neighborhood each year from prisons or jails. The collective impact of all these arrests, convictions, incarcerations, and returns can be a major destabilizing force in the neighborhood, exacerbating the effects of poverty, broken families, unsupervised youth, and unemployment. Without tackling these important aspects of community life in high-impact areas, traditional criminal justice is little more than a debilitating revolving door.

Community justice targets high-impact areas for another reason: these are where the problems are and where any progress made by community justice has the most payoff. A 10 percent reduction in crime in a neighborhood that has 10 crimes a year will barely be felt; but a similar impact in a high-crime location with, say, 1,000 crimes each year, will be a major improvement in the life of the community. This is the reason these areas are called high impact—the potential for impact by purposefully tailored strategies is much, much higher in these locations than in other areas in which problems are less severe.

Thus, community justice can be thought of as a broad strategy that includes the following priorities:

1. Community justice selects high-impact locations—places where there is a concentration of crime and criminal justice activity—for special strategies designed to improve the quality of community life, especially by promoting public safety.

2. Community justice approaches its tasks in these areas by working to strengthen the capacity of informal systems of social control: families, neighborhood groups, friends, and social supports. This means that instead of adopting the usual *reactive* strategy of merely responding to criminal cases as they occur, community justice undertakes a *proactive* strategy designed to work in partnership with these informal social control sources to strengthen the foundation for public safety.

3. In order to strengthen community capacity, community justice initiatives develop partnerships with residents, businesses, and other social services to coordinate the way public safety problems are addressed.

Community justice, therefore, is both a strategy and a philosophy. As a strategy, community justice broadens the responsibility of traditional criminal justice agencies to make room for partnerships with various citizen groups and other service providers so that a more comprehensive level of activity is sustained in the high-impact areas. Strategies of community justice are directed to deal with criminal events and to address the informal social control deficits that make crime possible. As a philosophy, community justice seeks to be evaluated for the way it responds to criminal events or even problems of public safety. It also accepts responsibility for helping to improve the quality of life and building social capital in the locations where community justice is most needed. Community justice brings important notions of social justice to the criminal justice agenda.

CRIMINAL JUSTICE
AND SOCIAL JUSTICE

Modern philosophers make an important distinction between criminal justice and social justice. Because both involve notions of justice, they are each based on the existence of a fair set of rules for how people treat each other and how citizens are treated by their government. Criminal justice is a type of "negative" justice. It is concerned with the way a society allocates undesirable experiences to its members. The study of criminal justice is the study of the rules, procedures, and practices under which citizens experience the application of a criminal label and the imposition of a criminal sanction. Criminal labels and criminal sanctions are considered just when they are imposed upon the guilty, but only when imposed within the rules of substantive and procedural due process.

By contrast, social justice is concerned with the distribution of "good" things within a society: opportunities for advancement, personal wealth, and other assets such as health care, housing, and basic goods of life. In a socially just society these benefits are provided by a fair set of rules and are applied to everyone equally.

Criminal justice and social justice, then, are both concerned with what people "deserve." Criminal justice is a set of institutions and procedures for determining which people deserve to be sanctioned because of their wrongdoing and what kind of sanctions they deserve to receive. Social justice is the set of rules by which people get the good things they deserve as a consequence of their talents and by the fruits of their efforts.

To a degree, criminal justice and social justice can be seen as flip sides of the same coin. When a person does something wrong, criminal justice ensures that the person gets the kind of punishment that goes with wrongful behavior. When a person's actions are meritorious—working hard and contributing to society—social justice requires that the person enjoy the benefits of having lived that way. We say that criminal justice is flawed when a person can break the law without suffering the consequences. Yet we also recognize that social justice is lacking when people are unable to get ahead, no matter how hard they might work or how much they might "play by the rules," because the cards are stacked against them.

Although perfect criminal and social justice is a laudable desire, we live in a society with well-known flaws in its criminal and social justice systems. Regarding criminal justice, we are troubled that innocent people are sometimes convicted of crimes and the guilty go free. In terms of social justice, some groups face unfair disadvantages that make it hard to succeed because of an uneven playing field. Both types of injustice make us ask hard questions about the fairness of criminal and social justice. We have a very strong cultural expectation that people should realize the consequences of their actions so that both those who break the rules and those who work hard and play by the rules get what they deserve.

Recently, we have come to see that criminal justice and social justice are related. The most obvious relationship is that places where people face the toughest odds against living out the American Dream are also the places where there is the most criminality. Crime and disadvantage are mutually reinforcing aspects of community life. The existence of disadvantage, in the form of an inadequate labor market, failing schools, and impoverished households, creates the foundation for drug markets and other criminal enterprise. At the same time, the existence of criminal activity makes neighborhoods less desirable places for people to live and for businesses to flourish, with the result that disadvantage becomes even more ingrained in these areas, and the people who try to live and work in these places find it harder to build successful lives.

The fact that social injustice and crime reinforce one another in high-impact areas has provided one of the main incentives for the development of community justice strategies with an objective of reducing crime, as well as the social injustices that accompany high rates of crime. Community justice brings together the two concepts of criminal justice and social justice to build a response to crime that takes both ideas into account. Community justice is a strategy of criminal justice because it is concerned with the problems that contribute to and result from crime. Yet the essence of community justice as a strategy is to strengthen the capacity of places that are hard-hit by crime; in that sense, community justice has a concern for broader matters of social justice.

The marriage of criminal justice and social justice is most evident in the way community justice approaches local areas with an eye toward building social capital. The aim of community justice is not merely to process criminal cases but to restore order, strengthen community cohesion, repair the damage from crime, and build partnerships that nurture a more beneficial community life. Taken together, these capacities represent social capital, which enables communities to act in defense of their interests and to pursue collective goals.

Community justice, therefore, is not simply about a desire to increase public safety. It is also concerned with the quality of public life and efficacy of collective community action. Using crime as a fulcrum for leveraging social capital, community justice seeks to improve the life of the community through attacking the problems that surround public safety and ultimately undermine the capacity of entire social groups in a place to advance their well-being. Criminal justice strategies are typically individual and negative: they remove residents, one by one, from their everyday lives and impose negative, undesirable sanctions upon each. Community justice gives attention to social justice, in that it is not merely negative and individual in its orientation. It seeks a positive, collective outcome as a response to crime: better communities. Because these aims are sought in the most disadvantaged areas of a jurisdiction, community justice is a vehicle of social justice.

THE IMPORTANCE OF "PLACE"

Community justice begins with an important insight about contemporary life: places matter. It is easy, in our modern society with its technological infrastructure, to think that space has constricted in size and that everything today is global. It is true that the advent of such everyday technologies as the telephone, television, and especially the Internet, has reduced the importance of distance as a constraint on daily living. Today, a person can talk to someone living thousands of miles away, see events as they are happening halfway around the globe, and chat by email with someone who is sitting at home on the other side of the country. Distance is no longer the all-encompassing limitation it was a century ago.

To recognize that space is no longer so impassable does not mean that local environments are unimportant. Where a person lives turns out to be one of the most important aspects of what that person's life is like. This is true in developing countries, where a person is born into a community that may become that person's environment for an entire lifetime, but it is just as true in a thoroughly modern society such as the United States. In this country, people commonly move from place to place precisely because where a person lives has so much to do with what a person's life is like. America, one of the wealthiest nations in history, is extremely segregated in the layout of its living areas—its neighborhoods. The poor, especially poor people of color, live in ghetto-like conditions where almost everyone shares a common dialect, dark skin, and poverty. Those with means move out to middle-class neighborhoods, where schools are better and expectations for life more optimistic. The affluent live in places where privilege dramatically expands the array of choices for spending their time and resources.

The place where a person lives greatly affects which schools that person's children attend, the leisure-time activities used to occupy time, the places the person eats, and so on. For the poor, who often lack easy access to transportation, there are other constraints. The neighborhood is the place that provides work opportunities (however meager) and is home to the friends that a person will have. Whatever is available in the form of recreation—and in poor areas, this is often very limited—will form the field of choices for spending free time. Shopping for groceries, clothes, and other amenities will be dominated by selections within walking distance. All this can be a bit easier in city settings, which is one reason that rural poor often migrate into dilapidated city areas.

Therefore, even though we live in the era of cell phones and Web searches, place matters. It sets the stage for how a person lives much of daily life and is especially important for those who lack the resources to easily leave their surroundings.

What Is Community?

In this book, we will commonly use the terms *community* and *neighborhood*. What do these words mean? Are they interchangeable? Do they have specific meanings we should keep in mind?

Much has been written in the attempt to define *community*, and there are numerous interpretations of the word *neighborhood*. In this book, we will often use the terms interchangeably. But these terms are not strictly the same, and it is useful to make some distinctions in the meanings as applied to the idea of community justice.

The term *neighborhood* is almost always used to refer to a particular geographic area within a larger jurisdictional entity. Neighborhoods of this type develop a reputation and an identity, and residents come to say, "I live in so-and-so." But the boundaries for these sorts of neighborhoods are not always concrete. People sometimes disagree about where one particular neighborhood ends and another begins. Over time, the boundaries of neighborhoods are fluid, and areas that were thought to be inside one area come to be thought of as belonging to another. Despite this definitional murkiness and spatial fuzziness—the idea of the geographical neighborhood is one of the more standard and traditional ways we understand the places where we live and work: downtown, north side, the Heights, west side, Maple Hills, the valley, Riverside, and so on—we learn to designate meaningful areas within larger jurisdictions, name them, and understand them as coherent neighborhoods, even though locating the actual boundaries of those places can be problematic. For the most part, when we say "neighborhood," we mean a coherent area within a larger jurisdiction that most people see as different in some meaningful way from the areas surrounding it.

The term *community* can be used to indicate a neighborhood, but it usually has more personal significance. Community refers to people more than places. Even when the community is a neighborhood, the term connotes people who live there, as in the Elm Avenue community or the West Atlantic community. When we hear these phrases, we think not only of location, but also of the people who live (or work) in those places. When we say "community," we also can mean more than just a location. Sometimes, the term is used to refer to a group of people who share a common personal identity, regardless of where they live: the Ukrainian community or the African American community. Used in this way, the term *community* designates a collection of people who see themselves as belonging together because of their backgrounds rather than their addresses. Another, broader use of the term refers to a group of people who share a common goal or set of interests. In this case, we would say that the student community, or the business community, has shared interests that, despite other differences, link them in the pursuit of collective goals.

Community and neighborhood are related in America because people who share common backgrounds or collective purposes often live near each other. Patterns of immigration have led to areas of cities dominated by people of like ethnicity: Little Italy and Chinatown are good examples. People who immigrated to the United States may have found it easier and more comfortable to live in areas where others from their country had already settled and where their native language was widely understood and spoken. Alternatively, they may have been victims of discrimination, and these areas were the only places they were allowed to live. Whatever the reason, ethnic enclaves typically developed in the urban centers as a consequence of waves of immigration.

This has also been true of internal patterns of migration, especially with regard to African Americans migrating northward from the South. These former slaves and offspring of former slaves came to America's Northern cities to find better work and to escape racism in the South; and when they arrived, they found themselves moving into areas populated by other urban African Americans. Again, this was a result of the dual pressures of housing discrimination and cultural comfort zones. Today in the Southwest, this pattern is repeating itself with regard to Spanish-speaking immigrants, legal and undocumented. Within cities, areas are coming to be dominated by those of Mexican descent, and these locations have the qualities of being both a neighborhood and a community.

It is important to stress that the neighborhood experiences of the last two centuries' waves of immigrants—Germans, Irish, Italians, Jews, and so on—emigrating here from Europe have not been the same as those of Blacks and Hispanics in the United States. Although many European immigrants have kept their identity as a community, they have been able to leave restrictive neighborhoods in a pattern of economically upward mobility. Over time, those whose parents were born outside the United States assimilated into neighborhoods where everyone's family did not hail from the same original location. Ethnic integration and even intermarriage have occurred, a process called the melting pot. However, people of color have not had the same experience. Many areas that were dominated by people of African descent nearly a century ago are still places where African Americans outnumber others by 20 or more to 1. This concentration of poor, economically immobile Black families has been referred to as "the Urban Underclass" (Wilson, 1980) and has not been broken down by the usual form of integration and assimilation that other ethnic groups experienced. Rather, it has experienced multiple generations of racial isolation from the mainstream and concentration in urban ghettos, without a reasonable expectation of any different circumstance. In the Southwest, the experience has not continued long enough to be determined the same, but there are troubling signs of a similar spatial concentration of Spanish-speaking poor in certain locations.

At the same time, communities of common interests, such as students or business owners, likewise suffer the effects of poverty, economic immobility, and social stigma. In socially isolated and economically disadvantaged districts, students endure run-down facilities, limited pedagogical resources, and an often disorderly and sometimes violent school environment. Similarly, local business owners experience fewer paying customers and lowered revenues and are unable to maintain their stores or provide quality products. When social isolation is coupled with economic disinvestments, we face a growing problem of concentrations of poor members of certain communities in certain neighborhoods, with little prospect of change.

How Do Neighborhoods Affect Community Life?

The problem of deteriorating urban neighborhoods is of deep significance to community justice. For people who find themselves born into these areas, place really does matter. There is diminished social mobility, economic viability, and personal possibility. Community justice, because of its concern for broader social justice, considers this aspect of poor places to be one of the most important issues that officials of justice must understand and confront. The place a person calls home affects the way a person lives.

Place and Life Chances   The most important way that a person's residence affects quality of life is through the way location influences later life chances. The term *life chances* refers to the possibilities people encounter in their lives and the likelihood that a person will be able to achieve personal and social goals. Being born to two, college-educated parents increases one's life chances, as does living in a wealthy family. On the other hand, being born into an impoverished, single-parent family or having a drug-addicted parent reduces one's life chances.

The idea of life chances is one way to keep the popular image of the American Dream honest. In this country, it is true that people who are born into deprived circumstances are free to work hard, apply themselves, and "make it." Some do. But people who start out with significant disadvantages find it hard to rise above them, and for most, there is little prospect of success in the upper ranges. The concept of life chances holds that most of the pivotal experiences of one's social and economic life—from getting into a college to landing a good first job; from developing social skills to meeting people who can help along the way—are established by the circumstances of one's birth.

One of these important circumstances is the place a person lives. "Bad" neighborhoods typically have a dearth of good choices: schools are usually below standard or worse, job prospects are limited, and positive youth activities are few. A short distance away, a "good" neighborhood will offer a youngster born there a good education, plenty of structured and safe leisure activities, and when the time is right, a convenient chance to make a little money while finishing an education. In the former area, kids, especially young males, find it easy to get involved in a gang, easy to start down the road of drugs and alcohol abuse, and easy to meet others who are involved in serious criminal activity; they find it hard to get reinforcement for keeping up in school, hard to envision a realistic road to a conventional life of success, and hard to develop the life skills that help a person succeed. In the good neighborhood, almost the exact reverse is true.

The way a person's place of residence influences that person's life chances challenges our sense of social justice. It does not seem fair that so much of a person's life is determined by the circumstances of birth, because where a person is born is a complete accident. Someone who happens to have a billionaire for a father will likely be wildly wealthy one day, but how can we say that this person's extreme wealth is deserved? Similarly, a child of a crack-addicted mother who grows up in homeless shelters will likely encounter the criminal justice system as a youth or even as a young adult; and even though we might all think that a criminal act requires a criminal justice response, it is hard to see how anyone could come from such circumstances unscathed.

Thus, place matters in life. It sets up a series of social circumstances that play out over time as a major part of a person's life story. If you disagree, try this exercise: Tell your life story to date. Make sure you try to do it in a way that helps explain why you are where you are and what is important about your life today. Then, notice that the significance of the role played by the circumstances of one's birth, including where you grew up and how you grew up there, is as determinative for everyone else as it is for you.

The Concentration of Crime and Criminal Justice Neighborhoods differ dramatically in the degree to which they experience crime and criminal justice. This is part of what makes the concept of community justice so important, because each neighborhood will face a series of different issues regarding crime and justice. A one-size-fits-all style of criminal justice may work in some places but will probably not be effective everywhere.

To understand how crime and criminal justice concentrate, we can use geographical analyses that show spatial distribution of each. For example, when we compare crime rates among police precincts in Brooklyn to incarceration rates among police precincts, the variations are remarkable (see Figures 1.1 and 1.2). The police precinct with the highest crime in Brooklyn has three times the amount of crime as the lowest. The difference in criminal justice activity is even more dramatic: the precinct with the highest incarceration rate has nine times more people per capita going to and from prison than the precinct with the lowest rate. These numbers tell a powerful story of what it must be like to live in these places. In the 73rd precinct, for example, crime is common, and a

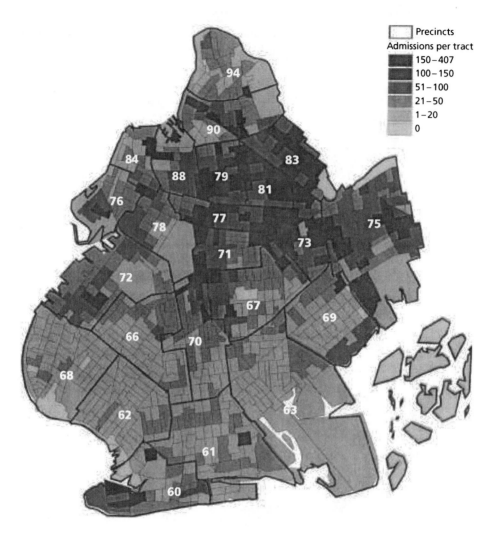

FIGURE 1.1 Jail and Prison Admission, Brooklyn, New York.

Map produced by Charles Swartz and Eric Cadora, Community Justice Project, CASES, copyright CASES, 2000. Data from New York City Department of Corrections, 1998; New York State Division of Criminal Justice Services, 1997.

large proportion of residents—one in eight adult males—is removed for incarceration. By contrast, both crime and criminal justice are comparatively rare in other locations only a few blocks away. In the former, crime and criminal justice are an everyday part of life; elsewhere, crime and justice are remote concerns (Cadora, and Swartz, 2000).

Place and Public Safety Recent scholarship has uncovered the importance of place as an element of public safety. This is most commonly understood through the idea of hot spots. For example, Lawrence Sherman (Sherman, Gartin, and Buerger, 1989) showed that in the places he had studied, the majority of crimes were committed in concentration in very specific locations—

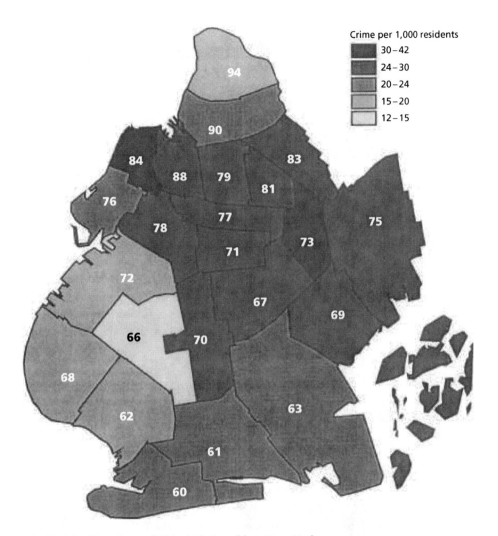

FIGURE 1.2 Crime Rates (FBI Index), Brooklyn, New York.

Map produced by Charles Swartz and Eric Cadora, Community Justice Project, CASES, copyright CASES, 2000. Data from New York City Police Department, 2000.

for example, street corners, blocks, or addresses—which he called hot spots. Crime is far more likely to occur in hot spots than in the immediate surrounding areas. Later researchers have found that the pattern uncovered by Sherman is the norm. A small number of specific locations account for a disproportionate number of police calls for assistance and reports of criminal events.

What are hot spots like, and how do they become problem locations? The answer is complicated because there is not a particular formula for a place becoming a hot spot. Often, but not always, there is a late-night tavern nearby; usually, there are dark streets or hidden alleyways. A couple of abandoned buildings or a secluded empty lot can also become a hot spot. What almost all hot spots have in common is not so much their physical attributes but the fact that they are configured to allow criminals to engage in crime with relative ease, and they exist in locations or neighborhoods where crime is generally higher than elsewhere.

The discovery of the existence of hot spots has had enormous impact on strategies of policing, as we describe in Chapter 2. The effective police administrator can target policing strategies surrounding these hot spots in order to cool them down or curtail criminal activity altogether. The first step is to use crime mapping to identify the hot spot; second, an analysis is made of what makes crime occur at the location; and third, a strategy is developed to overcome the factors in those locations that lead to crime.

The idea that crime concentrates in certain locations has led to new thinking about how to overcome crime there. Today, there are three main schools of thought about how to overcome problems of public safety that concentrate in certain areas: disorder, disorganization, and inadequate informal social control. These each make assumptions about the sources of crime and the circumstances that are thought to promote it. Although these models share some common themes, they are worth discussing separately in order to understand their core tenets.

Disorder Models: Broken Windows   The "broken windows" theory is one of the most popular ideas about the way crime comes about in urban settings. First enunciated by James Q. Wilson and George Kelling (1982) in an article in the *Atlantic Monthly,* the broken windows argument sees a link between urban disorder and crime that involves a process of deterioration in those areas. Disorder, in the form of trash, unsupervised groups of young men and boys, noise, and the broken windows that gave the theory its name, creates an atmosphere that makes people think a place is not being "taken care of." It becomes a distasteful environment, so the tendency is for people to stay away from an area where disorder predominates by avoiding it, moving to a new area, or simply staying indoors. This urban disorder also sends a signal to those inclined to engage in crime that such an area will not be cared for, so deviant or even criminal activity will not be stopped or otherwise hindered.

These two impressions of disorderly public space combine to make crime much more likely. Law-abiding citizens feel uncomfortable in disordered areas and do not remain there long. Offenders, however, feel empowered in these locations, and when they engage in minor deviance that seems to be allowed without formal controls, they interpret this as encouragement. Their deviance escalates from minor activity to ever more major crime. At least one study (Skogan, 1992) of the relationship between disorder and crime has supported this pattern.

Advocates of the broken windows idea should be and are the most interested in the repair of urban disorder. William Bratton was one of the first practitioners of the broken windows idea. When commissioner of the New York City subway system in 1990, he decided to keep the subway cars clean of graffiti and quickly stopped any other disorder in the subway. His strategy proved very successful, and the New York subways vastly improved.

Surprisingly, however, the broken windows idea has led to a different emphasis among law enforcement officials: arresting and jailing minor offenders. Their reasoning is that these are the people who break the windows in the first place; these are the people who create disorder and whose minor deviance in public space leads, inevitably, to an escalation of deviance and more serious crime. Many New Yorkers believe that the aggressive arrest policies of the New York City Police Department under Commissioner Howard Safir have played a major role in the dropping crime rates, although many citizens have been troubled by aggressive police tactics that affect young men of color more than other groups. Studies of crime in New York suggest that this strategy may have had less to do with the drop in crime than did new police practices targeting problem locations (Silverman, 1999) and changes in the socioeconomics and demographics of the city (Karmen, 2001).

Disorganization Models: Systemic Theory The first important theory of crime and place, called social disorganization theory, was developed in the 1940s by Clifford Shaw and Henry McKay (Shaw and McKay, 1942). Shaw and McKay were concerned with explaining why certain neighborhoods in Chicago seemed to produce the most juvenile delinquents, year in and year out. They theorized that something about those places made it more likely for kids to become delinquent. Their analysis highlighted three sociological characteristics that seemed to matter most: poverty, ethnic heterogeneity, and mobility. When these attributes are present, the society in these places becomes "disorganized," and young people fail to become adequately socialized.

It is easy to see why these characteristics might matter. Poverty has always been a foundation for crime, one reason being that poor people have less stake in the status quo. Shaw and McKay argued that ethnic heterogeneity led to a situation in which there was less acceptance and agreement about the norms of conduct in the neighborhood, because different groups would have different values. Mobility out of the neighborhood meant that there are more people entering and soon after leaving a place than there are long term residents; consequently, people did not stay long enough to form attachments to others and thus help build the strong sense of social interdependence that made crime less desirable among neighbors who knew one another.

Recent studies assessing the usefulness of the Shaw–McKay approach have found evidence that cuts both ways: not only have poverty and mobility contributed to crime, but reciprocally, crime itself has come to perpetuate poverty and mobility. Poverty continues to be such an important cause of crime that some scholars (see Wilson, 1980) have described an entrenched, inner-city poor so alienated from dominant economic and social forces that they form an urban underclass in which criminal activity becomes passed along intergenerationally and little hope exists for joining the economic mainstream. Ethnic heterogeneity is no longer thought to be as important as racial composition: areas where nearly 100 percent of the residents are African Americans living in multigenerational poverty are typically areas with very high crime rates. These are places where most people find it hard to gather up the resources to leave, and so mobility tends not to be the issue it was in 1940. Recent work on coercive mobility (Clear and Rose, 1999) suggests that the prison and jail system removes from and returns so many people to these areas that it has become the major source of destabilizing mobility in high-crime areas.

Social disorganization theorists seek strategies that "organize" neighborhoods by building social groups and creating political capacity. The idea is that a community that is organized can counter the forces of poverty, ethnic conflict, and outward mobility, which serve to promote disorganization in an area. Many studies have been conducted of community organization strategies (Moynihan, 1969), including the famous Back of the Yards Project of Saul Alinsky, which was designed to overcome the problems Shaw and McKay identified. So many community organization projects have been tried that it is impossible to summarize them in a few sentences; but it is fair to say that many of the community organization approaches end up in failure or attract strong resistance from city government, and getting the poorest communities to organize on their own behalf is very difficult.

Informal Social Control Models: Collective Efficacy A recent idea that borrows from both the disorder tradition and the social disorganization tradition is that of collective efficacy. Again, this work is based on studies in Chicago by Robert Sampson and his colleagues (Sampson, Raudenbush, and Earls, 1997), but it takes a different view of the way demographic forces work at the neighborhood level. The thesis of the collective efficacy idea is that crime is reduced when there are strong forces of informal social control at work in the neighborhood.

Informal social control comes from two sources: from families and other loved ones who exert controlling influences on the young people near to them; and from social groups and friendship networks that serve a similar function either in addition to or instead of families. Some neighborhoods have strong families or wide bonds of social relationships among adults and youth that lead to less criminal involvement by those youth. Other places have weak or "broken" families that exert inadequate control on the youth, and residents who neither know one another nor form social networks that have the capacity to support one another.

Thus, social networks—interpersonal relationships that people value and sustain—provide the ability for people to be collectively effective at producing control in the places they live. When social networks are weak or thin, there can be little collective efficacy. Research supports this view, finding that in neighborhoods where people know their neighbors and help each other, crime is lower regardless of poverty or racial composition (Sampson, Raudenbush, and Earls, 1997). Moreover, these studies find that disorder plays an insignificant role compared to that of collective efficacy.

Advocates of collective efficacy try to prevent crime by building social relationships in problem neighborhoods. They try to develop neighborhood organizations and centers that engage residents with one another, helping to develop social networks and strengthen social bonds. Unlike the externally directed community organizing that took place under the social disorganization model, which was aimed at organizing to get money and resources form city government, collective efficacy strategies try to build strength from within by forming groups that attend to neighborhood matters.

PLACE-BASED STRATEGIES AND PUBLIC SAFETY GOALS

This discussion of theories of community life and community safety leads us to a discussion of action strategies to produce greater public safety at the neighborhood level. We discuss two general types of strategies: community-oriented criminal justice strategies and community change strategies.

Community-Oriented Strategies in Criminal Justice

Because this book is devoted to the idea of community justice as a criminal justice approach, the chapters that follow discuss in detail criminal justice strategies of public safety directed at the community level. But it is important to recognize how these community-oriented criminal justice strategies for public safety are different from the traditional criminal justice approach, and we discuss five such ways. The themes we list here will be developed and elaborated in the chapters that follow.

Places, Not Just Cases The most important way that criminal justice changes its strategic approach in a community justice orientation is by focusing on the attributes and circumstances of places more than on cases. Because various aspects of places—neighborhoods and communities—are so important to forming and maintaining public safety, it makes sense to focus on places in order to produce safety. This focus means that physical aspects of areas afflicted with high crime are studied and, when necessary, altered: vacant lots are renovated into small parks or playgrounds, dark streets are lighted up at night, vacant buildings are torn down, streets that house open-air drug markets are closed off, and so forth. A concern for places also considers the importance of the people who live there. Residents are mobilized into action groups to provide support for one another and help reclaim public space. Child-care programs are created for unsupervised children. Job creation and placement programs are established for residents who need work. This, then, is a dual-track strategy: clean up the broken windows aspects of the neighborhood that tend to encourage criminal activity and organize residents so that more effective services can be provided to improve their prospects.

It is not easy or natural for criminal justice to change its level of focus from cases to places. Criminal events, and the people who are involved in them, are the inherent and, traditionally, only level to which the criminal justice system has attended. Police arrest suspects, prosecutors charge them, judges sentence them, and correctional officials supervise them. The expectation that all criminal justice action flows from criminal events and concerns itself with those events is deeply ingrained in traditional thinking. A concern for community-level issues does not replace the case-level action of criminal justice. After all, how individual criminal complaints are handled ultimately forms an important basis on which we evaluate criminal justice, even with a community focus. The concern for places, however, provides an additional target for criminal justice activity: to make neighborhoods and communities better places to live, work, and raise children.

Proactive, Not Reactive By adding a concern for places, community-oriented criminal justice begins by becoming proactive rather than simply reactive. By proactive, we mean that community-oriented criminal justice tries to head off problems before they occur, particularly by identifying the causes of public safety problems and overcoming them.

A case-level orientation is by its nature reactive. Nothing can be done about a criminal complaint until a crime has occurred (or is alleged to have occurred). But community-level problems, especially those that are cyclical in nature, can be dealt with *before* they happen. That is one priority of a community safety agenda, which seeks both to handle events that damage public safety after they have occurred and to prevent their occurrence in the first place.

Just as the focus on places does not replace a focus on cases, the concern for proactive strategies does not eliminate the need for effective ways of reacting to criminal events that occur despite the proactive work. Criminal justice will always be evaluated, at least partly, on how well it responds to crimes that have occurred. The advent of community justice has meant that criminal justice is also evaluated on the extent to which criminal justice has been able to build strategies that prevent crime from occurring in the first place. This is especially true for both individual-level and community-level strategies.

Problem Solving, Not Just Blaming Traditional criminal justice has been described as a "blaming" and "sanctioning" institution. Legal philosopher Andrew von Hirsch (1993) has pointed out that a criminal conviction requires both a finding of personal culpability and a finding of blameworthiness. In finding a person guilty of a crime, we hold not only that the person did the crime (culpability), but also that the person was wrong to have done it (blameworthiness). From this perspective, the "problem" of a crime is that a person appears to have committed one, and the "solution" is that the person needs to be punished.

Community-oriented criminal justice recognizes that a much broader view of the problem of crime is needed. How the crime affects the victim and the community is a potential problem that needs to be addressed; how the sanction might affect the offender and those close to that offender also matters. Just as significant is the need to gain an understanding of the problems that may have given rise to the crime, and then to try to address those as part of the prevention agenda of public safety.

Under a community-oriented criminal justice philosophy, it is quite reasonable to expect that wrongdoers will be found culpable and blamed for what they have done. It is also expected that the problems the crime has created for the community and the victim will be addressed, and the problems that a sanction will impose on those who are connected to the offender will be considered in determining how to sanction the offender. Another objective of the community justice orientation is to identify the problems in the community that make crime more likely to occur and to try to reduce their impact on community life. Building public safety is thus seen as a challenge to the system's problem-solving capacity at several levels.

Decentralization, Not Hierarchy Because criminal justice so often places a premium on the use of authority in response to crime, there is a tendency for criminal justice organizations to have a hierarchical, authoritarian style: a chief district attorney to whom everyone else is an assistant, and a chief probation officer to whom everyone else is a deputy. The same kind of hierarchical structure is common in law enforcement and institutional corrections, with chain of command, operations manuals, and standard rules and procedures. In this kind of organization, authority is concentrated at the top, and discretion is limited at the bottom.

Community-oriented criminal justice strategies cannot operate within a rigid, hierarchical organizational culture. There are several reasons for this, but two are prominent. First, because these strategies tend to be oriented to particular places—neighborhoods—that exist within larger legal jurisdictions, it is necessary to decentralize leadership to those subjurisdictional levels. Criminal justice officials who are responsible for services delivered in particular neighborhoods have to have a certain autonomy to work in those neighborhoods. This autonomy is made necessary by the second reason for decentralization: neighborhoods are not all alike, so a degree of flexibility is needed to tailor activity to fit the particulars of the given neighborhood. Even though it is essential that the law give all citizens equal protection, the justice official working in a particular neighborhood must form relationships with residents and businesses there, develop problem-solving strategies that meet neighborhood needs, and give priority to certain issues that are most important in that neighborhood. A command structure, where every decision emanates from the very top of the organization, simply does not fit this philosophy of service delivery at the neighborhood level.

Fluid Organizational Boundaries, Not Fragmented Organizational Accountability Traditional criminal justice organizations have a sense of their "turf" and work hard to protect it. Police do not like meddling by courts, prosecutors, or correctional officials; prosecutors are not concerned with how their work affects other parts of the system; and so forth. In classic organization theory, criminal justice organizations work hard to protect their boundaries from incursion by other organizations, even sister organizations serving the same constituency.

Community-oriented approaches form partnerships at the neighborhood level, and protecting organizational boundaries takes a backseat to the need to form and sustain cross-organizational strategies that produce public safety. Police and probation officers start to work together, and court services intermingle with traditional social services to provide a more comprehensive response to the problems arising from crime that are faced by victims, offenders, and other citizens. A premium is placed on effective coordination and cooperation, not effective separation.

Comprehensive Community Change Initiatives

Some neighborhoods face multiple problems besides those of public safety, including housing, employment, child care, and health. Each of these problems is difficult on its own, but together they can create a daunting situation for those who want to improve the neighborhood's prospects. These issues are not easy to deal with because they are interconnected. People with poor health find it difficult to obtain or maintain good jobs, for example, and single mothers cannot easily work without child care.

In recent years, a new strategy for addressing the multidimensional aspects of poor communities has emerged, called comprehensive community change (CCC). CCCs are systematic ways to confront the most entrenched problems communities face. In most cases, they work by establishing a local development corporation that operates under legal authority to build approaches that confront the communities' most pressing problems. CCCs that take the form of neighborhood development corporations composed of resident staff and volunteers are referred to as local intermediaries. They are local in that they do not address problems outside the specific neighborhood boundaries within which they work. They are intermediaries in that they build partnerships among business, services, and institutions operating inside the neighborhood, and they seek grants and other funds to establish new services or augment existing services for the neighborhood area. Sometimes, they provide the services themselves, but other times they help bring together organizations and individuals who are better positioned to provide the services themselves.

The starting place for CCCs, and their most successful area of work, has been housing. Working in neighborhoods where affordable housing was a real need, CCCs brought together investors, builders, and community groups to take advantage of federal tax credits and create a climate in which the renovation and construction of housing was more likely to succeed, both financially and socially. With a history of success in developing housing, CCCs have more recently turned their attention to creating jobs and improving services for children, especially health care for infants and expectant mothers.

Some people believe that a natural next step in this work is to undertake public safety concerns. This seems to be an obvious expansion of the CCC idea because the lessons learned by focusing on housing, employment, and youth fit well into the problems surrounding public safety. Following are three examples.

Political Empowerment Most people think of community organizing as a process by which residents band together and march on City Hall to demand new services, more resources, and attention for their political leadership. But one of the most important new lessons of the CCC movement has been that this form of confrontational organizing often does not work in the face of more insidious contemporary responses. As with any power-based confrontation, there is the ever-present prospect of confronting a more powerful opponent. City Hall can overcome this sort of pressure in a number of ways: build a counter pressure bloc, pit one neighborhood against another, or even buy off some of the leaders of the complaining group. The approach can even backfire if the neighborhood comes to be seen as a political problem and no political actors want to be associated with it. City Hall may dig in its heels to teach the organizing group a lesson or to avoid having to face similar claims from other sources. Confrontational strategies, although sometimes unavoidable, rarely work out as intended and usually lead to a series of countermoves by opposing political forces.

Therefore, some CCCs have developed a new understanding in recent years of what it means to be empowered and what empowerment requires. In these cases, rather than try to become powerful "against" some group, neighborhoods try to find a way to align themselves with interests that are strong, redirect the efforts of those interests toward mutually beneficial outcomes, and gain power through this coalition of interest groups. For example, a neighborhood that wants to renovate its schools will find that rather than march on City Hall, it will have more success by building a cooperative relationship among a firm that does renovation, a bank that wants to invest in improving the community, and a citizens' group willing to volunteer time working on the project. Rather than start a public outcry for more police protection—which, even if responded to positively, may not address the core issues and may produce other unintended consequences—the neighborhood will have more success by developing relationships among a local parents' group, the police precinct leadership, and some of the local faith leaders. Today, grassroots approaches to organizing are increasingly employing more sophisticated ways to create power by bringing together groups who share a common interest in solving the underlying problem.

Economic Development Economic development is one of the best areas in which mutual interests can lead to empowerment. Investors know that places where employment is low, people are poor, and businesses are few—as in most high-crime areas—are places where it is very hard to establish a profitable business. At the same time, these locations represent untapped markets because there is such a dearth of business that the competition is slim. If a few of the problems these places face can be alleviated, they will become wide open as potential markets for new businesses, especially businesses that provide basic goods and services to local residents.

Seeing these areas as opportunities for economic development rather than as economic disasters opens up an entirely new conversation about them. Instead of avoiding them, businesses should be encouraged to form partnerships to help cultivate these changes. For example, construction firms that renovate existing structures stand to benefit as partners when investors open up new businesses in these areas, and employers stand to benefit when housing improvements lead to a more stable residential population. For all parties, providing an environment where there are fewer public safety problems is an essential foundation for economic expansion. Therefore, CCIs have started fashioning a workable partnership among investors, housing interests, and renovators that can create a basis for economic improvement. Here again, it is the act of forging partnerships among those whose interests align that creates the empowerment needed to establish economic improvements.

Service Sector Improvements In most areas, services are provided by separate agencies operating in a fragmented manner. In multiproblem areas, residents often are in contact with more than one service provider at a time: it is not uncommon for a single family to have different members involved with welfare, housing support, child care, and health care. Again, this is an area where forging coalitions of organizations whose interests align can help solve problems. In a kind of one-stop-service-center model in these communities, local organizations have been facilitating the creation of service consortiums that work together in the same building, enabling them to coordinate and strengthen their services to those in need. CCIs often provide office space to these entities, and they channel residents to those comprehensive service centers.

Public safety organizations have observed these CCI-based strategies and have begun to see how these approaches can be adapted to the public safety agenda. They see, for example, the profound empowerment that occurs when private and public interests combine to create solutions to the problems that make public safety a priority. They can see how economic development and public safety go hand in hand, and making headway on one necessitates improvements in the other. They can also see how creating effective partnerships among justice service providers can increase the impact of those services. The CCC model, therefore, has lessons for those who would seek to promote community justice.

COMMUNITY JUSTICE WITHIN TRADITIONAL CRIMINAL JUSTICE FUNCTIONS

Community justice ideas are not new to the criminal justice system. The main criminal justice organizations—police, courts, and corrections—have been exploring various ways to improve community relevance with new programs and strategies, and these have formed the basis for a more comprehensive understanding of the possibility of community justice more broadly realized. The following discussion illustrates the ways some criminal justice agencies have been approaching community-oriented activity.

Police

In the mid-1980s, a small group of policing leaders and scholars convened at Harvard University's Kennedy School of Government to discuss the crisis facing American policing. This crisis was seen as stemming from lack of public confidence in the police and a long list of studies showing that the most commonly emphasized police strategies, from 911 calls to intensified patrol, had little effect on crime but carried severe, negative side effects, such as overemphasis of police response time and loss of public trust. This group was looking for a new paradigm for policing in America, and they developed the idea of community-oriented policing. Within a few years, this concept had swept across the country and soon became the standard operating theory, if not always the method, of police in America.

Along with the idea of community-oriented policing services came a renewed commitment to experimentation and innovation in police work. Police agencies became leaders in community organizing, developed new partnerships with businesses and civic organizations, and started trying to prevent the patterned recurrence of crime by using problem-solving methods rather than merely responding to crime with the traditional tools of investigation and arrest. In various departments around the country, place-based policing strategies began to pay off in reductions in crime: New York City's CompStat (computerized statistics), San Diego's Community Policing, and Boston's Operation Night Light (all of which are discussed in the chapters that follow) served as examples to the nation of what could be done to prevent crime if police put down their operations manuals and began working with the people and the problems that presented themselves in the neighborhoods they served.

Among the three arms of the criminal justice system—police, courts, and corrections—policing has undergone the most thorough philosophical reorientation toward community justice. There are two probable reasons for the prevalence of community justice ideas within policing. The first is that the inadequacies of criminal justice are most directly experienced by citizens as policing problems because the police are in more direct contact with community members. That visibility has led both to higher expectations and more available targets of praise and criticism. Second, the nature of policing has always been more oriented to geographical or place-based strategies and tactics. The fact that police departments have traditionally been organized according to more discrete geographical units than have the courts or corrections makes it easier to reorganize policing principles around the concerns of people in those places.

Courts

Because the court system operates on the basis of criminal law, which holds the U.S. Constitution as its foremost document and applies across all the neighborhoods within a given jurisdiction, there is a tendency to keep the courts centralized and located in the downtown area of a city near the other buildings of city, county, and state government. At the same time, judges and lawyers are among the least popular public officials, and the court system has been facing a substantial reduction in public approval in recent years.

Three innovations have begun to bring the court system into a community-relevant framework. A few innovative prosecutors, notably Michael Shrunk in Multnomah County (Portland), Oregon, and Amy Klobuchar in Hennepin County (Minneapolis), Minnesota, experimented with the assignment of a deputy to a particular area of the city, which met with huge success. Citizens living in those areas began to rely upon these prosecutors for a new range of legal assistance, and the prosecutors took a new view of how the courts could serve this population. To mirror this change in prosecution, a few jurisdictions experimented with community-based defense services, and these were found to increase the impact of defender activity as well as to change the focus of the defender's work on cases. The third innovation was the establishment of community-based courts to develop special legal approaches and targeted services to address problems that were specific to particular communities.

Corrections

Correctional services have come slowly to the community-oriented movement in criminal justice. For the most part, the community-based idea for correctional services has been upheld within the probation, parole, and community corrections aspects of correctional work, where there is a tradition of thinking about community in carrying out correctional activity. Some of these changes have been cosmetic, but there has been a very recent surge of interest in ways that correctional systems can forge meaningful partnerships with citizens, private-sector interests, and other services in order to work better with clients. This has followed directly from a correctional interest in serving "places" better.

Institutional correctional administrators are now beginning to understand how important their work is for community quality of life. Every time an offender is removed from a community and sent to prison or jail, members of the community area are affected; and every time an ex-inmate returns to a community, that community is affected by what the prison has (or has not) done. Many people believe that the new frontier of correctional work lies in helping communities deal with the dual impacts of removal and return of residents.

CONCLUSION

It is important to remember that community justice is still an emerging set of experiments that range widely in scope and practice. Policymakers and practitioners are inventing new applications every day. In some cases, these applications will be rooted in the broken windows theory of neighborhood disorder. In others, they will seek to address community weaknesses ascribed by theories of social disorganization. And in still others, they will look to strengthen informal social control and build social capital in a neighborhood, which is identified as crucial to public safety in theories of collective efficacy. What holds these differing initiatives together as community justice and distinguishes them from other criminal justice innovations is that they are rooted in two basic assumptions: (1) there are critically important differences between communities—as between rich and poor—that suggest the need to tailor criminal justice strategies to the particular problems and priorities of each; and (2) the influence of stable families, good neighbors, effective social organizations, positive peers, and other informal networks of social control are the most important foundation for public safety.

The result is that regardless of their scope or the particular form that they take, community justice strategies will be characterized by a unique set of common concerns. They will focus on the circumstances of particular places, not just on individuals. They will be proactive in that they will look to head off problems before they occur, rather than respond to them only after they have become critical. They will be enacted through collaborations within the criminal justice system that cross agency boundaries, and collaborations outside the system with new community partners, such as community development corporations. In so doing, community justice will adopt new priorities associated with community well-being that are not strictly limited to immediate concerns of public safety, but which also include factors that contribute to the underlying causes of crime. In neighborhoods that remain entrenched in poverty, improved employment prospects, health care, and housing all become the shared concern of community actors and the criminal justice system.

Because community justice is concerned as much with social justice as with traditional criminal justice, it will measure its success in new terms. Whether the operations of the police, courts, or corrections are being considered, community justice will seek to answer this question: Have justice activities improved the community's well-being and the capacity of its residents to affect the quality of safety in their own neighborhood?

REFERENCES

Cadora, Eric, and Charles Swartz. 2000. "Community Justice Atlas." Center for Alternative Sentencing and Employment Services (CASES). Unpublished Report.

Clear, Todd R., and Dina Rose. 1999. *When Neighbors Go to Jail: Impact on Attitudes about Formal and Informal Social Control.* Washington, D.C.: U.S. Dept. of Justice, Office of Justice Programs, National Institute of Justice.

Karmen, Andrew. 2001. *New York Murder Mystery: The True Story behind the Crime Crash of the 1990s.* New York: New York University Press.

Moynihan, Daniel P. 1969. *Maximum Feasible Misunderstanding: Community Action in the War on Poverty.* New York: Free Press.

Sampson, R. J., S. W. Raudenbush, and F. Earls. 1997. "Neighborhoods and Violent Crime: A Multilevel Study of Collective Efficacy." *Science* 277 (August 15): 918.

Shaw, Clifford R., and Henry D. McKay. *Juvenile Delinquency in Urban Areas.*

Chicago: University of Chicago Press, 1942.

Sherman, Lawrence W., Patrick R. Gartin, and Michael E. Buerger. 1989. "Hot Spots of Predatory Crime: Routine Activities and the Criminology of Place." *Criminology* 27:27–55.

Silverman, Eli. 1999. *NYPD Battles Crime: Innovative Strategies in Policing.* Boston: Northeastern University Press.

Skogan, Wesley G. 1992. *Disorder and Decline: Crime and the Spiral of Decay in American Neighborhoods.* Berkeley and Los Angeles: University of California Press.

Von Hirsch, Andrew. 1993. *Censure and Sanctions.* Oxford: Clarendon Press.

Wilson, J. Q., and G. L. Kelling. 1982. "Broken Windows." *Atlantic Monthly* 249 (3): 29–38.

Wilson, William J. 1980. *The Declining Significance of Race: Blacks and Changing American Institutions.* 2d ed. Chicago: University of Chicago Press.

FOR FURTHER READING

Social Justice

Barber, Benjamin. 1984. *Strong Democracy: Participatory Politics for a New Age.* Berkeley: University of California Press. A description of a civic democratic model of politics.

Braithwaite, John. 1979. *Inequality, Crime, and Public Policy.* London: Routledge and Kegan Paul. A theory of the impact of social inequality on crime.

Pettit, Philip. 1997. *Republicanism: A Theory of Freedom and Government.* New York: Oxford University Press. An explication of the "republican theory" of just governance.

Rawls, John. 1971. *A Theory of Justice.* Cambridge, Mass.: Harvard University Press. The classic description of a democratic theory of the just society.

The Concept of "Place"

Anderson, Elijah. 1991. *Streetwise: Race, Class, and Change in an Urban Community.* Chicago: University of Chicago Press. A description of how living in impoverished inner cities affects social capability and social life.

Bursick, Robert J., and Harold G. Grasmick. 1993. *Neighborhoods and Crime: The Dimensions of Effective Social Control.* New York: Lexington Books.

A summary of the literature on social disorganization theory and an integration of that theory with systemic social control theory.

Logan, John R., and Harvey L. Molotch. 1987. *Urban Fortunes: The Political Economy of Place.* Berkeley: University of California Press. A description of the analytical framework for thinking about "place."

Community

Etzioni, Amatia. 1993. *The Spirit of Community: Rights, Responsibilities, and the Communitarian Agenda.* New York: Crown. An explanation and advocacy of the philosophy of communitarianism.

Gottdeiner, Matthew. 1994. *The Social Production of Urban Space.* 2d ed.

Austin: University of Texas Press. How cities and local areas create space, and how space affects social life.

Putnam, Robert D. 2000. *Bowling Alone: The Collapse and Revival of American Community.* New York: Simon & Schuster.

Broken Windows Theory

Kelling, George L., and Catherine M. Coles. 1996. *Fixing Broken Windows: Restoring Order and Reducing Crime in Our Communities.* New York: Simon & Schuster. Description of broken windows theory and studies of broken windows policing in action.

Skogan, Wesley. 1990. *Disorder and Decline: Crime and the Spiral of Decay in American Neighborhoods.* New York:

Free Press. A study of the impact of disorder on crime in Chicago.

Taylor, Ralph B. 2001. *Breaking Away from Broken Windows: Baltimore Neighborhoods and the Nationwide Fight against Crime, Fear, and Decline.* Boulder, Colo.: Westview. A critical assessment of broken windows theory in Baltimore.

2

✦

Policing and
Community Justice

The police were in large part the first criminal justice agency to embrace the concepts of community justice, and so it is appropriate that we begin our discussion of the criminal justice functions with the police. The most obvious way that police serve as exemplars of community justice is in the deeply embedded community-oriented policing movement that began to sweep across America in the 1980s and 1990s. We will discuss this movement in more detail, but it is worth noting that community justice as a concept owes much of its momentum to the abundant success of community policing.

It is a bit of an understatement to say that community policing has swept the profession. Although the roots of community policing go back to at least the 1940s (Carter and Radelet, 1998), a groundswell of support for the idea materialized in the 1980s, and by the turn of the twenty-first century, most urban (and many suburban and rural) police departments in the United States openly described themselves as using community-oriented principles. This shift to the community level represents an attempt to bring the police closer to the public they serve. Instead of simply responding to crimes, the community police officer builds relationships and partnerships with local businesses, organizations, residents, and social-service agencies; and the officer uses these relationships to better understand the needs of the community and better address local problems.

However, the community policing movement, important as it has been, is not the same as the community justice movement. The latter has derived a number of its most important lessons from the former, but the differences between the two are important to bear in mind. Community policing is both a comprehensive strategy of policing and a philosophy of law enforcement. Community justice, on the other hand, is a strategy and a philosophy of criminal justice. The recent experiences of police innovation in the United States have tested many of the most important community justice concepts in the police setting and have illustrated why community justice has become such a popular new idea.

In this chapter, we describe the police as an agency of community justice. We begin with a review of some of the issues that face modern police, and we show why community-oriented policing seemed such a valuable way to deal with those issues. We then provide a detailed description of the community- and problem-oriented policing approaches and assess their effectiveness. We conclude with a discussion of the current agenda for community-policing advocates.

A BRIEF HISTORY
OF COMMUNITY POLICING

In the late 1800s and early 1900s, the police were under the control of those with political power—the police helped those who had power and punished those who opposed these powerful individuals. During this time, the public saw the police as corrupt and lawless. Eventually, after much public outcry, reformers of the 1920s managed to separate the police from political influence and created a professional, military-like administration system. In an effort to solve many of the problems of the past, and in order to appear more professional, the police became more distant from the public (Greene, 2000; Kelling and Moore, 1988).

Technological innovations also increased the rift between officers and the community. The use of automobiles severely decreased the number of neighborhood beat cops, and the widespread use of telephones and radios allowed residents to quickly and easily contact the police for assistance. The ease with which the police could be contacted significantly increased the number of calls-for-service, reducing the amount of time officers could spend on crime prevention and relationship building (in order to ensure public safety, police departments must respond to almost every call). The use of computers further increased the gap between officers and the community by increasing the importance of performance statistics and highlighting inferior policing, high crime areas, crime trends, and response times. Instead of listening to public concerns, officers and managers became slaves to crime statistics (Bureau of Justice Assistance, 1994).

The distance between residents and police officers culminated in the social and political unrest of the 1960s—a time when members of both the civil rights movement and the antiwar movement actively participated in civil unrest (Palmiotto and Donahue, 1995). During this time, the police were severely criticized for brutal behavior toward nonviolent protesters and blamed for instigating major riots through their aggressive, uncontrolled actions. These violent incidents, in addition to the well-publicized hostile relationship between minority communities and the police, sparked another set of reforms to improve the relationship between communities and police officers. After a few attempts to establish community policing had failed, the concept evolved and took root in the mid-1980s (Greene, 2000). These topics will be expanded upon later in this chapter.

POLICE AND THE COMMUNITY: A DUAL-TRACK RATIONALE

Community-oriented policing has two justifications that also apply to community justice in law enforcement. The two aims of community-oriented policing are better community relations and better crime prevention.

Better community relations are needed because police rely on the public in order to do their jobs, but there are several important impediments to good community relations. Some have to do with different images of the police by the public: citizens with advantaged social class tend to see the police in a very positive light; people who suffer significant social disadvantage do not have that same positive view. The problem is that the police mission is much more reliant upon the ability to sustain the confidence of the latter than the former, and therein lies a challenge: how to obtain and maintain positive interaction with citizens who may be predisposed to be suspicious of the police. But the problem is not only in the attitudes of citizens. Aspects of police culture and the police ethic also interfere with a capacity for positive relations—for example, when police develop cynicism about citizen groups and become negative about their work, and when the culture of the "thin blue line" prevents police from having confidence in citizens.

Better crime prevention relies on community-based practice. As we saw in the opening chapter, street crime concentrates in some locations more than others, and police therefore tend to be more active in these areas. However, if the policing approach is simply to be more active in response to crime—more investigations and more arrests—then the police will always be playing catch-up. If, on the other hand, the solution to high levels of crime is to take a proactive approach, there are more possibilities for public safety results. To do this, the police will have to change the way they act in the communities where the greatest police presence is called for.

THE COMMUNITY RELATIONS RATIONALE FOR COMMUNITY POLICING

To understand the need for a new orientation to policing, we must begin with a review of the main issues interfering with police effectiveness. We might be tempted to say offhand that the problem with police effectiveness is too many criminals. There is some truth to the idea that the sheer volume of criminal behavior makes police work a difficult assignment, but that discounts a profound and important truth: Police work faces a series of built-in problems that tends to frustrate the capacity of police to do their jobs well. This has to do with both the nature of the problem and the police themselves, at least in their traditional form.

We begin with a discussion of what we might call "the way things are," that is, certain factors in the job of policing serve to limit the way police can do their work. These are neither criticisms of the police nor complaints about the community. They are merely facts that set the stage for an understanding of the complexity of the public safety task. This discussion begins with a call for improved community relations as an essential first step in an improved police force and not simply as a desirable but less important goal. The importance of prioritizing community relations is explained by the nature of the policing job.

The Police: Essential Services Ensnared in Quandary

In most places in the United States, the police and the hospital emergency room are the only public service organizations available twenty-four hours a day, seven days a week for citizens in crisis. Hospitals help us when we are sick or have a medical emergency; the police deal with us for almost everything else — and they often get involved in medical emergencies as well. Although we see police around us routinely, we encounter them only when our lives are not routine: when we are stopped for a traffic violation, experience some form of victimization, or face an emergency that requires an immediate response from someone in authority.

The facts that police are a full-time community service and that their work almost always comes into play when people are in trouble of some sort provide an essential foundation for understanding the police as a part of community justice. In a democracy, where citizens have personal rights and the police exercise carefully limited powers, it is impossible to understand the police and the community without acknowledging a quandary. The most important services provided by police usually take place in the context of somebody being in trouble or in some sort of crisis, so it is quite natural to expect the police to arrive with special powers to intercede. Yet the powers of the police to act are carefully circumscribed by democratic law and tradition, so the immediacy of the predicament is always tempered by the limitations placed on police authority. This often leads to disappointment, because the police will often feel constrained in the actions they can take and citizens will often fail to grasp those constraints.

In police–citizen encounters, the reverse problem can also occur. A police officer may interpret the facts of a situation as calling for serious or even urgent action, while the citizen feels intensely that his rights ought to constrain the actions taken by the police.

Small wonder that police often feel in that classic double bind, "damned-if-I-do, and damned-if-I-don't." In this situation, it is easy for police to become cynical, believing that nothing can be done to satisfy the public. It is equally likely that the public can become indignant, either objecting to an overreach of authority or disputing a seemingly lackadaisical approach.

This predicament of police–citizen encounters provides a powerful backdrop to our understanding of contemporary policing. It helps explain why the topic of policing receives such strong, often opposing, opinion: some people seem to despise the police, while others hold them in extremely high regard. A major defining characteristic for how people feel about the police can be race and age: people of color have lower opinions of the police than do Whites, and young people (especially those of color) have lower opinions than do older people, regardless of race (Sampson and Bartusch, 1999). This makes sense, as these are the very people who are most likely to be stopped by the police. But it would be easy to exaggerate this problem, when the reality is more complex. Police consistently receive a more positive performance appraisal than do other sectors of the criminal justice system, even with all these built-in problems (Bureau of Justice Statistics, 2000).

How can it be that police are simultaneously so heavily criticized and also so deeply respected? The answer to this important question lies in an understanding of three aspects of contemporary policing. The police may be simultaneously thought of as a symbol of modern culture, a function of the legal system, and a function of power in society.

Police as a Symbol of Modern Culture

The police represent social control, and they stand for social order. As the main coercive arm of the state, they also represent the power of the government. As a consequence, the police generate strong feelings among the public.

Many see the police as the symbol of a safe and secure society. This view holds that all law-abiding citizens share a common interest in safe streets, and the police are one of the main sources of safety. When police face constraints on their powers, those who see the police as the mechanism of social control often fear that disorder and criminality will follow. Those who hold the symbolic vision of the police as the agency of social control typically support a strong police presence, and they object to "civil liberties" views of the police that emphasize citizens' rights. When police are viewed in this fashion, it is easy to think of society as composed of "good guys" and "bad guys"—the police come from the former group and are asked to control the latter group.

Yet the police also symbolize the raw power of the state, and in a democracy, such power is uncomfortable to citizens. It is especially disturbing to members of minority groups who receive more attention from the police: African Americans, Latinos, and the poor. To those who see the police as a symbol of power, the problem is not public safety but the way to place meaningful reins on that power. These people worry about police authority run amok, police action without controls. Because the most disadvantaged in our society are also the most likely to encounter police power used against them, this concern often arises along lines of social class and social status. People of color, especially young men, are very likely to be suspicious of police and less likely to accept their authority as legitimately exercised. There is a tendency to view the police as treating them and their neighborhoods differently than other people and locations.

It is easy to see how the symbolic importance of police carries community significance. The United States is today a residentially segregated society. Those who live in the residential areas occupied by dominant majorities see the police far more positively than those who live in poor, minority areas. Some of this opinion is related to the way the police treat people in those areas. In high-crime locations, suspects are numerous and suspicious situations routine; police often tend to take an aggressive stance, and the result is that many citizens feel deeply disrespected on account of the color of their skin. In the low-activity areas, police are less vigilant about crime, and citizens as a result feel under less scrutiny.

Thus, part of what determines the way citizens react to the police is how the police define the citizenry. When police see citizens as potential problems, those citizens often respond by seeing the police as a potentially unwelcome power in their lives. When police see citizens as "residents," those residents will see the police as a support system. The way in which police attitudes toward the public tend to create a public reaction was one of the original sources of the movement toward community policing.

Police as a Function of the Legal System

No matter what the police symbolize, they are first and foremost the initial stage of the criminal justice process. They take reports of criminal events, investigate suspicious situations, and make arrests. Few cases come into the criminal justice system without first encountering the police.

For this reason, police work has to be assessed on three different criteria: How do police actions affect willingness of citizens to report crimes? How do these actions encourage citizen cooperation with criminal investigations? And how effective are these strategies in identifying suspects accurately?

We would think that most law-abiding citizens would be anxious to cooperate with the police. But studies of police–citizen relations find that citizens who have had negative experiences with the police often become reluctant to assist the police in their investigations or report crimes to the police in the first place—even when they are the victims (Clear and Rose, 1999). Indeed, in places where police–community relations are poor, citizens show a marked reluctance to report crimes and a strong hesitation to trust the police response to problems.

For police, this lack of cooperation has two sides. Any police officer who has worked in a poor neighborhood, especially a poor minority area, knows the level of mistrust and even antagonism that can permeate the attempt to do the work. It is frustrating, because the police point of view is that they are only trying to protect the law-abiding citizens from the "bad guys," and the lack of cooperation makes the work that much harder. Then again, not everyone is uncooperative. Some of the residents have an unabashed enthusiasm for the police to do their work, and this positive response by many highlights the difficult behavior of the others. It is easy for the police to view all the residents who express suspicion as somehow being aligned with "the bad element."

Nonetheless, when folks are reluctant to report crimes and when those who are surrounded by crime are disinclined to assist the police, the job of law enforcement, difficult enough without citizen recalcitrance, becomes more untenable. After a while, some police can develop an attitude toward the residents of these areas of "since they don't care, why should I?" Under these circumstances, the basic work of policing becomes more and more difficult. To protect themselves from an all-too-often unfriendly public, police adopt a first-choice style of indifference. When a victim or a citizen shows an appreciation for a police officer's effort, this can energize activity on behalf of that citizen, but others may come to see this as a kind of favoritism. In the end, the credibility of the criminal justice system suffers, as citizens lose confidence in it and the police become more cynical about their work.

Police as a Function of Power in Society

In this context, the important distinction between authority and power can become blurred. *Authority* is the legitimate capacity to require compliance imbued in a role by law, standards, or custom. It is housed in the idea that some consensus of opinion exists that the person occupying a certain role ought to have a level of obedience to his or her directives, so long as they flow from legitimate exercise of duties within that role. Judges have authority in the courtroom, teachers in the classroom, supervisors in the workplace, and so on. So long as the person with authority is acting consistent with the expectations of the role, we expect voluntary compliance with the directives that emanate from the legitimate performance of that role. There is a certain expectation from all of us that people will *willingly* comply with the valid directives of a person with authority to give those directives.

Power, on the other hand, is the raw ability to compel compliance, regardless of the person's willingness to comply. When a person has power with regard to certain actions, it means that person can make others do what is wanted through some implied or actual coercive capacity. The ultimate source of power is the force of might—one who is stronger than another might be able to make that person do something, whether that person wants to or not—but power can also derive from the force of law or the force of group solidarity. For example, a police officer stops a person to ask a few questions, using authority, but then decides to detain that person, using the power of arrest.

The distinction between power and authority is important to bear in mind. Authority is a far more efficient means for getting a person to do something, since it works without any direct threat. Someone with the authority to ask simply does so, and on the basis of that recognized authority, the requested behavior follows. Power, by contrast, requires implied or demonstrated threat: we all know the implications of the statement "You are under arrest," and few of us will doubt the meaning of the order "Stop or I'll shoot," but it is the act of pulling out the handcuffs or revolver that communicates the meaning of the statement.

There is an important irony here. Authority, to work, is reliant on voluntary cooperation, whereas power can be exercised regardless of the other person's willingness to comply. In a very real sense, *authority is given* to the person exercising it by the person who has decided to comply, while *power is taken* by the person giving orders. Power, then, typically comes into play when authority is absent. Yet authority is absent not because of something missing from the police officer's role, but because of something missing in the citizen's response to that role. Authority exists because people voluntarily accept the dictates of the police.

Sometimes, of course, power and authority flow together, as when a judge oversees a courtroom, but usually there are important distinctions between them. Teachers, who hope to have broad authority in the classroom, in truth have limited power there. Police, who appreciate having broad authority over citizen conduct, exercise power only in ways that are very carefully constrained by law.

Thus, a police officer who is frustrated by a lack of authority cannot get authority through obtaining more power, even though this may seem to be the way to go. Authority is obtained by coming to be seen as legitimate in the eyes of the citizen, but obtaining power has almost nothing to do with the eyes of the citizen. Indeed, some might say that the more a person turns to power as the way to compel others' compliance, the less everyone would expect that person to have (or even eventually obtain) authority. Often, the exercise of power comes at the expense of authority.

This is one reason why *the police culture* is such an important force in the work world of the police. The police culture is a set of informal standards and norms that develop among police officers and influence how they approach the job (Crank, 1998). Volumes have been written about the origins and effects of police culture. The most common descriptions include the points we have made previously: police learn to approach the public with distrust and suspicion, expect that the public will not understand the job of policing, and view everyone as a potential problem (even dangerous). This cynical stance regarding the public is repeated when it comes to the criminal justice system, when the dominant view is some version of "the cops keep doing their job, but everyone else—from judges to probation officers—is soft on crime."

Three points must be emphasized here regarding the police culture. First, the police culture develops in response to the pressures of the job and the traditions of the department. Any problem with the police culture is much less an issue of "bad cops" than a human response to the difficulties inherent in police work. Second, police culture is not uniform across all departments and all divisions within departments. Important differences exist that make departments vary from deeply cynical and negative orientations to ones that are much less so, and these differences can even exist between, say, plainclothes detective units and the uniformed officers. Third, the police culture is not solely adverse in its effects. By adopting the informal norms of the police culture, newly hired police learn to support each other, avoid common mistakes, and deal with the pressures of the job.

But the police culture can, and often does, get in the way. Because it is typically cynical in its orientation, it tends to discount the value of authority and exalt the importance of power. Indeed, it is common for police to confuse the two, seeking an increase in formal power because of the weak potency of their authority. Most important, the dominant police culture puts the police officer at odds with the public. In high-activity areas, where public suspicions often match those of the officers, this is a recipe for alienation. Both the police and the citizens can come to feel that the officers in blue constitute an occupying army from an alien force, all parties at odds with one another, and little stake in common. What is often seen is a kind of a standoff.

The community-oriented policing movement came about as an antidote to this sense of a police–citizen standoff. Leadership in policing saw the considerable negatives facing the police: problems with citizen relations, especially in the most disadvantaged communities most needing an effective police presence; difficulties with authority; and concerns about the impact of the police culture on police practices. All of this came together to suggest a need for change. Almost nobody was happy with the way that many communities regarded the police, and there was increasing criticism of the way the police regarded the communities they served. But even with this widespread and growing distress about the relationship between the police and the public, it took an unforeseen development to usher in the police–community era: a string of studies suggesting that the traditional approach was not working.

THE CRIMINAL JUSTICE RATIONALE
FOR COMMUNITY POLICING

Improving police–community relations may be a central objective in the overall job of building a better police force, but there are other equally important reasons to change the relationship between the police and the community.

Studies have shown that without good police–community relations, the police face extreme difficulties in carrying out their work. These studies were concerned with a variety of different topics in policing, but they led to a consistent general conclusion: the traditional manner of business in police work was not producing good results.

To understand this line of studies, it is important to summarize the traditional model of policing. In this approach, police see themselves as professional crime fighters concerned with the problem of serious felonies. This model has two important elements. With regard to citizens, police are expected to be detached and impartial, working "beat assignments," not communities or neighborhoods. With regard to crime, police are reactive and investigative, responding to criminal events based on their seriousness and building the evidence for criminal cases after crimes have been reported.

This professional model was the dominant model of policing from the early 1900s until the late 1960s. For most of this time, there was little questioning of the professional model, and police reforms took consistent patterns: more training, an emphasis on investigation technologies and crime-prevention hardware, and the adoption of paramilitary thinking about command, police deployment, and accountability. The idea was to downgrade the importance of duties that had little to do with crime (traffic, emergency services), allocate the most resources to the most serious crime, focus on rapid responses to criminal events, and maintain a visible, deterrent presence on the streets.

The first signs that this orientation might be in trouble came with the 1967 President's Commission on Law Enforcement and the Administration of Justice, which pointed with concern to the increasing problem of urban unrest, often taking the form of riots that began in the wake of some violent encounter between the police and a young person of color. The commission pointed out the urgent need for improvements in the way police dealt with the public, and it called for a reassessment of the way the police defined their responsibilities and provided services to the community.

There was also a serious concern about police performance. Crime and fear of crime were both increasing, while clearance rates for crimes and public confidence in the police were decreasing. Although this context was becoming less hospitable to the traditional policing model, a series of studies was leading some to conclude that the old emphasis on command policing simply did not provide adequate results.

The first, and most important, such study was the Kansas City Preventive Patrol Study (Walker, 1992). This study employed a randomized field experiment to compare the effectiveness of standard policing patrol to proactive methods, in which two to three times as many police patrolled the streets, and to reactive methods, in which there was no police patrol and officers only responded to explicit calls for service. After these very different levels of police work had been compared for one year, the rates of crime in the areas were compared. The surprising result found no significant difference in the rates of serious crime, fear of crime, attitudes toward the police, or even police response time.

This study threw contemporary police thinking for a loop. The study not only failed to confirm all the usual arguments about the need for more police, but questioned the very assumptions underlying those arguments. Traditional police thinking received a further jolt when studies of police response time—the amount of time it took the police to get to the scene of a crime after a citizen called for help—had little relationship to the probability of apprehending a suspect and was unrelated to citizen satisfaction with the police response. What really mattered was how long it took the police to get to the scene compared to what the citizen thought should happen (Carter and Radelet, 1998).

Two other studies caused police to begin to rethink their strategies. A comparison of one-officer and two-officer patrol cars in San Diego tended to favor the use of single officers, both in terms of costs and citizen interactions. In addition, a series of studies of 911 calls for service found that by carefully explaining to citizens the priorities for calls and by helping citizens know how their case was going to be handled, the ascendancy of the 911 system over centrally managed priorities for services could be stemmed (Carter and Radelet, 1998).

This string of studies, together with the continuing rise in crime and increasing popular alarm about public safety, led to a rethinking of what should be the best philosophy of policing. That rethinking was heavily influenced by foot-patrol studies in Flint, Michigan, and Newark, New Jersey; and fear-of-crime studies in Newark, New Jersey, and Houston, Texas. The foot-patrol studies found support for the idea that face-to-face interaction with citizens was an important part of citizen satisfaction with police, and that the closer cooperation between citizens and police that resulted may have contributed to safer streets. The fear-of-crime studies found that citizen–police interaction resulting from foot patrols helped reduce the overall level of fear. Together, these and other studies of the emerging idea of community-oriented police work began to call attention to the possibilities of change in policing.

COMMUNITY POLICING

Community policing has three main sources of intellectual development. Robert C. Trojanowicz of Michigan State University was one of the more prominent scholars to write about the idea (Trojanowicz and Bucqueroux, 1990). He founded the National Center for Community Policing, which advanced the ideas of the community-based (sometimes called neighborhood-based) model. According to Trojanowicz, community policing is a full-service policing model where the same officer regularly patrols the same area and forms partnerships with residents to solve problems. Mark Moore, of Harvard's Kennedy School of Government, initiated a series of Police Executive Seminars in the 1980s that clarified the theoretical and practical basis of community-oriented policing and then helped spread the innovation across the country. The most significant

Community Policing in Brooklyn

In 1984 the NYPD created a demonstration project named CPOP (Community Patrol Officer Program) in the 72nd precinct of Brooklyn. Through this program, ten community patrol officers (CPOs) were assigned areas ranging from sixteen to sixty square blocks. The CPOs set their own patrol times to maximize their effectiveness, and they were exempt from responding to 911 calls-for-service. In addition, each CPO kept a "beat book" with information on local issues and problems, strategies for solving the problems, and lists of community organizations. A plan for addressing neighborhood problems was outlined each month (Pate and Shtull, 1994).

In 1990 the 72nd precinct was chosen to be a model precinct to test the feasibility of instigating a citywide community-policing initiative. The following goals of the model precinct project were stated (from Pate and Shtull, 1994, 387–389):

- Develop an organizational structure that facilitates the transition to community policing (increase staff; consolidate units; establish neighborhood beats).
- Develop an operational system that promotes and encourages the practice of community policing (improve communication among officers and develop monthly work plans).
- Develop an information system that would support community and problem-oriented policing (analyze crime "hot spots"; create daily calls-for-service reports).
- Develop a system that would allocate the calls-for-service workload between foot patrol and motor patrol officers (low priority calls will be routed to foot patrol officers whenever possible).
- Work with other departments to develop a comprehensive community policing model (detectives would be required to attend community meetings; introduce a fully staffed narcotics unit to the precinct that will work with foot officers).
- Develop a training program for all precinct personnel (teach concepts of community policing and problem-oriented policing).

Officers enjoyed the flexible hours and the opportunity to do something different and interact with community members. Interactions with residents in nonemergency situations made the job more interesting and more pleasant. Some officers did not want to join the unit because of the challenges of working outside in all types of weather, the feelings of being vulnerable without a partner, problems with responding to emergencies without a vehicle, the perceived lack of excitement, the lack of a clear reward structure, and uncertainties about the possibility of promotion (Pate and Shtull, 1994).

source of the change was the U.S. Department of Justice Community-Oriented Policing Office that worked closely with the Police Executive Research Forum (PERF) to conduct workshops, studies, and seminars while publishing numerous reports on the concept.

Police scholars have identified three different types of community-oriented policing: community-building strategies, which attempt to strengthen community capacity; problem-oriented strategies, which deal with the causes of crime; and broken windows strategies, which focus on minor crimes and physical disorder. We discuss the current status of community policing using these main approaches as guides (Mastrofski, Worden, and Snipes, 1995).

Community-Building Strategies

The most common form of community policing includes a range of tactics that help strengthen the community's own ability to reduce crime. Some of these are mundane and have proven to be of limited value, such as Neighborhood Watch or neighborhood meetings (Skogan, 1992). Others are of more durable impact, such as victim-assistance programs, police–minority relations initiatives, and the long-standing Police Athletic League. Variously, each of these types of strategies is theorized to improve crime-prevention effectiveness in three ways.

First, the effect of increased day-to-day interaction between community residents and beat officers is thought to promote community-based "intelligence." That is, the more police talk to local businesses and other neighborhood residents, the more information they are able to obtain about crime and criminals in the area. Second, the same contacts are thought to provide another way to reduce crime when the flow of information is reversed. That is, when police publicize information about trouble spots or crime events, residents are more informed and able to act to protect themselves. Third, and perhaps most broad, is the belief that "police legitimacy" within the neighborhood is crucial to effective local crime prevention because citizens are more forthcoming with information regarding crimes and some residents act in more law-abiding ways (Sherman et al., 1996).

What these strategies have in common is their attempt to improve some aspect of community life by increasing interaction among residents or creating a standing relationship between the community and the police. Community building is an intuitively attractive idea, as the communities hardest hit by crime are also the very ones that most need development. But attempts to develop these communities also meet major obstacles. Skogan's studies of community policing in Chicago show that it is difficult to sustain community interest in developmental activity, and even police who are enthusiastic about the idea sometimes find themselves like fish out of water when it comes to community organizing (Skogan and Hartnett, 1997).

These obstacles derive in part from the very premise of their goals. Hard-hit communities are the ones that struggle the most to make more time to meet after hours and increase their everyday obligations. Strategies that focus on building relationships with effective community networks suffer when those networks are weak or need to be developed. Thus, the communities most in need of assistance are also the least able to take advantage of this particular approach.

Problem-Oriented Strategies

Developed by Herman Goldstein (1991), problem-oriented policing (POP) strategies are based on the idea that crime emanates from particular, persistent circumstances that can be identified, documented, and then overcome through systematic action, and that police should be more thoughtful and innovative when dealing with neighborhood issues. The POP approach is very focused in its method, and although several problem-oriented techniques have been proposed, the SARA (Scan, Analyze, Respond, Assess) method is the most popular. Using SARA, the officer scans the community for problems, analyzes each problem in a systematic way, designs a specific response to each problem, and then assesses the usefulness and success rate of the response (Greene, 2000).

For example, an officer might scan the community and identify drug dealing as the main problem. The officer then analyzes the locations of drug-related activities, the times of day these activities take place, the opinions and feelings of community residents and businesses, and the capacity of neighborhood organizations, social services, and religious institutions to aide in the development of a solution. After careful thought and planning, the officer might decide that the best response is increased foot patrols by officers and citizen groups in certain locations, along with improved street lighting in these areas. The officer might also decide to contact the landlords of the buildings where the drug dealers live or work and attempt to get the offenders evicted, or arrange to have surveillance cameras installed. Once the response has been implemented, the officer assesses the change in drug dealing and any changes in resident perceptions in order to see if the initiative worked.

One of the more successful problem-oriented strategies has been hot-spots policing. This style of strategic policing is derived from the fact that a very small percentage of addresses in a jurisdiction account for a significantly disproportionate number of criminal events. These locations can be identified by mapping crimes, and strategies can be designed to ameliorate the problems that make these places more criminally involved. For example, a check-cashing store between two bars can become a problem, or a liquor store on a dark corner can invite crime. The hot-spots model is also closely related to a school of crime prevention called situational crime prevention (Brantingham and Brantingham, 1990), which is based on the idea that crimes occur when situations exist that make crime possible. Situational crime-prevention methods study the distribution of crime across time and space, with the aim of identifying the reasons why these two factors coincide so frequently.

Problem-solving methods seek policing tactics that are intelligence based. An elaborate version of intelligence-based policing is New York City's CompStat (computerized statistics) meetings. Credited by many as a major contributing factor in New York City's drop in crime (Silverman, 1999), the CompStat process involves the spatial analysis and mapping of crime at the precinct level (precincts are approximately the size of a neighborhood), and a report on any increases in criminal activity and the ways the local precinct will deal with these increases.

> These meetings are an integral facet of a comprehensive interactive management strategy that enhances accountability while providing local commanders with considerable discretion and the resources necessary to properly manage their commands. It also ensures that they remain apprised of crime and quality of life conditions within their areas of responsibility, and that the Department's ten Crime and Quality of Life Strategies are fully implemented throughout the agency. The meetings serve as a forum in which precinct and other operational unit commanders communicate to the agency's top executives the problems they face while also sharing successful crime reduction tactics with other commanders. The process allows top executives to carefully monitor issues and activities within precincts and operational units, to evaluate the skills and effectiveness of middle managers and to properly allocate the resources necessary to reduce crime and improve police performance. (NYPD Web site, 2001)

It should be noted that the CompStat process, and any use of computer mapping to locate crime hot spots, does not, by itself, represent community policing. This technique must be used in conjunction with community partnerships and community-level problem solving in order to form a complete community-policing initiative. Also, any current community-policing initiative could significantly improve its crime-fighting capabilities through the use of spatial analysis—knowing where crimes occur is one of the most important pieces of information for police departments.

Broken Windows Strategies

One of the most influential new ideas in policing is the broken windows thesis (Wilson and Kelling, 1982). We have described this thesis in detail elsewhere, but here we consider the implications of the concept for police practices. A detailed description of the broken windows philosophy of policing has been provided by one of its originators, George Kelling, along with Catherine Coles (1996). They describe the experiences of broken windows strategies in various locations of New York City, San Francisco, and elsewhere. In these locations, the broken windows idea has been credited with a reduction in crime and an increase in public order.

Because the broken window thesis holds that crime results from public disorder, the solution to crime is to use the police to create order. Under this assumption, the strategies are directed at people whose public behavior causes the general public to believe that order has disappeared: homeless are required to go to shelters or they are arrested; drunks are arrested and placed in jail; disorderly people—those playing loud music, drinking alcohol in public, or otherwise disturbing the peace—are required to stop or are arrested. In short, the power of arrest is used to enforce public order, especially by requiring that these people abide by public expectations for conduct. In some places, the emphasis on widespread "stop-and-frisk" tactics has led to accusations of racial profiling. In these accounts, it is not behavior alone that leads to police inquiry and action, but a combination of behavior and racial characteristics, which are said to fit a profile of prospective criminal offenders. The problems associated with accusations of racial profiling represent some of the civil rights limitations to crime-prevention techniques that depend too heavily on police intervention in the absence of citizen partnerships.

Another controversial form of community policing is evinced in broken windows policing as it has been implemented in New York City's "zero-tolerance" policing practices. The zero-tolerance method uses arrests of minor offenders—jaywalkers and those holding opened beer cans in public—as a means of quelling public disorder. While stopping a person for a public order violation, the police search and question the violator. Proponents claim that this routine questioning of public nuisance cases has resulted in large numbers of illegal weapons being seized and leads to the arrest of parolees who have absconded and others who are wanted on arrest warrants, and that the processing of these cases leads to a major reduction in crime. Critics of zero tolerance say that the rate of apprehension of serious offenders is actually very low (Karmen, 2001), and so most of the stops turn out to be a form of harassment. Many observers blame zero-tolerance policies in New York City for the tragically deteriorating relationships between minority youth (especially males, who are the most likely to be stopped) and the police.

COMMUNITY POLICING
AND COMMUNITY JUSTICE

Community-oriented policing services (COPS) have played a central role in the community justice movement. But community policing is not the same as community justice. The COPS movement in policing is, for the most part, particular to the traditional functions of law enforcement: investigation and arrest. Although some of the more elaborate community-policing methods move out of traditional police functions in attempting to prevent crime, community justice is a broad concept that applies not just to crime but to the quality of life in the community. It also embraces the nonpolice functions of adjudication, sanctioning, and correcting—discussions that we attend to in the following two chapters.

Thus, although we may think of community policing as the bellwether for change that has set the stage for community justice, integration of community policing into the broader community justice agenda will require still more

Levels of Community Policing

Greene (2000) provides an important summary of the types of changes brought about by community policing, as well as the expected outcomes as a result of these changes. This discussion serves as a useful framework for understanding both the potential effort needed for the development of a community-policing initiative and the potential rewards of such an initiative. The following table summarizes these levels and the expected outcomes.

Environmental Level

At the environmental level the police form relationships and partnerships with local organizations, residents, social services, and businesses and focus on problem solving and crime reduction in an effort to reduce fear of crime and improve quality of life. The mobilization of the community to address crime-related issues is thought to increase the social bonds, communication, and trust between neighborhood members, thus improving community cohesion and increasing informal social control (formal social control being the police, and informal social control being community conflict resolution through nonpolice involvement). Also, when residents have more contact with police officers, and when police officers illustrate an investment in neighborhood quality of life, the residents feel safer and empowered (Greene, 2000, 321–324).

Organizational Level

At the organizational level, community policing affects how the department defines problems and solutions, and how the actual organization is structured, including the organizational attitude toward the police subculture and the selection and training of officers (for example, the hiring of more minority officers and language training for officers in minority communities). The organization must accept a new set of values for seeing the community as a partner and developing new problem-solving techniques to create a true community-policing initiative. This new set of values also includes changes in

change in the way the police do their business, even within a community-oriented philosophy.

Community policing is not a panacea. Although it has been one of the most important systematic changes in criminal justice in the last one hundred years, it has also raised a series of questions about the functions of the police in modern society and the capacity of the police to accomplish those functions alone. As we see in the following chapters, the courts and corrections both face the same questions about an expanded mission that seeks to produce greater public safety through increasing community well-being.

internal communication practices and information sharing among officers (Greene, 2000, 322).

Individual Level

Organizational-level changes must also make their way into the rank and file and be inculcated by each police officer if community policing is to succeed. Officers must develop new problem-solving techniques and learn to view the community as a partner in their crime-fighting activities. Also, crime prevention must become a higher priority for the officer. Job satisfaction should improve as the officer becomes more connected with the community, and the officer will have to use a greater range of interpersonal and problem-solving skills in his or her new role (Greene, 2000, 323).

LEVEL OF INTERVENTION	ANTICIPATED CHANGES	COMMUNITY-POLICING OUTCOMES
Environmental	Form partnerships with local organizations and residents; increase public safety; improve social bonds	■ Reduced crime and fear ■ Increased level of trust ■ More communication ■ Better problem solving
Organizational	Redefine departmentwide problem-solving techniques; have officers adopt a new set of values, develop new internal communication practices	■ Improved training ■ More diverse hiring process ■ Improved internal communication ■ Improved analysis of problems ■ Change in information flow ■ New performance measures
Individual	Develop new problem-solving techniques and interpersonel skills; change view of the community role	■ Increased job satisfaction ■ Increased performance ■ More attachment to community ■ Wider role in community

Source: Adapted from Greene (2000, 324).

REFERENCES

Brantingham, P. L., and P. J. Brantingham. 1990. "Situational Crime Prevention in Practice." *Canadian Journal of Criminology* 32 (1): 17–44.

Carter, D. L., and L. A. Radelet. 1998. *The Police and the Community.* New Jersey: Prentice-Hall: Upper Saddle River, New Jersey.

Clear, Todd R., and Dina R. Rose. 1999. *When Neighbors Go to Jail: Impact on Attitudes about Formal and Informal Social Control.* Washington, D.C.: U.S. Dept. of Justice, Office of Justice Programs, National Institute of Justice.

Crank, John. 1998. *Understanding Police Culture*. Cincinnati, Ohio: Anderson Publishing Company.

Goldstein, Herman. 1991. *Problem-Oriented Policing*. New York: McGraw Hill.

Greene, Jack R. 2000. "Community Policing in America: Changing the Nature, Structure, and Function of the Police." In *Policies, Processes, and Decisions of the Criminal Justice System*. Vol. 3 of *Criminal Justice 2000*, edited by Julie Horney, pp. 299–370.

Karmen, Andrew. 2001. *New York Murder Mystery: The True Story Behind the Crime Crash of the 1990s*. New York University Press.

Kelling, G. L., and C. Coles. 1996. *Fixing Broken Windows: Restoring Order and Reducing Crime in Our Communities*. New York: Free Press.

Kelling, G. L., and M. Moore. 1988. "From Political Reform to Community: The Evolution of Strategy of Police." In *Community Policing: Rhetoric or Reality*, edited by J. R. Greene and S. Mastrofski. New York: Praeger.

Mastrofski, Stephen D., Robert E. Worden, and Jeffrey B. Snipes. 1995. Law Enforcement in a Time of Community Policing. *Criminology* 33 (November): 539–563.

NYPD Website. 2001. http://www.nyc.gov/html/nypd/html/chfdept/process.html

Palmiotto, M. J., and M. E. Donahue. 1995. "Evaluating Community Policing: Problems and Prospects." *Police Studies* 18 (2): 33–53.

Pate, A. M., and P. Shtull. 1994. "Community Policing Grows in Brooklyn: An Inside View of the New York City Police Department's Model Precinct." *Crime and Delinquency* 40 (3): 348–410.

Sampson, Robert J., and Dawn Jeglum Bartusch. 1999. *Attitudes toward Crime, Police, and the Law: Individual and Neighborhood Differences*. Washington, D.C.: U.S. Dept. of Justice, Office of Justice Program, National Institute of Justice.

Sherman, Lawrence W., Denise Gottfredson, Doris MacKenzie, John Eck, Peter Reuter, and Shawn Bushway. 1996. *Preventing Crime: What Works, What Doesn't, What's Promising: A Report to the United States Congress*. Washington, D.C.: National Institute of Justice.

Silverman, Eli. 1999. *NYPD Battles Crime: Innovative Strategies in Policing*. Boston: Northeastern University Press.

Skogan, Wesley G. 1992. *Disorder and Decline: Crime and the Spiral of Decay in American Neighborhoods*. Berkeley: University of California Press.

Skogan, W., and S. Hartnett. 1997. *Community Policing, Chicago Style*. New York: Oxford University Press.

Trojanowicz, R., and B. Bucqueroux. 1990. *Community Policing: A Contemporary Perspective*. Cincinnati, Ohio: Anderson Publishing Company.

U.S. Bureau of Justice Assistance. 1994. *Understanding Community Policing: A Framework for Action*. Washington, D.C.: U.S. Bureau of Justice Assistance.

U.S. Bureau of Justice Statistics. 2000. *Sourcebook of Criminal Justice Statistics. Section 2: Public Attitudes toward Crime and Criminal Justice–Related Topics*. Washington, D.C.: U.S. Department of Justice.

Walker, Samuel. 1992. *The Police in America: An Introduction*. New York: McGraw Hill College Division.

Wilson, J. Q., and G. L. Kelling. 1982. "Broken Windows." *Atlantic Monthly* 249 (3): 29–38.

FOR FURTHER READING

Community-Oriented Policing

Kelling, George, and William P. Bratton. 1993. *Implementing Community Policing: The Administrative Problem.* Washington, D.C.: National Institute of Justice. A prescription of ways to create and sustain community-oriented policing systems and cultures.

Greene, Judith. 1999. Zero Tolerance: A Case Study of Police Policies and Practices in New York City. *Crime and Delinquency* 45 (2): 171–187.

Nicholl, Caroline. 1999. *Community Policing, Community Justice, and Restorative Justice: Exploring the Links for the Delivery of a Balanced Approach to Public Safety.* Washington, D.C.: U.S. Department of Justice, Office of Community Oriented Policing Services.

Radelet, Louis A., and David Carter. 1994. *The Police and the Community.* 5th ed. Englewood Cliffs, N.J.: Prentice-Hall. A comprehensive review of literature on community and police interactions.

Zhao, J., and Q. Thurman. 1997. "Community Policing: Where Are We Now?" *Crime and Delinquency* 43 (3): 345–357.

Problem-Oriented Policing

Bayley, David H. 1994. *Police for the Future.* New York: Oxford University Press. A challenging prescription of the methods and philosophy of policing in the coming decades.

Goldstein, Herman. 1990. *Problem-Oriented Policing.* Philadelphia: Temple University Press. The classic description of problem-oriented police theory and practice.

Police Culture

Repetto, Thomas. 1978. *The Blue Parade.* New York: Free Press. Analyzes what it is like to be a police officer and the problems facing urban police reform.

Rubenstein, Jonathan. 1973. *City Police.* New York: Farrar, Straus & Giroux. The classic description of urban police culture.

Police Authority and Power

Bittner, Egon. 1990. *Aspects of Police Work.* Boston: Northeastern University Press. A summary of the literature of police behavior and the forces affecting police effectiveness.

Davis, Kenneth Culp. 1969. *Discretionary Justice: A Preliminary Inquiry.* Baton Rouge: Louisiana University Press. The classic essay on police power and police discretion.

3

⠿

The Courts and
Community Justice

Of the three main divisions of the criminal justice system—police, courts, and corrections—the middle justice function, the courts, has the furthest conceptual distance to travel to become community oriented. As we shall see, one reason for this is that the natural subject matter of the courts is the problems in criminal cases, not the problems of difficult places. Another reason has to do with the way the courts work, processing defendants through what looks a bit like an impersonal assembly line of decisions, from charging to sentencing. And yet another has to do with the traditional values of detachment and impartiality in the courts, which tend to disconnect judges and lawyers from their clients and the communities in which they live.

Despite these impediments, the courts have been in recent years a setting for enthusiastic experimentation with community justice concepts and strategies. After decades in which change was very slow in the courts and traditional models of court processing remained virtually undisturbed by pervasive changes elsewhere in the system, courts have become a beacon for community justice thinking, especially with regard to the handling of vexing problems that seemed intractable under the usual methods, such as drug abuse or minor crime.

In this chapter, we explore the way the courts have embraced major concepts of community justice and particular strategies of community-oriented court practices. We will see that innovation in the courts has resulted in fundamental changes in the way the court system relates to citizens, including victims, offenders, and their families. As extensive as these changes have been, however, we will also see that some advocates call for even more far-reaching reform, and the courts have only barely begun to address the needs of multiproblem communities.

CRIMINAL CASES, COMMUNITIES, AND COURTS

The subject matter of the criminal courts is criminal cases, not communities, and this has been one of the main practical and conceptual impediments to community justice in the courts. The focus on individual cases is completely understandable, as courts were established to deal solely with criminal cases. Each unit of the court's business, the criminal case, is defined by a complaint filed by the state against a defendant. What is at stake is the legal status of a defendant's conduct, and the efforts of the professional lawyers in the court triumvirate—prosecutor, defender, and judge—are designed to assess the legal consequences of the accused actions. These key actors in the court system perform their functions in interaction with one another, without much direct activity by nonprofessionals. Courts are traditionally insulated from outside forces, and emphasis is given to creating an environment in which professionally trained lawyers can use their skills in a formal, solemn setting to create outcomes that are seen by the public as just.

We will discuss whether this view of the courts, as a formal, somber institution of deliberation about criminal accusations, is wholly accurate. Accurate or not, the image of an independent, detached judiciary has a hallowed place in American jurisprudence, and it has operated as a counterforce to community justice thinking. Whereas the traditional view of the courts is that they are stately and detached, community justice is seen as informal and involved. Whereas traditional court procedures are dominated by professionals with everyday citizens silent, except when asked to testify, community justice is open to the views of citizens and supplements the professional practice of the law with informal participation by people who are not lawyers.

Perhaps most important, whereas the traditional courts serve legal jurisdictions, such as states, districts, or municipalities, community justice devotes its attention to a particular location, such as a neighborhood, that is part of a legal jurisdiction. Courts give a high premium to the concept of equal justice under law, which means that every person within that legal jurisdiction is to be treated the same way by the court workers. Community justice accepts the foundational importance of the concept of equal justice, but sees within that idea a broad range of flexibility to tailor programs and legal strategies to fit the particular circumstances of communities affected by the law. Equal justice is important, but justice that addresses the needs of people most affected by the court system is seen as even more central to what the courts are called upon to do.

These two conceptual challenges have made it complicated for the court system to adopt community-oriented strategies. How can the courts shift their traditional focus on due process of law given to specific criminal cases so that they include a concern for the community-level impact of court case outcomes? Without violating well-established and profoundly important constitutional rights that have evolved over two centuries of litigation, how can the courts embrace a growing concern for the quality of life in the communities the courts serve? These are difficult questions. Our review of the current efforts to bring community-oriented ideas to the courts will show that today's court innovators are successfully creating strategies that embrace the new court's concerns without violating its traditional values. There is nowhere a perfect community justice court on which to model all community-based court innovation, but neither is there a perfect traditional court. What court reformers have been doing involves rebuilding court processes, procedures, and jurisdictions so that community-oriented values can emerge within the broader context of individual protections. In the end, courts still apply the law from a larger political jurisdiction to individual criminal cases, but community-oriented courts do this in a way that takes into account the need for community justice in the way these decisions are produced and carried out.

THE TWO FUNCTIONS
OF CRIMINAL COURTS

Courts have two main responsibilities: they adjudicate disputes, and they determine the sanctions that will apply in cases that have been adjudicated. In each of these two areas, issues arise concerning two core values underlying the way the courts do their work: justice and rights. Justice issues are concerned with outcomes, asking the question "What results best fit the circumstances of the case?" Rights issues are concerned with the procedures used to determine the outcomes of cases, asking a different question, "What practices should be employed (or prohibited) in developing the outcome for the case?"

Table 3.1 illustrates the different rights and justice issues related to the two functions of the courts. As we see for the discussion that follows, the concern for rights and the criterion of justice each pose quite different challenges for community-oriented strategies of adjudication and sanctioning in the courts.

Adjudication of Complaints

The first function of the criminal courts is to adjudicate a criminal complaint. The criminal complaint is a formal document, called an indictment, or an information, filed by the prosecution accusing a citizen of violating the law. This document brings the case to the attention of the court. The criminal complaint

Table 3.1 Balancing Concerns for Rights vs. Justice in the Court

	Adjudication	Sanctioning
Rights	Concern that the defendant receives due process under the law and that the innocent are not mistakenly found guilty	Concern that the "punishment fit the crime" and is equally applied in like cases
Justice	Concern that the guilty are not mistakenly exonerated	Concern that sanctions take differing circumstances into account and are not counter-productive

alleges certain conduct in violation of the law, and it calls upon the defendant to answer the allegations. In the courtroom, the defendant answers those charges, and, if the defendant claims to be "not guilty," demands that the prosecution offer evidence in proof of the allegations.

One way of looking at the criminal complaint is that it brings about a dispute between the citizen and the state. (That is why criminal cases are referred to, for example, as *State v. Jones.*) At the technical level, the dispute is about the legal status of the defendant, whether the label "offender" may be applied to the defendant by virtue of conduct. In terms of practical implications, the dispute is about whether the defendant may be sanctioned for the alleged conduct. Before the person can be labeled an offender and prior to the imposition of punishment, guilt must be proven. The citizen's status must be shifted from "defendant" to "offender."

In adjudicating the dispute, the values of "justice" and "rights" play a powerful role. Two types of unjust outcomes are possible in adjudication. One occurs when an innocent person is mistakenly found guilty, the other when the case against a person who committed the crime is not proven, and the verdict is "not guilty." Although both values of rights and justice are important, the adjudication function seems to place a higher priority on rights, especially defendant's rights, than on justice. The Constitution gives the defendant the right to reject taking the witness stand and prevents the state from using evidence that has been obtained in violation of the defendant's rights. Legal traditions require that guilt be established "beyond a reasonable doubt."

The emphasis placed on rights is meant to make it difficult for the state to prove its case, and it suggests that when it comes to adjudication, not all forms of unjust outcomes are to be considered equal. This is illustrated by the commonly repeated aphorism, "Better for a hundred guilty men to go free than for one innocent to be convicted" (Justice Learned Hand).

Community justice advocates do not view the adjudication function as a contest. As a consequence, the community justice strategy tends to be less formal in its approach and tries to bring a concern for rights and a belief in outcomes that are just into a better balance. This poses one of the most difficult challenges for community justice as a strategy of the courts. America has a long-standing and immensely important tradition of individual rights as a starting point for adjudication of criminal complaints. How the courts can embrace a concern for community-oriented justice without discarding or depreciating the enormously important tradition of rights is, as we shall see, a significant challenge.

Sanctioning Wrongdoers

For those who are found guilty, the courts must determine the appropriate sanction. The term *appropriate* is not easily defined, in practice, because a penal sanction that seems right to one person may seem too lenient or too severe to another. We all may want a court system that imposes penalties that fit the circumstances of the case, but there may be little agreement about the facts of the case that the penalty should be fitted to. Do the offender's personal characteristics matter? Which ones? Does it matter that the defendant is young, or intellectually limited, or poor, or a mother? What aspects of the crime itself are to be considered? Do we care if the offender was provoked? Does it matter if the way the crime occurred was particularly wanton?

When it comes to imposing a sanction, the concern for an outcome that is just rises in importance, and the prominence of rights is diminished. Of course, the offender's rights are still intact and may not be violated, but we recognize that the sanctioning process is mostly about selecting a penalty that fits the case. Whereas adjudication is about a process of law, sanctioning is about determining the right legal outcome of that process.

Among legal scholars there is some disagreement about the outcome the sanction ought to be tailored to achieve. An eloquent case can be made that the purpose of a sanction is primarily to punish, to impose a penalty that fits the seriousness of the crime (Von Hirsch, 1993). But equally persuasive arguments exist in favor of sanctions that rehabilitate (Cullen and Gendreau, 1989) and incapacitate (Zedlewski, 1987). With this kind of disagreement about the basic aims of a penal sanction, it is not surprising that people frequently disagree about the best penalty to impose upon a newly convicted offender.

In selecting a penalty, the conversation turns from rights to justice: What penalty fits the circumstances of this offender and the offense? The formal process of the courts allows for various opinions to be expressed on the matter before the judge decides. The offender speaks, then the victim and the prosecutor. Sometimes family members of the victim and the offender are also encouraged to offer an opinion; and occasionally experts, such as psychiatrists, give testimony. Whatever penalty is eventually selected, however, must conform to the requirements of the law, and some choices are not allowed in a given penal code. Certain crimes are so serious that at a minimum, a sentence to prison is required; other crimes are sufficiently mundane that financial or community penalties can be imposed.

In the last thirty years, many reformers have become concerned about disparities in penal sanctions (Allen, 1996) and have tried to develop penal codes that resulted in more consistency in sentencing. These new sentencing approaches, whether sentencing guidelines or determinate sentencing (Tonry, 1993), have been seen by some as successful and by others as a mistake. But they all have had the result of reducing the range of penalties a judge may consider when imposing sentence. In most jurisdictions across America, judges today have far fewer choices available to them when determining the sentence than they did a generation ago, because legal reforms have restricted those choices.

Community justice challenges the sanctioning function of the courts in two ways. First, those who advocate for community-oriented penalties tend to desire a broader array of possible case outcomes than are now available to judges. They approve of creative sanctioning that builds a penalty based partly on the crime, but also very much on the circumstances of the offender. They also call for a sentence that takes into account the desire of the community for a long-term investment in public safety. Community justice advocates also give a very high priority to what is thought of as "voice": the victim, the offender, and the community ought to have an opportunity to explore and explain what is desired as the best outcome of the sanction, once it is selected. Perhaps the biggest way community justice challenges the sanctioning function of the courts is that, under its model, sentences are not "imposed" by a judge who is remote to the circumstances of the case; rather, the penalty is determined in interaction with those who were affected by the crime, including the offender.

HOW COURTS WORK TODAY

We have a view of the courts as a very formal, dignified process. Judges sit high above the courtroom, donned in severe black robes. Lawyers, dressed with professional respect, speak only when allowed. Decorum is at a premium. A kind of ritual occurs, starting with the "Oyez, oyez," and punctuated by the ringing authority of the judge's gavel. The courtroom is purposefully designed to symbolize the somber majesty of the law, standing in for the historical prerogative of the omnipotent Crown. Each detail of the way the court is arranged speaks of the power and dignity of the law, and the comparative insignificance of those who are assembled under its austerity.

Is That the Way the Law Really Operates in Practice?

The contemporary courtroom maintains elements of this stylish, symbolic instrument of power and authority. But for the vast majority of cases, what happens bears only a minuscule resemblance to this picture. To understand the way the criminal trial courts work today, we must begin with four concepts: caseload pressure, informality, exchange, and stages of decision making.

Caseload pressure is a dominant force in contemporary courts because the number of criminal cases to be processed by the courts has grown over the last thirty years without a commensurate increase in the number of judges, prosecutors, and defenders. State courts experienced a 45 percent increase in criminal filings between 1984 and 1997 (Ostrom and Kauder, 1998). Court players have felt this growth. State prosecutors reported that the volume of their caseloads has increased because more offenders are being prosecuted (Nugent and McEwan, 1988); and public defenders, who receive on average 80 percent of all criminal cases, have not had increases in staff commensurate with increases in caseloads (Spangenberg, 2001). Specifically, this means that there is a premium on avoiding jury trials, which are five to ten times more costly in time and personnel than guilty pleas or even (in many cases) bench trials. Even though defendants have a Constitutional right to select a jury trial, the realities of case pressure mean that lawyers on all sides will try to resolve a case without resorting to an expensive and in many cases, unnecessary, jury trial.

Jury trials are not necessary in many cases because the factual guilt of the defendant is often not in question. Of course, the state must be able to prove the defendant's guilt in a trial, but often there is incontrovertible evidence of guilt, and the prospects of acquittal are less than slim. In such cases, what defendants have at stake is less the question of adjudication than the eventual sanction to be imposed. Here, *informality* is in the interests of all parties. Rather than simply leave the sanction up to the judge, it is often thought better for the state and the defendant to reach a general agreement about a sanction acceptable to both parties. To do this requires informal conversation and negotiation outside the inflexible confines of the courtroom.

Flexibility is reinforced by the reality of *exchange,* which means that each party has something to offer the other in the process of negotiating a case outcome. The defender can promise not to demand an expensive jury trial and can promise the unparalleled efficiency of a guilty plea instead of a trial. The prosecutor can offer an opportunity to avoid some of the harsher penalties available under the law, either through reducing the charges or agreeing to make a recommendation to the court for a lenient sentence. The judge, by accepting this negotiated settlement, can avoid tying up the courtroom with an unneeded criminal trial in which guilt is not at issue and can thereby avoid further delay in proceeding to more pressing cases.

The *stages of decision making* in the courts facilitate this less formal processing of cases. In most courts, there is an initial hearing in which the charges are registered and the basic evidence in behalf of those charges is listed. Often an arraignment follows, with a more formal reading of charges and evidence, a formal plea by the defendant, and a date set for a trial. There are pretrial hearing dates that deal with questions such as bail and the admissibility of evidence. All this occurs prior to the actual trial, and each event offers an opportunity for the parties to discuss, informally and outside the presence of the judge, a way of resolving the charges without going to trial. Each stage accelerates the pressure on the parties to work out a nonjury decision, and each stage offers a new opportunity to discuss a way to make a nonjury agreement work.

The combination of caseload pressure, exchange, and a tradition of informality dominates the stages of the court process. Because there are repeated op-

portunities to reach an agreement, a trial is usually avoided in favor of a negotiated guilty plea. This means that most defendants eventually waive their Constitutional rights to a trial, to proof of the charges "beyond a reasonable doubt,"
to avoid self-incrimination, and to have all the prosecution's evidence tested
against rules of admissibility. The defendant trades these Constitutional rights
in expectation of a penalty that is less onerous than the one threatened by full
force of the law.

It is against this backdrop that the contemporary community justice movement in the courts must be evaluated. Critics of the community justice model
argue that a defendant's rights are imperiled by the informality of decision making in community-oriented courts, and the basic protections of the law are lost.
They also say that negotiated decision making results in compromises that de-
tract from the symbolic importance of the formal criminal law. There is also a
concern that too much discretion will lead to sanctions in a community justice
framework that suffer from extensive sentencing disparity.

In fact, the current system encourages these same problems because its procedures in full expression are so expensive, and because those who are involved
in the system have very good reasons for avoiding the most extreme implications of the provisions of the penal law. The question is not whether community justice has too much informality and negotiation of its practices but
whether the informality and negotiation activity within community justice
practices leads to case outcomes that are more acceptable to all parties.

THE VICTIM OF CRIME

The last two decades have seen increasing importance placed on the victims of
crime. This concern has expressed itself in two forms. First, there has been
strong pressure to increase the severity of sanctions in the belief that tougher
penalties show respect for the impact of crime on victims. Second, there has
been pressure on the formal criminal justice system to listen more to victims
regarding the way cases are handled. Thus, prosecutors have opened up victim-
assistance offices, and penal-code reforms have created a basis for victims to
speak at sentencing and parole hearings, and even to be informed of the way
charges are changed during plea negotiations.

The addition of the voice of the victim has changed the dynamics of the
criminal court case-management practices. Victims are given a very limited
role when they are encouraged to testify at trial and allowed to make a sentencing recommendation. But a more aggressive stance regarding victims lets
them have a say about the case at every stage. It includes them as a voice in the
charging process, the negotiations of a guilty plea, and the selection of the
eventual penal sanction. Nowhere are victims as fully involved in the criminal
justice process as they could be, but every criminal court hears much more
from victims today than was the case twenty years ago.

Now that we have become more understanding of the needs of victims and more willing to give them a substantial voice in the criminal justice process, we have become more sophisticated in our appreciation of what victims need in order to begin to recover from the emotional and material costs of the crime. It is not always what we might think. Studies of victims find that they differ in their needs (Office for Victims of Crime, 2000). Some want a kind of revenge, while others are more interested in restitution. Some want to meet and confront the offender; others do not. Some want to understand why the crime happened, and these victims often look for a way for the offender to be rehabilitated so that future criminality will not occur. Others care little about what is in the offender's head or heart. They just want a meaningful punishment to be imposed by the court.

Almost all victims want to be able to speak on their own behalf, and being able to give voice to their experiences in the formal justice process is often an important part of recovery from crime. By far, most victims, when given a choice, would prefer a sanction that leads the offender to a productive, law-abiding life, over a sanction that merely punishes. But almost all victims think that some form of punishment is called for in order to bring the case to closure. Contemporary critics of the way the court system handles victims point out that there is little capacity for the justice system to undertake the variety of strategies required to meet the diverse concerns of crime victims, and there is almost no provision for handling cases differently based on the desires of the victim.

We know as well that the reality of the victim's circumstances does not always correspond to the popular image of the victim. We often think emotionally about the victim of crime, and in our image we see an entirely innocent stranger, victimized by a cavalier felon. However, most victims are not strangers to their victimizer—many are family members, and others are acquaintances. In these cases, there is often an understandable ambivalence about harsh punishment for the perpetrator of the offense. Just as important, crimes such as drug abuse or prostitution have no obvious victim. How to represent the voice of the victim in these quite common circumstances is an essential part of a broad victims movement in criminal justice.

The increasing role of the crime victim in the justice system is a critical development in the advent of community justice, because those who believe in community justice have had to invent new ways to incorporate victim sentiments and interests into the community justice ethic. From the community justice standpoint, of course, the broader community suffers from crime, so delivering justice in the community helps deal with the problem of victims insofar as they are community members. Moreover, the process of sanctioning offenders affects their families and their communities, and the community justice approach makes room for these issues. There is, however, a need for more—a need for community justice to embrace the specific concerns of specific victims of crime.

THE COMMUNITY COURT

The idea of community-oriented strategies in the courts has become a new and very important force in recent years. Today, community courts are a popular idea, with many urban areas experimenting with community-based specialty courts. As we shall see, the community court concept applies to courts that serve particular neighborhoods within larger jurisdictions, and it also refers to courts that deal with a particular community of clients, such as domestic-violence cases. But the contemporary idea of community courts borrows some concepts from an era long past in the court system when municipal courts held extraordinary power over adjudication in communities that were isolated from other governmental sectors. The environment for community courts has changed a great deal in modern times, but some of the values we expect of them have not.

A Historical Look at Community Courts

During most of U.S. history, trial courts have been community based. Until the early part of the twentieth century, American society was a rural society in which county legal government was the dominant political force. Counties had a criminal court, located in the county seat, and justice emanated from that venue. The benefit of these courts was their fit to the community. The judges who determined criminal cases lived in their communities, knew many of the residents, and had a sense of the values that the community held. Their activity was far from impersonal and held strongly to themes of community values.

This was also the main weakness of the community-friendly rural court. People who were community outcasts or whose status in the community was suspect may have found it hard to receive equal justice. This charge held particularly in the South, where Blacks encountered an often-hostile court system run exclusively by the dominant White majority. The all-too-common lack of sympathy for poor Blacks in trouble with the law exposed the dark underbelly of community-friendly courts: if you were not seen as a legitimate part of the community, you might have had a little trouble getting justice.

This concern fueled a professional version of the courts that became the dominant idea in the latter half of the twentieth century. Several key issues figured in this change; chief among them was that the work of the courts was not community work but was a professional task requiring technical skills. The law, it was felt, needed to be uniform across all places, and a community-friendly judiciary was inconsistent with the vision of an unvarying criminal law. Part of this sentiment came from an evolving commitment to equal protection under the law, which arose as part of an emerging concern for civil rights and rights of the powerless. Another concern came from the sense that "amateur" justice was inadequate, often stemming from a faulty understanding of the law and a parochial application of its principles. There was also, in the last third of the century, a new concern for equality in punishments. Punishment disparity was identified as a serious problem in criminal law, and the remedy was thought to be the reduction of sentencing discretion in favor of application of a set of sentencing standards in every location of the jurisdiction.

The romantic vision of a community-friendly court, as existed in the early rural and agrarian United States, is forever gone, replaced by professional civil servants highly trained in the legal process. Yet the community court is not extinct. Most Americans may live in urban and suburban settings, where a sense of personal anonymity is a common part of legal procedures. But most of the jurisdictions in the United States remain small and medium-sized, and many of America's courts serve populations that are not the urban, disenfranchised poor. The state of Indiana, for example, has ninety-two counties, and each has a county seat with a county court that handles criminal cases arising in that jurisdiction. Of those ninety-two courthouses, perhaps a dozen serve populations that can be considered primarily densely urban.

However, the contemporary community court movement is not designed for the rural or even the suburban courthouse. The way people describe the mission of the community court places its relevance directly within the troubled neighborhoods in our densely populated urban areas. The neighborhoods served are discrete locations existing wholly within larger, more heterogeneous jurisdictions. The communities served within those neighborhoods are typically poor groups lacking access to legal resources. What has happened is that the logic of the bygone community court, which can tailor its efforts to better meet the needs of the community it serves, has been reformulated as an urban solution to distinctly urban problems.

Thus, we can make a distinction between community-friendly courts that operate in smaller community settings and are composed of community leaders who handle cases involving people who, for the most part, know each other, and the modern community-oriented court. This latter version is not a happenstance of the nature of a community, but is an intentional innovation designed to help create a sense of community and improve the feel of the community it serves.

The Contemporary Community Court Movement

The breakthrough example was the Midtown Community Court in New York City. Developed in 1993, the Midtown Community Court was the brainchild of the Midtown Business Improvement District (BID) coalition of businesses, prominent residents, and social services operating in the Times Square area of New York City. The Times Square area has a concentration of entertainment-based businesses—theaters, restaurants, hotels, and recreational game centers—and therefore attracted a large number of one-day "tourists." By the late 1980s, misbehavior by some of the more disagreeable visitors had become a serious concern: drunken and disorderly, the "tourists" would urinate in the streets and alleys, openly solicit prostitutes, get in fights with each other, and engage in other loud and rowdy activity. The increasingly undesirable nature of these visitors made living in the residential areas surrounding the businesses an ever more distressing experience.

One of the problems was that the criminal justice system was largely unresponsive to the situation. Arrests would be made, and perpetrators would spend the night in a holding cell nearby. Then they would be released, only to return to Midtown and engage in the same disruptive behavior. The sentences imposed were typically for "time served," and referrals to treatment were never given, so the problem people and their problem behaviors remained. And in a classic broken windows pattern, their presence in the area attracted others like them.

Led by criminal justice innovator Gretchen Dykstra, who was the CEO of the BID, a new strategy was invented. People arrested in the Times Square area would not be taken elsewhere to be processed by courts having no accountability to the Midtown community. Instead, they would be booked, arraigned, and adjudicated locally by the Midtown Community Court, newly established solely to serve cases arising from this area of Manhattan. Not only would these cases be handled locally, but they would also be sanctioned locally. Sanctions would include requirements of public service—a typical offender sentenced by the court does community service cleaning the Midtown streets—but the offenders would also be placed in court-administered treatment programs. The latter, involving substance-abuse treatment, job-training assistance, job-placement assistance, anger-management treatment, and so forth, set the Midtown Community Court apart from the other courts in New York City. Whereas those courts focused their attention on serious felonies that made citizens fearful of their streets and often did next to nothing about nuisance crimes, the Midtown Court reasoned that it was precisely these public order offenses that led to deterioration in the Midtown area.

Residents and businesses banded together to form the Midtown Community Court, and they were wildly enthusiastic about its accomplishments. The popularity of that experimental court with its core clients—the businesses and residents of Midtown—was matched by the appreciation many of the court's criminal clients expressed for the services they received. Soon, the experiment was seen as such a complete success that community courts began to spring up in other urban locations. The Center for Court Innovation, which designed and ran the Midtown Community Court, began to assist other locations in developing their own community courts for problem locations. In 1999, the National Institute of Justice funded a series of community courts across the nation on an experimental basis.

The Midtown Community Court is not without its critics, some of whom argue that locating social services within the courthouse merely serves to strengthen judicial institutions at the expense of the community institutions the court was ostensibly created to help. This criticism is more meaningful in

---

Center for Court Innovation

The Center for Court Innovation (CCI), established as a public-private partnership, serves as the research and development arm of the New York State Unified Court System. CCI pioneered the first community court in Midtown Manhattan in 1993 and has since been in the fore-front of the movement to develop and promote community and prob-lem-solving courts. Building on their success with the Midtown model, CCI tested the flexibility of its community court approach in two dis-parate neighborhoods: Red Hook, Brooklyn, and Harlem, New York. In each of these sites, CCI worked to be responsive to local concerns. The Red Hook Community Justice Center, which houses the nation's first multijurisdictional court, also incorporates an adult job-training pro-gram and a youth court. Harlem residents were primarily concerned about the impact of youth crime on the neighborhood. Consequently, in addition to being a housing and re-entry court, the Harlem Commu-nity Justice Center is home to a youth court, a youth mediation pro-gram, and a juvenile treatment court. Thus, by incorporating outreach to the community during the planning process, CCI ensured that the courts were truly responsive to community public safety issues and had laid the groundwork for ongoing community involvement.

---

light of the unavoidable added expense of establishing a community court. There are ancillary costs associated with decentralizing court services, such as the extra personnel costs for defense, prosecution, and corrections. Some crit-ics have claimed, in fact, that only in business-rich Midtown Manhattan can a community court garner sufficient resources to be able to create a true prob-lem-solving court, one that disposes of cases on a local level and is actually able to provide the care needed to address the complex problems faced by low-level offenders. Consequently, the community court model is not truly replicable. Community courts, most of which target low-level offenders, are also subject to the charge that they engage in "net-widening" activity. By bringing into the criminal justice arena a whole class of offenders who otherwise would have little if no contact with the justice system, community courts may be serv-ing to criminalize and punish individuals who might be better served with more informal, community-based censure for their behavior. Moreover, by displacing normal venues for informal, community-based censure, community courts actually serve to debilitate the inherent social institutions that are the foundation of public safety in neighborhoods. But even with the validity of these concerns, the community court movement has become a bellwether for reformulating courts to make them more accountable to the communities they serve.

COMMUNITY-ORIENTED
COURT FUNCTIONS

The two main functions of the courts are adjudication and sanctioning, and each has been open to an infusion of community justice concepts. We will explore how community justice principles have been incorporated into traditional court functions.

Community-Oriented Adjudication

Adjudication consists of three roles: prosecution, defense, and judiciary. Each can be adapted to a community context, though the most experience exists with community-oriented prosecution. Because the three roles are so tightly linked, it makes sense to consider the ways that creating one as a community-based model leads to the logic of the other.

Community Prosecution Michael Shrunk of Multnomah County (Portland), Oregon, had been elected as district attorney and served for nine years, and most people thought of him as having a "safe" seat. He enjoyed the wide respect of the electorate, the confidence of business leaders, and political independence. Yet he had a problem. In the highest crime area of Portland, the Lloyd District, people had little confidence in the criminal justice system, and his prosecutors often faced difficulty obtaining citizen support for investigations and prosecutions of everyday offenders from that area.

Shrunk decided to try something new. He opened up a district attorney branch office in the neighborhood and assigned one of his more talented assistant district attorneys (ADA) to that office. While most of his "downtown" ADAs were specialists in particular types of offenses—frauds, homicide, drugs—this ADA would handle all the cases emanating from that neighborhood. It was an experiment to see how this energetic ADA could change the relationship between the prosecutor's office and the residents of that area of Portland.

The innovation worked. After a few months, the ADA had gained the confidence of many of the residents of the area, and new, productive relationships were formed between the citizenry and the prosecution. No longer did the residents of that area have an alienated, or even hostile, relationship to the work of the prosecutor. The residents wanted legal help with their community problems, especially problems that related to public safety and community quality of life, and the new community prosecutor could help them with that.

Just as interesting was the way the prosecutor's job changed when the office was moved to the problem neighborhood. In the downtown office, the emphasis was on major cases, the kinds that make headlines and involve severe violence to victims: rape, murder, and assault. It was natural for the downtown prosecutors to focus on these cases because they seemed to be the most important. The public also considered these cases important, but there was an even more avid interest in the kinds of criminal activity that were less likely to make headlines in the local newspaper. Citizens wanted crack houses to be closed down, street drug markets to be moved off public space, open prostitution to be removed from their streets, and landlord violations to be prosecuted. They also wanted their kids who were in trouble with the law to get help, by being placed in treatment programs and getting assistance with education and employment.

What the community ADA learned was that serious crime may be a high priority to outsiders, but the people who live in those problems places may have a different priority. Most people think that people in high-crime areas want tough prosecution of serious criminal cases, but this idea misses the myriad, everyday indignities that people in these places must confront. What they want is something like a legal service; they need access to the courts to press for solutions to their community-level problems. They have asked for help in problem solving in addition to the prosecution of individual criminal cases. They want a legally relevant support system for their community priorities, and the prosecutor, as an official of the court, has a unique ability to provide that service. Because this kind of law is so different, some people have referred to it as "community safety law" (Conner and Griffin, 1998).

The Portland lesson has been repeated in numerous other jurisdictions where community prosecutors have begun to reshape the prosecution function in multiproblem neighborhoods. The problems vary from location to location because in each community, there is a slightly different set of issues to be tackled. But the big picture is the same everywhere. Whenever a centralized prosecution service has opened up specialized offices to serve a particular, troubled location, there has been an increase in citizen confidence in the prosecutor's activity, and there has been a shift in that activity to better match the needs and desires of the citizenry who live there.

However, there have been problems with community prosecution. Community-based prosecutors are open to co-optation by community groups by developing too close or comfortable a relationship with a select number of citizens. This co-optation jeopardizes their neutrality and inhibits their ability to see the full range of problems that need to be addressed in a neighborhood. Community prosecutors must also be careful about burnout. In the face of the multiple and varied problems that communities face, prosecutors may try to take on too much. But it must be recognized that community prosecution has emerged as a new way to provide prosecutorial services so that communities' needs for legal assistance with public safety problems can be addressed.

Community Defender Services Much newer than the idea of community prosecution is the development of community defenders, also called neighborhood defender services. As a result, there are very few studies of this application of the community justice idea in the court area.

Neighborhood Defender Service

Launched in 1990 by the Vera Institute of Justice, the Neighborhood Defender Service (NDS) in Harlem, New York, completely altered the traditional nature of indigent legal representation. Based in the community, NDS does not wait for the court to assign it cases; rather, through community outreach it encourages residents to call when they are first arrested—much the way wealthy clients call their attorneys. This gives NDS more time to develop cases and potentially resolve them before they go to court. Using a team approach that includes an attorney, community worker, administrative assistant, intern, and senior attorney, NDS shifts the priority of legal representation from cases that are in trial to the up-front work that occurs when defendants first walk in the door. As a result, teams handle far more than the case at hand and help to mediate and dispose of community problems that are often shunted through the court system for lack of a community-based response. NDS finds that their clients lead complicated lives; many do not perceive their criminal case as a priority among the many others they face. By listening to their clients, NDS adopts a more holistic approach to legal representation, which often takes a backseat to addressing other concerns, such as implications of the case for the family. NDS also works proactively to improve public safety in the community. Recognizing a need in the community for legal education, NDS leads workshops with young people, teaching them how to prevent potential conflict with police from escalating.

Neighborhood defenders would seem to have several advantages over the traditional, downtown and centralized defender services. For example, the neighborhood defender is closer to the community where the defendant lives, and it is often easier to obtain witnesses in support of the defendant at trial and to speak on behalf of the defendant at sentencing. Because many of the crimes occur in the same neighborhood where the defendant lives, it is also easier to gather evidence in those cases that result in a trial.

An equally important advantage of neighborhood-based defender services is that the defender gets to know the neighborhood. Relationships are established with important private-sector interests—such as businesses and churches—and these can translate into valuable supports for clients. Businesses can provide jobs for clients, and churches can provide other types of assistance. Familiarity with social-service providers can also establish a foundation for clients to deal with the problems that led to their criminal involvement.

This point highlights one of the key differences between neighborhood-based defender services and traditional services. In the latter, the lawyer sees the job as getting the best deal possible for the client—a finding of not guilty, if possible, and a short sentence, if necessary. But the neighborhood defender looks at the broader interests of the defendant, helping the defendant get into drug treatment, for example, or arranging child care and family services for the family members who are not under scrutiny of the court.

As happens for neighborhood-based prosecutors, defenders who work at the neighborhood level find that their job changes. They are no longer exclusively concerned with the tactics of the criminal case. Instead, they also develop an interest in the defendant's relationships to the neighborhood, and they look for ways to strengthen the client's integration into the neighborhood.

Community Judiciary We have discussed the concept of the community court, and the head of that court, the judge, might represent a type of community judiciary. As yet, however, there is no official role for a community judiciary beyond what we described for community courts. However, as community courts gain acceptance, there is reason to think that a kind of community-oriented judiciary will also grow.

Such a judiciary would be very different from the centralized, disconnected judges of today. They would work closely with citizen groups and neighborhood interests to develop a judicial practice on behalf of neighborhood concerns. This role would constantly test their commitment to judicial impartiality, but it would also open a door to a deeper and more effective level of citizen participation in the work of the courts.

In effect, the judiciary can follow the orientation of the defender and prosecutor. If they have devoted themselves to a community justice model, the way they develop their cases and the way they hope to resolve disputes will be oriented to the community. The judicial role will then be presented with case decisions and caseload priorities that reflect the orientation of the attorneys.

Community-Oriented Sanctioning

It is one thing to identify and prioritize criminal complaints with an eye to community issues; it is quite another to try to resolve them with that same vision. Community justice sanctioning offers a significant departure from the usual strategy, because both the aims of the sanction and the stakeholders to the outcome are different.

Under traditional models of sanctioning, the aims of the criminal sentence are primarily punitive, especially for serious crime. The sentence may include recognition of the possibility of rehabilitation, if an offender is required to attend a treatment program or placed under some form of community supervision with treatment conditions. But the overarching value expressed by the sentence is punitive, as its centerpiece is a loss of freedom. Secondary aims of traditional criminal sentences may be incapacitation or deterrence, depending upon the circumstances of the case. The main point is that the object of the sentence is to do something *to* the offender that will communicate blame and reprobation through a penalty that is intentionally unpleasant. (For a discussion of this idea, see C. S. Lewis, *The Abolition of Man*.)

In this model, the sentence is determined with little attention paid to anyone but the offender. There may be sympathy expressed to the victim and an emotional appeal to community values, but the sentence is about the offender's conduct and the requirements of the law. In a very real sense, the crime is seen as a trespass against the laws of the state, and the resolution of the crime is for the state to reassert its authority by imposing a penalty for the trespass.

Community justice changes the aims of the sentence. Punishment of the wrongdoer is not eliminated as a goal, but it takes a second priority to the needs of the community for an outcome that restores some of the losses suffered as a result of the crime. Instead of viewing the crime as a legal dispute between the accused and the state, a criminal act is seen as an unfair loss (or harm) imposed by one citizen upon another. The problem to be solved is to overcome the unfairness by restoring the loss and repairing the harm. In most crimes, there are multiple victims—a citizen, the community, relatives of the offender and the victim—and finding a way to restore all their losses is a priority. In this way, the stakeholders to a criminal event are not just the state and the accused, but everyone affected by the crime.

The Role of Victims In this philosophy of sanctioning, the role of the victim is radically changed. Traditional justice models tend to see the victim as aligned with the punitive agenda of the state. They stand mostly at the sidelines of the criminal case, offering testimony in support of the conviction and being given the opportunity to argue for the most punitive sanction available to the court. To the extent there has been harm or loss as a result of the crime, it tends to be expressed as anger at the offender and a call for a more punitive penalty.

Studies of victims find that many have a much more complex view of how they would like the sanctioning process to proceed and what they expect from the penalty (Office for Victims of Crime, 2000). Most want the offender to be punished for the crime, but they also want to be able to tell their story so the offender can see how the criminal act was harmful. They want to understand why the offender committed the crime and to see a sanction that makes it less likely that the offender will repeat the crime. If some sort of rehabilitation program is in order, the victim usually supports its inclusion in the sanction; and victims want some support that will help to repair the harm they have encountered as a result of the crime.

These views are similar to those of citizens at large (Gorczyk and Perry, 1997). Most people want a penalty that "makes sense," in that it will help to restore the victim. They also want the offender to recognize the harmfulness of the act and regret it. This desire translates into an "instrumental penance," where the offender is so sorry for the act that he or she takes strong steps to deal with the problems that led to the act so it will not be repeated. In this sense, the community expects an offender to repent, make restitution to the victim

---

Parallel Justice

The movement toward incorporating victims' voices in the justice process is best represented by Susan Herman, the executive director of the National Center for Victims of Crime, who has called for a system of parallel justice for victims. She argues that most victims don't get a chance to participate in the justice process because their offenders were never arrested or prosecuted, and even those that do participate are likely to be disappointed because the justice system is focused primarily on instituting appropriate treatment of offenders. Rather than tie the dispensation of victims' services to the court process and offender restitution, local government authorities should provide all victims with resources ranging from counseling to new door locks to victims' compensation. Herman sees the creation of this parallel system for victims taking place on the local level. Local leaders would be "challenged to assess the needs of victims in their community, establish a process for meeting those needs, and combine federal and local resources to make parallel justice a reality" (Herman, 2000).

---

and the community, and become a better citizen. The desire is for a three-way restoration—of the victim, the community, and the offender.

To achieve this three-way restoration, community justice has to place the victim and the community in the center of the sanctioning process, not at the sideline. Instead of a process that emphasizes the voice of the prosecution and the protests of the offender, community justice seeks a process that gives voice to victims, offenders, and communities, and moves the role of the judge and prosecutor to the sideline. This approach is known as "restorative justice."

Restorative Justice Restorative justice is a new version of an ancient idea: the outcome of a transgression against the community ought to be some process that restores the community from the effects of that transgression and thereby allows the transgressor to be restored as well. There are four main versions of restorative justice (Bazemore and Umbreit, 2001).

Victim–offender mediation is an approach to sanctioning that enables the victim to confront the offender with the harm that has been done, and then invokes a process whereby the victim and offender come to an agreement about the appropriate sanction to be imposed as a consequence of the wrongful conduct.

Community reparative boards are citizen tribunals that receive criminally convicted referrals from the court, for which they determine the appropriate sanctions through a process of conversation with the offender and others affected by the crime.

Family group conferencing is derived from ancient practices of the Maori people of New Zealand, in which the family of the offender, the victim, and the community come together with a trained facilitator to develop an appropriate sanction for the offender's misconduct.

Circle sentencing is based upon traditional practices of aboriginal peoples of North America, in which community leaders, the offender, and the victim come together in a circle to seek sanctions that will lead to healing from the crime on everyone's part.

There is a growing body of research on restorative justice approaches. These studies find that most restorative justice processes are limited to non-violent, less serious crime, although there are a handful of projects that apply these principles to interpersonal violent crime. Almost all studies report a significant improvement in the satisfaction of both victims and offenders with the process and the sanction it produced. Several studies show that offenders who go through restorative sanctions have lower failure rates than those who go through the traditional process, though other studies find no difference. Interestingly, there is some evidence emerging that the most successful restorative justice projects are those that allow cases involving serious interpersonal violence and that are not restricted to property crime (Coates and Umbreit, 1999).

COURTS FOR SPECIALIZED COMMUNITIES

As new adjudication practices emerged and sanctioning schemes broadened, more attention came to be paid to the way the courts were structured to accommodate these processes. When increasing specialization of treatment and intervention protocols that address the needs and circumstances of specific populations, such as substance abusers or juvenile delinquents, were added to the mix, courts began to tailor their work to these special communities of offenders.

Drug Courts

Drug courts emerged in response to the crack epidemic of the late 1980s, which flooded court dockets with drug offenders. The initial drug-court models were established to overcome the backlog of cases through expedited case processing. These courts, however, did not address the "revolving-door" phenomenon of the many addicted offenders who inevitably became recidivists upon release. Drug courts as commonly implemented today coordinate legal case processing with a range of treatment modalities. These courts build on the experience of pioneers such as Treatment Alternatives to Street Crime (TASC), which brought a link of treatment into the courtroom, but take this treatment intervention one step further through a codified model of "therapeutic jurisprudence." There are now more than six hundred drug courts in operation across the country, a number that includes juvenile treatment courts and family treatment courts, as well as drug courts (see Federal Department of Justice,

Office of Justice Programs, Drug Court Clearinghouse and Technical Assistance Project at http://www.ncjrs.org/drug_courts/training.html#2).

In a drug court, the judge plays an active role in helping defendants conquer their addiction by teaching consequential thinking through a series of graduated sanctions and rewards. Defendants are required to appear in front of the judge at frequent and regular intervals, at which point they recount how they are progressing with their treatment and other life goals. Compliance with the court requirements is celebrated by rewards, such as having to appear in court less frequently, and noncompliance is marked by sanctions that vary in severity depending on the gravity of the violation. Low-level rearrest might trigger a temporary remand to jail, while a urine test positive for drugs will bring a day spent in court watching the proceedings. These graduated sanctions incorporate an understanding that relapse is an almost unavoidable component of the recovery process, and rather than terminate someone from treatment for relapse, the court incorporates an appropriate therapeutic response. Defendants who successfully complete the drug court often receive a reduced sentence, a lowered or dismissed charge, or some combination.

As in most community justice models, the justice player roles are redefined. In order to operate a drug court effectively, the traditionally adversarial roles of the prosecutor, defense, and judge are shifted so that the three represent a coordinated team. This team then acts both to safeguard public safety and to treat defendants for their addiction problems. Drug courts also serve as community justice models, not because they are located within a geographic community and therefore concern themselves with the problems of that community, but because their approach to justice problems incorporates a context much larger than the case at hand. Drug courts work to solve the problem of drug-addicted offenders who cycle in and out of the justice system. To do this, the court must form strong links to community-based treatment programs by bringing them into the courtroom and the justice process. Additionally, drug courts often develop connections to other community-based support services such as job training and education. In the ideal drug-court model, community volunteers would be brought into the court to provide continual support for defendants in court and upon their return to the community.

Domestic-Violence Courts

Domestic violence continues to be one of the most intractable public safety issues with which communities and the justice system grapple daily. The National Crime Victimization Survey revealed that in 1998 an estimated one million violent crimes were committed against intimate partners (Rennison and Welchans, 2000). The justice system has responded to this crisis by developing specialized court processes to handle domestic-violence cases. These courts, which are still in their infancy, vary widely in their structure and goals (Keilitz, 2000). One court that has received national attention was implemented in 1996 in Brooklyn, New York, by the New York State Unified Court System in partnership with the Center for Court Innovation.

The Brooklyn Domestic Violence Court was designed to promote swift and certain responses to domestic-violence offenders while also ensuring the victim's safety. Defendants must appear regularly in the court, where they are subject to ongoing monitoring of court-ordered programs, such as batterers' intervention programs and compliance with orders of protection. Defendants remain accountable to and continue to appear in front of the same judge, even after case disposition and during the term of probation. A resource coordinator helps the judge monitor compliance by obtaining information from the district attorney, the department of probation, and batterers' programs. A victim advocate, who works in partnership with the prosecutor, ensures that victims have a safety and housing plan and are linked to counseling and other social services. Domestic-violence courts provide a critical step in a continuum of response that begins with local police intervention and continues through ongoing community correction monitoring of the offender and community-based services for victims.

Teen Courts

Teen courts turn peer pressure on its head, using young people to censure teens who have broken the law. With the earliest documented teen court established in Grand Prairie, Texas, in 1976 (Godwin, 1996), teen courts have recently blossomed with 675 across the United States (Butts and Buck, 2000). These courts, by providing an alternative to more formal case processing for young offenders, serve to craft a more meaningful response to low-level teen offending, as well as positively involve young people in the justice process. Teen courts fit into the rubric of community justice by creating a "community of teens" that work to promote and enforce appropriate standards of behavior for young people in their neighborhood.

Although there are many types of teen courts, in the basic model, young offenders who have already admitted their guilt to low-level offenses such as vandalism, truancy, shoplifting, and trespassing, participate voluntarily in a process in which their case will be heard by a judge and jury of their peers, who determine the appropriate sanction. Schools, probation departments, police, nonprofit agencies, and courts all may operate a teen court. Some teen courts use adult judges with youth juries and/or youth "attorneys," while other courts are fully staffed by young people. Typical sanctions might include community-service hours, essay writing, a letter of apology, service on the teen-court jury, and/or restitution. Teen courts may also work to incorporate family participation, with parents being required to take the stand or with mandated parental attendance at the hearing. Teen courts frequently draw on the principles of restorative justice by incorporating a social-service assessment of the young person prior to or after the hearing and subsequent linking to social services.

The most common evaluations of teen courts focus on the recidivism of the young offender, which disregards the multiple functions teen courts fulfill. These recidivism analyses fail to indicate a clear connection between lowered recidivism and teen-court participation. A recent summary (Butts and Buck,

Red Hook Youth Court

Dave sits facing a jury of ten at-risk neighborhood youth all wearing Red Hook Youth Court T-shirts in a basement of a local church. The community advocate has already made an opening statement about the harm done to the community by Dave's recent truancy, mentioning that Dave not only is jeopardizing his own future but has also set a bad example for other young people in the neighborhood. The youth advocate has also made an opening statement stressing that Dave is generally well behaved and promises not to do it again. The judge just opened the questions to the jury. In a freestyle manner, the jurors start asking about Dave's life—what he does instead of going to school, what he likes and doesn't like about school, how his relationships are with his family. During the course of their wide-ranging questions, they discover that Dave is frequently truant, that he smokes pot at home when he's not at school, and that he really likes art but doesn't like his teachers. Upon finishing their questions, the jury exits to deliberate and returns with a sanction that incorporates a letter of apology to Dave's mother, a drug assessment, and a goal-setting workshop. Several weeks later, some of the jurors talk about seeing Dave in the neighborhood and asking how he is doing; one juror said that he took Dave to his after-school art class. After completing their six months of service, many of the jurors mention that they feel more responsible for their neighborhood and will stop other kids when they see them writing graffiti or doing other vandalism.

2000) of studies of youth courts found inconsistent results from recidivism analyses: some supported the idea that teen courts are more successful than regular juvenile courts, and others found no differences between the two in overall outcome. However, teen courts also serve to make justice processing more accessible to communities, to provide a community-based forum for the handling of youth crime, to increase public awareness of the legal system, to teach young people about the justice system, and to help young people feel responsible for their neighborhoods. The realization of these last goals will serve the most valuable community justice function by planting positive seeds in the community that will grow into increased community engagement in overall public safety.

Re-entry Courts

Re-entry courts take the drug-court model of intensive court monitoring, therapeutic jurisprudence, graduated sanctions and rewards, and the combination of services with justice case processing and then apply it to offenders returning to the community from extended stays in jail or prison. Their goal is

Multicultural Community Justice

One of the promises of community justice is its ability to be responsive to cultural and racial differences among community residents. For community police it might mean looking at a group of people hanging out in front of a building not as potential drug dealers, but as community members seeking companionship and cooler air outside cramped apartments. For community defenders it might mean treating a client as a member of an elaborate family network who will not make decisions about the case without considering the needs of this network. Community mediators must regularly grapple with racial and cultural differences as they facilitate the direct communication of parties in conflict. Mediators must be adept at helping parties understand each other through a fog of disparate communication styles. They must also be sensitive to the role that racism can play in initiating and escalating conflicts and then in inhibiting the fair and reasonable resolution of conflict (Umbreit and Coates, 2000).

to stabilize parolees and probationers in the community when they first exit prison so as to prevent future recidivism. Recently spearheaded by an Office of Justice Programs initiative, there are only a few re-entry courts extant, with a handful more still in development. Although still too new to evaluate, re-entry courts hold the promise of alleviating the pressures of one of the fastest growing prison populations across the United States: technical parole violators.

Even though models of re-entry courts differ, they tend to combine similar elements. Offenders are assessed prior to release, at which point a re-entry plan is developed. Once released, the offender appears in a "court" established in partnership with parole or probation, which is often headed by a magistrate or administrative law judge rather than a sitting judge, because the offender's case has already been adjudicated. At the court, the offender is mandated to attend appropriate social and drug-treatment services, be law abiding, and engage in education or employment training. The offender will return frequently to court for parole and judicial monitoring and will be subject to a graduated system of sanctions and rewards in response to compliance with the court's mandates.

Re-entry courts may be located in a downtown courthouse, but they necessarily concern themselves with the successful reintegration of offenders into their home communities. To achieve this, the courts must draw on neighborhood-based community supports, which might include community-based social-service agencies, family networks, or faith–based institutions. Ideally, in drawing on these informal community institutions, re-entry courts will also serve to strengthen them, improving future prospects for overall public safety in the neighborhood.

The community court movement is at the center of tension that surrounds the idea of community justice. Do concerns about rights or concerns about justice take priority when they are in conflict? In practice, community courts are splitting the difference. The concern for rights during the adjudication process still predominates in the courtroom, while a concern for justice is gaining pre-eminence during the sanctioning process. One important reason for the increasing concern for justice during the sanctioning process is that the argument for rights has become steadily weaker as the cumulative effects of individual sanctioning decisions have become more apparent. In communities where people suffer poverty, substandard education and health services, and few economic opportunities, the same sanctions given to offenders add up to a more disproportionate impact on the community and the individual than they do in communities characterized by more resources and healthier community well-being. Despite continuing and prospective conflicts, community courts are showing that a fair balance can be struck between individual rights and community justice.

REFERENCES

Allen, Francis. 1996. *The Habits of Legality: Criminal Justice and the Rule of Law.* New York: Oxford University Press.

Bazemore, G., and M. Umbreit. 2001. "A Comparison of Four Restorative Conferencing Models." *Juvenile Justice Bulletin* (February). Washington, D.C.: U.S. Department of Justice, Office of Justice Programs, Office of Juvenile Justice and Delinquency Prevention (OJJDP).

Butts, Jeffrey A., and Janeen Buck. 2000. "Teen Courts: A Focus on Research." *Juvenile Justice Bulletin* (October). Washington, D.C.: OJJDP.

Coates, R. B. and M. S. Umbreit. 1999. *Research & Resources Review: Victim Offender Mediation Empirical Studies.* Minneapolis: Center for Restorative Justice & Peacemaking, University of Minnesota.

Conner, Roger, and Patrick Griffin. 1998. *Community Safety Law: An Emerging Legal Specialty.* National Institute of Justice.

Cullen, F., and P. Gendreau. 1989. "The Effectiveness of Correctional Rehabili-tation: Reconsidering the 'Nothing Works' Debate." In *American Prisons: Issues in Research and Policy,* edited by L. Goodstein and D. MacKenzie. New York: Plenum.

Godwin, Tracy. 1996. *Peer Justice and Youth Empowerment: An Implementation Guide for Teen Court Programs.* Lexington, Ky.: National Highway Traffic Safety Administration and the American Probation and Parole Association.

Gorczyk, John F., and John G. Perry. 1997. "What the Public Wants from Corrections." *Corrections Today* (September).

Herman, Susan. 2000. "Seeking Parallel Justice: A New Agenda for the Victims Movement." Speech given at the National Press Club luncheon, December 15, Washington, D.C.

Keilitz, Susan. 2000. *Specialization of Domestic Violence Case Management in the Courts: A National Survey.* Williamsburg, Va.: National Center for State Courts.

Nugent, H., and J. T. McEwan. 1988. *Prosecutors' National Assessment of Needs.* Washington, D.C.: National

Institute of Justice, U.S. Department of Justice.

Office for Victims of Crime. 2000. New Directions from the Field: Victims' Rights and Services for the 21st Century, Strategies for Implementation. Tools for Action Guide Series: Training Manual. Washington, D.C.: U.S. Department of Justice.

Ostrom, B. J., and B. Kauder. 1998. *Examining the Work of State Courts, 1997: A National Perspective from the Court Statistics Project*. Williamsburg, Va.: National Center for State Courts.

Rennison, Callie, and Sarah Welchans. 2000. *Intimate Partner Violence*. Washington, D.C.: U.S. Dept. of Justice, Office of Justice Programs, Bureau of Justice Statistics.

Spangenberg Group. 2001. *Keeping Defender Workloads Manageable*. Washington, D.C.: U.S. Dept. of Justice, Office of Justice Programs, Bureau of Justice Assistance.

Tonry, Michael. 1993. "Sentencing Commissions and their Guidelines." *Crime and Justice* 17.

Umbreit, Mark, and Robert Coates. 2000. *Multicultural Implications of Restorative Justice: Potential Pitfalls and Dangers*. Washington, D.C.: U.S. Department of Justice, Department of Victims of Crime.

Von Hirsch, Andrew. 1993. *Censure and Sanctions*. Oxford: Clarendon Press.

Zedlewski, Edwin M. 1987. *Making Confinement Decisions*. Washington, D.C.: U.S. Department of Justice.

FOR FURTHER READING

Courts Culture and Caseload

Eisenstein, James, and Herbert Jacob. 1977. *Felony Justice: An Organizational Analysis of the Courts*. Boston: Little, Brown. Still the best description of the social organization of the courts and how it affects court processes.

Harlow, Carol. 2001. *Defense Counsel in Criminal Cases*. Washington, D.C.: U.S. Department of Justice, Office of Justice Programs, Bureau of Justice Statistics.

Lewis, C. S. 2001. *The Abolition of Man*. San Francisco: Harper.

McCoy, Candace. 1993. *Politics and Plea Bargaining: Victims' Rights in California*. Philadelphia: University of Pennsylva-

nia Press. An analysis of the ways court culture affected the implementation of victims' rights in California.

National Association of Drug Court Professionals, Drug Court Standards Committee. 1997. *Defining Drug Courts: The Key Components*. Washington, D.C.: U.S. Dept. of Justice, Office of Justice Programs, Drug Courts Program Office.

Rosset, Arthur, and Donald R. Cressey. 1976. *Justice by Consent*. Philadelphia: Lippincott. Classic study of the way the courts' caseload affects court processing.

Sentencing Reform

Byrne, James M., Arthur J. Lurigio, and Joan Petersilia. 1992. *Smart Sentencing: The Emergence of Intermediate Sanctions*. Newbury Park, Calif.: Sage. A description and evaluation of various alternatives to incarceration.

Griset, Pamela. 1991. *Determinate Sentencing: The Promise and Reality of Retribu-

tive Justice*. Albany: SUNY Press. A critical assessment of the determinate sentencing movement.

Tonry, Michael. 1996. *Sentencing Matters*. New York: Oxford University Press. An explanation and analysis of contemporary issues in sentencing in the United States.

Innovation in the Courts

Feeley, Malcolm. 1983. *Court Reform on Trial: Why Simple Solutions Fail.* New York: Basic Books. A special report on the reasons why court reform in the United States has not succeeded in improving court performance.

Shapiro, Martin. *Courts: A Comparative and Political Analysis.* Chicago: University of Chicago Press. A classic description of various court systems and the social and political issues they raise. 1986.

Stone, Chris. 1996. "Community Defense and the Challenge of Community Justice." National Institute of Justice Journal, *Communities: Mobilizing Against Crime, Making Partnerships Work.* August.

4

❖

Corrections and
Community Justice

Compared to law enforcement and the courts, the correctional function has
been a latecomer to community justice. As Chapter 3 indicated, community-oriented policing activity has a long history but did not become a core aspect of American policing until the 1980s; community-based courts have had
a long tradition in America, but the community court movement did not
gather momentum until the early 1990s. Corrections, by contrast, has begun
to embrace community justice ideas only very recently.

Correctional operations are generally grouped into two types: (1) institutional
corrections and (2) field-service corrections. Institutional corrections encompass jails (usually locally run by the city or county and where defendants await
the disposition of their cases or serve short sentences of incarceration), prisons
(usually run by states and where offenders serve longer-term sentences), and
federal penitentiaries (where offenders convicted of usually more serious federal crimes serve the terms of their sentence). In contrast, field service corrections usually encompass two sorts of activities carried out by two types of
agencies. Probation is a nonincarcerative form of community supervision that
is often understood as an alternative to jail (in some jurisdictions, a probation
sentence is termed a suspended jail sentence). Parole is a form of community

supervision that is meant to monitor the reintegration of offenders into their home communities as they return from prison.

This late arrival of the corrections field to the community justice arena is understandable, yet also ironic. It is understandable because to most people, the correctional functions call forth the imagery of prison and jail, and these seem to have a problematic relationship to everyday community life. Yet there is an irony because the most commonly used forms of corrections occur in the community (probation, parole, and community corrections), and these aspects of correctional activity would seem to be naturally related to the ideals of community justice. As we will see, correctional activity has a historical focus on individual offenders that makes a community justice orientation difficult to sustain, and this is as true for community as for institutional correctional strategies.

Even though correctional leaders have come late to the community justice scene, there is now an energetic interest in the way community justice principles apply to essential correctional tasks. In this chapter, we begin with a brief review of traditional correctional services. We then explore community justice in the correctional setting, and we describe ways in which correctional services are changing to incorporate community justice ideas. We conclude with a description of the challenge of community justice for correctional functions.

THEMES IN TRADITIONAL CORRECTIONAL SERVICES

Many volumes have been written about corrections, and we must simplify a broad, complex topic to come up with a handful of themes that characterize traditional correctional activity. We summarize traditional themes to provide a starting place for talking about community justice versions of corrections in contrast to traditional corrections. The five themes we describe are dominant topics in traditional correctional thought, but they also have relevance to community corrections. In the latter case, they emerge not as core ideas, but as subtopics within larger concerns.

Offender Management

In traditional corrections, the technical core is developed to manage offenders through the process of criminal sanctions. Correctional workers are held accountable for the way they deal with individual offenders. Computerized information systems track offenders from the point they are sentenced by the judge to the point they are terminated from correctional programs. Indeed, every aspect of correctional activity is designed with regard to the way it assists correctional workers in managing the offenders assigned to their care.

The offender-management theme determines the level of focus of correctional attention to be on the individual offender, not the community, the victim, or the system. The offender orientation permeates correctional action: institutional officers are assigned to work cell ranges or housing units populated by individual offenders, and they are accountable for what happens to (and is done by) those offenders; community supervision is organized into caseloads that are collections of offenders, perhaps grouped depending upon the way a classification system suggests they be handled. Under correctional authority, offenders are processed through stages of correctional work—pretrial, post-conviction, and community re-entry. The meaning of corrections is operationalized by the way each of its clients is dealt with by correctional staff.

Risk

The central concern correctional officials emphasize in managing offenders is their risk. High-risk offenders are treated one way—managed with care and with an emphasis on control; and low-risk offenders are dealt with in another—given less restrictions and controls. Average-risk cases fall in the middle. Most correctional programs enable the risk assessment of a given offender to change as he or she is managed through the penal process, so that an offender-management strategy of tight controls may be followed by a much less restrictive approach as the offender demonstrates through behavior that risk is less than the close control requires.

Risk permeates correctional thinking. When a case fails, especially when a new crime is committed by a person under correctional authority, questions usually follow about why the risk was not anticipated. This means that it is unwise to underestimate risk, and correctional officials are encouraged to treat any risk indicator as important. At the same time, however, there are far too many cases under correctional control to allow them all to be handled as high risk. Correctional leaders are therefore caught in a bind—they have to find a substantial body of low-risk cases that justify diverting their attention to the more problematic cases. But whenever there is a problem with any of these cases, correctional officials are made to answer for not anticipating the risk.

Treatment

The idea of rehabilitation has received less support in recent years than it did for most for the twentieth century, but the idea of correctional programming is still very important. Almost all offenders have significant personal problems that, left unchanged, bode poorly for subsequent adjustment to community life after correctional authority ends: drug abuse, poor impulse control, lack of job skills, educational deficits, and so on. All correctional settings are asked to assess offender needs for treatment and provide basic programs that meet those needs.

Unfortunately, the success of correctional treatment programming is notoriously poor. It is not so much that "treatment doesn't work," but rather that even the best treatment programs work for only some of the clients, and all treatment programs have some failure. There is no "silver bullet" in correctional rehabilitation. Treatments are at their most successful when they address the needs of high-risk (rather than low-risk) clients, so we can see that treatment programming poses an inherent dilemma for corrections: the treatments are all going to have failures, and if they are applied correctly (to high-risk cases) to start with, they will have a larger number of failures overall.

Surveillance and Control

Traditional correctional programs have a basic concern for safety of the community. This implies the need for a minimum level of surveillance and control and suggests that as program failures mount and as risk levels of clients get higher, the need for surveillance and control also increases. For correctional administrators, there are no excuses for losing control of cases. A basic requirement is to know where a client is supposed to be and to know if the client is actually there. Institutional correctional officials do counts several times a day to ensure surveillance and control, and community corrections workers employ home visits and drug testing to achieve similar knowledge.

With the advent of new technologies, the emphasis on surveillance and control has grown in recent years. From electronic monitors that identify a person's whereabouts to drug screens and lie detector tests, correctional officials now employ an ever increasing array of methods to assert control and aid surveillance. Whenever there is a problem in a particular offender's case, the question always seems to be, "Why wasn't this person's behavior under closer scrutiny?" It isn't possible to watch every offender all the time, but it is possible to give greater emphasis to watching particular offenders more closely, especially those of high risk or those who have complicated or significant treatment needs—in the former case, to make sure that the rules are being followed, and in the latter, to make sure the treatment program is working.

Punishment

If there is anything that citizens expect from corrections, it is that offenders will be sanctioned for their misconduct. This has two levels of meaning for correctional officials. First, it is assumed that correctional workers will make sure that punishments imposed by the court will be carried out as indicated by the judge. Second, when offenders fail to conform to the rules of correctional programming, there must be unpleasant consequences that will tend to persuade the recalcitrant to rethink their errant ways.

The metric of punishment has changed in recent years. Sentences are longer, correctional program conditions are more stringent, and expectations for compliance are higher than they used to be only a scant generation ago. This has caused some observers to consider punishment as the most important function of corrections. It is certainly true that the public's expectations of effective punitive approaches have been accepted by correctional authorities as an important force in the correctional agenda.

These five themes of traditional corrections—offender management, risk, treatment, surveillance and control, and punishment—form something of a modern language in the field. Any useful description of contemporary correctional policy will necessarily consider these issues. Yet they are not the dominant themes in community justice as it applies to the correctional arena.

THEMES IN CORRECTIONAL COMMUNITY JUSTICE

The strains of community justice call forth a different set of correctional themes. It is important to emphasize that these themes are different from those enumerated above, but not opposite to them. The most significant difference is that community justice seeks to align itself with and build the capacity of informal social controls at the community level. Formal social controls—police, courts, and correctional enforcement—are seen as of secondary importance in building a safer society than the informal social controls of families, personal associations, social organizations, and the private sector. Community justice recognizes the importance of the latter, and seeks to work with and through them to create a stronger community capacity for public safety.

Below we describe five community justice themes in corrections. We then discuss how community justice officials integrate traditional themes into the concerns emphasized by community justice proponents.

Neighborhoods and Communities

Under a community justice model, corrections maintains a focus on neighborhoods and local communities. This focus stems from recognition that neighborhoods are a central aspect of contemporary life, and the correctional responsibility for public safety requires treating neighborhoods as a client. That is, the community justice model is not merely about the offenders assigned to correctional supervision and control, but is also concerned with the places where those offenders live and work and the people with whom they live and work.

The importance of neighborhood and community is straightforward for correctional functions that operate when the offender is residing in the community, such as probation and parole. The activity of these clients has enormous significance for community life, especially in relation to their struggle to remain crime-free. Beyond public safety, the presence of offenders in the community connects to the circumstances of many other residents, as offenders are also family members, employees, neighbors, parents, peers, and friends to those around them. As we pointed out in Chapter 1, the concentration of offenders in some locations is great enough that correctional authorities may have a role in the lives of a large percentage of people living there.

But the neighborhood connection also applies to the institutional correctional function. Communities comprise interwoven connections of interpersonal social networks. These social networks are the basis for collective community activity—it is through the social networks that groups form, resources are shared, and supports are provided. Criminologists agree that informal social controls form the basis for public safety in community life: the capacity of a community to achieve a degree of public safety through collective activity is referred to as collective efficacy (Sampson, Raudenbush, and Earls, 1997). Without strong, broad networks, there is little collective efficacy.

Every time an offender is removed from the community for incarceration, those networks are affected. Whatever that person was doing that damaged the capacity of the network to support those enmeshed within it is eliminated by incarceration, but whatever that person was doing to assist the networks is also eliminated. Likewise, when an offender re-enters the community from prison or jail, those networks are called upon to absorb the person back as a resident. Thus, high rates of incarceration can become significant forces in the capacity of social networks in these communities to perform their public safety functions (Sampson, Raudenbush, and Earls, 1997). When large numbers of men are locked up from a particular area, their children suffer from lack of adult male supervision, and their parental partners are forced to do double duty as financial and personal supports for those youngsters. When many residents are fresh from prison or jail, an area is forced to develop its informal capacities in the face of a large concentration of people struggling in the workforce and under close law enforcement scrutiny.

For these reasons, correctional functions under a community justice approach are concerned with particular neighborhoods and the people who live there. The issue concerns not only how an offender is behaving, but also how that offender's situation—in or out of prison—affects the people who are not under correctional authority.

Partnerships

Community justice organizations, including correctional agencies, do not work in isolation. Those organizations responsible for a special set of objectives, such as public safety, partner with other organizations to carry out their functions. The reasons for partnerships are fairly simple: the problems of community life are so complex and so interconnected that working on one set of issues in isolation from the others is not likely to produce much overall change. When organizations begin to work together, greater change can occur.

The most common correctional partnerships are formed with other criminal justice organizations, particularly the police. Under community justice, police become natural partners to probation and parole officers, and public defenders can work alongside correctional authorities to pursue the interests of the client—especially regarding treatment, employment, and family relationships. However, when it comes to forming partnerships in community justice, institutional corrections face the greatest challenge, but the idea that careful transition planning can improve re-entry success automatically suggests a role for community partners, even with institutional correctional functions.

Operation Night Light

Operation Night Light began in November 1992 as a partnership between probation officers in the Dorchester, Massachusetts, district court and Boston police officers in the Anti-Gang Violence Unit (which later became the Youth Violence Strike Force). This alliance was created at a time when Boston was experiencing heightened gang violence, a rise in homicide victims under the age of seventeen, public alarm, increasingly bold behavior of gang members in courthouses, and criticism by minority community leaders and judges of police stop-and-frisk tactics. Probation officers worked independently of police, and curfews were not commonly imposed by the court and were difficult to enforce. In response to those problems, a few probation officers and police officers met informally to develop the Operation Night Light model as a more effective way of deterring juvenile violence.

Operation Night Light pairs one probation officer with two police officers to make surprise visits to the homes, schools, and work sites of high-risk youth probationers during the nontraditional hours of 7 P.M. to midnight, rather than from 8:30 A.M. to 4:30 P.M., which was previously the norm. In Dorchester, where Operation Night Light started, probationer surrenders based on new arrests declined 9.2 percent between January 1994 and June 1996, compared with a statewide increase of 14 percent during the same period (see http://ojjdp.ncjrs.org/pubs/gun_violence/profile33.html).

Non–criminal-justice agencies also stand as good partners. For example, treatment providers become natural partners for the jail, as offenders prepare for release and seek to maintain continuity in treatment programming. Social services, such as welfare, child-protective services, and employment-related services, may also work closely with correctional activity under community justice approaches. Juvenile correctional workers align themselves closely with the schools. Overall, partnerships with nonjustice agencies are designed to encourage "seamless" service systems in which comprehensive strategies are concentrated in communities whose residents suffer from significant deficits.

Finally, community justice strategies seek private-sector partners. Among the most important partners are for-profit businesses that operate (or might operate) in the neighborhoods targeted by community justice initiatives. In making community quality of life a priority, community justice seeks to help transform troubled communities into places where businesses can succeed because this helps create employment opportunities (for offenders and non-offenders alike) and bolsters a solid economic foundation for residents. In addition, community justice organizations build partnerships with private nonprofit organizations, such as foundations, to carry out community-development initiatives that build a firmer foundation for public safety.

Victims and Communities

Unlike traditional justice services, community justice initiatives concern themselves with clients other than the offender under direct correctional supervision because the community justice agenda accepts responsibilities that go beyond the management of the offender. Community justice strategies recognize that crime and its consequences are profoundly important concerns for both victims and communities. For these clients, crime is a significant problem that needs to be overcome.

Traditional correctional practices will claim a concern for victims and communities that is indirect—by advancing public safety interests, traditional corrections indirectly benefit victims and their communities. Community justice embraces the interests of victims and communities directly. The problems victims encounter as a result of the crime and the difficulties encountered by communities resulting from the removal and return of resident offenders are made a part of the community justice agenda. The approach to these issues taken by community justice is one of problem solving.

Problem Solving

Community justice is a problem-solving philosophy. The orientation contrasts with traditional criminal justice, which is adversarial. Under community justice, preference is given to amelioration of problems and long-range solutions to entrenched difficulties rather than the mere adjudication of legal disputes. This concern for identifying problems and finding solutions enables community justice strategies to embrace a concern for victims and communities.

The problem-solving orientation of community justice means that an unusual set of questions may be addressed by community justice through its partnerships. The community justice orientation allows correctional agencies to consider diverse questions: How do we occupy our youths' time in the immediate hours after school when trouble is so common? What can we do about all the trash along the streets of this neighborhood? How can we facilitate a neighborhood organization to deal with landlord–tenant problems? What can be done to decrease school truancy? What should be done about store owners' complaints about youth groups hanging on the street corner?

One of the reasons partnerships are so important to community justice is that problem solving is so important. Rarely are important problems simple. The important problems faced by communities and their residents are sufficiently complex that no single organization can resolve them in isolation. Therefore, the community justice orientation requires correctional agencies to reach out to other groups—police, social services, and the private sector—to fashion solutions to complicated problems.

Restoration

To some extent, every solution to the problem of crime involves some level of restoration because crime is destructive to society. It is destructive in tangible ways, as victims lose property and suffer personal injury. It is destructive in meaningful but less tangible ways, as citizens lose faith in societal institutions and residents isolate themselves from one another in order to remain safe (Zehr, 1989).

This dual level of loss—tangible and social—suggests that restoration has two aims. One aim is to repair the losses suffered by victims of crime. This is accomplished by restitution, usually from the offender but often from the community as well. But the social damage of crime can be ameliorated only through social reparation. This involves offenders "giving back" to society by recognizing that the crime they committed was a wrong done, not just to the victim, but to everybody.

As an objective of community justice action, restoration replaces punishment at the top of the priority list. Community justice correctional action will include punishment, because community justice advocates recognize that one of the ways reparation is achieved is through legal sanction. But in selecting sanctions, there is often significant latitude, and, all else being equal, community justice strategies give highest preference to sanctions that restore the victim and repair the frayed social fabric that results from crime.

INTEGRATING TRADITIONAL CORRECTIONAL THOUGHT INTO THE COMMUNITY JUSTICE FRAMEWORK

The traditional concerns of corrections do not disappear under community justice; rather, they are incorporated into the community justice priorities. The most important of these priorities is the neighborhood and community focus of community justice, and most of the traditional correctional agenda is shaped by this orientation.

For example, *offender management* becomes community focused. The question is not how offenders may be processed through the criminal sanction, but how to best reintegrate offenders into the community. For this reason, community corrections apply most powerfully to the traditional activity of probation and parole, with more complex implications for institutional corrections. Because offenders live with their families and in relationships with their neighbors and others who share their context, the way offenders fit into community life is a concern of community justice offender-management strategies. Correctional workers become involved with key members of the offender's interpersonal network, and they also work to establish and strengthen new network

---

Vermont Restorative Justice

The crime problem in Vermont is not the incidence of crime, but the fear of crime and the lack of confidence among the citizens in their criminal justice system. That fear has created a decade of increased reliance on incarceration as the dominant response to crime, and the corrections' budget has quadrupled as education aid declines. As government has become increasingly centralized, a major source of citizen frustration is the inability to define what is being achieved by the justice system, both on an individual case basis and from the perspective of the community. As the media focus on the spectacular failures and the extremes of the spectrum, government is caught between overwhelming caseloads of minor criminals and the need to target resources to protect the public from the dangerous criminals. In the rush to efficiency, the government bypasses the most effective agents, the community and the family, instead focusing on the individual cases that squeak the loudest.

In the reparative probation program, ordinary citizens of Vermont make sentencing decisions about adult criminal offenders from their community. Board members meet with offenders and victims, resolving their disputes by providing the offenders with the opportunity to acknowledge their wrongdoing, apologize to their victim, and make amends to their community. The court sentences the offenders, having pleaded guilty to a nonviolent crime. The sentence is then suspended, pending their completion of a reparative agreement.

For the past two hundred years, the fundamental purpose of sentencing and corrections has been retributive. For the past one hundred

---

ties—associates, organizations, and family members are important sources of support for reintegration.

In working with those in the offender's social network, community justice workers must bear in mind the *risk* the offender represents to people in that network and to others in the community. Building strong community ties cannot ignore the fact that offenders have shown, by their past behavior, a willingness to damage those ties through criminal behavior. Part of what makes working with offenders under supervision so complex and challenging is the need to balance a realistic concern for risk with the direct need to establish supports and interdependencies that are vulnerable to that risk. Community justice workers thus give a significant importance to the need to monitor the progress of those relationships, both to make sure that they are remaining supportive of continuing progress toward full reintegration and to pick up signals of potential problems that may put those networks at risk. Offenders can hardly be expected to achieve the aims of repairing broken relationships and restoring the costs of their past crime unless criminal behavior has stopped. And neighborhoods and years, judges have had only two choices in sentencing: to punish, or not. For the past twenty-five years, we have known that not only does punishment not work, but that it also makes most offenders more likely to reoffend. We have attempted to ameliorate the effects of punishment with rehabilitative strategies and alternative forms of punishment in the community. None of these has been spectacularly successful in reducing the demand for incarceration.

The reparative probation program represents a different approach. The boards are focused on the minor crimes—the "broken windows" in James Q. Wilson's phrase (Wilson, 1982)—the crimes that are too petty to be dealt with by the system and that both diminish the quality of life and are committed by criminals who learn that we do not care enough about their behavior to do anything about it. They are the crimes committed by our children and young people. Reparative boards give citizens an opportunity to do something about their neighborhoods and their communities. By involving citizens directly in decision making about individual cases, they are forced to look at the offenders not as strangers, not as numbers, and not as monsters. The offenders are forced to confront the reality of their offense and its impact on the community and their victims. This confrontation, with a restorative outcome, shifts the paradigm from punishment to reintegration. The offender is held accountable, the victim is restored, and the community is repaired.

Perhaps even more important, the dispute is resolved by the community, and the community is empowered (see http://www.doc.state.vt.us/gw2/overview.htm).

---

communities have a legitimate expectation that offenders have desisted criminal behavior.

The two most significant ways that community justice workers ensure the progress toward reintegration is through the combined strategies of *treatment* programs and *problem-solving* efforts. Treatment programs control and reduce risk. Problem-solving strategies identify ways that risk may be overcome through new offender and community approaches. For example, an offender who has difficulty finding and keeping a good job can benefit from job-training programs, but these can be carried out in such a way that the offender earns some wages during on-the-job training in work that also benefits the wider community. Some of those wages can go to restitution, while some of the work can translate into community improvements, such as trash removal or housing renovation. Thus, community justice workers may try to develop on-the-job training programs that provide a beginning level of wages and include some degree of community service.

Finally, both *punishment* and *surveillance and control* are aspects of community justice, but they are used as tools to achieve eventual reintegration rather than as ends in themselves. By the fact that the offender is placed under correctional authority, punishment has occurred. Any losses of liberty (for instance, jail time or a prison sentence) and restrictions on freedom (through conditions of supervision) are deemed to be aspects of the punishment, and their imposition is the sanction for the offense. No additional sanctions need be imposed. By the same token, any surveillance or control that a case encounters is used as a means to facilitate reintegration. Surveillance and control are not seen as having value except that they are necessary to lead, eventually, to a fully reintegrated status for the offender. Risk levels, therefore, may dictate a need for certain kinds of surveillance or control, but these flow from special consideration in a case and the community, and are not a general part of the overall correctional program for every offender under community justice supervision.

Thus, under a community justice orientation, traditional correctional themes remain but are subverted to dominant, central considerations of community justice. It is possible to see indications of traditional correctional thinking when observing a community justice system in action. What is different is the larger and broader sense of client—including victims and the community—and the central concern for reintegration as the offender-management aim. Moreover, the question posed to assess the value of particular actions (Will this strategy help the offender adjust to the community more successfully?) is not directed mainly at the offender but is instead focused on the question of community quality of life (Will this strategy help strengthen this community and the offender's circumstances within it?).

HOW COMMUNITY JUSTICE CHANGES THE TRADITIONAL CORRECTIONAL FUNCTIONS

The ideals of community justice can operate within traditional correctional functions, but they change the look of those ways of doing business. There are two main locations for corrections: the community and the institution. For each of these locations, traditional corrections has two types of functions: regarding the community, there are probation and parole (re-entry); regarding institutions, there are jails and prisons. This classification of correctional functions is a bit oversimplified, but it will enable us to consider the different ways that the concepts of community justice alter the tasks of corrections.

Community Justice and Probation

In many ways, probation is the correctional function ideally suited to incorporate the values of community justice. Probation (along with parole) involves community supervision, meaning that its operations occur in the community, and its clients reside in the community. Indeed, the phrase "community-based corrections," which denotes probation and parole functions, as well as residential community facilities, indicates the degree to which these functions have a natural relationship to the community.

Despite this seeming relevance to community, traditional probation has not realized a community justice orientation. In contrast, what most probation agencies practice is a form of "Fortress Probation" (Manhattan Institute, 1999). Under Fortress Probation, the probation office is located adjacent to the courthouse, downtown, far away from the communities in which the clients live. Probation officers rarely visit clients in their homes or jobs, but instead see them in regularly scheduled visits to the downtown office. Caseloads are organized to make the reporting process easier: the caseload either has a balanced number of high-, moderate-, and low-supervision cases to make the workload of those cases manageable or has "specialized" clients representing particular problems or supervision issues (such as intensive supervision) to make management of those special requirements easier. Fortress Probation requires the clients to come to the office, report on their activities since the previous office visit, and provide a urine sample for testing to determine compliance with the restrictions on alcohol and drug use.

There are plenty of critics of the Fortress Probation approach. They point out that studies of probation effectiveness continually show the futility of the traditional caseload system of supervision (Manhattan Institute, 1999), and they complain that the reactive style of Fortress Probation means that problems are not prevented but simply managed. One of the most significant criticisms of this traditional approach is that office-bound probation officers cannot engage in the kinds of community services that are needed to support adjustment to the community, and they fail to get to know anything meaningful about the offender's family, work circumstances, or living situation. Yet, these are the factors that will have more effect on the offender's eventual adjustment than almost any others.

Under a community justice model, probation moves out of the office and into community branch offices opened up in the neighborhoods where the majority of clients live, and probation officers operate from these neighborhood offices. Sometimes they work in the office, but more often they are in the community, working not just with offenders, but also with others who live and work in that neighborhood. The activities of the community justice probation officer go beyond mere supervision, but the strategy of community justice probation begins by locating the probation function in the places where clients live and work.

Being "in the field" makes it much easier for community justice probation to expand its correctional tactics and targets to include more than just supervision and surveillance of offenders under sentence of the court. The community justice probation officer recognizes that offenders often succeed or fail largely on the basis of the nature of informal social controls in their lives, and that probation can work to strengthen and augment those informal social controls.

Informal social controls are the prosocial relationships that strengthen an offender's connection to a conventional lifestyle: family members, employers, associates, and community organizations. Probation can help enhance the role those informal relationships play in the offender's life by reinforcing their importance, supporting the offender's bond to them, and showing ways that they can assist the offender's adjustment.

A neighborhood-based probation system, therefore, does not concern itself with just the person on probation. It is also concerned with others in the neighborhood who might play a role in the offender's adjustment. Community justice probation seeks to build ties to various community organizations, such as neighborhood councils, social clubs, and churches, and it relies upon those various organizations to develop a better relevance to residents who are under criminal justice authority. Each of these targets can be a part of a probationer's "making it": business managers can become employers, churches can become support groups, and community organizations can become advocates for community services and even host them.

Community justice probation seeks ways to establish support systems in the community for probationers. Some offenders live in isolation, of course, and it is particularly important for probation to help these clients develop support in the community by turning to churches, civic organizations, and other community groups. But for most probationers, the key target for community justice probation is the family. When the offender's primary relationships are supportive of the offender's overall adjustment, chances of success improve. Family members do not automatically know what they need to do, however, so community justice probation officers can work with them to understand how they can help the offender succeed in the community.

Community justice probation is also concerned about victims of crime, as they are also residents of the community. In many cases, probationers are required to provide restitution to their victims, and community justice probation recognizes that ensuring restitution can go a long way to increasing community willingness to participate in this form of probation. From this perspective, the community is also a victim of crime, and offenders can be expected to make some form restitution to the community, not just to the specific victim. Restitution to the community is usually some type of community service, such as repairing property, cleaning parks, or restoring damages in the neighborhood infrastructure.

By locating in the neighborhood, community justice probation tailors its efforts to the particular neighborhood. For example, if a location is struggling with truancy, community justice probation will work with police and child-protective services to develop truancy-prevention strategies, knowing that the children who are having the most trouble in school are often those whose older siblings or parents have been in trouble with the law. A place with a large population of elderly might develop a community-service system of delivering food and medicine to them, using the clients of the criminal justice system to make the deliveries. By accepting the responsibility to work on problems such as these, which extend beyond working with actual clients, community justice probation embraces a truly preventive function.

Community Justice and the Jail

Most jails are community based in that they operate within the confines of a particular community, but turning a jail into a community justice correctional operation is not a simple matter. Jails handle offenders that are confined for various reasons: some are in lockup for only a night or two, until they make bail; others stay incarcerated until they are sentenced, then go to probation or prison to complete their sentences; still others receive jail terms as sentences and switch from being detained to doing time for a few months before they are released. Jails are very important to the community. There are almost 10 million admissions to jails each year, and a similar number of releases (U.S. Department of Justice, 1995). If the processes of removal and return are important to community life, then jails are a major part of those processes.

Most often, the typical jail inmate stays inside for only a few days or weeks and then returns to the community. What can be done about those cases from the perspective of community justice? Three principles would seem to be important in the application of community justice to the jail: informal social controls, transition planning, and restoration/restitution.

The jail stay, no matter how short, always represents a disruption in the offender's life, and the disruption can imperil the ties to informal social controls (family and others) that will prove so important after the offender leaves jail. If the person serves a reasonable period in jail—several weeks or a few months—there will often be profound consequences with regard to informal social controls and community supports: loss of a job, break in relationships, eviction from housing, conflict with intimates, and so forth. These can be quite problematic for later adjustment, even if they are very recent changes. A community justice orientation to a jail will try to minimize these losses. It will work to keep employment prospects strong, reach out to family members so they may retain contact with the person in confinement, assist community groups in reaching out to the jailed offender, and so forth. The broad aim of targeting these informal social controls is to try to create a situation in which the inmate, upon release, will be surrounded by supports that will tend to reinforce a positive adjustment. Perhaps most important, the jail staff can help set up treatment programs for drug and alcohol abuse or anger management that will continue to be a part of the offender's life after release.

Transition planning, therefore, is very important. In the typical case, a jailed inmate is simply released with no particular supports or assistance. In New York City, for example, inmates are released in the wee hours of the morning and put on a bus to the center area of the borough where they live. They dismount the bus into an awaiting gathering of drug dealers and prostitutes. Under community justice, the plan for return to the community—especially its impact on family, neighbors, and potential employers—is carefully factored into the way

Maricopa County Neighborhood Probation Centers

The Maricopa County (Arizona) Adult Probation Department operates neighborhood-based probation services in the Phoenix area. Each service is a partnership between the probation department, the Phoenix Police Department, and community organizations in various neighborhoods. In 1996, the Maricopa County Adult Probation Department established its first neighborhood probation project in the Coronado district of Phoenix. Two other neighborhood probation projects soon followed. Neighborhood probation projects have two goals: to reduce recidivism and to expand the role of probation to include problem solving in the community.

Unlike intensive supervision programs, which define their target populations by offense, neighborhood probation partnerships define their target populations by existing neighborhood boundaries. For example, the Garfield neighborhood probation office targets all probationers living in the Garfield neighborhood of central Phoenix, an area a little more than two miles in diameter. Targeting established neighborhoods affords the partnerships easier access to community boards and churches.

Although each of the Maricopa County Adult Probation Department's three neighborhood probation partnerships adjusts its activities to fit the needs of its particular neighborhood, each shares several attributes. Each office maintains a strong relationship with local law enforcement. Informally, police officers spend time in neighborhood probation offices familiarizing themselves with probationers in the neighborhood and discussing cases with probation officers. Formally, police and probation officers coordinate roundups and probationers' participation in community-service projects. Police officers also provide backup for probation officers making home visits and aid in the observation and supervision of probationers, serving as an extra set of eyes while they are on patrol. In return, probation officers use their broader search powers to aid in police investigations, and police officers receive increased cooperation from the community because residents know they are working with probation officers.

Partnerships maintain a strong relationship with the community. Both probation officers attend all community board meetings. Probation officers and police officers coordinate projects in which probationers perform their community service in the neighborhood. Sometimes, maintaining a strong relationship with the community requires a deep understanding of the neighborhood. Staff from the Garfield neighborhood probation office visit regularly and provide services (such as running errands) for several elderly women in the area who are considered the neighborhood matriarchs. In exchange for these visits, staff receive valuable insight into the history of the neighborhood and the roots of any problems. Like police officers, community members often visit the neighborhood probation offices to talk with the officers about the neighborhood and its issues. Finally, each partnership maintains a strong relationship with probationers. Geographic proximity allows probation officers more contact with their probationers. In addition, probationers receive supervision from local law enforcement officials who are aware of their probation conditions. Because they are seen as part of the community, probation and police officers believe the contacts are more productive and that they have better rapport with the probationers. The community also assists in the supervision of probationers. Because probationers are heavily involved in community-service projects, residents see probationers performing valuable services for the neighborhood and, in turn, these residents are more likely to perform services (such as job placement) for the probationers.

The following example illustrates how these three functions interact. While attending a neighborhood board meeting in Coronado, probation officers learned that the biggest concern for the community was the condition of one particular home. The owner of the home had been accumulating garbage in his yard for years. Community members complained about its appearance and its odor. Further, they believed the condition of the home was responsible for lowering property values and for discouraging working families from moving into the neighborhood. Police officers explained that they would continue to issue citations, but they could not force the owner to clean his property. The newly established Coronado Neighborhood Probation Office volunteered to have probationers clean the house as part of their community-service obligations. The community board was thrilled and volunteered to provide extra equipment and labor, as did the local police precinct. The house was cleaned within a month. As yet, Maricopa County's neighborhood probation partnerships have not been evaluated. Nonetheless, officials believe the programs are meeting some of their goals. They note that there has been a 45 percent decrease in crime in Coronado, and that turnover is lower among neighborhood probation officers than among traditional probation officers.

Travis County Community Justice

Ronald Earle was first elected district attorney in Travis County (Austin, Texas) in 1976, after working previously in judicial reform, as a municipal court judge, and in the state legislature. Over two decades, Earle transformed the Travis County District Attorney's Office from a small office of about 10 attorneys to one that in 1996 employed 157 staff, including 57 assistant district attorneys, with a Felony Trial Division, a Family Justice Division (that coordinated the investigation and prosecution of child and family-related cases, and child-protection actions), and a highly developed Special Prosecutions Unit (that investigated and prosecuted public-integrity and fraud cases). During his entire time in office, Earle has seen himself—and acted—as a leader whose mission was to involve the community in criminal justice processes.

From early on, Earle led much of criminal justice planning and established many integrated initiatives among public and private agencies in Travis County and the city of Austin. For example, he wrote state legislation for and then helped to create a Community Justice Council and Community Justice Task Force, bodies that bring together elected officials, appointed professionals, and private citizens to oversee all criminal justice operations in the county. Along with his first assistant, Rosemary Lehmberg, who headed the Family Justice Division for many years, Earle was largely responsible for founding the Children's Advocacy Center in Austin. Here, as in other initiatives, the District Attorney's Office brought people in the community together, obtained support from the necessary agencies, helped find sufficient resources to get the project off the ground, and then when it became self-sustaining, passed it over to community control.

In 1996, Earle set up the first of several Neighborhood Conference Committees (NCCs), in which adult volunteers, cleared by Austin authorities and trained, serve on panels that hear cases diverted from juvenile court. After intensive hearings that involve the juvenile offenders and members of their families, the panels offer individualized contracts to offenders that include restitution, community service, counseling and/or treatment, and mentoring by adults in the community. Participating adults in the NCCs say they welcome the opportunity to take responsibility for directly addressing crime and working with juvenile offenders in their own neighborhoods. Anecdotal accounts of individual offenders' experiences suggest that one outcome

---

the release is conducted, and the idea is to use release as the first positive step in the overall adjustment to the community.

Jails can also play an important role in restoration and restitution. One of the ironies of incarceration is that offenders who are locked up cannot make restitution to their victims. But a community justice jail finds ways to make restitution possible: inmates are allowed to work for income that partly goes to

of the NCC process is the creation of strong relationships between the offenders and adults in the local community that survive the period of their contracts.

Earle ran for re-election against his first contender in twenty years. He used the campaign as an opportunity to inform the public about his record and the rationale that informed it. For example, he put forward a mission that included a commitment to fashioning criminal justice processes, including prosecution, in accord with principles of restorative justice. Within the District Attorney's Office, even the prosecution of cases was seen as an opportunity to help victims heal. Victim–witness advocates and assistant district attorneys work closely with victims throughout trials, and a number of programs, such as victim–offender mediation and restitution sessions, are available. Earle also pursues programs and processes that he believes will cause offenders to change their behavior, to take responsibility for their actions, and to make restitution. Diversion and treatment programs supported by the DA's office offer counseling, treatment and rehabilitative services, mediation, and community-service alternatives for both adults and juveniles. In 1997, a new Community Justice Center opened in Austin to house offenders from the local community and offer programs that would help them to work toward becoming part of the community upon release. Vigorous prosecution and punishment of offenders is secondary to, but accompanies, each of these goals.

Although Earle and his top staff in the District Attorney's Office have been involved for years in leading most of these efforts in the community, by 1998 they were engaging the entire office in sometimes heated discussions about changes that might be made to decentralize prosecution efforts and build accountability to local neighborhoods. Earle had hired a police officer experienced in community policing as program manager for a new "community prosecution" effort and was working with a new police chief in an attempt to build police/prosecutor collaboration by geographical area. He also moved into the area of quality-of-life offenses, publicly supporting an ordinance prohibiting camping in public spaces, designating assistants in the office to handle nuisance-abatement suits, targeting gangs and porn shops—all of which provoked considerable controversy and public debate (see http://www.ksg.harvard.edu/criminaljustice/publications/cross-site.pdf).

a victims' fund, trustee programs are created that allow the offender to perform restorative services in the community, and inmate programs that benefit the community are encouraged.

The jail can also be decentralized to local levels, and facilities similar to halfway houses can be a part of the offender's initial stay in the community. These facilities enable offenders to work during the day, sustain their family contacts, and provide income to the family and restitution to the victim, all while becoming gradually more involved in the neighborhood and its system of informal social controls. Jails are not community-based correctional facilities, but they can be reconfigured to have a community justice relevance.

Community Justice and the Prison

Of all the correctional functions, the prison is the most removed from a community justice orientation. Yet prisons are an important part of community justice, even though they seem to be remote from community life. One reason is that each prisoner comes from a community, and concentrations of inmate populations often come from certain communities. On any given day, about 12 percent of the African American males in their twenties and early thirties are in a prison or a jail (U.S. Department of Justice, 2001); in some inner neighborhoods, such as in sections of Brooklyn, 15 percent of the adult males go to prison or jail each year (Cadora and Swartz, 2000). These kinds of concentrations of removal (and return, which we discuss later) pose important issues for the communities in which the effects are most concentrated.

The typical prisoner is away from the community between two and three years. This is a long enough time to suffer severe disruptions in ties to informal social controls back in the community, and long enough to allow significant changes in the circumstances of those left behind. Children grow, spouses form new relationships, families move, loved ones die, jobs dry up, and society slowly changes in the technologies and everyday practices the released offender will encounter. For many prisoners, the seriously disrupted social ties are a major obstacle to overcome in the eventual adjustment back to the community.

Prisons can help make that process of adjustment easier. An emphasis can be placed on facilitating the maintenance of family ties through visitation programs and access to long-distance telephone services. (Currently, operator-assisted collect calls from prisons to home are among the most expensive calls in the industry.) Prisoners can receive the kinds of wages that enable them to contribute some money back to the family and to pay a portion of the necessary restitution as well. Inmates can also be allowed to interact with community groups and communicate with outsiders who might play a role in social supports upon release.

As the offender nears release, a process of planning for transition can occur. This process can help create linkages to the community by involving family members, employers, and residents' groups (such as churches) in the preparation for the transition. Prison time can shift to the community, as offenders move from the secure confinement of the remote facility to semisecure halfway-house facilities in transition neighborhoods. Treatment programs can be located in the community, and other supportive resources can serve both halfway-house inmates and community members equally.

The point of any community justice initiative in prison is to reduce the isolation of prisons from community life. Prisoners are being incarcerated because

Oregon Correctional Program

The Oregon Department of Corrections is changing the business of offender incarceration. The department is implementing a systematic approach to developing safe and secure institutions, developing a productive inmate workforce within institutions, and providing essential treatments, education, and workforce skills for transition to Oregon society. Oregon's population has increased in the last ten years. Corresponding increases in violent crime, drug, and sex-offender statistics have pushed Oregon voters to pass a number of "get tough on crime" initiatives. These have dramatically increased Oregon's prison population. Two key initiatives from this period are Measure 11 and Measure 17.

Measure 11 requires that all offenders serve the full duration of their sentences. The result is that Oregon's prison population has expanded even more. Measure 17 requires that all inmates work forty hours per week, and through a combination of institution-based businesses and private-sector partnerships, the department is expected to develop business enterprises that generate excess revenue and thereby "reduce the cost of government." To accomplish this, the department must evaluate effective means to develop and efficiently manage a productive workforce from an inmate community, 77 percent of which has alcohol and drug problems and 70 percent with less than a high school diploma. The implementation of Measure 11 and Measure 17 has prompted Oregon's Department of Corrections to consider new ways of doing business.

The Correctional Programs Division has taken up this challenge. It has developed and is currently implementing the incarceration/transition plan to integrate an automated intake-assessment process with a scheduled, progressive, automated incarceration plan. In the short term, the incarceration/transition plan coordinates the development of skilled workers within the institutional work environment while, in the long term, builds entry-level workers and productive citizens capable of re-entry into Oregon's society.

Incarceration/transition planning begins with an automated intake-assessment program designed to identify risk factors, education, treatment, and work-skill deficiencies of each inmate. The assessment process develops an individualized set of risk factors and subsequent priorities, which become the action items for the inmate's incarceration plan. The intake center forwards the assessment and corresponding priorities to institutional counselors. Counselors receive the assessment and priority information and then—in the context of the education, treatment, and workforce capacity of their institution— begin to develop the inmate's action plan. The inmate's action plan is designed to systematically address personal and professional barriers, such as alcohol and drug addictions, anger-management issues, health

Continued

Oregon Correctional Program (Continued)

issues, education, and work-skill deficiencies. Inmates are scheduled up to twenty hours a week in education and treatment programs designed to overcome these barriers. They also begin to build positive workforce habits by working the remaining twenty hours of the workweek in institution jobs for which they qualify. The inmate progresses through his or her individualized incarceration/transition plan, step by step toward "graduation" or, more appropriately, "readiness" to reenter the community. The new automated incarceration planning system has a "one stop" screen that displays summary data available from intake assessment. In addition, it identifies priorities, projected and actual entry dates, and outcomes for each specific treatment, basic education, work-based education, and work assignment. Further, the automated computer program offers point-and-click access to related data, such as education, health services, alcohol and drug use, work schedules, mental-health services, gang management, and summary data on compliance under Measure 17 requirements for an inmate to work forty hours per week. The screen for the automated incarceration plan is accessible by all applicable institutional personnel.

The institution counselor functions much like a college counselor who oversees the successful completion of a college student's program to graduation. The counselor brokers the systematic progress of the inmate through a prescribed set of priorities to a defined objective: a productive member of the workforce with qualified work skills, capable of prosocial behavior in the community. The plan's systematic approach to building prosocial skills reflects a belief that transition to the community begins the moment the offender enters the system. The department's goal, the moment the offender arrives, is to consider, evaluate, and plan the offender's transition back to the community.

There are additional active ingredients to the success of the incarceration/transition plan. The plan is integrated with the department's inmate Performance Recognition and Award System (PRAS) that reinforces work, education, and prosocial behavior. Each day an inmate earns points for successfully completing the defined incarceration plan activities. These points are accumulated and applied to a matrix at the end of the month. A failure in one day's activity loses all point accumulation for that day and significantly impacts the potential PRAS award. The PRAS program alone has reduced major disciplinary reports in Oregon institutions by an average of 20 percent in 1996. Linking the incarceration plan to PRAS (and eventually the incentive program in the fall of 1998) will increase the effective ability of the department to motivate most inmates to successfully complete their plan, and, ultimately, become productive members of the institution community and general society upon release. This is truly a systematic step forward for correctional programming in Oregon (see http://www.doc.state.or.us/programs/bp.shtml?bp_incarceration_plan).

of their crimes, but with only minor exceptions, they will eventually return to the community. It is common sense to organize the incarceration term in a way that makes return to the community more likely to be successful.

Community Justice and Parole (Re-entry)

Each year, almost six hundred thousand inmates are released from prison (Travis, Solomon, and Waul, 2001), and their collective impact on the communities they re-enter is significant. Studies show that the rate of crime in a given community is associated with the number of prisoners returning to that community (Clear, Rose, and Ryder, 2000). Obviously, community safety is an important consideration in the re-entry of offenders.

Community justice in re-entry can function in much the same way as community justice in probation: through a neighborhood center that provides an array of services to newly released offenders, their families, and other residents. Indeed, in most communities with high concentrations of offenders as residents, the re-entry services will be a part of the community justice neighborhood center operated by probation. Because the same sorts of relationships are needed with employers, social services, community groups, and victims as were described for neighborhood probation centers, re-entry services fit right in with the approach of such a center.

The main additional function of a neighborhood-based re-entry center is participation in the transition planning process that begins with the last stages of incarceration. Family members, potential employers, and others are consulted in the release decisions and the circumstances of the offender's return. A discussion is held regarding the supports that will be used to maximize the opportunity for successful adjustment, and the responsibilities of the offender in re-entry are explained. The role of key people in the offender's re-entry is developed and mutually understood by the local residents and the offender alike. When re-entry occurs, everyone is prepared for it.

Community Corrections and Restoration

One of the values that sets community justice apart from traditional criminal justice is a concern for restoration. Crime is understood as impairing community. It damages the fabric of mutual trust that is necessary to the very idea of community, and it generates fear of association that makes community harder to achieve. Doing something to prevent crime is a part of building community, but doing something about the damage that results from crime is an essential part of community justice.

Community justice approaches restorative justice as problem solving. It is significantly different from the "contest" version of traditional criminal law, which is illustrated by the very name given to its cases: for example, *State v. Wilson*. By contrast, community justice conceptualizes a criminal case not as a contest between two disputants, but a problem between three parties: the offender, the victim, and the community. What is needed is a way to design case

Rhode Island Family Life Center

The Rhode Island Family Life Center is a collaborative project of the Rhode Island Department of Corrections and local community-based and civic organizations. In 1999, the project laid out a detailed plan for how it would merge correctional operations with community participation as described below:

Discharge Planning: The Family Life Center (FLC) will incorporate a strengths-based approach to case management, employing Community Living Consultants (CLC) in lieu of case managers. The CLC will first meet with the offender, who participates in the process voluntarily, to begin building a relationship through the discharge planning process ninety days before release. The CLC will spend time with the offender to create a workable discharge plan that capitalizes on the offender's assets while addressing any outstanding service needs. In this way, offenders will feel a sense of ownership over the process and will develop a relationship with the CLC that will be continued upon release. This early relationship building and buy-in will be the seeds that will grow into offenders' long-term engagement with the FLC. At the same time, the CLC will work with the offender to identify family members and other familial networks, which can serve to support the offender as he or she returns to the community. The CLC will reach out to these support systems to help prepare them for the offender's return and will also help address any service needs that they may have.

Case Process: Each CLC will handle approximately twenty to thirty active cases at any one time, taking in seven new participants a month. The most intensive engagement will take place six weeks prior to release and six weeks after release to the community. While the CLC will intake forty cases a year, the natural flow of adjustment to the community and client attrition will allow for an active case load of thirty clients, with a much smaller number taking up the majority of the CLC's time. The FLC will house five CLCs who will retain a generalist perspective—understanding that offenders and their families have complicated lives that require holistic responses. The FLC's program coordinator will have the clinical expertise to assess offenders for mental health and substance-abuse services. The bonding relationship between the CLC and the offender is critical to the offender's successful reintegration, so CLCs will remain engaged with those offenders who are temporarily remanded. CLCs will meet weekly as a group with the program coordinator to review all current cases, share information, and ensure that offenders and their families are receiving the best possible care. CLCs will follow up with their clients for a period of eighteen months in order to help them access services as new needs arise and to gather data that will help assess the efficacy of the FLC's interventions.

Offender progress in stabilizing in the community will be celebrated at quarterly ceremonies. Offenders who have maintained a period of stability in the community as defined by the commission—having no new criminal offenses and meeting the majority of their self-defined goals—are eligible to become alumni of the FLC.

Criminal Justice Partnerships: The FLC will have two on-site probation and parole officers who will be supervising offenders returning to the four zip codes. The community supervision officers will work as a team with the CLCs, holding regular meetings to discuss offenders' progress meeting their goals. Community supervision officers will work together with the CLCs to devise alternative responses to technical violations in order to help offenders remain within the community, rather than be remanded.

Social Service Partners: The FLC planning committee has selected five major service agencies to provide services to the FLC's clients. During its transitional phase, the FLC will develop Memoranda of Understanding with each of these providers. The following five agencies have agreed to provide services to offenders involved in the FLC: Amos House; The Providence Center; Phoenix House; The Urban League; and Miriam Hospital.

- Amos House is a multipurpose agency located in South Providence specializing in providing shelter for the homeless. It provides case management and a variety of social-service programs for this population and will support Family Life Center participants through the provision of transitional housing and job-readiness training.
- The Providence Center will provide services for returning offenders who require treatment for mental illness, chemical dependency, behavioral disorders, and emotional problems. The Providence Center's services include medication, case management, and psychotherapy services.
- Phoenix House will provide substance-abuse treatment services for offenders at the FLC. Phoenix House runs a long-term residential therapeutic community and an outpatient clinic. Phoenix House has designed treatment specifically for Latino/Latina clients and provides counseling for youth at the Rhode Island Training School, the youth detention facility.
- The Urban League is a community-based nonprofit organization with a sixty-two-year record of service to the Black and other minority populations in Rhode Island. Its mission is the elimination of racial discrimination and segregation and the achievement of parity for minorities. The Urban League has developed a special expertise in employment and training issues and will provide employment training and job-readiness training to participants of the FLC.
- Miriam Hospital will provide health-care services for returning offenders, who typically have health problems related to hepatitis C, HIV/AIDS, diabetes, and hypertension.

outcomes that best meet the legitimate interest of each party to the problem
at hand.

In community justice, the offender has a legitimate interest in being allowed to find a way to re-establish ties to the community; the victim has an interest in having the losses suffered at the hands of the offender restored; and the
community has an interest in developing some confidence that the offender
will refrain from this kind of conduct in the future. Each interest connotes an
obligation, as well. The offender is obliged to repair the damage and to provide
some tangible assurance that criminality will not recur. The victim has an obligation to identify the losses that need to be restored and to entertain the possibility of a reconstituting community with the offender (note that this is not
an obligation to rebuild community with the offender, just to entertain the
possibility of this rebuilding under the "right" circumstances, regarding which
the victim has a voice). The community has an obligation to identify the circumstances under which both the victim and the offender can be restored to
community.

Restorative community justice is an important, different way to conceive of
justice. It gives both the community and the victim an active role in determining the appropriate sanction in a case, and it gives the offender a voice in
that same process. By opening the process to those who are most affected by its
outcome, the restorative model seeks to develop solutions both to the problems
that result from crime and to the impediments to community that accompany
the existence of crime.

COMMUNITY JUSTICE CENTERS
IN THE NEIGHBORHOOD CONTEXT:
A VISION FOR THE FUTURE

As it stands, the prevailing criminal justice system is almost entirely focused
on responding to individual crimes, prosecuting individual cases, and managing individual offenders. Despite the myriad experiments in community justice, taken as a whole, the criminal justice system—particularly corrections—
is dominated by the individual case orientation and has not made a *systematic*
shift toward organizing its operations around the circumstances of places. But
what would corrections look like if it were systematically oriented to do business in neighborhoods? A common expression holds that "if you don't know
where you're going, you probably won't get there." To that end, it is probably
important to develop an anticipatory picture of how corrections might look if
it were neighborhood based.

Although everyone's vision for community justice might not look the same,
the community justice "movement" is at a stage in its development in which it
can only benefit from a diverse set of ideas. We offer one, brief scenario of how

a corrections system infused with the ideas of community justice might look in a particular neighborhood.

One way in which corrections might incorporate community justice principles is in the form of a neighborhood community justice center located inside the neighborhood, ideally in the hardest-hit area of the community. The center serves as a resource both for residents being supervised by corrections agencies and for their families, victims of crime, and other residents in need of assistance. To overcome the fragmentation of services that traditionally prevails between criminal justice agencies, the center houses offices for transitional staff from the state's prison system and local jail, supervision staff from the probation/parole department, and police officers from the local precinct. To facilitate working partnerships with the community, the center also makes space available for the local housing-development organization, substance-abuse treatment agency, local YMCA, vocational training and job-placement assistance program, victim-assistance agency, and other local faith-based or community social-service institutions.

In addition to the daily interactions that close physical proximity encourages, the center's staff meet monthly to assess progress in the neighborhood, identify new priorities, and plan how to implement its strategies. At the same time, the center serves as a meeting place for a variety of community discussions and forums. Residents under the supervision of the justice system report here, as do ex-prisoners making the transition back to the community; but other residents also use the center. When there are questions about illegal dumping or trouble corners, residents know that the center will help refer them to the proper authorities who can best address their problems.

While the center is a locus of activity in the neighborhood for community justice, not all the activities it sponsors take place there. Indeed, the majority of programs and activities, which are only planned and coordinated by the center, take place all around the neighborhood. These neighborhood programs include community guardianship, civic leadership, workforce development, and supportive health care and housing.

Community Guardianship The community guardianship program teams up probation and parole officers with local tenant associations, home owners, parks employees, and block associations. Together, they sponsor civic, recreational, social, and other community-service activities in areas of the neighborhood that have been identified as hotspots of trouble. Instead of depending entirely on police to respond to complaints by conducting sweeps and arrests, the guardianship program establishes proactive social events that make delinquency and other drug and public order crime difficult to take place. At the same time that it targets trouble locations, the guardianship program brings together mentors from faith-based and other social-service organizations, like the YMCA, and probation/parole officers. These mentor teams work closely with high-risk residents who are on probation/parole to ensure that they have the sufficient guidance and support to avert opportunistic illicit activities.

Civic Leadership The civic leadership program is a project-based series of neighborhood revitalization initiatives that combine obligatory community service for residents under probation/parole supervision and service by other residents who volunteer their time to community improvement projects. The civic leadership program brings together organizations like Habitat for Humanity, the local community-service society, public schools, local businesses, and the municipal parks agency with probation/parole and corrections officers. The coalition targets vacant lots, trash-strewn streets, broken-down and graffiti-covered storefronts, and dilapidated housing for beautification and rehabilitation. Resident volunteers are teamed up with resident offenders to create community gardens, murals, and other public-space projects with technical support from the participating agencies and supervisory services from corrections officers.

Workforce Development A priority of the community justice center is the financial stability and informal social control that comes from stable employment. The probation/parole department works in partnership with a coalition of local businesses, the community employment agency, schools, and public libraries. Together they offer vocational literacy, employment training, and job programs to both resident offenders and other residents in need of employment. Local employers are provided with tax credits for employing probationers and parolees. The local employment agency sponsors a job club to help employed probationers and parolees keep their jobs. They work with a probation/parole officer who offers specialized support around employment obstacles typically encountered by residents with criminal records. At the same time, job-skills training is integrated with vocational-literacy education and tailored to the kinds of jobs that the local businesses offer. These services are also offered to local residents who are in need of literacy services.

Supportive Health Care and Housing The center sponsors a stable housing program because it is well documented that one of the greatest impediments to crime-free living is lack of housing for returning ex-prisoners. Among the numerous housing initiatives sponsored by the center, two are of particular note. The first focuses on the eviction from public housing of family members who have a criminal record. To overcome this obstacle, the center brings together a coalition from its guardianship program and public housing officials to petition for exceptions to the public housing prohibition. The program recruits members of the tenant association and the mentor teams to sponsor the return of ex-prisoners to their former public housing apartments. In another of its housing programs, the center works with the local housing development organization to establish tenant-managed, affordable-housing apartment complexes. Through an innovative funding strategy, the center combines federal funding for housing with state correctional tax credits traditionally given to construction firms that build prisons, and use these funds to build supportive, mixed-use housing for low-income residents and residents involved in the criminal justice system.

Together, these programs provide only a glimpse of the possibilities that a community justice–oriented correctional agenda could accomplish if it became committed to these principles. The possibilities are endless, but these are some of the kinds of partnerships and coalitions that could arise if corrections shifts its attention from an exclusive concern for the individual to one that takes into consideration the community's priorities, needs, and inherent strengths.

REFERENCES

Cadora, Eric, and Charles Swartz. 2000. "Community Justice Atlas." Center for Alternative Sentencing and Employment Services (CASES). Unpublished Report.

Clear, Todd R., Dina R. Rose, and Scott R. Ryder. 2000. "Coercive Mobility and the Community: The Impact of Removing and Returning Offenders." Paper prepared for the Urban Institute Reentry Roundtable, Washington D.C., October.

Manhattan Institute. 1999. "'Broken Windows' Probation: The Next Step in Crime Fighting." *Civic Report* 7 (August).

Sampson, R. J., S. W. Raudenbush, and F. Earls. 1997. "Neighborhoods and Violent Crime: A Multilevel Study of Collective Efficacy." *Science* 277 (August).

Travis, Jeremy, Amy Solomon, and Michelle Waul. 2001. *From Prison to Home: The Dimensions and Consequences of Prisoner Reentry.* Washington, D.C.: Urban Institute.

U.S. Department of Justice, Office of Justice Programs. 1995. "Jails and Jail Inmates 1993–94." *Bureau of Justice Statistics Bulletin* NCJ 151651. Washington, D.C: U.S. Department of Justice.

———. 2001. "Prison and Jail Inmates at Midyear 2000." *Bureau of Justice Statistics Bulletin* NCJ 185989. Washington, D.C: U.S. Department of Justice.

Wilson, James Q., and George L. Kelling. 1982. "Broken Windows." *Atlantic Monthly* (March).

Zehr, H. (1989). "Justice: Stumbling toward a Restorative Ideal." In *Justice: The Restorative Vision,* New Perspectives on Crime and Justice, no. 7, edited by P. Arthur. Akron, Penn.: Mennonite Central Committee Office of Criminal Justice.

FOR FURTHER READING

Risk Assessment

Zamble, Edward, and Vernon L. Quinsey. 1997. *The Criminal Recidivism Process.* New York: Cambridge University Press. A comprehensive review of what is known about the causes of recidivism.

Public Safety

Crawford, Adam. 1998. *Crime Prevention and Community Safety: Politics, Policies, and Practices*. Harlow, England: Longman. A critical assessment of the social and political context of community-based public safety activity.

Lab, Steven P. 1997. *Crime Prevention at the Crossroads*. Cincinnati, Ohio: Anderson Publishing Company. A study of effective techniques for preventing crime.

Tonry, Michael, and David P. Farrington, eds. 1995. *Building a Safer Society: Strategic Approaches to Crime Prevention*. Chicago: University of Chicago Press. A collection of comprehensive studies of the effectiveness and usefulness of various approaches to crime prevention.

Offender Re-entry

Maruna, Shadd. 2001. *Making Good: How Ex-convicts Reform and Rebuild Their Lives*. Washington, D.C.: American Psychological Association. A study of the ways offenders change and desist from crime.

Travis, Jeremy, Amy Solomon, and Michelle Waul. 2001. *From Prison to Home: The Dimensions and Consequences of Prisoner Reentry*. Washington, D.C.: The Urban Institute. A review of the research and statistics on prisoner re-entry, including an assessment of impacts on family and community.

5

⠿

The Future of
Community Justice

Community justice is a new idea. Although many of the elements of community justice have a rich heritage in social thought—reparation, community, pragmatic problem solving—the idea of community justice as an expression of criminal justice is barely a decade old. We are in a time of rapid changes in criminal justice, but nobody can know in certainty where the changes will lead. What role, if any, will community play in the development of criminal justice in coming years?

To answer this question, we must shift our level of analysis from the specific to the general. The preceding chapters investigated particular applications of community justice to the three main functions of the criminal justice system: apprehension of offenders, adjudication of charges, and imposition of sanctions—police, courts, and corrections. In this analysis, we saw that community justice concepts have begun to receive broad and serious application in each of the traditional criminal justice functions. Throughout the apparatus of criminal justice, community justice ideas are increasingly common and increasingly important as foundations for new projects and innovative practices. To understand the significance of community justice as an idea, however, requires that we reach beyond these new projects to consider the core of the idea of community justice and how it transforms the current system. In this concluding

103

chapter, we first consider the core ideas that compose the community justice model. We then address a series of questions about community justice as a new way of doing justice. We conclude with a comment on the future of community justice.

THE ESSENTIALS
OF COMMUNITY JUSTICE

It might fairly be argued that community justice is far from a brand-new idea. Police have always walked beats, courts have for years tried to impose sanctions that restore the victim, and corrections has worked with offenders in the community since its earliest existence. Therefore, what makes community justice such a new thing?

A great variety of activity is offered under the community justice label: from community policing to drug courts, from neighborhood probation to zero tolerance. Does it all count as community justice? For a new idea to qualify as a community justice initiative, what must it offer as a new way of doing business?

There are three essential components of community justice: place, adding value, and public safety. Throughout this book, we have described and analyzed a large number of additional ideas important to particular community justice applications: among them are partnerships, problem solving, reinvestment, and citizen involvement. These are all key ideas in community justice thinking, but there are good examples of community justice initiatives in which one or more of these is not present. It is possible (though not necessarily advisable), for instance, to build a community justice court without community involvement; one could build a community-oriented policing approach without partnerships, and so forth. But community justice cannot occur without the three components of place, adding value, and public safety. It is the fact of place that makes the approach one of "community." It is the commitment to adding value that enables the community approach to do justice. Finally, the ultimate aim of all community justice is a better experience of public safety.

Place

Community is often used as an abstraction: the fellow feeling among people who share a personal characteristic, such as ethnicity; the sense of belongingness that comes from close associations and common experiences; the mutuality of interests that binds people together in a shared destiny. These abstractions are important, for they help us understand the intuitive appeal of the term *community.* But the term *community justice,* while it calls to mind these abstract notions, also has a concrete meaning. Community justice refers to actions that take place in a designated location, a neighborhood or section where people who live see themselves as sharing life together. Community justice takes place in a specific place.

Adding Value

Most of criminal justice is about a kind of "subtraction." The police investigate crimes with the intention of finding perpetrators so that they may be removed from the streets; the courts determine who should be removed and for how long; corrections confines those who have been removed and oversees others who are in risk of removal. Communities may benefit, of course, when problematic members are removed—a kind of "adding by subtracting." But community justice stands for two additional points. First, almost all of those removed eventually return, so the question of what to do about the people who live in the community, some of whom are ex-offenders, cannot be avoided by policies that only try to remove offenders. Second, and more important, dealing with offenders is not enough. Justice requires consideration of the broader and deeper quality of life in the community. From this perspective, public safety is not just a matter of strategic subtraction, but requires attention to the improvement of what is left intact. Community justice attempts to overcome the problems that produce crime, reduce the impediments to a good quality of life that communities face, and improve the capacity of communities to become safer, better places to live and do business.

Public Safety

It is possible to add value to places without doing community justice. What sets the community justice ideal apart from other philosophies of community life is that community justice is involved squarely with questions of public order and public safety. But community justice does not embrace a narrow conception of public safety, as might be suggested by simple rates of crime. Community justice is interested in public safety as a broad idea: people feel free to walk the streets without fear of harassment by anyone, criminals or agents of the state. Parents have confidence that there are good options for their children's daily activity, and young people feel that they have good choices of safe and satisfying ways of passing the time. There is vibrant social (and economic) commerce, and people feel free to pursue their dreams and aspirations. From the standpoint of community justice, public safety is not represented by an electric fence, a metal detector, or a barred window; rather, public safety exists where there is open and free social commerce without personal fear. Essential to the idea of community justice is the belief that achieving such a version of public safety is a prominent public aim.

VARIETIES OF COMMUNITY JUSTICE

These three essential elements of community justice leave plenty of room for many different ways of doing the work. We can visualize many varied strategies that seek to promote public safety by adding value to places. To help illustrate this, we can investigate further the core elements described above. Place is the *setting* for community justice, and this can be any neighborhood or

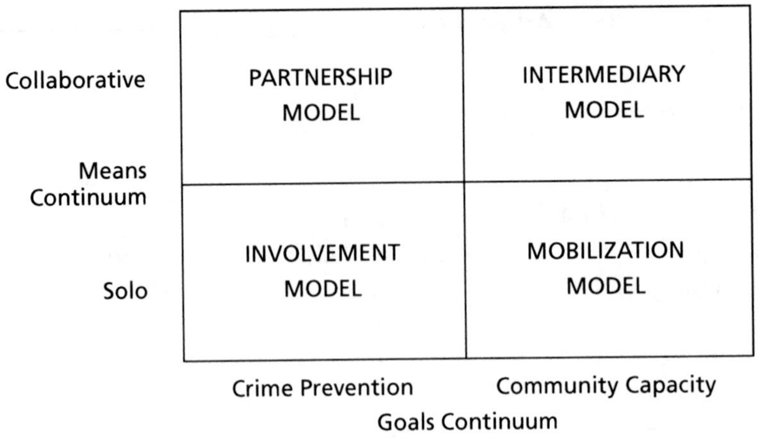

FIGURE 5.1 A Conceptual Model of Community Justice Strategies

community small enough to have an identity as distinct from other locations (especially within the same larger town or city). Public safety refers to the *goal* of community justice; adding value refers to the *means* of community justice. This enables us to investigate various differences in means (adding value) for particular community justice locations and goals (public safety). Figure 5.1 is a depiction of a conceptual model of community justice approaches based on goals and means.

Goals Continuum

The goals continuum provides two extreme values. On the one hand, there is an emphasis on the goal of crime prevention; on the other, is community capacity. Community justice initiatives that emphasize the goal of crime prevention tend to identify particular types of criminal activity that trouble a community and then seek to resolve problems that make that crime tend to occur. When community justice initiatives work at this end of the continuum, they may target serious crime (such as burglaries or robberies) or broken windows offenses (such as prostitution or open drug markets) or even try to break up gangs, but their aim is always to eradicate a criminal activity. At the other end of the continuum, the concern for community capacity aims to create better community life by improving some aspect of the community's functioning. A prime example is the desire to promote the kind of collective efficacy that seems to make some communities safer places.

Means Continuum

Most governmental organizations work solo in that they attend to their own responsibilities with little direct concern about the way other organizations affect and are affected by their work. Criminal justice is no exception. Working solo has its advantages. An agency working this way can quickly implement its own policies and procedures without having to consult other organizations, and it is easy to hold staff accountable for their obligations when no other organization is around to be blamed for things not going well. These advantages explain why most organizations seek to do much of their work solo, without having to deal with the involvement of other, potentially complicating, organizations. When complicated issues such as public safety are involved, there is a recognition that one organization, working alone, can have only limited success. This has led to an increasing interest in various forms of collaborative efforts to achieve community justice, where agencies form some sort of partnership or coalition that spans organization boundaries so that organizations trying to deal with similar (or related) problems can more easily work together.

FOUR PROTOTYPES OF COMMUNITY JUSTICE PROGRAMS: THE MODELS OF COMMUNITY JUSTICE

Figure 5.1, which arrays the two continua of goals and means, identifies four prototypical strategies of community justice. These can best be seen not as actual examples of existing programs, but as ideal types of community justice approaches that help us develop a critical understanding of some of the variation in community justice activity. In the following discussion, the underlying importance of each of the prototypes is described, and the pros and cons of each are presented.

Involvement Model

The initial form of community justice was to seek greater citizen involvement in the work of public safety. From its first days, the community-policing movement was a call for citizens and police to work together to deal with the problems of crime and disorder in urban settings. The idea of community policing developed from an interest in having members of the community meet with the police to develop priorities for police activity in their neighborhoods. The belief was that police would be more effective, and the community better served, if the people who needed police assistance worked together with the police.

A prototype of the Involvement Model of community justice is problem-oriented policing, developed by Herman Goldstein (Goldstein, 1991). In this approach, police work together with citizen groups to identify problems affecting public safety in a particular location, gather data about that problem, design a strategy to solve the problem, and implement that strategy. At each of these stages of the problem-solving approach, there is a role for citizen involvement, ranging from consultation regarding local priorities to providing feedback about the effectiveness of the implementation of solutions.

As a community justice approach, the Involvement Model has a number of advantages for police and citizens alike. For police, the model provides another source of information about local public safety problems, and it is therefore a superior way to gather information about policing priorities. It also gives the police a support system in the community for police practices. Citizens who have been consulted about the priorities for police activity are more likely to understand why the police do what they do and to support the police when inevitable problems arise. Working with a closer connection to the community, police are more likely to feel community encouragement for their work, and there is a direct sense of satisfaction for police officers who are engaged with, rather than estranged from, members of the community they serve.

Inherent within this strategy is a bilateral orientation involving the community—usually represented by some leaders and spokespersons—and the justice agency, working in tandem. The fact that the justice agency is working independently of other agencies can be a strength of this approach as well. There are no boundary concerns or turf battles, one person can speak for the interests of the justice agency, and changes in justice practices or procedures can be relatively quickly achieved.

The Involvement Model is not solely a policing strategy, although that is where it has its most apparent expression. Probation departments have established community advisory boards, and community courts often work closely with citizen leadership groups. Vermont's Reparative Justice Boards are fairly pure forms of involvement, in which the citizens themselves determine the sanctions to be implemented by the corrections system. In each of these involvement strategies, the community justice managers experience a flow of information from the community to the justice process guiding their efforts, and there is a strong sense of support from the community for the actions of community justice.

However, the Involvement Model has weaknesses. Indeed, one of its strengths—that a single agency can act unilaterally with citizen groups—is also a weakness. Often, a neighborhood suffering from deficient public safety faces complex problems, and other agencies—social services, child protection, the courts, and so forth—have responsibilities that bear on the problem at hand. Moreover, the local residents may not always speak for all the groups affected by public safety concerns in those areas. For instance, businesses, churches, and schools typically have important interests to consider in any public safety agenda facing a troubled neighborhood. For a single agency, such as the police or probation, to try to confront those problems without considering the interests of the other groups involved can reduce the impact of the community justice work and lead to frustration for the justice agency and disappointment for the citizens. The recognition that public safety problems extend to relationships beyond those between community residents and a single justice agency has led to an increasing interest in strategies involving multiple partnerships.

Partnership Model

Under the Partnership Model, justice agencies such as the police work in collaboration with citizens and other public- and private-sector interests to identify problem priorities and generate strategic solutions to prevent crime. This approach recognizes that almost any crime or disorder problem facing a community raises the practical concerns of groups other than justice agencies and residents. If there is a problem of homelessness, for example, the local shelters will be involved, as will welfare agencies and religious groups. If there is a problem involving gangs, there is a need to consult with schools, family services, and juvenile probation. In both cases, problems of unemployment and inadequate job skills raise the possibility that businesses (as employers) and job-development services will need to be a part of the solution.

There are four layers of partnerships that justice agencies engage in. The first is the most obvious: the resident groups. Justice agencies may align their efforts with neighborhood councils, neighborhood development corporations, or citizen volunteer groups and use these partnerships to gain credibility with the community. This layer of partnership is essential to community justice: without the involvement of the community, any new initiative is not likely to represent community justice.

A second level of partnership occurs when one criminal justice agency aligns with another to try to increase the effectiveness of public safety efforts. A common example is police–probation partnerships to work with offenders under supervision in the community. A community court can also form a centerpiece for a collaborative effort between probation and police to improve the services to a neighborhood. Police–prosecution partnerships are also common.

A third level of partnership involves nonjustice governmental agencies in public safety collaborations. Probation will often work with mental-health agencies in a particular neighborhood, police will become aligned with child-protective services in a given housing project, or the domestic-violence prevention services will become a partner with police and probation in a troubled section of a city. Community schools are another common partner for police, probation, and even the courts. In these collaborations, agencies that share some responsibility for a given problem in a particular neighborhood or local setting will, instead of working independently, coordinate efforts through a cross-agency management team or a local coalition.

The final level of partnerships involves the private sector. Businesses are natural public safety partners because they have a strong interest in safe environments for commerce. Moreover, community foundations and other philanthropies can also become active in supporting innovative community justice practices that require new funding for start-up. It is also possible to have private volunteer groups, such as the chamber of commerce or the Kiwanis Club, become an active sponsor in this kind of effort.

A good example of the collaborative type of public safety effort is the Ten Points Coalition in Dorchester, Massachusetts. Led by a group of ministers, the coalition brings criminal justice representatives from all parts of the criminal justice system (police, courts, and corrections, including local, state, and federal) together with an array of social services, local citizen leaders, and private-sector representatives to combat gang violence. The criminal justice involvement was to target gang gun violence by focusing efforts to investigate, prosecute, and punish those gang members who used guns. Social-service agencies provided gang members with viable alternatives to gang membership and involvement, so that when pressured, they could see ways out of their gang memberships. Citizens, led by ministers, supported the families whose children were involved in gangs and mobilized community understanding and support for the initiative. The private sector lent financial assistance to the effort (Van Beiman, 1998).

The results of the Ten Points Coalition in Dorchester demonstrate the comparative advantage that the Partnership Model has over other models: it has a much stronger capacity for overcoming the public safety problem it is designed to reduce. In Boston, partly as a result of the work of the coalition, gang homicides went from more than ten per month to less than ten per year. Partnerships work because they bring to bear on a complex problem an array of resources, finding multiple avenues for addressing the full range of complex issues involved in public safety.

The great advantage of the Partnership Model, that it offers a far more sophisticated response to complicated and sometimes entrenched problems, is now widely accepted. Most community justice initiatives today are not enterprises of single justice–citizen partnerships, but rather employ multiple partnerships to achieve their ends. Police rarely work alone, but typically work with one or more partners—probation, schools, businesses, religious groups—to increase the scope and flexibility of what can be done.

Partnerships have proven to be quite successful, but they are not without their own problems. Many of the agencies trying to work together are funded by the same sources, and there is a natural sense of rivalry among them for public support and funds. Moreover, years of isolation from one another may have created a history of conflict: police may distrust social services, and private businesses may distrust the justice system. Finally, there is a natural tension between organizations whose mission is to "help" and organizations set up to investigate, accuse, and punish, and this conflict in missions has to be resolved.

The main difficulty, however, relates to the limited capacity of those neighborhoods with the greatest public safety problems. Places that suffer great deficits in public safety are also usually quite poor. They lack economic infrastructure because they have few businesses and serve as home to many people who are unemployed. Drugs are far easier to obtain than jobs. Few families are intact, and adults who work generally face severe demands for their time. They spend most of their time trying to make ends meet and engaging in child care. There is little time available for voluntary participation in community projects, and there may also be very limited confidence in the ability of service agencies and justice to affect problems of the neighborhood. Morale is low.

In such places—places with insufficient *collective efficacy*—there is not much basis for collective action. People tend to mind their own business. There is often suspicion of the government and its agencies, but widespread suspicion or indifference to their neighbors, as well. People are frequently cynical about the motives of social services and justice, and they have plenty of experience to justify the cynicism. Getting participation in these locations is always hard work, and it takes time.

For these reasons, newer community justice initiatives have sought not simply to prevent crime, but to strengthen the capacity of the communities within which they work. These approaches see public safety as a long-term issue of community functioning rather than a short-term issue of community circumstances.

Mobilization Model

The earliest form of community action was community mobilization, which traces its roots to Saul Alinsky's Back of the Yards Project (Alinsky, 1991) in poor Chicago neighborhoods. Mobilization seeks to counter the most prominent problem underlying poor neighborhoods: disorganization. The essence of the mobilization approach is to bring people together to confront their own problems, to organize people with respect to the quality of their lives. The idea is that people who live in poor places cannot rely upon outsiders' altruism for an improvement of their conditions. They have to take their destiny into their own hands.

With regard to public safety, mobilization is an attractive idea. The image of residents of poor places coming together to make their neighborhood safer is an appealing one, and numerous attempts to do so have occurred. The archetypal mobilization strategy is Neighborhood Watch. Here, citizens band together to keep an eye on one another's property and children, making sure that strange people and "undesirables" are not able to put them in danger. Usually, a Neighborhood Watch campaign is kindled by the work of a single authority—the police, a neighborhood citizen's group, or another governmental agency.

The theory underlying mobilization strategies is that these approaches work by creating new capacity within neighborhoods. Neighborhood Watch, for example, builds new relationships among neighbors, even if that means no more than the occasional communication about some event that occurred in the area. Other Mobilization Model public safety programs have impact on community capacity. The neighborhood probation centers in Phoenix, Arizona, offer literacy programs for residents who are not themselves on probation. La Bodega de la Familia, a family drug-treatment center operating in the Lower East Side of Manhattan, provides drug-rehabilitation services to children and partners in families with someone under supervision of the criminal justice system.

Neighborhood-organization strategies have a spotty history. For one thing, any attempt to improve a neighborhood's capacity must build upon something, and the places that most need improvement are also places that have the least foundation to start with. It is an uphill battle to get residents of these places ready and able to come together to work on their area's problems. When the people who live or work in these places are struggling just to make it from day to day, it is unrealistic to expect them to easily make room in their lives for a whole new set of activities, especially when they do not see a likelihood for immediate payoff to their community involvement.

Often, the way to get a poor community mobilized is to inflame a sense of anger about an event or the conditions that exist, and to use the anger to get a group to "march on City Hall" and demand changes. Such confrontational strategies can generate a lot of interest and action by residents at first, but it is very hard to sustain interest or motivation after the first few public happenings. People work out their anger, and it subsides; or they see that the protest seems to bring only resistance, with little evidence of changes. They easily become discouraged. The "protest" ends, and things go back to the way they were.

This is the reason why those who seek to produce public safety through improved community capacity today seek to build coalitions of efforts aimed at improvements in multiple aspects of community life. In this strategy, a central group working on behalf of the neighborhood seeks to bring various interests together to help improve community life and works to coordinate the activities of groups and resources already involved in the community. The role is one of developmental intermediary, serving to link external resources to local interests.

Intermediary Model

The Intermediary Model operates under two assumptions. First, what troubled neighborhoods need most is investment in capacity so that new strengths can be created and the natural base can be augmented. Second, ironically, what troubled neighborhoods have is a large contingent of uncoordinated, largely ineffective agencies and services involved in community life but not affecting it very much. From this point of view, what is needed most in any strategy to improve community capacity is not really *new* services, but *reinvestment* of existing resources to more directly target the needs of the community.

For the most part, intermediaries comprise local groups with resident leaders, such as a neighborhood development corporation or a local development council, that have already been active in advancing other neighborhood interests, notably housing, health care, and economic development. The intermediaries now address the problem of public safety in the same way as previous problems, by working with governmental and nonprofit groups to develop strategies for neighborhood improvement in the particular priority areas. The intermediary group then turns its attention to the work of criminal justice agencies in its community and builds collaborations with police, courts, and corrections representatives to the neighborhood, seeking ways to reorganize the efforts of those agencies to deal with particular public safety problems.

The Intermediary Model, therefore, does not spring up spontaneously, nor is it born in the planning of a particular criminal justice agency. Rather, this model represents a natural evolution of action for both the neighborhood group and the criminal justice (and other) services working in that neighborhood. (A description of how this model works is provided in the Appendix.) These approaches do not emanate from outside the neighborhood but come from a natural interest of the neighborhood in taking action on public safety priorities.

Because intermediaries are not from the criminal justice system, they tend to develop public safety strategies that are different from typical crime-prevention approaches of criminal justice. They might initiate a new recreational program to occupy the free time of local youth; develop a drop-in center and a mentoring program for youth with insufficient parental supervision; provide educational day care so single parents can work; or support a police–probation partnership that provides employment to those in re-entry and makes sure they obtain decent housing under circumstances that will reintegrate them into community life. Local intermediaries can also work closely with local resources, such as businesses and religious institutions, to find places for ex-offenders to have positive community ties. Because the intermediary is operating in a neighborhood where ex-offenders are familiar to the residents and where they probably have family, the level of antioffender sentiment in the community can often be lower, and it is easier to generate support for reintegration programs. The work of the intermediary, then, is to help criminal justice and other governmental agencies to shift from business-as-usual methods of merely dealing with criminal events to a new way of working that seeks to strengthen the neighborhood. There is little evaluative track record for the Intermediary Model, because it is the newest approach to community justice. On the positive side, most community initiatives are moving in the direction of this approach. Rather than making unilateral efforts, criminal justice agencies are increasingly working in partnership with existing community groups and important nonprofit and public collaborators. More and more, the orientation of justice innovation is to strengthen the capacity of the community to deal with its public safety issues in addition to providing crime-prevention services. On the negative side, coordinating the agendas of the multiple agencies involved in serving a single location is a difficult task. For a local neighborhood group to be able to devote sufficient effort to the task requires more than just a handful of eager volunteers; it needs a core leadership for the long term. This implies a funding source, usually some form of governmental grant or subsidy, and once again the problem arises that the neighborhoods most in need of gaining this new capacity are also least capable of securing the kind of funding that enables the capacity to be built.

WHICH COMMUNITY JUSTICE
MODEL IS BEST?

These four models serve as stereotypes for a wide range of community justice initiatives around the country. Which is best? There is no right answer to this question, because there is no obviously superior community justice approach. Each of these models has strengths and weaknesses. The "right" way for a community to do community justice depends upon a number of factors facing that community, including those related to the following questions.

- *How difficult is the public safety problem?* Long-term, complex problems require a larger investment from more resources working in partnership in order to achieve change. Targeted, new problems may be overcome with simpler strategies developed by a single organization.

- *How ready are the justice agencies to collaborate?* Turf battles abound in local criminal justice activity: police distrust the courts (and probation), parole is at odds with treatment providers, and so on. Unless these organizations, which often compete with one another for funding, can share a vision for community justice, effective collaboration faces long odds.

- *Is there an active, effective community leadership available to take on the problem?* In communities with strong community leaders, government agencies can rely upon those leaders to effectively involve the community. When leaders (or their organizations) are not present, it is much more difficult to develop strong, reliable partners for public safety initiatives.

- *What natural private partners exist?* Are there local businesses in the neighborhood that have an interest in promoting public safety? Is there a community foundation that can contribute to the effort?

- *What has been tried before; what are the untapped ideas?* In places where there is a history of failure, it can be difficult to generate an interest in new attempts to change the circumstances that cause problems in the community. Moreover, it is important not to try ideas that have already failed: new ideas are at a premium, and new partnerships can help to seed them.

In the end, the key strategy for community justice is the one that best fits the needs and assets of the community. This means that any successful community justice effort will begin with a careful assessment of the needs and assets a community offers, so that promising opportunities can be identified and probable dead ends avoided.

ISSUES IN COMMUNITY JUSTICE

Community justice is an attractive idea but is not always accepted as a solution. Critics of community justice raise the following questions.

Is it fair to have poor places take on their own crime-prevention issues? Some people say that community justice puts too much of the public safety burden on the poorest places, where the least capacity exists to take on the problems that lead to crime. Instead of the traditional approach, they say the community justice approach turns some of this responsibility over to the people who live there, asking that they provide assistance to various agencies that engage in public safety activity.

To some people, this seems like "blaming the victim." In those areas where the public safety needs are the greatest, and where the formal criminal justice system has most failed in its community mandate, it seems somewhat unfair to expect people to promote their own safety. This is especially problematic, because as we have repeatedly noted, these are precisely the locations that have the fewest social resources and where residents are most challenged to make it from one day to the next. Placing some of the responsibility for public safety on these citizens will, some say, inevitably set the stage for the criminal justice system to point the finger at them when crime rates fail to drop. When the crime rates stay high because the community lacks the capacity to eradicate the social problems that produce crime, they suffer a cycle of crime and get the blame for it.

Community justice approaches cannot be used as an excuse for abandoning an interest in these troubled neighborhoods. The reverse must be true. The current criminal justice approach is not working, and so a greater investment is needed. What is required is a redoubling of traditional justice system efforts, not a divestment of them to community members.

Can there be equality across places? The essence of community justice is to deal with different neighborhoods in a given jurisdiction differently, depending upon the problems that each location faces. It is dangerous to start making distinctions across communities that are covered by the same laws, especially when one of the main characteristics distinguishing some communities from others is the level of concentration of minority groups and the poor. Critics of community justice wonder if "different" treatment will eventually lead to "lesser" treatment" for these places.

This is a realistic concern. The places targeted for community justice initiatives have limited political and social resources. Compared to more advantaged locations, these areas have trouble getting their fiscal and programmatic priorities at the head of the line for resources. There are often few strong advocates for these locations, and other areas are typically more easily able to influence the policies that affect their lives. The nature of advantages in social capital is that some places can exert influence on their critical environment more than others. Without social capital, poor places infused with disadvantage have trouble competing for public resources.

This means that community justice initiatives could easily become common in the less troubled areas, where citizens are organized enough to demand responsiveness from the criminal justice system. Because community justice embraces the need for criminal justice to operate differently from one place to another, the fear is reasonable that for poor places, these differences will not work out to their advantage.

The criticism based on inequality raises an important, indeed a central, issue: inequality causes crime, and so public safety cannot be promoted by policies that further exacerbate the consequences of inequality. If community justice stands not just for different attention to some troubled areas, but also means more resources for those locations, then it can provide hope for a better justice system response to public safety concerns. Otherwise, areas already suffering from reduced official impact will be likely to receive not just different services, but below-standard services.

Can there be impartiality in cases? One of the most important values that underlies our contemporary criminal justice system is impartiality. This is the most democratic of our basic values because it requires that all people be treated equally without regard for their status: rich or poor, famous or ordinary. An impartial justice system is one that will have no social axe to grind, no political agenda to advance. It will merely enforce the law. The right of impartiality gives every citizen a guarantee of fairness and the expectation that no one's status will be elevated above anyone else's.

Some wonder if community justice can be impartial, considering the target at which it aims. Because the target is the quality of life in a particular location, it has to be, say some, partial to the people who live in that location. It has to place the needs and interests of the people who live and work in the community justice area as superior to those of others living or working elsewhere. In this way, community justice faces an impartiality challenge. In cases where a community justice area resident faces a conflict with a person from somewhere else, the community justice approach will, it is said, naturally tend to give higher consideration to the resident.

The loss of impartiality would be a severe price to pay for community justice, if this were true. Nobody wants a criminal justice system that gives one person an advantage over another merely because of where the person resides or who the person's neighbors are. Community justice initiatives need to find ways to advance the interests of the community without giving some people privileges. The paradox is that community justice seeks to give the residents of some communities a head start in achieving public safety, but this cannot be done at the expense of some other area. There is no obvious way to prove that community justice does not advantage some places at the expense of others, but any other situation would also raise problems of fairness.

How do you protect the rights and interests of individuals and community minorities? We all live in communities, and we all live better lives when our communities are strong, but few of us want to subjugate our personal dreams and aspirations to the community's quality of life. Community justice seeks to establish a stronger foundation of collective life so that individuals may prosper. Critics wonder if systems of government that emphasize the interests of the collective are likely to undermine the purposes of individuals to achieve the broader focuses of community life.

Trying to advance the interests of communities always raises the possibility of affecting the rights of individuals, especially when those individuals are somehow "different." Should a community be allowed to come together to stop some individuals from engaging in activities that are entirely legal but are upsetting to the dominant majority of the community? This is an issue that continuously arises in America, where personal freedom is so important. If the neighbors generally like peace and quiet, should they be able to prevent young people from getting together on a street corner? If local residents do not like activity late at night, can they prevent businesses from staying open past a certain "reasonable" hour? And if the residents can band together to enforce these types of preferences, what happens if the majority do not want some particular religious group to establish its temple, or they resent the presence of some ethnic group's social club?

Community justice is about public safety through community capacity, but it cannot be a way for a community to act out its prejudices and bigotry. Community justice can never supersede the basic protections of the Constitution and the Bill of Rights. After all, a community that does not allow *all* its residents' basic rights to be protected can never be considered "just." The ultimate aim of community justice is not merely safer places, but places where justice prevails. Safety is an essential element of justice, but achieving a safer environment at the expense of justice is no bargain.

Aren't there big problems in reinvestment strategies? Community justice seeks to reallocate public safety investments from traditional criminal justice activity toward community-focused activity. This is easier to accomplish with some justice functions than with others. For example, police already expend their resources at the community level, so for them the community justice movement is primarily a matter of shifting from traditional paramilitary policing models toward more community-oriented models, and this shift has been occurring broadly. For the courts, the shift to community can bring up additional costs, when new courtrooms are opened up to serve community and neighborhood interests. But these costs are in fact reduced because the new courts handle their fair share of cases and reduce the caseloads of other courts.

The toughest resource-redistribution problem arises in regard to corrections. The greatest correctional costs apply to prisons; by comparison, probation and parole—the obvious community options—are as little as one-twentieth the cost per case. As the preceding chapter showed, the most correctional dollars, by far, go to support incarceration. This means that the only way to reinvest this money into community settings is to move offenders, who would otherwise have been in prison, to the community. Without this, community justice correctional programs require new funding.

Moving offenders from the prison to the community happens, of course, every time an offender completes the prison sentence, and this will apply to at least 95 percent of sentenced offenders. The problem comes when trying to change the sentence either by keeping the offender in the community instead of going to prison or by getting the release to occur earlier in the sentence. There are two reasons why this is not easy to do. First, community pressures often make it harder to choose community sanctions in place of incarceration.

Second, there are powerful financial interests that want to maintain a large prison population: the "prison-industrial complex" that constructs and staffs the prison. As long as prisons remain a boom industry, these interests remain strong.

In order to overcome these impediments, community justice leaders must deal with each directly. To confront community attitudes, there is a need to involve residents in the planning of the community justice correctional strategies. This will reduce the impact of fear and give residents confidence they can build community justice programs that enhance community safety rather than endanger it. Second, the resources that go to incarceration need to be thought of as being shifted to new investment opportunities with financial interests at stake in the community context. This provides incentives for an interest group coalition to push for community justice reinvestment.

Will it work, or will it backfire? The point of all these criticisms is that community justice represents a change in and a challenge to the status quo. As long as we are aware of what the status quo really is, some of these criticisms are less compelling. For example, it is easy to wonder if disadvantaged areas will suffer if the new approaches allow them to be treated differently from the more advantaged places, but the truth is that they are *already* treated differently than those areas. People who live in those places know they are treated less well than people who live elsewhere: they get less enthusiastic, less effective service from the justice system; they have more trouble meeting their individual needs; they get less consideration in political circles than do other places. Community justice can backfire, but the current system, it must be admitted, already leaves these places at a disadvantage in terms of services and safety. This cannot be changed without upsetting the status quo.

Nevertheless, there remains an all-too-common theme in justice reform that highly touted reform efforts often fall far short of their promise. This, too, could be the fate of community justice. Surface changes in criminal justice are common, but purposeful, fundamental changes in criminal justice are much harder to achieve. The criminal justice system tends to respond more readily to external forces, such as Supreme Court decisions or shifts in public opinion, than it does to the decisions of criminal justice planners and managers. To the extent that community justice remains an initiative of the criminal justice system, it risks being reconciled to this pattern of failed promises. If community justice can be a manifestation of the interests and influences of the community movement that is so prominent in other arenas, fundamental change in criminal justice may occur.

THE FUTURE OF COMMUNITY JUSTICE

There is no question that community justice is no longer an emerging idea but a prominent new conceptualization of the way criminal justice ought to be delivered. Community justice has developed deep roots in police practice, informs most of the current innovation in courts, and has become an important new force in correctional practice. Almost all of the new ideas in criminal justice contain some aspect of community justice thinking: place, problem solving, partnerships, restoration, and so forth. Overall, the underlying value of community justice has developed salience in criminal justice thinking.

Yet the appeal of traditional criminal justice remains very strong. Television offers another cop chase-and-capture show every night, punitive sentencing strategies are very popular in the public mind, and the idea is widely held that public safety comes from no-holds-barred criminal justice. Criminal justice insiders know that traditional methods have significant limitations, and their growing interest in community justice stems from a sense that the practices of community justice can overcome some of those limitations. There is also a prevailing desire to work in more close cooperation with the community, rather than in isolation. These beliefs within the system have made the formerly cautious and even defensive criminal justice establishment increasingly interested in the possibilities that arise when community justice approaches are employed.

Community leaders have also started to recognize the potential of the underlying principles of community justice. Leaders seek locally relevant justice practices in which citizens have a role and for which the quality of community life is an aim. As new initiatives develop offering this as a way of providing justice services, many community leaders see the advantages and seek even wider application of these principles. With each success in community justice, resident resistance to innovation fades, and mutual support for more of these new ideas grows. The community justice movement has been strong partly because it meets the various needs of a changing justice system and an insistent public.

Community justice has been a popular idea despite the fact that evaluative evidence in support of it is scant, at best. As the previous chapters have shown, community justice makes sense from the standpoint of what we know about public safety and strong communities. There are a few significant evaluation studies that confirm the wisdom of some of the community justice conceptual foundations: community policing has paid dividends in law enforcement; community courts and special courts (such as drug courts) have developed impressive track records; restorative justice offers sufficient benefits to encourage expansion of the idea. The empirical foundation for a community justice movement, however, is not as strong as any of these parts.

A core aspect of the future of community justice, then, is evidence. New initiatives must be studied and their results more fully understood. The relative benefits of different strategies of community justice need to be documented so that an informed conception of community justice priorities can be developed. This will not happen rapidly but will require sustained attention to the benefits and costs of community justice activity.

A second aspect of the future of community justice is political. A great deal will depend upon whether the current coalescence of opinion in favor of community justice concepts will continue. Today, there is a broad consensus of opinion among criminal justice leaders, researchers, and community leaders that the potential of community justice justifies continued interest and experimentation. New programs have solid support among the key constituencies needed to sustain community justice action. But the criminal justice system has a way of shifting its attention from time to time, and when the inevitable shift occurs, the momentum of community justice will be tested. If the basic support for community justice continues, this shift in interest will not be a problem; if the support evaporates when the attention shifts, community justice will struggle to survive.

Finally, there is the question of whether this new idea called community justice can retain its quality of creativity and innovation. Central to the idea of community justice is a challenge to the inventive capacities of collaborative partnerships of citizens and justice officials working together on the problems that face a particular geographic area. The idea is to avoid the routine response to crime and instead to invent new ways of responding to the challenge of public safety. It is easy to develop a copycat version of community justice, where local partnerships try to re-create the experiences of other areas rather than produce their own. Community justice will endure so long as the innovative and inventive spirit that fueled its inception supports its continuation.

In some ways, this book has been entirely about the future of community justice. Every idea presented in this book is a conception about how the future of criminal justice could be changed by a commitment to the values and vision of community justice.

REFERENCES

Alinsky, Saul. [1946] 1991. *Reveille for Radicals*. Reissue, New York: Random House.

Goldstein, Herman. 1991. *Problem-Oriented Policing*. New York: McGraw Hill.

Van Bieman, David. 1998. "In Search of Moses." *Time Magazine* 152 (December 14).

FOR FURTHER READING

Bazemore, Gordon. 1995. "Rethinking the Sanctioning Function in Juvenile Court: Retributive or Restorative Responses to Youth Crime." *Crime and Delinquency* 41: 296–316.

Clear, Todd R., and David R. Karp. 1999. *The Community Justice Ideal: Preventing Crime and Achieving Justice*. New York: Westview Press.

Clear, Todd R., and Dina Rose. 1999. *When Neighbors Go to Jail: Impact on Attitudes about Formal and Informal Social Control*. Washington, D.C.: U.S. Dept. of Justice, Office of Justice Programs, National Institute of Justice.

Decker, Scott H., and Barrik Van Winkle. 1996. *Life in the Gang: Family, Friends and Violence*. New York: Cambridge University Press.

Karp, David R., ed. 1998. *Community Justice: An Emerging Field*. Lanham, Md.: Rowman and Littlefield.

Rose, Dina R., and Todd R. Clear. 1998. "Incarceration, Social Capital and Crime: Examining the Unintended Consequences of Incarceration." *Criminology* 36 (3): 441–479.

Sampson, Robert J., Jeffrey D. Morenoff, and Felton Earles. 1999. "Beyond Social Capital: Spatial Dynamics of Collective Efficacy for Children." *American Sociological Review* 64: 633–660.

Smith, Margaret, and Todd R. Clear. 1997. "Fathers in Prison: Interim Report." Draft report to the Edna McConnell Clark Foundation by the Rutgers University School of Criminal Justice.

Smith, Michael E., and Walter J. Dickey. 1998. "What If Corrections Were Serious about Public Safety?" *Corrections Management Quarterly* 2 (3): 12–30.

Mobilization

Merry, Sally E., and N. Milner. 1993. *The Possibility of Popular Justice: A Case Study of Community Mediation in the United States*. Ann Arbor: University of Michigan Press. Investigates the circumstances leading to and consequences of a community-based alternative to the formal legal system for solving local conflicts.

Podolefsy, Aaron. 1983. *Case Studies in Community Crime Prevention*. Springfield, Ill.: Charles C. Thomas. Demonstrates a series of ways that communities can systematically come together to prevent crime.

Partnerships

Crawford, Adam. 1997. *The Local Governance of Crime: Appeals to Community and Partnerships*. Oxford, England: Clarendon. Describes the conceptual and practical limits of community-based crime-prevention partnerships.

Politics of Crime Prevention

Chambliss, William J. 2001. *Power, Politics, and Crime*. Boulder, Colo.: Westview. A critical analysis of the way political interests affect the formulation of crime policy.

Miller, Lisa L. 2001. *The Politics of Community Crime Prevention*. Burlington, Vermont: Ashgate Dartmouth. Description of the politics of the Federal Government's Weed and Seed program, in which law enforcement (Weed) is coupled with community services (Seed).

Index

N

National Center for Community Policing, 36

National Center for Victims of Crime, 64

National Crime Victimization Survey, 66

National Institute of Justice, 57

Native Americans, circle sentencing practices, 65

Neighborhood-based probation, 84–87

Neighborhood community justice centers, 98–101

Neighborhood Conference Committees (NCCs), 90–91

Neighborhood defender services, 60–62

Neighborhood development corporations, 18

Neighborhood-mobilization strategies, 111–112

Neighborhood probation centers, 88–89, 111

Neighborhoods

collective efficacy and, 110–111

concentration of crime and criminal justice in, 9–10

concerns about equal treatment under community justice, 115–116

concerns about public safety burden for, 115

in correctional community justice, 77–78

defined, 6

economic development and, 20

historical experiences of immigrants and African Americans in, 7–8

life chances and, 8–9

political empowerment and, 19–20

public safety and, 10–15

relationship to community, 7

service sector improvements, 20–21

Neighborhood Watch, 38, 111

New York City

"broken windows" theory, 12–13

CompStat process, 39–40

Midtown Community Court, 56–58

"zero-tolerance" policing, 41

See also Brooklyn; Harlem; Manhattan

911 system, 36

O

Offender management

in correctional community justice, 81–82

in traditional corrections, 74–75

Office of Justice Programs, 69

Operation Night Light, 79

Oregon, correctional program in, 93–94

P

Parallel justice, 64

Parole

community justice and, 95

crime rates and, 95

defined, 73–74

See also Re-entry

Partnership Model, 109–111

Partnerships

CASES Model and, 125

in correctional community justice, 78–80

Penal sanctions. *See* Sanctioning

Performance Recognition and Award System (PRAS), 94

Phoenix (AZ), neighborhood probation centers, 88–89, 111

Phoenix House, 97

Place

community justice and, 104, 105–106

community-oriented criminal justice strategies and, 15–16

importance to contemporary life, 5–6

life chances and, 8–9

public safety and, 10–15

See also Communities; Neighborhoods

Police

authority and, 33, 34

community-oriented strategies and, 21–22

culture of, 33–34

essential services of, 29–30

as a function of power in society, 32–34

as a function of the legal system, 31–32

hot spots concept and, 12

Involvement Model of community justice and, 107–108

main issues interfering with effectiveness of, 29–34

perceptions of citizens, 31

professional model of, 35

response time, 36

studies on effectiveness of command policing, 35–36

as a symbol of modern culture, 30–31

Police Athletic League, 38

Police-citizen relations

citizen distrust of police, 31–32

citizen perceptions of police, 31

in crisis situations, dynamics of, 30

issues of power and authority, 32–34

origins of community policing and, 34

Community Policing

Partnerships for Problem Solving | Sixth Edition

Table of Contents

CHAPTER 6
Communicating with a Diverse Population

DO YOU KNOW . . .

○ What the communication process consists of?

○ What individual characteristics are important in the communication process?

○ What two critical barriers to communication in a diverse society are?

○ Why police officers may have more barriers to communication than other professionals and what these barriers consist of?

○ What dilemma law enforcement officers face when interacting with immigrants?

○ What is needed to avoid discrimination?

○ The difference between prejudice and discrimination?

○ What disabilities police officers frequently encounter?

○ What disabilities can mimic intoxication or a drug high?

○ What special challenges are posed by persons suffering from Alzheimer's disease?

○ What youths with special needs police officers should be familiar with?

○ Why communicating effectively with victims of and witnesses to crime is essential?

CAN YOU DEFINE . . .

acculturation
Alzheimer's disease (AD)
Americans with Disabilities Act (ADA)
assimilation
attention deficit hyperactivity disorder (ADHD)

bias
communication process
crack children
crisis behavior
EBD
ethnocentrism
fetal alcohol syndrome (FAS)
jargon

kinesics
nonverbal communication
posttraumatic stress disorder (PTSD)
poverty syndrome
racial profiling
stereotyping

> What we are communicates far more eloquently than anything we say or do. There are people we trust because we know their character. Whether they're eloquent or not, whether they have human-relations techniques or not, we trust them and work with them.
>
> —*Stephen R. Covey*

Introduction

A woman executive at a shopping center discovered a minor theft of company property from her company car. The car had been parked outside a police office where several traffic officers took breaks between shifts. The office was not accessible to the public but had an identification sign on the locked door.

The woman knocked on the door and asked the sergeant who opened it who was responsible for watching the parking area. She also commented on the officers she could see sitting inside the room and suggested they were not doing their jobs. The officers in the room stopped talking with each other and turned their attention to the conversation at the office door.

The sergeant and the woman never got around to discussing the missing item. Instead he responded to her comments with questions. "What do you mean by that?" "What are you trying to say?" She left to tell her supervisor, refusing to file a police report. She soon returned, however, and encountered another officer just outside the office. Their conversation, later characterized as "heated" by witnesses, centered on the woman's suggestion that the officers should do more to prevent theft in the parking lot. She implied they were lazy and shirked their responsibilities.

At this point the woman asked to file a police report, and the officer asked her to enter the police office with him to do so. They entered the office, but when the officer suggested they enter a private office away from the hubbub of the break area, she refused to do so. She later said the officer intimidated her by slamming drawers, moving quickly, and ordering her into the room. She feared being alone with him.

The officer's perception of the incident was entirely different. He commented that the woman had a "chip on her shoulder" and an "attitude." She was demanding, and dealing with her was "impossible."

After refusing to enter the office to file the report, the woman sat down on a chair in the break area. She was told to either go into the other room and file the report or leave. When she refused to do either, she was escorted from the office and left outside the locked doors. The woman filed a complaint against the police department.

With better communication, this problem and thousands like it could be avoided. Effective communication with the public is vital to good police–community relations. In fact, at the heart of police–community relations are the one-on-one interaction between an officer and a citizen. This interaction becomes even more challenging when it involves individuals from different backgrounds and cultures. As our society becomes more diverse, communicating effectively requires an understanding not only of the communication process but also of the differences among individuals that affect communication.

This chapter begins with a discussion of the communication process, including nonverbal communication and body language, communication barriers and active listening. Then the discussion turns to community policing in a diverse society, beginning with a description of the multicultural diversity in the United States, including racial and ethnic diversity. Next, racism is discussed, including racial disparity, racial profiling, and strategies to overcome barriers based on racial or ethnic differences. Religious and socioeconomic diversities are examined briefly, with more extensive attention paid to persons in the lower socioeconomic class, the homeless, and the powerful and privileged. The discussion of diversity concludes with a consideration of the challenges facing police as they strive to "serve and protect" an increasingly diverse society. The third major area of discussion is communicating effectively with individuals with disabilities, including those with physical and mental disabilities, and interacting with elderly persons and youths. The final discussion focuses on communicating with victims of and witnesses to crime.

Keep in mind while reading this chapter that although various groups are presented separately to keep the discussion organized, in real life it is rare for individuals to be neatly compartmentalized. Americans embody every overlapping combination of diversity characteristics imaginable—from the young Hispanic girl who is deaf; to the middle-aged Jewish man who is homeless; to the elderly black woman with bipolar disorder.

The Communication Process

Communication is basically the transfer of information.

 The **communication process** involves a sender, a message, a channel, a receiver and, sometimes, feedback.

communication process
Involves a sender, a message, a channel, a receiver and sometimes feedback.

Communication involves transferring thoughts from one person's mind to another's. The people involved, the accuracy of the message in expressing the sender's thoughts and the channel used all affect communication. A simplified illustration of the process is shown in Figure 6.1.

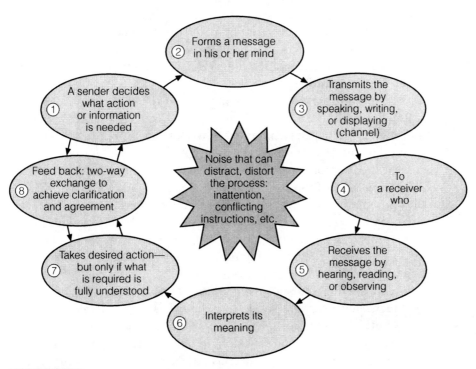

Figure 6.1 The Communication Process

The sender encodes the message in words—spoken or written—and then transmits the message by phone, by texting, by fax, by letter, in person or in some other way. The receiver decodes the message. The receiver may then provide the sender with some kind of feedback indicating the message has been received. Many factors will influence the message.

Important individual characteristics in communication include age, education, gender, values, emotional involvement, self-esteem and language skills.

Surprisingly, police departments rarely train their officers in communication skills. They assume that the people they hire know how to communicate. It is an erroneous assumption. In its 2003 report, "Training the Twenty-First Century Police Officer: Redefining Police Professionalism for the Los Angeles Police Department," the RAND Corporation noted: "To communicate effectively is to be skilled in the overt and the subtle, to make one's intentions known whether the recipient is deaf, unable to understand English, mentally handicapped, enraged, under the influence of drugs or alcohol, or simply unfamiliar with normal police procedure" (Miller, 2008, p.62). Skilled officers can communicate effectively even when they are under tremendous stress. The skill is critical for successfully gaining compliance or cooperation from subjects and for managing situations where arrest, search and seizure or use of force, scenarios that are "intricately related," are required.

Nonetheless, the RAND study notes: "Tactical communications as currently taught are too limited in scope and poorly integrated with other instruction. Officers need to learn how, when, and with what type of person certain communication techniques are more effective. This is particularly important when deadly force might be applied. A person who does not understand English or a person with a mental illness might inadvertently send aggressive signals to the officer. The officer needs to be adept at selecting from and effectively applying various modes of communication, verbal and nonverbal, under conditions of extreme stress" (Miller).

Dr. George Thompson, the name behind the effective and popular police training company the Verbal Judo Institute, asserts that the use of courtesy and respect is the safest and most powerful way for police officers to interact with even dangerous or explosive members of the public (2009). Thompson, a college English professor who became a cop, calls the technique tactical civility. According to Dr. Thompson, when officers respond to verbal attacks in kind, they give up their own personal and professional power and allow themselves to be controlled by others. A display of anger also reveals weakness and indecision, something most officers cannot afford to show in public. If officers react with rudeness or threatening comments, they put the other person on notice of pending attack, a tactical mistake.

Thompson recommends not giving such an early warning. Just remain civil, get tough if necessary and return to civility. Politeness does not equal weakness, but the other person may mistake it for that, causing him or her to play into an officer's hands. "My operating axiom has always been, 'the nastier you become to me, the more polite and courteous do I become to you because it is good for me, good for me at the moment, and good for me later, in court or when called before a supervisor or IA (internal affairs). Don't use words that will betray you later!" (Thompson)

Thompson (2006) stresses that community policing can only work if officers handle people with dignity and respect: "The people in affluent, successful America do not want a police presence, except indirectly. The people who need us bar their windows and hope for the best. They fear the gang bangers and the drive-by shooters, but they fear us—the police—as much, perhaps more, and they typically 'see nothing, hear nothing and know nothing' when crimes occur. People mistreated do not give intelligence to those who mistreat them" (Miller). According to Thompson, the "gap" between the police and many areas in the community needs to be eliminated. If that gap can be closed, the crooks have nowhere to commit their crimes. In communities where people see the police as protectors, they work in concert with the police to "take out the bad guys."

Giles and colleagues (2005), in a similar vein, stress that in a democracy an effective police force requires the consent and cooperation of the citizens. When that consent and cooperation exists, witnesses to crimes willingly come forward with information; citizens are more likely to follow police directives in an emergency; and citizens are also more likely to support the police legislatively—for example, in increasing funding for police departments.

How can that consent and cooperation be achieved? Research by Skogan and Frydl (2004, p.305) found that police are most likely to obtain cooperation if they engage in *process-oriented policing*—that is, they are attentive to the way they treat people, behaving in ways that positively influence the degree to which people perceive the procedures used as fair. Several elements influence people's judgments regarding fairness of procedures (Skogan and Frydl). One

Interactions between officers and citizens are at the heart of police-community relations. This relationship can be put to the test during challenging or tense situations, particularly those involving clashes between citizens' personal beliefs and constitutional rights.
© AP Images/Noah Berger

key element is participation; procedures are perceived as fairer if people are allowed to explain their situation. A second key element is neutrality. Evidence of evenhandedness and objectivity increases perceived fairness. Third, people value being treated with dignity and respect. Finally, people perceive procedures as being fairer when they trust the motives of decision makers.

Treating people fairly with dignity and respect involves not only the words officers speak but also their nonverbal messages.

Nonverbal Communication and Body Language

nonverbal communication

Includes everything other than the actual words spoken in a message, such as tone, pitch and pacing.

Nonverbal communication includes everything except the actual words spoken in a message, such as tone, pitch and pacing. Body language refers to messages conveyed by how a person moves. To test the power of body language, consider what the following actions say about a person.

Walking—fast, slow, stomping

Posture—rigid, relaxed

Eye contact—direct, indirect, shifting

Gestures—nod, shrug, finger point

Physical spacing—close, distant

Police officers' nonverbal communication was discussed in Chapter 2. Officers communicate with the public most obviously through the uniforms they wear and the equipment they carry. Other forms of body language are equally important. How officers stand, how they look at those to whom they are talking, whether they smile or frown—all convey a message.

Eye contact is a powerful nonverbal communication tool. Eye contact inspires trust and shows confidence, even if it is merely the illusion of confidence. It can buy you time if you are caught off guard and need to form a response. Eye contact quietly keeps control while deftly wielding power.

Usually, police officers want to convey the impression that they "know their way around." However, this may actually interfere with effective communication. When interviewing a truthful witness, police officers may want to modify their body language and soften their language. A relaxed manner may result in more in-depth communication and better understanding.

Reading Nonverbal Messages and Body Language

kinesics

The study of body movement or body language.

In addition to understanding nonverbal messages, many police officers develop an ability to interpret body language, also called **kinesics**, to such an extent that they can tell when a person is lying or about to become aggressive or flee. This is what some call a "sixth sense," and it alerts officers when something is not as it appears or when someone is suspicious, untruthful, afraid or hesitant.

Criminals are often apprehended because an officer thought they looked suspicious or because something did not feel right about a traffic stop or other contact. Many law enforcement officers develop an uncanny ability to spot stolen cars in traffic based on a driver's actions and driving maneuvers. Officers also learn to read their own hunches. Acting on a hunch can save lives. Police officers can tell story after story of nagging and intuitive feelings on which they acted.

Barriers to Communication

Two critical barriers to communication in a diverse society are language barriers and cultural barriers.

Roughly 47 million people in this country, or 18 percent of the U.S. population, speak a language other than English at home. Nearly 30 percent of all Spanish speakers, 25 percent of all Asian and Pacific Islander language speakers, and 15 percent of Indo-European language speakers classify themselves as having limited English proficiency (Venkatraman, 2006, p.40). The implications for law enforcement are obvious. Failure to communicate effectively can be disastrous in a variety of police functions from the routine to the deadly. It can compromise the integrity of the judicial process, interfere with crime control and undermine the core purpose of police work (Venkatraman, p.41). In addition, federal law requires police departments to address the language barrier.

The spoken language is not the only barrier. Gestures can also be misinterpreted. For example, making the A-Okay sign (a circle with the thumb and forefinger) is friendly in the United States, but it means "you're worth zero" in France, Belgium and many Latin American countries. The thumbs-up gesture meaning "good going" in the United States is the equivalent of an upraised middle finger in some Islamic countries. The amount of eye contact also varies with different racial and ethnic groups. For example, in the United States, Caucasians maintain eye contact while speaking about 45 percent of the time, African-Americans about 30 percent, Hispanics about 25 percent and Asians about 18 percent.

Moy and Archibald (2005, p.55) note that another significant communication barrier is some immigrants' lack of understanding of law enforcement practices and their fear of police. Among the misunderstandings they describe are recognizing law enforcement officers (some residents do not know the difference between police officers, security guards and firefighters), using the emergency 911 system and responding to a traffic stop (some people stop in the middle of the road and others refuse to sign the traffic citation). In addition, domestic violence calls are complicated not only by families' limited English but even more so by their lack of understanding of American laws and the legal ramifications of domestic violence.

For example, in some Asian cultures, only the oldest family member will deal with the police on behalf of the entire family. But older Asian immigrants are the least likely in the family to speak English. The only way for officers to communicate, in many cases, is by using one of the elder's grandchildren as an interpreter, which the elder usually considers to be a loss of face.

In the last few years, thousands of immigrants have come to the United States from Southeast Asia and Africa. Often victims of discrimination and crime, they tend not to seek police assistance or report crimes. In fact, many, especially elderly immigrants, fear the police. Compounding this communication problem is the fact that many immigrants from Asian and other Third World nations mistrust U.S. banks and keep their money and other valuables at home. Their cultural backgrounds leave them extremely vulnerable to scams, burglaries and robberies, but even after they are victimized they hesitate to talk to the police.

Police officers may have more barriers to communication because of the image they convey, their position of authority and the nature of their work. Other barriers include lack of time, use of police jargon, lack of feedback and a failure to listen.

Lack of time is another barrier to effective communication. Police officers and citizens are busy. Often, neither want to take the time to communicate fully and to establish high empathy. Bad timing can also interfere with communication. Police officers frequently are interrupted by calls for service and need to cut short conversations with others.

jargon
The technical language of a profession.

The use of **jargon**, the technical language of a profession, is another barrier to communication. Law enforcement has its own special terminology—for example, alleged perpetrator, modus operandi, and complainant. Officers should avoid using such terms when talking with the public.

Lack of feedback can also reduce effective communication. The old adage sums up this problem well: I know that you believe that you understand what you think I said, but I am not sure you realize that what you heard is not what I meant.

A failure to listen is one of the most common and most serious barriers to effective communication. Our educational system concentrates on the communication skills of reading and writing. Some time is devoted to speaking, but little or no time is devoted to listening. It is simply assumed that everyone knows how to listen.

Law enforcement officers need to receive information more than they need to give it. A major portion of their time is spent receiving information for forms and reports, taking action in arrests, eliciting information in interviews and interrogations and many other duties requiring careful listening. As important as listening is, many people lack good listening skills.

Listening skills *can* be improved. The effective communicator is skilled not only at speaking (or writing) but also at listening (and reading). In addition, the effective communicator recognizes personal biases likely to occur in a society as diverse as the United States.

Ethnic Diversity: A Nation of Immigrants

Dealing effectively with diversity is important to community policing because community outreach, communications, trust and activism are all necessary to community partnerships, and none of these can be achieved without accepting—indeed, embracing—diversity. Police officers and their agencies can accomplish much by working in partnership with citizens to implement the American vision of diverse and tolerant communities that offer freedom, safety and dignity for all (International Association of Chiefs of Police).

Culture is a collection of artifacts, tools, ways of living, values and language common to a group of people, all passed from one generation to the next. Diversity is most obvious and sometimes most problematic when groups with different "ways of living" coexist in the same community. The culture provides a framework or worldview, a cultural window through which events are interpreted. **Ethnocentrism** is the preference for one's own way of life over all others. People are naturally attracted to others who are similar to themselves

ethnocentrism
The preference for one's own way of life over all others.

because they feel less uncertain about how similar people will respond to them and more certain about the likelihood that similar people will agree with them. Ethnocentricity and segregation are consequences of a desire to avoid uncomfortable uncertainty.

During the seventeenth and eighteenth centuries, several different cultures came to the New World and established the United States. With the exception of Native Americans and Mexican Americans, the population was made up of immigrants. Skogan and associates (2002, p.1) stress: "The influx of immigrants and the corresponding changes in the racial and ethnic composition of the nation's population have placed significant demands on the infrastructure of the nation's public service sector, particularly the criminal justice system." They (p.3) report that Hispanic and Asian groups—younger and with larger families—are projected to account for more than half of the nation's population growth over the next 50 years: The U.S. Census Bureau projects that by 2050 non-Hispanic whites will constitute a bare majority at 52 percent.

The sociologic literature on ethnic and racial diversity contains three theories on the consequences of two or more cultures inhabiting the same geographic area: assimilation, cultural pluralism and cultural conflict. These are not mutually exclusive and may occur at the same time, creating problems for the transition to community policing.

Assimilation theorists suggest that our society takes in or assimilates various cultures. Assimilation, also referred to as **acculturation**, was, indeed, what happened among the early colonists. Initially the colonists came from various countries with different religions. They settled in specific geographic areas and maintained their original culture—for example, the Pennsylvania Dutch.

assimilation
A society takes in or assimilates various other cultures to become a "melting pot." Also called *acculturation*.

Over time, the triple forces of continued immigration, urbanization and industrialization turned the United States into a "melting pot" with diverse cultures from the various colonies merging. The melting pot was accomplished relatively painlessly because of the many similarities among the colonists. They looked quite similar physically; they valued religion and "morality"; most valued hard work; and, perhaps most important, there was plenty of land for everyone. The "homogenization" of the United States was fairly well accomplished by the mid-1800s. The formerly distinct cultures blended into what became known as the American culture, a white, male-dominated culture of European origin.

acculturation
A society takes in or assimilates other cultures. Also called *assimilation*.

Unfortunately, the colonists excluded the Native Americans. Like animals, they were herded onto reservations. Native Americans have only recently begun to enter into the mainstream of American life. Some Native Americans do not want to be assimilated—they seek to maintain their culture and heritage. The same is true of many African Americans. Consequently, cultural diversity will continue to exist in the United States. Assimilation does not always occur.

An alternative to assimilation is *cultural pluralism,* with diverse cultures peacefully coexisting. One example of cultural pluralism is Native American culture. There are more than 450 recognized tribes and bands of Native Americans in this country, with populations ranging from less than 100 to more than 100,000. Before colonization of the United States, the tribes had distinct territories, languages and cultures. Later, as the settlers took their lands, Native Americans joined together in self-defense. Today, Native Americans are often referred to as a single entity, although the individual tribes still maintain their unique identities.

Cultural pluralism is particularly noticeable when new immigrants arrive in the United States. Usually, instead of attempting to assimilate into the mainstream of U.S. culture, immigrants seek out and live near others from their homelands, forming Chinatowns; Little Italys; Little Havanas; Little Greeces; and, most recently, Hmong and Somali communities. This has resulted in what is sometimes referred to as the *hyphenated American:* the Italian-American, the Polish-American, the African-American, the Asian-American and so forth.

Cultural pluralism rests on the assumption that diverse cultures can co-exist and prosper; but peaceful coexistence is not always the reality. The cultural conflict theory suggests that diverse cultures that share the same territory will compete with and attempt to exploit one another. Such cultural conflict was common between the early settlers and the Native American tribes. Conflict was also common between the white immigrants and the more than 6 million slaves imported from Africa between 1619 and 1860. The hostile treatment of Japanese Americans during World War II was rooted in cultural conflict. Following Japan's attack on Pearl Harbor, many U.S. citizens saw Japanese Americans as a national threat. More than 110,000 Japanese Americans, the great majority of whom were American-born citizens, were forced by the government to sell their homes and businesses and then were placed in internment camps.

Cultural conflict can currently be seen in growing tensions between specific ethnic groups as they compete for the limited remaining resources available. In Minnesota, for example, a controversial law permits only Native Americans to harvest wild rice or spear fish. The Mille Lacs band of Chippewa has sued the state of Minnesota, claiming treaty rights allow them to fish outside their reservation without state regulation. Native Americans are also lobbying to be allowed to take motorboats into wilderness areas to enhance their guide business.

The Immigration Issue

"Give me your tired, your poor,/Your huddled masses yearning to breathe free,/The wretched refuse of your teeming shore,/Send these, the homeless, tempest-tost to me,/I lift my lamp beside the golden door!" These words appearing at the base of the Statue of Liberty once reflected a welcoming philosophy of a country developed in large part by immigrants, primarily of European descent. Today the situation has changed.

A study by the Pew Research Center (*America's Immigration Quandary*, 2006) found that Americans are increasingly concerned about immigration, with a growing number of respondents believing immigrants are a burden to the country, taking jobs and housing and straining our health and educational systems. Of particular concern is the burgeoning Hispanic population. According to the U.S. Census Bureau, in July 2004 the estimated Hispanic population of the United States was 41.3 million, making those of Hispanic origin the nation's largest ethnic minority, constituting 14 percent of the nation's total population. The Census Bureau projects that by 2050 Hispanics will make up 24 percent of the nation's total population. It is not the numbers alone that alarm many Americans but the fact that millions of immigrants are in the country illegally.

An estimated 11 to 12 million illegal immigrants reside in this country and have become an increasing focus of controversy: "Since early spring of [2006], illegal immigration has evolved from a peripheral political issue to one of the most important, and most contentious issues being faced by America since the first battles in the War on Terrorism" (Eggers, 2006, p.31). In the wake of the September 11, 2001, attack on America, carried out by hijackers who entered the country on student or tourist visas, Americans have become ultra-aware of the porous borders and lax enforcement of immigration laws as security threats, and in Congress both parties have pushed for a tougher line (Babington and Murray, 2006, p.A01).

Chaddock (2006) reports on the rift in the Republican party caused by immigration reform: polls show that a strong majority of Republican voters are opposed to amnesty for illegal immigrants, whereas business groups, an important Republican constituency, back amnesty, wanting to ensure a supply of low-wage workers for agriculture, the construction industry, and restaurant and other service industries. Jonsson and Chaddock (2006) report that business groups say immigrants do jobs that whites and blacks have stopped doing. The study by the Pew Research Center found that 53 percent of respondents say those who are in the United States illegally should be sent home. But nearly half of those respondents stated some could stay under a temporary work program.

A *Washington Post*–ABC News poll shows that three fourths of Americans think the government is not doing enough to prevent illegal immigration, but three in five said they favor providing illegal immigrants who have lived here for years a way to gain legal status and eventual citizenship (Balz and Fears, 2006, p.A01). However, Congressman Tom Tancredo (R-Colorado), an advocate of cracking down on illegal immigrants, cautioned: "Today's rallies show how entrenched the illegal alien lobby has become over the last several years. The iron triangle of illegal employers, foreign governments and groups like LaRaza puts tremendous pressure on our elected officials to violate the desires of law-abiding Americans" ("Should They Stay," 2006, p.32).

Communicating with New Immigrant Populations

The Vera Institute of Justice stresses: "Developing the trust and confidence of new immigrant populations is essential for effective policing. This is particularly true for the growing number of police departments that view communities and law enforcement as partners and incorporate community-oriented policing techniques" (*Strengthening Relations between Police and Immigrants*, 2006).

The 2000 U.S. Census revealed that 47 million people in the United States speak a language other than English at home. Many of them do not consider themselves proficient in English. About 30 percent of Spanish speakers, 25 percent of Asian speakers, and 15 percent of Indo-Europeans identified themselves that way to census takers. Bilingual officers are still rather rare in American law enforcement, but police departments, especially in major metropolitan areas, are interested in hiring officers who speak a second language. Bilingualism is even more sought after in many federal agencies, including the Department of Homeland Security and the Drug Enforcement Administration (DEA) (Hoffman, n.d.).

Knowing another language can be a life saver. For example, in one incident, an officer in Washington, DC, conducting a late-night stop in a Spanish-speaking neighborhood, knew enough Spanish to understand when the driver instructed a passenger in Spanish to shoot the officer when he got close. The officer called for backup and ordered the occupants out of the car. When one suspect opened fire, the officer was prepared and shot back (Venkatraman, p.46).

As discussed, cultural and language barriers make it difficult for police to reach out to immigrants and persuade them to report crimes, be witnesses, provide information to police or become law enforcement officers. In addition, immigrants are now more reluctant to seek police assistance or to cooperate with them because they fear being detained or deported (Vera Institute). Henderson and colleagues (2006, p.7) note that since September 11, 2001, some policing scholars and practitioners have encouraged local agencies to leverage their street-level position to become more involved in intelligence gathering and immigration enforcement, observing that in some jurisdictions local police have responded by embracing surveillance and intelligence gathering.

 A dilemma facing law enforcement regarding the immigration issue is whether police can build trusting partnerships with immigrant communities if they are also to gather intelligence and enforce immigration law.

In an effort to improve relations between new immigrant communities, the Vera Institute began working with the New York Police Department, organizing working groups with representatives from New York City's Arab, African and emerging Latin American immigrant communities. A series of facilitated forums focused on such topics as the relationship between the police and the community; the community's crime, safety and policing needs and concerns; and strategies for improving police–community relations. They also tested several initiatives, including developing fact sheets for police officers and coordinating public education and outreach campaigns on legal rights and responsibilities, reporting crimes and police procedures. According to the institute, by cultivating alternative communication channels such as the police immigrant working group forums, the project demonstrated new, more effective, more culturally sensitive ways to reach out to and serve New York City's immigrant communities.

Henderson and associates (p.21) also report on the "shock waves" that the September 11, 2001, attacks sent through local and federal law enforcement agencies and Arab American communities alike. Law enforcement's role in immigration enforcement was stepped up and their interactions with people of Arab descent became much more intense. Before the attacks, Arab Americans were "largely unnoticed in the fabric of American life," but after the attacks, these persons found themselves at the center of attention that was mostly unwelcome. The Vera Institute tried to build relationships with Arab American communities and found that the number one barrier, as perceived by community leaders, police personnel and Federal Bureau of Investigation (FBI) personnel, was distrust of law enforcement. Among the top six solutions for overcoming barriers to working together, improving or initiating communication and dialogue was the most commonly suggested solution by police and FBI personnel. Improving or initiating communication and dialogue was the second most commonly suggested solution by community leaders, with cultural awareness training being the most commonly suggested (p.23).

Communication is also a key factor in recognizing one's own and others' biases and prejudices.

Recognizing Prejudice and Discrimination

No one can be completely objective. Everyone, consciously or unconsciously, has certain preferences and prejudices.

It is critical to recognize prejudices and stereotypes to avoid discrimination.

A *prejudice* is a negative judgment not based on fact; it is an irrational, preconceived negative opinion. Prejudices are often associated with a dislike of a particular group, race or religion. They represent overgeneralizations and a failure to consider individual characteristics.

Prejudice is also referred to as **bias**, a belief that inhibits objectivity. Taken to an extreme, a bias becomes hatred. It is important for law enforcement to understand bias and its extreme form—hate—to deal with bias and hate crimes, discussed in Chapter 14. Prejudices or biases are the result of overly general classification or stereotyping.

Stereotyping assumes that all people within a specific group are the same; they lack individuality. Simply because a person is a member of a specific group, that person is thought to have certain characteristics. Common stereotypes associated with nationalities include the French being great lovers, the Italians being great cooks and the Scots being thrifty. Often the stereotype of Americans is very negative, as illustrated in the novel *The Ugly American.*

Many people stereotype police officers based on what they see on television—scenes showing cops in car chases and shootouts. Officers are not shown standing on the street corner in late January directing traffic after a car crash or being tended to at the medical center because they were bitten on the arm by a prostitute who resisted arrest.

Police officers may also stereotype those with whom they come in contact. In the traditional mode of policing, officers spend a considerable amount of time dealing with criminals and their victims. Some officers may begin to categorize certain types of individuals as perpetrators. Police officers focus so much attention on crime that they may develop a distorted view of who the "bad guys" are. Generalizing from a few to the many is a serious problem for many police. It is a very natural tendency to stereotype people, but it is a tendency that can be fatal to effective communication.

Preconceived ideas about a person's truthfulness or "worth" can result in strained relationships with individuals and little or no interchange of ideas. The very language used to refer to others can interfere with communication. For example, would you rather be called a "cripple" or a "person with a disability"?

Prejudices may lead to discrimination, which can be manifested in two ways: (1) some individuals or groups may be treated preferentially or (2) persons of equal stature may be treated unequally. Illegal unequal treatment may be based on race, religion, sex or age.

Prejudice is an attitude; discrimination is a behavior.

This difference between attitude and overt behavior was summed up by an English judge in his comments to nine youths convicted of race rioting: "Think what you like ... But once you translate your dark thoughts into savage acts, the law will punish you, and protect your victim." Unfortunately, prejudices may result in racism.

bias
A prejudice that inhibits objectivity; can evolve into hate.

stereotyping
Assuming all people within a specific group are the same, lacking individuality.

Racism

For the community policing philosophy to become a reality, racism, wherever it exists, must be recognized and faced. Racism is a belief that a human population having a distinct genetically transmitted characteristic is inferior. It also refers to discrimination or prejudice based on race. The racist idea that some groups (ethnic groups) are somehow genetically superior to others has no scientific basis.

The issue of racism as it relates to community policing is multifaceted and extremely emotionally charged. Furthermore, racism flows in both directions between the police and the citizens within the communities they serve. Some officers make the critical mistake of trying to achieve rapport by using terminology they hear members of a minority group using among themselves.

Racial Profiling

A survey by the Police Foundation found race to be a divisive issue for American police, with black and nonblack (white and other minority) police officers in strong disagreement about the significance of a citizen's race in how they are treated by police. When police use certain racial characteristics such as skin color as indicators of criminal activity, the practice is commonly referred to as **racial profiling**. The contention that police single out subjects based solely on the color of their skin is a serious concern for any department engaged in such a practice and for the credibility of the police profession as a whole.

The *Sourcebook of Criminal Justice Statistics* (2004, p.128) states: "It has been reported that some police officers or security guards stop people of certain racial or ethnic groups because these officials believe that these groups are more likely than others to commit certain types of crimes." It then asks those surveyed if they believe such racial profiling is widespread in three specific circumstances: at motor vehicle stops, at airport security checkpoints and in shopping malls (to prevent theft). Fifty-three percent believed racial profiling was widespread during motor vehicle stops; 49 percent believed it was widespread in shopping malls; and 42 percent believed it was widespread at airport security checkpoints. In all three circumstances, blacks and Hispanics saw racial profiling as more widespread than whites perceived it to be.

Prior to the September 11, 2001, attacks on the World Trade Center and the Pentagon, the practice of racial profiling was being denounced by one police chief after another across the country. Suddenly, after the attacks, the debate was renewed, as police chiefs tried to decide if racial profiling was not only necessary but also the only sensible thing to do in view of the threat to the United States and its citizens. With the heightened threat of more terrorist attacks, people who appeared to be of Arab or Middle Eastern descent began reporting that they had been singled out for stops, questioning, searches or arrests solely on the basis of their appearance. In some areas of the country, it seem that motorists of certain racial or ethnic groups are being stopped more frequently by police; oftentimes, the drivers claim, it is for no apparent reason.

However, profiles of certain serial crimes have been used for decades. Police have relied on profiles of drug couriers and serial rapists. Many practitioners argue that race is often part of a perpetrator's description and that to deny police this information because it might offend someone's sense of political correctness does a great disservice to law enforcement.

racial profiling

A form of discrimination that singles out people of racial or ethnic groups because of a belief that these groups are more likely than others to commit certain types of crimes. Race-based enforcement is illegal.

Closely related to the issue of racial profiling is the issue of whether our criminal justice system discriminates against racial minorities, resulting in a disproportionate number of members of minority groups being incarcerated.

Racial Disparity in the Criminal Justice System

Racial disparity is an unfortunate reality of the criminal justice system for both juveniles and adults. Although "Equal Justice Under Law" is the foundation of our legal system and is carved on the front of the U.S. Supreme Court building, the criminal justice system does not always dispense equal justice. Throughout the system, minorities—especially African American youths—receive different and harsher treatment. Walker and colleagues (2007, p.423) contend: "Our analysis of race and crime in the United States suggests that those who conclude that 'the criminal justice system is not racist' are misinformed. Although reforms have made systematic racial discrimination—discrimination in all stages, in all places, and at all times—unlikely, the U.S. criminal justice system has never been, and is not now, color blind."

Strategies to Overcome Barriers Based on Racial and Ethnic Diversity

Various strategies have been proposed to help agencies attack bias and overcome racial or ethnic barriers between the police and the community. Some are very general, whereas others are quite specific.

One of the first steps to take is implementing a zero tolerance policy for bias within police ranks and publicizing that philosophy. Another strategy is to develop an outreach effort to diverse communities to reduce victimization by teaching them practical crime prevention techniques. A critical part of this effort involves training and education for both police and citizens, as well as the formation of key partnerships between law enforcement and community groups.

Police must often rely on the services of translators, interpreters, community liaisons, religious leaders and other trusted members of an ethnic community to develop an effective crime prevention program for that group. Schools can also assist by including crime prevention techniques in classroom instruction and special English as a Second Language classes.

Ethnic or racial diversity is usually visually obvious, but other forms of diversity within the United States may also pose a challenge to law enforcement and community policing, including religious and socioeconomic diversity.

Religious Diversity

Many of those who came to America in the 1600s did so to escape religious persecution, and the colonists' desire for religious freedom is evident in our Bill of Rights. The First Amendment protects, among other freedoms, freedom of religion. The First Amendment was drafted and adopted to protect the establishment and practice of different religious communities in the early colonies: Congregationalism in New England, Quakerism in Pennsylvania, and Catholicism in Maryland. Over the years, these distinctions have become much less important, with the term *Christians* taking on the meaning of a melting pot for people of similar religious beliefs. However, religious tension still exists between many Christians (the majority religious group) and those of Jewish faith (the minority religious group). Anti-Semitism is a problem in some communities and may result in hate crimes.

Arab Americans may also be discriminated against because of their religious beliefs. Although often considered a monolithic group, they come from 22 different countries, and whereas the media usually associates them with Islam, an estimated two thirds of Arab Americans are Christian (Henderson et al., p.5).

A national survey by the Pew Research Center showed:

"Public attitudes about Muslims and Islam have grown more negative in recent years. About four-in-ten Americans (43 percent) say they have a favorable opinion of Muslims, while 35 percent express a negative view. Opinion about Muslims, on balance, was somewhat more positive in 2004 (48 percent favorable vs. 32 percent unfavorable). As in previous surveys, Muslim Americans are seen more positively than Muslims (53 percent vs. 43 percent); however, unfavorable opinions of Muslim Americans have also edged upward, from 25 percent in 2005 to 29 percent currently" (*Public Expresses Mixed Views of Islam, Mormonism*, 2007).

Opinions about Muslims and Muslim Americans continue to differ widely according to a person's age, educational level, political views and religious background. Young people and college graduates express more favorable views of Muslims than do older people and those with less education.

The biggest influence on public impressions of Muslims, particularly among those who express an unfavorable opinion of them, is what people hear and read in the media. About a third of the public (32 percent)—including nearly half of those who offer a negative opinion of Muslims (48 percent)—say that what they have seen or read in the media has had the biggest influence on their views. Other factors, such as personal experience and education, are less influential, though they are cited far more often by those who have favorable impressions of Muslims than those who express negative views. Public opinion about whether Islam is more likely than other religions to encourage violence has fluctuated in recent years. In 2005, 47 percent said Islam does not encourage violence more than other religions and 36 percent said Islam is more likely than other religions to encourage violence among its believers. In the current survey, the balance of opinion has shifted: 45 percent said Islam is more likely to encourage violence, while 39 percent disagreed. The current measure is similar to public views on this issue in 2003 and 2004.

Religious diversity continues to increase, presenting unique challenges to community policing efforts aimed at enhancing citizens' levels of trust, communication and activism. Cults may pose special challenges to community policing efforts because they zealously advocate unorthodox beliefs.

In Oregon a group lobbied for an exception to the general drug laws to make it legal for Native Americans to smoke peyote during their rituals. In this case, the Supreme Court ruled that such an exception need not be granted. Smoking peyote was illegal for all citizens; Native Americans had not been singled out as a special group.

Socioeconomic Diversity

Even the casual observer recognizes social and economic differences in the United States. Sociologists usually divide individuals within the United States into three basic classes, based primarily on income and education: the lower, middle and upper classes. These basic classes may be further subdivided. As noted, the middle class is shrinking, and the gap between the rich and the poor has become wider, resulting in tension.

The Lower Socioeconomic Class

Poor people have more frequent contact with the criminal justice system because they are on the streets and highly visible. A poor person who drives an old car may get a repair ticket, whereas a wealthier person is more likely to drive a newer car not requiring repairs. In addition, the repair ticket issued to the poor person is likely to be a much greater hardship for that person than a similar ticket would be to someone in the middle or upper classes.

Immigrants and certain races and ethnic groups are frequently equated with poverty and crime in an interaction described as the poverty syndrome. The **poverty syndrome** includes inadequate housing, inadequate education, inadequate jobs and a resentment of those who control the social system.

poverty syndrome
Includes inadequate housing, education and jobs and a resentment of those who control the social system.

The Homeless Carrying their worldly goods and camping everywhere from laundry rooms to train and bus stations, the homeless pose a challenge for law enforcement. In many cases, homelessness is temporary; people who are homeless one month may not be the following month. Thus, it is difficult to accurately measure the number of homeless on any given day.

Many of those who are homeless are women and children, veterans, alcoholics, drug addicts and mentally impaired persons. Police need to balance the safety and other needs of the homeless with the need to protect the public from interference with its rights. The needs of the homeless are as varied as the people who comprise this group. Besides needing the obvious—a place to live and an income to support themselves—other needs include better nutrition; medical care; clothing; chemical addiction treatment; and, especially for children, an education.

In a study on homeless children, the National Center on Family Homelessness found that one in 50 children, a total of about 1.5 million youths, in America is homeless (*America's Youngest Outcasts*, 2009). And according to Duffield, policy director for the National Association for the Education of Homeless Children and Youth, homeless families did not become a problem until the mid-1980s. Homeless families now represent 34 percent of the homeless persons in the United States. "With the economic downturn, people who have not been poor before are now facing the situation," says Duffield. "Homelessness is becoming more of a middle-class issue" (Delaney, 2009).

For some children, the mental and physical stress of being homeless spawns a host of other difficulties. According to the National Alliance for the Mentally Ill (NAMI), nearly 25 percent of homeless people in the United States are children, few of whom escape emotional, behavioral and academic problems. Furthermore, few receive help for such problems. In one study, more than one third (37 percent) of the homeless children had depression scores high enough to warrant a psychiatric evaluation, and 28 percent were in the borderline range for serious behavioral problems.

Although being homeless is not a crime, the activities of some homeless people do violate laws and local ordinances. Such activities include public drunkenness; public urination and defecation; loitering; trespassing;

panhandling; littering; disorderly conduct; or more serious offenses such as vandalism, theft and assault. Cities across the nation have tried numerous legislative and other tactical measures in their efforts to eliminate or minimize the problems presented by the homeless:

○ Anticamping laws that make sleeping in public places illegal and in some cases make it illegal to possess camping equipment in the city.

○ Laws against soliciting employment in public places.

○ Removal of park benches.

○ Locking public restrooms.

○ Laws prohibiting providing food to homeless people.

○ Curfews for homeless people.

○ Laws against sitting, lying or sleeping on sidewalks.

In communities where sleeping on the streets is illegal, what begins as a social problem becomes a criminal justice problem, and the officer on the beat is expected to enforce the law.

The Las Vegas City Council passed an ordinance that bans providing food or meals to the indigent for free or for a nominal fee in parks, in effect outlawing feeding the homeless (Schwartz, 2006). The Orlando, Florida, City Council also banned the feeding of homeless groups in Lake Eola Park and other city property downtown (McKay, 2006). It is interesting to note that one of the councilmen, a retired police officer, was quoted as saying that, although the ordinance was being cast as a public-safety issue, he thought it was more about covering up the city's homeless problem: "We're putting a Band-Aid on a critical problem" (McKay). In fact, a common criticism of laws that effectively criminalize homelessness is that such legislation ignores the underlying reasons why people live on the streets and can even cause the problem to spread. Ordinances that prohibit panhandling and sleeping in public places force many homeless people to become transient, simply displacing the problem.

According to "Out of Sight—Out of Mind?" (n.d.), a report published by the National Law Center on Homelessness and Poverty, police in half of the 50 largest U.S. cities have engaged in sweeps of the homeless in the past few years. However, laws affecting the homeless are facing increased scrutiny as to their constitutionality. In *Pottinger v. City of Miami* (1992), a U.S. district court judge found the city's practice of conducting "bum sweeps" (i.e., making minor arrests of transients and confiscating and destroying the property of the homeless) was a violation of their constitutional rights. The central question in this case was whether the government can lock up a person for being outside when that person has no place to go. The U.S. Ninth Circuit Court of Appeals has ruled that cities cannot enforce any laws that broadly ban sitting, lying or sleeping in public unless there are available shelter beds (Geluardi, 2006). The U.S. Court of Appeals for the Ninth District has ruled that the Los Angeles homeless ordinance violates the Eighth Amendment against cruel and unusual punishment by "criminalizing the unavoidable act of sitting, lying or sleeping at night while being involuntarily homeless" (Sampson, 2006).

In October 2005, the city of St. Louis agreed to settle a lawsuit filed against it by 25 homeless and impoverished people who claimed they were illegally "swept" from the downtown area and jailed prior to the city's Fourth of July celebration in 2004. The city, the police department and the Downtown Partnership—all named defendants in the case—shared in paying a combined $80,000 in damages to the plaintiffs, $20,000 of which was to go toward meals and other services for the area's homeless. An attorney for the plaintiffs stated: "This agreement makes it clear that sweeps violate the law and human dignity" (Shinkle, 2005, p.B4). Following the settlement, the police department implemented several changes in the way it addressed the homeless issue, such as avoiding arresting homeless people or removing them from downtown areas without probable cause that a crime had been committed; instituting a policy where, under most circumstances, a summons to court is issued for "quality-of-life" violations rather than arrest; emphasizing to officers that an "individual's residential status (homeless or nonhomeless) is not to be considered in any of [their] decisions"; and affirming that begging is not a crime if it is not "aggressive" (*A Dream Denied*, 2006, p.42).

Further complicating interactions with those who are homeless is the fact that they are often victims rather than perpetrators of crime. *Hate, Violence and Death on Main Street USA* (2006), a report from the National Coalition for the Homeless, reports that in 2006, 85 homeless individuals were victims of violent acts, with 13 resulting in death; 73 were victims of nonlethal attacks. The victims' ages ranged from 22 to 70 years.

As with other diversity issues, training for officers can be a valuable step toward improving relations with a community's homeless population. Unfortunately, many departments do not provide the means, training, or tools necessary for officers to successfully reach out to the community's homeless. However, in jurisdictions where police are trained and empowered to address the issue of homelessness, their intervention can benefit both the homeless and the neighborhood. A New York City police officer, Fran Kimkowski, developed an innovative approach to the homeless problem for a group of men who were homeless in the Long Island City section of Queens, New York. Assigned to calm the fears of residents when the Salvation Army opened a shelter for homeless veterans in the neighborhood, Kimkowski wanted to show the residents that the homeless men could and would contribute to the community if given a chance. She organized V-Cops, a group of homeless veterans who volunteer to help prevent crime in the neighborhoods. Partnerships to address the issue of homelessness are also discussed in Chapter 7.

The Powerful and Connected

At the opposite end of the socioeconomic scale are powerful, privileged and politically connected people. In the traditional role of crime fighter, the police seldom interact with the upper class, but when they must, problems can arise. One of the most common is providing accommodation and/or special treatment to powerful people in those rare circumstances when one might be arrested. It often results in public outrage and bad press for the police department involved, and yet, it happens time and again. Much of the public assumes such actions to be the norm and imagines that many in this category are never arrested in the first place unless it is unavoidable.

In community policing, the personal and financial resources of those in the public eye and upper socioeconomic level can be invaluable. A population's socioeconomic profile can reveal much about the balance of power within a community.

Ideas in Practice

FORT LAUDERDALE, FLORIDA, HOMELESS OUTREACH PROGRAM

The city of Fort Lauderdale was experiencing a dramatic increase in individuals suffering from a crisis of homelessness, substance abuse and mental health issues. These crises, whether real or perceived, were affecting not only those in crisis but Fort Lauderdale citizens as well. To address the problem, the Fort Lauderdale Homeless Outreach Unit was created, with two officers given the task of improving the quality of life for both the residents and those in crisis.

The following problems were identified:

○ Panhandling in major intersections that created fear among drivers and exposed panhandlers to accident injuries or deaths.

○ Tourist beaches frequented by homeless individuals sleeping and camping.

○ Homeless camps openly created on public and private property.

○ Disorderly intoxicated individuals sitting at business entrances.

○ Open use of alcoholic beverages in public.

○ Petty crime to support alcohol and substance abuse.

○ Abuse and assault upon homeless individuals by area youth or other homeless individuals.

○ Lack of social service support.

○ Difficulty with gaining entry to alcohol/substance abuse programs.

○ Lack of housing assistance upon jail release.

○ Lack of understanding and education within the residential, business, and police communities in terms of crisis recognition, deescalation, and assistance.

The wide diversity of issues made it obvious that partnerships and teamwork were needed to address the problems. Many private, county and state agencies had been addressing these issues unsuccessfully for years. A vast amount of funding, resources and knowledge was available through compassionate programs, but in order for them to be successful they needed to work in partnership rather than in isolation.

The Homeless Outreach Unit began building partnerships. The first step was documentation and tracking of individuals in crisis and the services they received The nonprofit Task Force for Ending Homelessness, Inc. (TFFEH) and the neighboring Palm Beach County high-quality Housing and Urban Development (HUD) data program formed a partnership, with TFFEH supplying a social worker and Palm Beach County creating, supplying and adapting a HUD tracking program. The Homeless Outreach Unit created a shelter services pickup location and sent flyers to the medical hospitals, behavioral health hospitals, social service contractors and area detention facilities. Additional partnerships were created with detoxification programs and substance abuse programs to send individuals from discharge to a shelter program. The Homeless Outreach Unit and TFFEH created documents to distribute to individuals in need of assistance, including information about and directions to veteran services, social security benefits, food stamp assistance, mental health medication and elderly services.

Next, the partnership began monitoring streets, alleys and wooded locations for individuals in crisis. The program began in 2000 with 2,300 individuals contacted and 1,300 placed into shelter assistance. As the years continued, the numbers of homeless and mental health consumers increased; in 2007, 5,800 individuals were contacted and 4,000 placed into shelters. The Fort Lauderdale Police Department saw a tremendous decrease in the recidivism of municipal ordinance arrests as well as a decrease in quality-of-life issues.

The second Homeless Outreach Unit focused on education, partnering with the National Alliance on Mental Illness and becoming a coordinator for the Crisis Intervention Team (CIT) to educate the police agencies in Broward County. The Homeless Outreach Unit also partnered with agencies across the state, assisting them in developing their own homeless outreach programs. The Homeless Outreach workers began actively engaging in community speaking forums for local churches, businesses and homeowner associations to provide education on and obtain understanding of the homeless/mental health crisis. The Fort Lauderdale Police Department added a brief section on the homeless/mental health crisis to the curriculum of the police officers' annual in-house training unit and, additionally, required all new recruits to ride along with Homeless Outreach Unit workers.

The Homeless Outreach Unit continues moving forward to help individuals in crisis through a new program titled "Missing Link," in which businesses offer financial assistance for reunification and job assistance. The local shelters have gone beyond offering only sleeping quarters by adding dental reconstruction, hygiene preparation, job skill training and counseling.

This program's success has not only reduced jail recidivism and quality-of-life issues but it has further enhanced the direction of police work by assisting and serving individuals at a time of true crisis, as was confirmed when the Fort Lauderdale Police Department was recognized as the number-one department in the country for homeless assistance by the National Coalition for the Homeless (Ft. Lauderdale Homeless Program, 2002).

Facing the Challenge of Diversity

Keeping the peace and serving and protecting a society as diverse as the one in the United States presents an extreme challenge to police officers. To meet the challenge, police might consider the following guidelines:

○ Each person is, first and foremost, an individual.

○ Each group, whether racial, ethnic, religious or socioeconomic, consists of people who share certain values. Knowing what these values are can contribute greatly to effective police–community interactions.

○ Each group can contribute to making the community safer.

○ Communication skills are vital. Empathy, listening and overcoming language barriers are crucial to implementing the community policing philosophy.

○ An awareness of personal prejudices and biases can guard against discrimination. An awareness of the language used to talk about different groups is extremely important.

The term *minority,* for example, has subtle secondary, if not caste-status, implications that are the opposite of the implications of *majority,* which is frequently a polite code word for "white." *People of color* also places distance between those so designated and Caucasians. Officers should consider the terms they use and how they might be perceived by those being labeled. Of course, in an emergency, when officers need to communicate with each other rapidly, a descriptive term such as *black* or *white* is appropriate and, indeed, necessary for a rapid response. It is important for officers to know when to use certain terms.

A Cultural Diversity Value Statement

The Aurora (Illinois) Police Department's cultural diversity value statement is a model of what departments might strive for (reprinted by permission):

As professional police officers, we commit to:

○ The fair and impartial treatment of all individuals, placing the highest emphasis on respect for fundamental human rights.

○ Nurturing and protecting the individual dignity and worth of all persons with whom we come into contact.

○ Understanding the differences of all people.

○ Zero tolerance for racially, sexual, gender or religious biased behavior.

○ Maintaining a welcoming environment of inclusion through which communication is open to all people whose problems become our priorities to resolve.

In addition to the racial, ethnic, religious and socioeconomic subcultures found in the United States, another subculture exists in the United States—those with physical and mental disabilities. These are populations that provide even more diversity and challenge to community policing efforts.

Persons with Disabilities

Estimates of disability prevalence in the United States vary, but the U.S. Census Bureau puts the figure at 51.2 million, or 18 percent of the population, making those who are disabled the nation's biggest minority (*Americans with Disabilities: 2002*).

Understanding Physical and Mental Disabilities and the Americans with Disabilities Act

A police officer asks a woman to perform some field sobriety tests. She cannot do so even though she is not under the influence of any drug, including alcohol. Another person ignores the direct order of a police officer to step back on the sidewalk. Yet another person approaches an officer and attempts to ask directions, but his speech is so slurred he is unintelligible. These common occurrences for police officers can often be misinterpreted. In each of the preceding instances, the individual interacting with the officer has a disability: a problem with balance, a hearing impairment, and a speech disability. A disability is a physical or mental impairment that substantially limits one or more of a person's major life functions. This includes people with mobility disabilities; mental illnesses; mental retardation; epilepsy or other seizure disorders; and speech, hearing and vision disabilities.

Greater recognition of this "minority" came on July 26, 1990, when then-President Bush signed into law the Americans with Disabilities Act (**ADA**), calling it "another Independence Day, one that is long overdue."

The ADA guarantees that persons with disabilities will have equal access to any public facilities available to persons without disabilities. In addition, the ADA affects virtually everything that law enforcement officers do—for example, receiving citizen complaints; interrogating witnesses; arresting, booking and holding suspects; operating phone (911) emergency centers; providing emergency medical services; enforcing laws; and various other duties ("Justice Department Offers Local Police Guidance for Complying with ADA," 2006, p.2).

The ADA does not, however, grant special liberty to individuals with disabilities in matters of law, nor does it dictate that the police must take a "hands off" approach toward people with disabilities engaged in criminal conduct. Lyman (2005, p.81) asserts that under the ADA a person with a disability need not be accommodated if that person poses a direct threat to the health or safety of others: "This exception also applies if the individual is a threat to him- or herself."

Because the ADA guarantees access to government services, it helps build partnerships for community policing. Under the ADA, all brochures and printed material must be available in Braille or on audiotape if requested. To include people with disabilities in community partnerships, the police must be able to communicate with them and should conduct their meetings in barrier-free places.

Many people in our communities have made treatment of those with disabilities a priority and are available and willing to work with law enforcement agencies to ensure that people with disabilities are treated respectfully and protected from those who would victimize them. The outcome of increased awareness and service in this area will not only make police officers' jobs easier when they encounter people with disabilities but will also help reduce their fear and vulnerability. The focus on those with disabilities will make the community a better and safer place for everyone and help to build police–community relations.

ADA
The Americans with Disabilities Act of 1990.

ON THE BEAT

Police officers frequently encounter people with disabilities while working in the field. I recall one experience where I was on routine patrol on a busy stretch of roadway and saw a man in an electric wheelchair stopped in the middle of the sidewalk. The day was overcast, and rain was imminent. I glanced in my mirror and saw that the man in the wheelchair was not moving. I turned around and headed his way, parking my vehicle on the side of the road. When I approached him on foot, I asked him if everything was all right. The man began to speak slowly and softly. I could barely hear the words he was saying, so I leaned in closer. After several minutes, he was able to communicate to me that his wheelchair had broken down, and he wasn't sure what to do. I offered him a ride home and arranged for a pickup truck to take his wheelchair home. He got home safely that day, and he thanked me when he arrived.

It is important for officers to be tuned in to what is going on around them. In this case it was a man in a wheelchair who could have been overlooked had I not been paying attention and noticed that he was immobile.

-Kim Czapar

Frequently Encountered Disabilities

Disabilities police officers frequently encounter include mobility impairment, vision impairment, hearing impairment, impairment as a result of epilepsy and mental or emotional impairment.

The first three types of disabilities may hinder communication but seldom pose a significant hindrance for community policing efforts. Likewise, those who have epilepsy do not pose a problem unless their symptoms are mistaken for intoxication, as both conditions may elicit similar behavioral symptoms in affected individuals (*Epilepsy: A Positive I.D.*, 1991).

An epileptic seizure may be mistaken for a drug- or alcohol-induced stupor because the person may have incoherent speech and a glassy-eyed stare and may be wandering aimlessly.

Individuals with mental or emotional disabilities, in contrast to the preceding disabilities, pose a significant challenge to community policing efforts.

Mental Disabilities

Historically, society institutionalized people who were mentally ill or mentally retarded. In the mid-1960s, however, treatment in the community replaced institutionalization. *Deinstitutionalization* refers to the release of thousands of individuals who were mentally disabled into society to be cared for by family or a special network of support services.

This was the result of several factors, including development of medications to control mental illness; research showing that people who were institutionalized did not receive adequate treatment and could do better in the community; federal programs to build and operate mental health centers; and patients' rights litigation and state legislation.

Community-based mental health service rests on the premise that people have the right not to be isolated from the community simply because they are mentally disabled. This premise works only if a support system for them exists. Unfortunately, the network of support services has developed slowly. As a result, thousands of mentally disabled people are on the street and homeless and hundreds more are living with families ill-equipped to provide the necessary care and assistance.

Mental Illness Mental illness has been defined as a biopsychosocial brain disorder characterized by dysfunctional thoughts, feelings and/or behaviors that meet diagnostic criteria (Cordner, 2006, p.1). It includes schizophrenia, major depression and bipolar disorder; obsessive-compulsive disorder; and posttraumatic stress disorder. Cordner (p.1) notes that mental illness is not, in and of itself, a police problem; instead, it is a medical and social services problem. However, police officers frequently encounter people with mental illness—about 5 percent of U.S. residents have serious mental illness, and 10 to 15 percent of incarcerated individuals have severe mental illness.

Problems associated with mental illness often become police problems, including crimes, suicides, disorderly behavior and a variety of calls for service. Unfortunately, the traditional police response to people with mental illness has often been "ineffective and sometimes tragic" (Cordner).

crisis behavior

Results when a person has a temporary breakdown in coping skills; not the same as mental illness.

Mental illness should not be confused with crisis behavior. **Crisis behavior** results when a person who is not mentally ill has a temporary breakdown in coping skills. Anyone can suffer from a crisis. The people that police encounter who are mentally ill frequently lack social support. They are difficult to manage and may have complications such as alcohol or drug abuse. Often people who feel threatened by the strange behavior of a person who is mentally ill may call the police to handle the problem.

Officers become involved with people who are mentally ill because the police are the only responders who have around-the-clock, mobile emergency response capacity, as well as the authority to detain and arrest persons and use force when needed. When police are called to manage people who are mentally ill, the behaviors they most frequently encounter are bizarre, unusual or strange conduct; confused thoughts or actions; aggressive actions; or destructive, assaultive, violent or suicidal behavior. Suicide is the eleventh leading cause of death in the United States and the third leading cause of death among people age 15 to 24.

According to the National Institute of Mental Health (NIMH) in 2002, 31,655 (about 11 per 100,000) people died by suicide in the United States. More than 90 percent of people who kill themselves have a diagnosable mental disorder, most commonly a depressive disorder or a substance abuse disorder.

A 1998 report by the American College of Emergency Physicians examined all deputy-involved shootings that occurred in the Los Angeles County, California, Sheriff's Department and found that suicide-by-cop incidents accounted for 11 percent of all deputy-involved shootings and 13 percent of all deputy-involved justifiable homicides. The report concluded that suicide by cop constitutes an actual form of suicide and defined it as "an incident where a suicidal individual intentionally engages in life-threatening and criminal behavior with a lethal weapon or what appears to be a lethal weapon toward law enforcement officers or civilians specifically to provoke officers to shoot the suicidal individual in self-defense or to protect civilians" (Pinizzoto, 2005, p.9).

One natural outgrowth of a mental health system that withholds needed treatment until a person with a mental illness becomes dangerous is that police officers and sheriff's deputies are forced to become frontline mental health workers. The safety of both law enforcement officers and citizens is compromised when law enforcement responds to crises involving people with severe mental illnesses who are not being treated (*Law Enforcement and People with Severe Mental Illness,* 2006). Or, if they are being treated, Moore (2006, p.134) suggests: "Most of the violent individuals with whom police deal are mental patients whose treatment plans have lapsed." Or they have simply stopped taking their medication.

Police in one city shot and killed a suspect who had just robbed a gas station. The suspect turned out to be a mentally disturbed female who they had dealt with often over the past year. After robbing the gas station, she ordered the clerk to call 911 and stayed there until he did. The confrontation and subsequent shooting seemed orchestrated, forced by the depressed, suicidal woman. She claimed to have a gun, threatened to shoot the officers and advanced toward one with an object in her hand. The object turned out to be a comb. This is a tragic situation where a person who is suicidal arranges to die at the hands of the police.

"Research on the extent to which police interact with people with mental illness made it a priority to improve services for dealing with unique populations such as the mentally ill by developing Crisis Intervention Teams (CIT)" (Dodge, 2005, p.84). The CIT model combines police officers with mental health professions and includes extensive training. Hill and associates (2004, p.18) explain: "The purpose of a crisis intervention team (CIT) is to provide law enforcement officers with the skills they need to safely deescalate situations involving people with mental illness who are in crisis, *not* to turn officers into mental health workers." As Anderson (2006, p.14) puts it: "CIT is not just about training. It is about building relationships between law enforcement and the mental health community and working together to improve the effectiveness of the response to mental health 911 calls. CIT is about humanizing people with mental illness and understanding that mental illness is first and foremost a health care problem."

Law enforcement members of a CIT team learn that people who are severely mentally ill need an entirely different approach; an entirely different voice tone, voice volume and personal space; and both observational and questioning skills (*Tactical Response* Staff, 2006, p.55).

Another challenging and frequently misunderstood mental disability that police encounter is mental retardation, which is often, and incorrectly, equated with mental illness.

Mental Retardation Mental retardation is the nation's fourth-ranking disabling condition, affecting 3 percent of the U.S. population. Mental retardation means that normal intellectual development fails to occur. Unlike mental illness, mental retardation is permanent. It is diagnosed when three criteria exist: (1) significant subaverage general intellectual functioning (as measured by IQ tests); (2) resulting in, or associated with, defects or impairments in adaptive behavior, such as personal independence and social responsibility; (3) with onset by age 18.

People who are mentally retarded are usually aware of their condition and may be adept at concealing it. Thus, it may be more difficult to recognize mental retardation than mental illness. Communication problems, interaction problems, inability to perform tasks and personal history can help officers make this determination.

Yet another communication challenge is posed when police officers must interact with those who are much older or much younger than they are.

Age Diversity

Law enforcement officers deal with individuals of all ages and must be able to communicate effectively with them. In 2004, more than one third (37.4 percent) of the U.S. population was older than 65 or younger than 15 years of age (*U.S. Census Bureau: State and County QuickFacts*). Although it is rare for most people in these age groups to be involved in criminal behavior, they are among the most vulnerable of our populations and, because of that, police officers will have considerable contact with them. Most contact will take the form of providing assistance and protecting their welfare.

The Elderly

In 2004, 36.3 million people were age 65 and older, accounting for 12 percent of the total U.S. population (U.S. Census Bureau). The country is "graying," with childbearing rates remaining low and baby boomers (those born between 1946 and 1964) beginning to turn 65 in 2011. The U.S. Census Bureau predicts that by 2030 one in five people will be age 65 or older. Many individuals age 65 and older do *not* consider themselves elderly and, in fact, are in better physical and mental condition than other individuals much younger than they are. Police officers need to understand and empathize with the physical and emotional challenges of the aged so they may deliver the best possible service.

Older people tend to admire and respect authority and are often grateful for any help the police may offer. They are usually in contact with the police if they become victims of crime, are involved in an automobile crash or are stopped for a traffic violation. Many older people have serious medical problems for which they may require emergency medical assistance. In fact, more than half of the U.S. population older than age 65 are disabled in some way.

Alzheimer's disease (AD)

A progressive, irreversible and incurable brain disease with no known cause that affects four million elderly Americans; the classic symptom is memory loss.

Some older people suffer from **Alzheimer's disease (AD),** a progressive, irreversible, incurable disease of the brain that adversely affects behavior.

Approximately 4 million elderly Americans have AD, and it afflicts people of all social, economic and racial groups. Officers should know the symptoms, the most classic of which is gradual loss of memory. Other symptoms include impaired judgment, disorientation, personality change, decline in ability to perform routine tasks, behavior change, difficulty in learning, loss of language skills and decline in intellectual function. A number of behavior patterns common to patients with AD may bring them to the attention of police officers.

People with AD may wander or become lost, engage in inappropriate sexual behavior, lose impulse control, shoplift, falsely accuse others, appear intoxicated, drive erratically or become victims of crime. Many symptoms of AD and intoxication are identical: confusion and disorientation; problems with short-term memory, language, sight and coordination; combativeness and extreme reactions; and loss of contact with reality.

People with AD are often physically able to drive a car long after the time when their memory, judgment and problem-solving ability make it safe. Drivers who have AD may drive erratically; "lose" their car and report it stolen; leave the scene of a car crash because they forget it happened; and wander the streets in the car because they are lost or have forgotten their destination. Sometimes drivers with AD are found several hundred miles from home.

People afflicted with AD may become victims of crime because they are easy prey for con artists, robbers and muggers. Also, police may become aware of patients with AD as a result of legal actions such as evictions, repossessions and termination of utility service as a result of the patients' forgetfulness or inability to make payments.

The Helmsley Alzheimer's Alert Program, started in 1991, provides information on missing patients to public safety agencies. When a person with AD is reported missing, the Alzheimer's Association sends an alert and identifying information to a fax service that transmits it simultaneously to hundreds of locations, including police, hospital emergency rooms and shelters. When the patient is found, another fax is sent to inform the agencies that the search is over.

Just as older people may pose communication challenges, youths, particularly those with special needs, may also present challenges.

The Young

A frequently overlooked segment of the population important to community policing implementation is youths. Just who is classified as a youth is established by state statutes and varies in age from 16 to 18 years. Because youths lack economic and political power, their problems and concerns may not receive the attention they deserve. But our nation's future depends on the values they form—they are the future decision makers of our country. As you read this part of the chapter, do not become discouraged about the future of our youths. Most young people (95 percent, according to FBI statistics) have not been in trouble with the law. Almost certainly some juveniles have been arrested multiple times, so that the actual percentage of youths who have been arrested is even lower than it appears at first glance.

The overwhelming majority of "good kids" should not be forgotten in community policing efforts. They can be valuable as partners in problem solving and, if provided opportunities to become active in areas of interest to them, will most likely continue to be good citizens. The following discussion, however, focuses on those youths with whom law enforcement most often interacts.

Youths with Special Needs and the Police Police officers may have to deal with youths who have special needs.

Youths with special needs include those who are emotionally/behaviorally disturbed; who have learning disabilities; who have an attention deficit disorder; or who have behavior problems resulting from prenatal exposure to drugs, including alcohol, or to human immunodeficiency virus (HIV).

EBD

Emotionally/ behaviorally disturbed.

Emotionally/behaviorally disturbed children, often referred to as **EBD**, usually exhibit one or more of the following behavioral patterns: severely aggressive or impulsive behavior; severely withdrawn or anxious behavior such as pervasive unhappiness, depression or wide mood swings; or severely disordered thought processes reflected in unusual behavior patterns, atypical communication styles and distorted interpersonal relationships.

Parents and teachers in some communities have expressed concerns that children labeled as EBD have fewer coping skills to deal with police contacts than other children and may be traumatized by such contacts. A large percentage of youths suspected of crimes are EBD, and that condition is one cause of their unlawful behavior. It is impossible, however, to arrange for an EBD specialist to be present at all police contacts because a majority of contacts are unplanned events that occur on the street.

Attention deficit hyperactivity disorder (ADHD)

A common disruptive behavior disorder characterized by heightened motor activity (fidgeting and squirming), short attention span, distractibility, impulsiveness and lack of self-control.

Attention deficit hyperactivity disorder (ADHD) is one of the most common disruptive behavior disorders in youths, with an estimated 5 to 10 percent of all children having it. Occurring four times more often in boys than girls, ADHD is characterized by heightened motor activity (fidgeting and squirming), short attention span, distractibility, impulsiveness and lack of self-control. (*Note:* The disorder of being easily distracted *without* the presence of hyperactivity is ADD, or simply attention deficit disorder. The two disorders, ADHD and ADD, are commonly confused and the terms used interchangeably; the absence of hyperactivity is the primary distinguishing feature between them.) Children with ADHD may do poorly in school and have low self-esteem. Although the condition often disappears by adulthood, by then those who had ADHD as children may have other behavior problems, including drug abuse, alcoholism or personality disorders.

Other children may present special challenges because of some form of learning disability, which the Association for Children with Learning Disabilities (ACLD) (p.4) defines as "one or more significant deficits in the essential learning processes." Essential learning processes are those involved in understanding or using spoken or written language and do not include learning problems that result from visual, hearing or motor handicaps; mental retardation; or emotional disturbance.

The ACLD (p.3) identifies the most frequently displayed symptoms of learning disabilities as short attention span; poor memory; difficulty following directions; disorganization; inadequate ability to discriminate between and among letters, numerals or sounds; poor reading ability; eye–hand coordination problems; and difficulties with sequencing. Such children are often discipline problems, are labeled "underachievers" and are at great risk of becoming dropouts.

Although learning disabilities are usually discussed in an educational context, the ACLD (p.8) notes: "The consequences are rarely confined to school or work." Characteristics that may bring a youth with a learning disability into conflict with the law include responding inappropriately to a situation; saying one thing and meaning another; forgetting easily; acting impulsively; needing immediate gratification; and feeling overly frustrated, which results in disruptive behavior. Those who interact with such children need to be patient and communicate effectively. Youths with learning disabilities look like their peers. Inwardly, however, most are very frustrated, have experienced failure after failure and have extremely low self-esteem.

Prenatal exposure to drugs can also cause serious problems. The term **crack children** is sometimes used to refer to children exposed to cocaine while in the womb. They may exhibit social, emotional and cognitive problems. Children who were exposed to drugs prenatally may also have poor coordination, low tolerance levels and poor memory. Police officers should be aware of these symptoms and recognize that they reflect a condition over which the youth has limited or no control.

Another pressing problem is that of **fetal alcohol syndrome (FAS)**, the leading known cause of mental retardation in the western world. FAS effects include impulsivity; inability to predict consequences or to use appropriate judgment in daily life; poor communication skills; and high levels of activity and distractibility in small children and frustration and depression in adolescents.

Yet another group of at-risk children who present special problems to law enforcement are children prenatally exposed to HIV. Such children may have mental retardation, language delays, gross- and fine-motor skill deficits and reduced flexibility and muscle strength.

Children with special needs are likely to be in contact with the police, and many may become status offenders, committing offenses based on age such as underage smoking or drinking or violating curfews. Others may become more serious offenders. Many youths with special needs are also likely to join gangs, as discussed in Chapter 13. A final population presenting communication challenges are victims of and witnesses to criminal acts.

crack children
Children who were exposed to cocaine while in the womb.

fetal alcohol syndrome (FAS)
The leading known cause of mental retardation in the Western world; effects include impulsivity, inability to predict consequences or to use appropriate judgment in daily life, poor communication skills, high levels of activity, distractibility in small children and frustration and depression in adolescents.

Victims and Witnesses

> IF YOU HAVEN'T BEEN THERE, YOU DON'T KNOW THE FEELINGS OF
> EMPTINESS AND FEAR AND HOW IT CHANGES YOUR LIFE. I WAS IN
> A STATE OF SHOCK. I WALKED AROUND IN A DAZE FOR WEEKS. I WASN'T
> FUNCTIONING. NO ONE REALLY UNDERSTOOD HOW I FELT.
>
> —*Sherry Price, rape victim*

Understanding others is particularly important in police work. Understanding others does not, however, mean that you sympathize with them or even that you agree with them. *Sympathy* is an involuntary sharing of another person's feelings of fear, grief or anger. *Empathy* is an active process involving trying to *understand* another person's feelings. Empathy requires effective communication skills.

It is essential for law enforcement officers to communicate effectively with victims and witnesses because they are a major source of common crime information known to law enforcement.

Results of Being Victimized

People who become victims of crime often come out of the experience feeling victimized by both the perpetrator and the system. The entire criminal justice system is focused on the criminal. Victims are sometimes blamed for being victimized and many times are left in the dark about progress on their case. Perpetrators, on the other hand, have an attorney representing them every step of the way, ensuring that their rights are not violated. Many victims are shocked to learn that the prosecutor represents the state, not the victim. If the crime was a violent one, victims are often frightened, traumatized and feel very much alone. They may suffer physical injury, financial and property losses, emotional distress and psychological trauma. Some suffer from **posttraumatic stress disorder (PTSD)**, a persistent reexperiencing of a traumatic event through intrusive memories, dreams and a variety of anxiety-related symptoms.

posttraumatic stress disorder (PTSD)

A persistent reexperiencing of a traumatic event through intrusive memories, dreams and a variety of anxiety-related symptoms.

Nonreporting of Victimization

Many victims feel it is their civic duty to report victimization and hope doing so will bring offenders to justice. Others report crimes simply because they want to recover their property or file an insurance claim. In the absence of such motivators, however, a large percentage of robberies, aggravated assaults, burglaries and rapes go unreported to the police. Victims may consider the matter private, feel ashamed or believe the police will be unable to do anything. In the case of victims of sexual assault, they often feel they will not be believed and all too frequently, they are right.

When crime is underreported the police do not know there is a problem or may think it is only a minor problem. They do not have a true picture of the situation, which makes it difficult to problem-solve effectively.

Some victims and witnesses fear threats or retaliation from the offender(s). Many victims of violent crimes are warned by their attackers that going to the police will result in dire consequences for either the victims themselves or people they care about.

One reason gangs flourish is that they operate through intimidation, both inside and outside of court. Police must often deal with courtroom intimidation. Sometimes the court is packed with gang members who give threatening looks and suggestive signals to witnesses. Some departments counter this tactic by taking classes of police cadets into the courtroom. Confronted with this law enforcement presence, gang members usually give up and leave. It is important for law enforcement to encourage reporting crime by reassuring victims and witnesses they will be protected against threats, intimidation or reprisals by the victimizers.

Assisting Victims

Society has made progress in assisting victims of crime. In 1981 then-President Ronald Reagan proclaimed National Victims of Crime Week, putting the full weight and influence of his office behind the victims' movement. Since then, a variety of organizations and programs have been created to help victims.

Organizations Providing help to crime victims originated as a grassroots effort in the 1960s and 1970s to help battered women and victims of sexual assault. Organizations dedicated to helping victims include the National Organization for Victim Assistance (NOVA), founded in 1976; the Office for Victims of Crime (OVC), founded in 1984; and the National Victim Center, founded in 1985.

Other victim organizations have been formed, including Mothers against Drunk Driving, Students against Drunk Driving, Parents of Murdered Children, the National Organization of Victim Assistance and Victims for Victims. In addition, victim compensation laws and victim advocacy and protection programs attempt to address what is widely perceived as the system's protection of the accused's rights to the victim's detriment.

Programs Implemented Numerous programs also have been implemented to help victims deal with the financial and emotional fallout of victimization. The two main types of programs provided for victims are victim compensation programs and victim/witness assistance programs. *Victim compensation programs* help crime victims cope with crime-related expenses such as medical costs, mental health counseling, lost wages and funeral or burial costs. *Victim/witness assistance programs* provide services such as crisis support; peer support; referrals to counseling; advocacy within the justice system; and, in some cases, emergency shelter.

Crime victim compensation programs have been established in every state. Programs are based on identified needs of victims and witnesses.

Victims' Bill of Rights Victims and witnesses have two basic rights: the right to obtain certain information from the criminal justice system and the right to be treated humanely by the system. Most victims' bills of rights include both informational and participatory rights. They commonly require the victim to be informed about available financial aid and social services, as well as the whereabouts of the accused; advised of case status and scheduling; protected from harassment and intimidation; provided with separate waiting areas during the trial; and granted a speedy disposition of the case and return of property held as evidence.

Police officers can help victims by letting them know their rights, including the right to become active in the case processing and to prepare a victim impact statement (VIS). They can also tell victims what services are available.

Some departments are using innovative approaches to reach out to victims and maintain lines of communication. For example, in some lower-income communities where few residents can afford telephone service, cellular phone links have been established to help crime victims reach the police. Cell phones have no lines to cut and can be preprogrammed with 911 and the general information number of the police department whereas all other calling capability can be locked out. An example of how communications are maintained with prior victims is seen in Jefferson County, Kentucky, where the Victim Information and Notification Everyday (VINE™) system automatically alerts victims with a telephone call when an inmate is released from custody. VINE could serve as a national model for using technology.

Agencies That Can Assist

Agencies usually included in a victim/witness assistance referral network are community groups, day care centers, domestic violence programs, food stamp distribution centers, job counseling and training programs, mental health care programs, physical health care programs, private sector allies, private and community emergency organizations, rape crisis centers, unemployment services, victim assistance or advocacy organizations, victim compensation boards, volunteer groups and welfare agencies.

The Direction of Victims' Rights and Services in the Twenty-First Century

Examples of "promising practices" transforming victim services include children's advocacy centers; community criminal justice partnerships; crisis response teams; technologies to benefit crime victims (such as VINE); community police, prosecutors and court programs; initiatives of allied professionals (such as partnerships between criminal justice agencies, schools, the medical and mental health communities, religious communities and the business community); comprehensive victim service centers; and specialized programs for diverse crime victims (including disabled victims and victims of gang violence).

SUMMARY

The quality of police–community relations depends on effective communication. The process involves a sender, a message, a channel, a receiver and, sometimes, feedback. Important individual characteristics in communication include age, education, gender, values, emotional involvement, self-esteem and language skills. Two critical barriers to communication in a diverse society are language barriers and cultural barriers. Police officers may have more barriers to communication because of the image they convey, their position of authority and the nature of their work. Other common communication barriers include prejudices and stereotypes, time, use of jargon, lack of feedback and failure to listen.

A dilemma facing law enforcement and the immigration issue is whether police can build trusting partnerships with immigrant communities if they are also to gather intelligence and enforce immigration law. One challenge facing our increasingly diverse society is discrimination. It is critical to recognize prejudices and stereotypes to avoid discrimination. Prejudice is an attitude; discrimination is a behavior.

Disabilities police officers frequently encounter include mobility impairment, vision impairment, hearing impairment, impairment as a result of epilepsy and mental or emotional impairment. An epileptic seizure may be mistaken for a drug- or alcohol-induced stupor because the person may exhibit incoherent speech, glassy-eyed staring and aimless wandering. Officers may also encounter individuals who are mentally disabled, some of whom may need institutionalization. Another population the police encounter daily is the elderly, people age 65 and older, who may be victims of Alzheimer's disease (AD). Police contact with people with AD is likely because these people may wander or become lost, engage in inappropriate sexual behavior, lose impulse control, shoplift, falsely accuse others, appear intoxicated, drive erratically and become victims of crime. Many of the symptoms of intoxication and AD are identical: confusion and disorientation; problems with short-term memory, language, sight and coordi-

nation; combativeness; and, in extreme reaction cases, loss of contact with reality.

Young people are a frequently overlooked segment of the population important to implementing community policing. Youths with special needs include those who are emotionally/behaviorally disturbed (EBD); have learning disabilities; have an attention deficit hyperactivity disorder (ADHD); or have behavior problems resulting from prenatal exposure to drugs, including alcohol, or to HIV.

Finally, it is essential for law enforcement officers to communicate effectively with victims and witnesses because they are a major source of common crime information known to law enforcement.

DISCUSSION QUESTIONS

1. In what ways might a person become a victim and need assistance from the police?
2. What role do euphemisms ("soft" words) play in communication?
3. In what ways might the general public be perceived as "customers" of a police department? What implications does this have?
4. How diverse is your community?
5. Have you ever tried to communicate with someone who does not speak English? What was it like?
6. How would you describe the American culture?
7. Would you favor eliminating the word *minority* when talking about diversity? If so, what term would you use instead?
8. Do you consider yourself "culturally literate"? Why or why not?
9. Have you encountered instances of racism? Explain.
10. Have you or someone you know ever been a victim of crime? Was the crime reported to the police, and if not, why?

GALE EMERGENCY SERVICES DATABASE ASSIGNMENTS — ONLINE Database

• Use the Gale Emergency Services Database to help answer the Discussion Questions as appropriate.
• Research at least one of the following subjects and write a brief (three- to four-page) report of your

findings: discrimination, Verbal Judo Institute, non-verbal communication, prejudices or stereotypes.
• Research and report on at least one of the following subjects: cultural conflict, hate crime, homelessness, racial profiling.
• Research how mental retardation affects the likelihood of criminal activity, conviction, incarceration and rehabilitation. What systemic changes, if any, would you recommend based on your research?
• Research the police services that are available for mentally ill persons in your area.

REFERENCES

Americans with Disabilities: 2002. Washington, DC: U.S. Census Bureau, July 19, 2006.

America's Immigration Quandary. Washington, DC: Pew Research Center for the People and the Press, March 2006.

America's Youngest Outcasts. Newton, MA: The National Center on Family Homelessness, 2009.

Anderson, Mark. "The C.I.T. Model in Minnesota." *Minnesota Police Chief,* Spring 2006, pp.13–14.

Association for Children with Learning Disabilities. "Taking the First Step to Solving Learning Problems." Pittsburgh: Association for Children with Learning Disabilities (no date).

Babington, Charles and Murray, Shailagh. "Immigration Deal Fails in Senate." *Washington Post,* April 8, 2006, p.A01.

Balz, Dan and Fears, Darryl. "'We Decided Not to Be Invisible Anymore.'" *Washington Post,* April 11, 2006, p.A01.

Chaddock, Gail Russell. "A GOP Faceoff over Illegal Immigration." *The Christian Science Monitor,* March 29, 2006.

Cordner, Gary. *People with Mental Illness.* Problem-Oriented Guides for Police Problem-specific Guides Series, No. 40.

Washington, DC: Office of Community Oriented Policing Services, May 2006.

Delaney, Arthur. "Recession Increasing Interest in Homelessness." *HuffingtonPost.com*. March 26, 2009.

Dodge, Mary. "Reviewing the Year in Police, Law Enforcement, Crime Prevention." *Criminal Justice Research Reports*, July/August 2005, pp.84–85.

A Dream Denied: The Criminalization of Homelessness in U.S. Cities. A Report by the National Coalition for the Homeless and the National Law Center on Homelessness and Poverty, January 2006.

Eggers, Ron. "Immigration Issues Present a Complex Set of Considerations for Public Safety." *9-1-1 Magazine*, August 2006, pp.30–37.

Epilepsy: A Positive I.D. Epilepsy Education, University of Minnesota, 1991.

Ft. Lauderdale Homeless Program. Washington, DC: Community Oriented Policing Services, 2002.

Geluardi, John. "Much of City Ruled Off Limits." *Contra Costa Times* (Walnut Creek, California), May 18, 2006.

Giles, Howard; Fortman, Jennifer; Dailey, Rene; Barker, Valeria; and Hajek, Christopher. *Hate, Violence and Death on Main Street USA: A Report on Hate Crimes and Violence against People Experiencing Homelessness, 2005*. Washington, DC: National Coalition for the Homeless.

Henderson, Nicole J.; Ortiz, Christopher W.; Sugie, Naomi F.; and Miller, Joel. *Law Enforcement and Arab American Community Relations after September 11, 2001: Engagement in a Time of Uncertainty*. New York: Vera Institute of Justice, June 2006.

Hill, Rodney; Guill, Guthrie; and Ellis, Kathryn. "The Montgomery County CIT Model: Interacting with People with Mental Illness." *FBI Law Enforcement Bulletin*, July 2004, pp.18–25.

Hoffman, Allan. "Wanted in Law Enforcement: Foreign Language Skills." Monster.com.

Jonsson, Patrik and Chaddock, Gail Russell. "A Nation Divided on Immigration." *The Christian Science Monitor*, April 6, 2006.

"Justice Department Offers Local Police Guidance for Complying with ADA." *Criminal Justice Newsletter*, May 15, 2006, pp.1–3.

Law Enforcement and People with Severe Mental Illness. Arlington, VA: Treatment Advocacy Center, 2006.

Lyman, Stephen W. "How to Handle Disability Issues." *Security Management*, October 2005, pp.75–82.

McKay, Rich. "Feeding of Homeless Banned." *Orlando Sentinel*, July 25, 2006.

Miller, Christa. "The Art of Verbal Judo." *Law Enforcement Technology*, August 2008. pp.62, 64, 66–71.

Moore, Carole. "Policing the Mentally Ill." *Law Enforcement Technology*, August 26, 2006, p.134.

Moy, Jones and Archibald, Brent. "Talking with the Police." *The Police Chief*, June 2005, pp.54–57.

"Out of Sight—Out of Mind." Washington, DC: National Law Center on Homelessness and Poverty, no date.

Pinizzoto, Anthony J. "Suicide by Cop: Defining a Devastating Dilemma." *FBI Law Enforcement Bulletin*, February 2005, pp.8–20.

Public Expresses Mixed Views of Islam, Mormonism. The Pew Research Center for the People and the Press, September 2007.

Sampson, Greg. "Ninth Circuit Rules Los Angeles Homeless Ordinance Violates Eighth Amendment." *Jurist*, April 15, 2006.

Schwartz, David McGrath. "Feeding Homeless Outlawed." *Las Vegas Review–Journal*, July 20, 2006.

Shinkle, Peter. "City Settles Lawsuit Brought by Homeless." *St. Louis Post-Dispatch*, October 13, 2005, p.B4.

"Should They Stay or Should They Go?" *Time Magazine*, April 10, 2006, p 32.

Skogan, Wesley and Frydl, Kathleen, eds. *Fairness and Effectiveness in Policing: The Evidence*. Washington, DC: National Academies Press, 2004.

Skogan, Wesley G.; Steiner, Lynn; DuBois, Jill; Gudell, J. Erik; and Fagan, Aimee. *Community Policing and "The New Immigrants": Latinos in Chicago*, 2002.

Sourcebook of Criminal Justice Statistics 2004. Washington, DC: Bureau of Justice Statistics, 2004.

Strengthening Relations between Police and Immigrants. New York: Vera Institute of Justice, July 25, 2006.

Tactical Response Staff. "Crisis Intervention Team." *Tactical Response*, May–June 2006, pp.54–59.

Thompson, George. "Community Policing: The Gap Theory." Auburn, NY: Verbal Judo Institute, 2006.

Thompson, George. "Tactical Civility: The Path of Power and Safety." *PoliceOne.com News*, March 27, 2009.

U.S. Census Bureau: State and County QuickFacts. Online: http://quickfacts.census.gov/qfd/index.html.

Venkatraman, Bharathi A. "Lost in Translation: Limited English Proficient Populations and the Police." *The Police Chief*, April 2006, pp.40–50.

Walker, Samuel; Spohn, Cassia; and DeLone, Miriam. *The Color of Justice: Race, Ethnicity and Crime in America*, 4th ed. Belmont, CA: Wadsworth, 2007.

CHAPTER 7

Building Partnerships: A Cornerstone of Community Policing

 **DO YOU KNOW...**

○ Why police are asking the community to help them identify and prioritize crime concerns?

○ What four dimensions of trust are?

○ Whether beats and shifts should be permanent?

○ What kind of beats community policing officers should be assigned to? Why?

○ What may impede a shared vision and common goals?

○ In addition to commonalities, what must be recognized when forming partnerships?

○ What the common criticisms of community policing are?

○ How these common criticisms can be addressed?

○ How some cities are diverting nonemergency calls from 911?

○ What purposes are served by citizen police academies?

○ What key collaborators may be overlooked in community policing efforts?

○ What some benefits of using citizens as volunteers are?

○ Why it can be more difficult to build partnerships in a lower-income neighborhood?

 **CAN YOU DEFINE...**

call management
call reduction
call stacking
collaboration
stakeholders
TRIAD
working in "silos"

Introduction

The Office of Community Oriented Policing Services (COPS) Web site states: "In community policing, citizens are viewed by the police as partners who share responsibility for identifying priorities and developing and implementing responses." In community policing, the term *partnerships* refers to the collaboration that takes place between police officers, community members, government

> **Problem-solving without partnerships risks overlooking the most pressing community concerns. Thus, the partnership between police and the communities they service is essential for implementing a successful program in community policing.**
>
> *—Chief Darrel Stephens, Charlotte-Mecklenburg (North Carolina) Police Department*

Former Massachusetts Governor Mitt Romney holds up an educational pamphlet during a news conference in Boston to announce the program Transit Watch. The security awareness campaign encourages passengers to report suspicious activity or packages to transit employees. At right is Chief Joseph Carter of the Massachusetts Bay Transit Authority Police. © AP Images/Angela Rowlings

agencies and other stakeholders: "The police become an integral part of the community culture, and the community assists in defining future priorities and in allocating resources. The difference is substantial and encompasses basic goals and commitments" (*Understanding Community Policing*, 1994). Community partnership means adopting a policing perspective that exceeds the standard law enforcement emphasis. This broadened outlook recognizes the value of activities that contribute to the orderliness and well-being of a neighborhood (Community Policing Consortium Web site).

This chapter begins with a discussion of why partnerships are important in community policing and the core components making up successful partnerships. This is followed by a discussion of the benefits of partnerships as well as some criticisms that have been raised. Next is a look at how departments can make time for partnerships through call management and how citizens can become educated partners through citizen academies. Some key partners are identified: criminal justice partners, including prosecutors, courts and corrections; government agencies; the private security sector; victims; and volunteers. Community policing partnerships in diverse neighborhoods are discussed. The chapter concludes with a look at some effective partnerships in action.

Why Partnerships?

Community partnerships are crucial for police agencies serious about community policing. Community policing cannot succeed without them. Collaborations may be with businesses, schools, youths, residents, organizations and other government agencies, depending on the problem and who the stakeholders are.

Traditional policing expected the community members to remain in the background. Crime and disorder were viewed as police matters, best left to professionals. That meant most citizen–police interactions were *negative contacts*. After all, people do not call the police when things are going well. A citizen's only opportunity to interact with officers was as a victim of crime, as being involved in some other emergency situation or as the subject of some enforcement action such as receiving a traffic ticket.

Some people may question why the police would consult the public about setting police priorities and why they would ask them to work with them to solve neighborhood problems. Some feel that the police are paid to deal with crime and disorder and should not expect communities to take any responsibility or do their job for them. Others feel that until something is done about the causes of crime (poverty, teen pregnancy, racism, homelessness, single-parent families, poor schools, unemployment) the crime problem will remain.

 Partnerships usually result in a more effective solution to a problem because of the shared responsibilities, resources and goals.

Core Components of Partnerships/ Collaborations

Partnerships are often referred to as collaborations. **Collaboration** occurs when several agencies and individuals commit to work together and contribute resources to obtain a common goal. Figure 7.1 illustrates the core components of a partnership or collaboration.

collaboration
Occurs when a number of agencies and individuals make a commitment to work together and contribute resources to obtain a common, long-term goal.

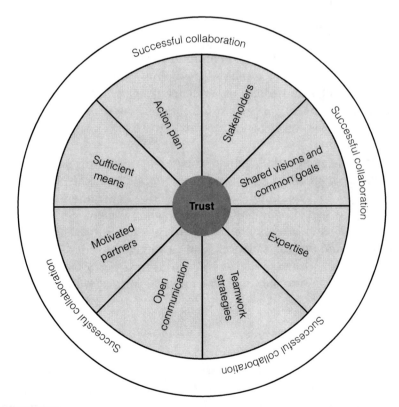

Figure 7.1 Core Components of a Successful Collaboration/Partnership
Source: Tammy A. Rinehart, Anna T. Laszlo and Gwen O. Briscoe.
Collaboration Toolkit: How to Build, Fix and Sustain Productive Partnerships.
Washington, DC: U.S. Department of Justice, Office of Community Oriented
Policing Services, 2001, p.7.

Stakeholders

Partnerships are made up of **stakeholders**, those people who have an interest in what happens in a particular situation. This might include school board members, business leaders, elected officials, neighborhood-watch/block clubs, community activists, the attorney general, trade organizations, social service organizations, federal law enforcement agencies (e.g., Federal Bureau of Investigation, Drug Enforcement Administration, Bureau of Alcohol, Tobacco and Firearms, United States Citizenship and Immigration Services), the media, private foundations and other charitable organizations. For example, a project to reduce thefts from cars on a college campus could involve stakeholders from several groups: students, administrators, teachers, the maintenance department and police. Stakeholders will change depending on the problem being addressed, but when possible the collaboration should reflect the diversity of the community.

Active Community Involvement

Community policing relies on active community involvement, recognizing that such involvement gives new dimension to crime control activities. While police continue to handle crime fighting and law enforcement responsibilities, the police and community work together to modify conditions that can encourage criminal behavior. The resources available within communities allow for an expanded focus on crime prevention activities.

Patrol officers are the primary providers of police services and have the most extensive contact with community members. In community policing efforts, they provide the bulk of the community's daily policing needs and are assisted by immediate supervisors, other police units and appropriate government and social agencies. Upper-level managers and command staff are responsible for ensuring that the entire organization backs the patrol officers' efforts.

Effective community policing depends on optimizing positive contact between patrol officers and community members. Patrol cars are only one method of conveying police services. Police departments may supplement automobile patrols with foot, bicycle, scooter and horseback patrols and add mini-stations to bring police closer to the community. Regular community meetings and forums will afford police and community members an opportunity to air concerns and find ways to address them. Once the stakeholders are enlisted in partnerships, the focus becomes building trust among all collaborators.

Building Trust

Establishing and maintaining mutual trust is a central goal of community policing and community partnership. Police have recognized the need for cooperation with the community. In the fight against serious crime, police have encouraged community members to come forth with relevant information. In addition, police have spoken to neighborhood groups, participated in business and civic events, worked with social agencies and taken part in educational and recreational programs for school children. Special units have provided a variety of crisis intervention services.

So then how do the cooperative efforts of community policing differ from the actions that have taken place previously? These actions include helping accident or crime victims, providing emergency medical services, helping resolve domestic and neighborhood conflicts (e.g., family violence, landlord–tenant disputes or racial harassment), working with residents and local businesses to improve neighborhood conditions, controlling automobile and pedestrian traffic, providing emergency social services and referrals to those at risk (e.g., adolescent runaways, the homeless, the intoxicated and the mentally ill), protecting the exercise of constitutional rights (e.g., guaranteeing a person's right to speak and protecting lawful assemblies from disruption) and providing a model of citizenship (helpfulness, respect for others, honesty and fairness). Although these are all services to the community, none are true partnerships, which require sharing of power and responsibility to identify and respond to problems.

Nonetheless, these services are important because they help develop trust between the police and the community. This trust will enable the police to gain greater access to valuable information from the community that could lead to the solution and prevention of crimes, will engender support for needed crime control measures and will provide an opportunity for officers to establish a working relationship with the community. The entire police organization must be involved in enlisting community members' cooperation in promoting safety and security.

Four dimensions of trust are shared priorities, competency, dependability and respect.

Building trust will not happen overnight; it will require ongoing effort. But trust must be achieved before police can assess community needs and construct the close ties needed to engender community support. The use of unnecessary force and arrogance, aloofness or rudeness at any level of the agency will dampen the willingness of community members to ally themselves with the police. In addition, how officers have been traditionally assigned needs to be changed.

Changing Beat and Shift Assignments

Traditional shift and beat *rotation* works to the detriment of building partnerships.

Officers whose assignments continually change have no chance to develop the relationships and trust needed for community policing. Communities also do not have the opportunity to get to recognize and know officers who work in their neighborhoods.

According to the Community Policing Consortium: "Having officers periodically rotate among the shifts impedes their ability to identify problems. It also discourages creative solutions to impact the problems, because the officers end up rotating away from the problems. Thus, a sense of responsibility to identify and resolve problems is lost. Likewise, management cannot hold the officers accountable to deal with problems if the officers are frequently rotated from one shift to another."

ON THE BEAT

Building trust with community members takes time and can occur in a variety of ways. One way is to have designated police districts. It is important that officers be assigned a particular geographic area so they can get to know the unique characteristics of that area. This creates ownership in a sense. By working in the same area day after day, you begin to see patterns and develop a better understanding of the location's needs.

Our city is divided into four police districts. Officers bid to work in one district for an entire year. Some officers end up working in the same district for several years. Residents and businesses in your area get to know you and see you regularly. They learn who they can go to with an issue or concern. You begin to get a complete picture of what the needs are for the area and where your time is best spent.

An example of this is when you see many crimes occurring in a particular neighborhood. Based on what you see, you begin to do more directed patrols in the area—perhaps some foot or bike patrols. You are able to get others involved in problem solving and perhaps find people who are willing to report suspicious activity as it occurs. These conversations can happen when you are able to work in the same area for an extended period of time.

—Kim Czapar

The goal of community policing is to reduce crime and disorder by carefully examining the characteristics of problems in neighborhoods and then applying appropriate problem-solving remedies.

 The community (beat) for which a patrol officer is given responsibility should be a small, well-defined geographic area.

Beats should be "configured in a manner that preserves, as much as possible, the unique geographical and social characteristics of neighborhoods while still allowing efficient service" (Community Policing Consortium Web site). Officers who have permanent assignments become experts about their beats.

Beat officers know the community leaders, businesspeople, school personnel and students. They know the crime patterns and problems and have the best chance to develop partnerships for problem solving. Community members will become accustomed to seeing the permanent beat officers working in the community.

This increased police presence is an initial move in establishing trust and serves to reduce fear of crime among community members, which, in turn, helps create neighborhood security. Fear must be reduced if community members are to participate actively in policing. People will not act if they feel that their actions will jeopardize their safety.

Police work proactively, often identifying and addressing issues before they become problems. They often collaborate with other agencies and community members to solve problems and identify potential trouble spots or situations and act on them instead of waiting for the radio calls that will surely come if the situation is ignored. They are able to respond to questions about crime in their area—for example, why burglaries or auto thefts have increased in a particular time period and what is going to be done about them. Of course, they still take all the enforcement action necessary and respond to calls as well. It is a far more challenging job and provides more job satisfaction because officers can see they are making a real difference. They are affecting a neighborhood, helping make it a safer, better place to live and work, and are building trust.

A Shared Vision and Common Goals

Although the delivery of police services is organized by geographic area, a community may encompass widely diverse cultures, values and concerns, particularly in urban settings. A community consists of more than just the local government and the neighborhood residents. Churches, schools, hospitals, social groups, private and public agencies and those who work in the area are also vital members of the community. In addition, those who visit for cultural or recreational purposes or provide services to the area are also concerned with the safety and security of the neighborhood. Including these "communities of interest" in efforts to address problems of crime and disorder can expand a community's resource base.

Concerns and priorities will vary within and among these communities of interest. Some communities of interest are long lasting and were formed around racial, ethnic or occupational lines or a common history, church or school. Others form and re-form as new problems are identified and addressed. Interest groups within communities can be in opposition to one another—sometimes in violent opposition. Intracommunity disputes have been common in large urban centers, especially in times of changing demographics and population migrations.

These multiple and sometimes *conflicting interests* require patrol officers to function not only as preservers of law and order but also as skillful mediators.

Demands on police from one community of interest can sometimes clash with the rights of another community of interest. Such conflicting interests may impede establishing a common vision and shared goals.

For example, a community group may oppose certain police tactics used to crack down on gang activity, which the group believes may result in discriminatory arrest practices. The police must not only protect the rights of the protesting group but must also work with all community members involved to find a way to preserve neighborhood peace. For this process to be effective, community members must communicate their views and suggestions and back up the negotiating efforts of the police. In this way, the entire community participates in the mediation process and helps preserve order. The police must encourage a spirit of cooperation that balances the collective interests of all citizens with the personal rights of individuals.

When forming partnerships, the conflicts within communities are as important to recognize as the commonalities.

The Remaining Core Components of Successful Collaboration and Partnerships

The remaining components, although vital, are not described, either because they are self-explanatory or because they have been discussed elsewhere in the text. With this understanding of the core components of partnerships, how can stakeholders be convinced to participate in collaborations? One way is to point out the personal benefits they might attain.

Benefits of Partnerships

This brings us back to the key question: Why partnerships? The benefits of participating in a partnership include:

- A sense of accomplishment from bettering the community
- Gaining recognition and respect
- Meeting other community members
- Learning new skills
- Fulfilling an obligation to contribute

Despite these benefits, partnerships have been criticized by some.

Criticisms of Partnerships

Partnerships are time consuming and therefore cost money. Most police agencies do not have extra personnel available for community policing–type projects. Many departments are 911 driven. Officers respond to one call after another and have a difficult time keeping up with the demand for service. When would they have the time to meet with stakeholders and develop plans to solve problems?

 Criticism of the partnerships in community policing usually centers on time and money.

Working as partners with the community may take time and cost more in the short run, but continuing to treat the symptoms without solving the problem has its own long-term costs. It will mean responding again and again to the same calls, often involving the same people, and using temporary tactics to resolve the problem. One way many departments free up time for officers to problem-solve with community members is to manage the volume of 911 calls and to ultimately reduce the number of calls through call management or call reduction.

Making Time for Partnering and Problem Solving: Call Management

In most departments, calls for service determine what police officers do from minute to minute on a shift. People call the police to report crime, ask for assistance, ask questions, get advice and many other often unrelated requests. Police departments try to respond as quickly as possible, and most have a policy of sending an officer when requested.

 Departments might free up time for partnerships without expense through effective call management or call reduction.

Table 7.1	Call Prioritizing Scheme		
Priority	**Designation**	**Response**	**Numbers of Units**
1	Emergency	Immediate; lights and siren; exceed speed limit	2
2	Immediate	Immediate; lights and siren; maintain speed limit	2 if requested
3	Routine	Routine	1
4	Delayed	Delay up to 1 hour; routine	1
5	Telephone report units (TRUs)	Delay up to 2 hours	TRUs

Source: Tom McEwen, Deborah Spencer, Russell Wolff, Julie Wartell and Barbara Webster. *Call Management in Community Policing: A Guidebook for Law Enforcement.* Washington, DC: U.S. Department of Justice, Office of Community Oriented Policing Services, February 2003, p.50.

When using **call management** or **call reduction**, departments take a fresh look at which calls for service require the response of one or more officers and, regardless of past practice, which do not. In call management, calls are prioritized based on the department's judgment about the emergency nature of the call (e.g., imminent harm to a person or a crime in progress), response time, need for backup and other local factors. Priority schemes vary across the country, but many have four or five levels. Table 7.1 presents a typical call priority scheme.

Call management usually involves **call stacking**. A computer aided dispatch system is used to rank calls. Nonemergency, lower-priority calls are held (stacked), and higher-priority calls always receive attention and response ahead of the stacked calls. Using an officer to take telephone reports of nonemergency, low-priority calls is one change that has helped. Reports of minor thefts occurring days or even months in the past and made for insurance purposes are an example of incidents that could be handled completely by phone.

Similar results can be obtained by taking reports by appointment. If the reporting party is willing, an appointment can be set up to have an officer take a report at a time that is less busy for the department but still convenient for the caller. Many people find this method agreeable. Certain kinds of reports can be made on an agency's Web page, by mail or by fax. Figure 7.2 illustrates the type of intake and response common in call management.

Another method of call management is to have civilians handle certain calls that do not involve dangerous situations, suspects or investigative follow-up. These calls might include reports of abandoned vehicles, complaints about animals, bicycle stops, building checks, burglary, criminal mischief, funeral escorts, lost and found property, park patrol, parking issues, paperwork relays, runaways; subpoena service, theft, traffic crashes (with no injuries), traffic control, vandalism and vehicle lockouts. However, police unions may take issue with such an approach unless reserve officers are used.

Call management may also involve dealing with the 911 system, which was set up for emergency calls for assistance. Large numbers of callers use 911 to ask for information or to report nonemergency situations. Most agencies field hundreds or even thousands of phone calls a year from citizens seeking information, often unrelated to police services. Keeping the public informed in other ways, such as on a Web site or through newspapers and newsletters, about city policies, services and procedures and when and when not to call police can reduce the volume of calls.

call management
Calls are prioritized based on the department's judgment about the emergency nature of the call (e.g., imminent harm to a person or a crime in progress), response time, need for backup and other local factors. Also called *call reduction*.

call reduction
Calls are prioritized based on the department's judgment about the emergency nature of the call (e.g., imminent harm to a person or a crime in progress), response time, need for backup and other local factors. Also called *call management*.

call stacking
A process a computer-aided dispatch system performs in which nonemergency, lower-priority calls are ranked and held or "stacked" so the higher priorities are continually dispatched first.

Intake   **Response**

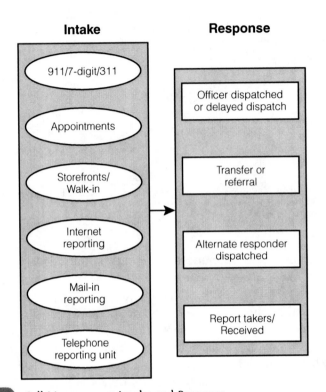

Figure 7.2   Call Management Intake and Response
Source: Tom McEwen, Deborah Spencer, Russell Wolff, Julie Wartell and Barbara Webster. *Call Management in Community Policing: A Guidebook for Law Enforcement.* Washington, DC: U.S. Department of Justice, Office of Community Oriented Policing Services, February 2003, p.12.

People call the police for nonpolice matters for a variety of reasons: because they do not know who can help; because they believe the police know or should know the answers to all questions; because they know the phone number (911); and because, no matter what day of week or time of day it is, they know the phones will be answered. Every 911 call center fields calls asking why the electricity is out, what the weather conditions or driving conditions are, when the snowplows will start plowing, what time the shopping center opens, what time the neighborhood-watch meeting begins, what the driving directions are to a distant state, what the juvenile curfew hours are, where to pay a utility bill and why there is no stop sign or semaphore at a certain location. Calls reporting pothole locations or complaining about raccoons, deer and other wildlife and even about noisy church bells are clogging 911 lines across the country.

 Large cities have begun to implement 311 lines to divert nonemergency calls from 911.

Mazerolle and colleagues (2005, p.ii) explain that in the mid-1990s some jurisdictions introduced the 311 nonemergency number to relieve overburdened 911 systems. Calls can be switched immediately between 911 and 311 and forwarded to other city agencies, or citizens can call 311 directly rather than 911. The goal is to provide an easy-to-remember alternative number for nonemergency matters, thus reserving 911 for true emergencies: "The relative ease of marketing and remembering 311, a decrease in 911 calls and the less measurable effect of empowering citizens to decide whether a call should be considered an emergency" will hopefully reinstate the intended function of 911 (Mazerolle et al., pp.1–2). Disadvantages, however, include high implementation costs, lack of caller ID or location identifiers for 311 as are provided by most 911 systems, failure to record information, underuse of neighborhood policing resources and a common dispatch policy for both 311 and 911.

An increasing number of cities across the United States are implementing 311 call centers, at which trained employees field a wide range of questions from citizens or forward requests to an appropriate agency.

A survey by the International City/County Management Association of Local Government Customer Service Systems (311) found that, of the 710 cities that responded to the survey, 104 reported using a centralized 311 system. Interestingly, thirty-two of those were small cities with less than 30,000 in population (Moulder, 2008). Central call centers provide savings in reducing 911 calls, improving customer service and information management.

According to the call center manager for Minneapolis 311: "We have a first-call resolution of over 80 percent, meaning that more than four out of five calls do not need to go any further than our customer service professionals because their service request has been entered or their question has been answered.... That's a tremendous improvement over what the experience was before, when people had to choose from one of 275 city phone numbers in the blue pages" (Hayes, 2008).

Results in Baltimore

Baltimore has implemented a 311 nonemergency call system to reduce the response burden on police and improve the quality of policing. Researchers note a 34 percent total reduction in calls to 911 (Table 7.2) and widespread community acceptance of 311 as an alternative number (Mazerolle et al., p.3). Most low-priority calls have moved from 911 to 311. Certain types of calls in particular migrated from 911 to 311, such as reports of larceny, parking violations and loud noise complaints.

Not all of the results of the study were positive, however. The number of priority 1 calls *increased* by more than 27 percent after the 311 system was introduced. Researchers believe this increase was unrelated to implementing the system, because their analysis showed that priority 1 calls for specific categories

Table 7.2 The Impact of 311 on Calls to the Police

	Pre-311 implementation	Post-311 implementation		
Call priority	911 only	911 only	311 only	911 + 311
1	417,728	470,263	62,534	532,797
2	902,565	633,706	184,931	818,637
3	415,133	177,967	138,722	316,689
4	201,043	66,169	103,878	170,047
5	111,500	375	50,454	50,829
Total	2,047,969	1,348,480	540,519	1,888,999

Note: Preintervention period was 730 days, from October 1, 1994, to October 1, 1996, excluding February 29, 1996 (leap year). Postintervention period was 730 days, from October 2, 1996, to October 1, 1998.

Source: Alberto R. Gonzales, Tracy A. Henke, Sarah V. Hart. Managing Calls to the Police with 911/311 Systems. Washington, DC: U.S. Department of Justice, Office of Justice Programs, February 2005, p.3. http://www.ncjrs.gov/pdffilesl/nij/206256.pdf.

of serious crime had begun to increase several months before the 311 system was installed.

The large reduction in priority 5 calls to 911 was partly offset by an increase in nonemergency calls referred to other city agencies. Citizens may have stopped calling the police about priority 5 matters because the department stopped dispatching patrol cars in response to these calls after 311 was introduced.

Unrecorded calls were estimated to be about 8 percent more frequent after the introduction of 311. This small but significant increase may have resulted from a greater inclination by 311 operators to handle calls about nonpolice matters without recording them.

Impact on Policing Many elements of Baltimore's approach were successful—the overall burden on 911 was reduced, and citizen use of and satisfaction with calling 311 were high. The 311 system's impact on policing was muted because the department's response and dispatching protocols were not changed when the system was implemented. The research noted three key areas the 311 system was expected to have affected that actually showed little impact (Mazerolle et al., pp.3–4):

> *Response time* for priority 1 calls to 911 was not lowered; rather, patrols were dispatched a bit more slowly following the introduction of 311. The increase in total number of priority 1 calls may account for this. Overall, after implementing 311, police responded to most categories of 911 calls in the same way as before.

> *Dispatch policy* remained unchanged, with officers being dispatched, except on priority 5, whether 911 or 311. Either officers did not know or were indifferent about whether a call had been placed through 911 or 311.

> *Officer discretionary time* increased only marginally. Almost two-thirds of the officers surveyed did not perceive a change in how much discretionary time they had available, most likely because time gains were spread out over shifts and obscured by the failure to dispatch 311 and 911 calls differently. Officer perceptions were about equally split on whether 311 implementation had changed their work routine. Sector managers, however, were certain 311 had decreased their patrol officers' 911 call response load.

Despite these mixed results, researchers concluded that linking 311 call technology with changes in policy and practice can advance a department's community-oriented policing agenda.

Online Reporting

Another way to make time for partnerships and problem solving is to have complainants report priority 5 calls online. Minneapolis, for example, has an e-report Web site. When people sign on, they are cautioned that the site is not monitored 24 hours a day and that, before they begin, they should make sure they do not need a police officer to take the report. The site also directs them to call 911 immediately if:

Table 7.3 Percent of Departments Using Problem-Solving Measures*

Measures	Currently Doing	Plan to Do	No Plan to Do
Identifying top problem locations	92	7	1
Reporting/analyzing frequency of call types	84	13	3
Conducting "hot spot" analysis	66	23	12
Identifying repeat callers	65	17	18
Capturing and using premise history	61	27	12
Predicting emerging problem locations/areas	58	32	10
Assessing problem-solving efforts through change in number of calls	50	29	22
Determining which officers are performing problem-solving efforts	44	30	26
Assessing problem-solving efforts through displacement	32	28	40

*Totals may not equal 100 percent because of rounding.
Source: Tom McEwen, Deborah Spencer, Russell Wolff, Julie Wartell and Barbara Webster. *Call Management in Community Policing: A Guidebook for Law Enforcement.* Washington, DC: U.S. Department of Justice, Office of Community Oriented Policing Services, February 2003, p.104.

○ A crime is in progress

○ Someone is hurt or threatened

○ They can provide information about someone who may have committed a crime

The e-report site then asks specific questions such as who is reporting the incident, what happened, where it happened and the like. Information from dispatch and online reports can be of great assistance in a department's problem-solving efforts.

Calls for Service and Problem Solving

The data that departments obtain using computer-aided dispatch can be valuable in problem-solving efforts and can help identify top problem locations, hot spots and repeat callers. The data can also help predict emerging problem locations. Table 7.3 shows the percent of departments using problem-solving measures or planning to do so using call-for-service data.

In addition to call management, many departments are finding they can improve citizens' participation in community policing and build trust through citizen police academies.

Citizen Police Academies

 A citizen police academy educates the public about the nature of police work and encourages public involvement in crime prevention and problem-solving efforts.

The typical citizen police academy (CPA) is held for 10 or 11 weeks, meeting one evening a week for 3 hours. CPAs are popular among community members, with many agencies having waiting lists for admission to the next academy. Designed to give the participants a basic view of crime and policing in their community, many chiefs and sheriffs believe CPAs improve public relations and help build partnerships between the citizens and the police. Little research has been done to learn what impact CPAs are actually having.

Most academies include lectures, demonstrations, a ride-along with an officer and an opportunity for participants to try their hand at some police technical skills. For participants, the experience is a rare opportunity to get an insider's view of the police or sheriff's department; learn about the challenges faced by police officers and the complex nature of the job; and come to better understand police procedures. Does the experience change community attitudes or improve the relationship between the police and the community? Bonello and Schafer (2002, p.19) describe what has happened with the CPA in Lansing, Michigan.

The Lansing, Michigan, Citizen Police Academy

The Lansing Police Department, which has had a CPA since the early 1990s, used a survey of all its CPA graduates to evaluate its program. Key findings are as follows:

○ Participants increased their knowledge, by large percentages, of crime, safety, community policing and police activities.

○ The number of participants motivated to volunteer to support police department programs increased modestly.

○ Seventy-four percent of respondents changed their view of media reports about the police.

○ All respondents had positive or very positive views of the police department. Five stated they had a negative view when they started the program. Four of those had a positive or very positive impression of the department after completing the academy. Seventy-seven percent stated they viewed the department differently after attending the academy and, overwhelmingly, their views changed in a positive direction.

○ Ninety-eight percent told others of their experience.

○ Ninety-four percent were more likely to collaborate with the police to solve a problem.

The survey results indicated that the Lansing Police Department was meeting its goals with its CPA program. They decided the program would have an even greater impact if they recruited future participants in different segments of the community because, in Lansing and elsewhere, typical participants in CPAs hold positive impressions of the police before they enroll in a CPA.

Candidates for CPA programs are usually screened before being accepted, and anyone with a criminal history is usually excluded. Some have suggested that CPAs might want to reconsider this practice in the case of very minor offenses or where the offenses occurred many years ago. In Lansing's case, the survey results revealed that the department needed to capitalize on many CPA graduates' willingness to volunteer and collaborate with the department to solve neighborhood problems, yet there was only a modest increase in graduates being involved in these ways.

Bonello and Schafer (p.6) note:

The LPD has begun to take steps to recruit their detractors to join the CPA. Such efforts include providing CPA applications to those who contact internal affairs about minor complaints or misunderstandings which stem from a lack of knowledge about police procedures; encouraging leaders in minority communities to attend the academy; and discussing the CPA on a radio talk show that has a large minority audience. . . . For agencies hoping to strengthen community alliances, the challenge for the future is to begin including a broader range of the public in their citizen police academy programs. . . . Agencies need to improve relationships with those citizens who mistrust or feel alienated from their police, which is especially important if an agency hopes to succeed in carrying out community policing.

Numerous variations on the traditional CPA have been developed, including special academies for teens, older people and limited English proficiency residents such as the one developed in Durham, North Carolina, for Hispanic speakers.

The Durham, North Carolina, Spanish-Speaking Citizen Police Academy

The nation's first Spanish-speaking CPA was introduced in Durham, North Carolina, in 2003. The academy was successful beyond expectations, with 46 Spanish-speaking city residents graduating from the 6-week session. In 2004 a second academy was offered and was again met with a high level of community support and enthusiasm from within the Durham Latino community.

This initiative helped strengthen the Durham Police Department's community policing philosophy and the level of trust between law enforcement and the rapidly expanding local Latino community. Typical academy sessions have police commanders discussing their core mission and explaining how police efforts support the community. Extensive interaction, discussion and questions abound, with translators assisting, as necessary, in the communication process (Chalmers and Tiffin, 2005, p.59).

Effectiveness and Impact of Citizen Police Academies

A study of the Bowling Green (Kentucky) Police Department CPA indicates that, overall, opinions about CPAs are favorable, with data showing that citizen participants and police personnel gain a number of benefits (Pope et al., 2007). A preliminary survey found that participants began the program with generally positive attitudes toward police but with limited knowledge about the daily job of police officers and the department's programs. A survey taken after the CPA had ended showed that graduates left the program with increased positive attitudes and significantly increased knowledge about the job of officers and the department's programs (Pope et al.).

The study seemed to show that CPAs are designed to preach to the converted. CPAs reach a very small segment of the population, and that segment has little diversity. Stringent backgrounding of applicants keeps out any with past law violations. It might be helpful for CPAs to reach out to those who are neutral or even hostile toward the police. One way to increase diversity might be to move CPAs away from the police department, as some potential attendees may be unable to travel far due to lack of transportation. In addition to providing CPAs, police departments might identify local key collaborators and be certain they are included in community policing efforts.

Key Collaborators

 Key collaborators who should not be overlooked include prosecutors, courts, corrections, other government agencies, private security providers, victims, the volunteers and even such groups as taxi drivers.

The first group of collaborators discussed are those within the justice system itself. The trend to involve the community is affecting all aspects of the system, with many researchers and practitioners advocating the move toward community justice. Wolf (2006a, p.4) suggests three ways to measure the success of an idea: (1) measure how rapidly an idea catches on, (2) measure the idea's staying power and (3) measure how far the new concept travels. According to Wolf: "By all three measures, community justice—the idea that the justice system should be more aggressive in engaging communities and more reflective about its impacts on neighborhoods—has been highly successful." Wolf notes that the idea has spread to South Africa, England, Sweden, the Netherlands, Australia, British Columbia and Scotland.

In the United States the community justice emphasis has influenced prosecutors, courts and corrections.

Community Prosecutors

As community policing evolves, new collaborations continue to emerge. Including the prosecutor as a partner is one collaboration gaining popularity, and for good reason. Community members' concerns are often not murder or robbery but the types of things that contribute to neighborhood decline and fear of crime, such as abandoned buildings, heavy neighborhood traffic or street-drug dealing. These neighborhood stability issues are frequently addressed by police, but prosecutors tend to see them as a low priority.

Cunningham and associates (2006, p.203) note: "Community prosecution seeks to change the traditional orientation of prosecutors by more fully integrating them into the community and removing barriers between the office and those it is designed to serve." Campbell and Wolf (2004, p.1) suggest that the community prosecution philosophy calls on prosecutors to think of themselves as problem solvers "who seek not only to prosecute individual offenders but also develop lasting solutions to public-safety problems."

As in community policing, community prosecutors focus not on specific cases but on community issues and problems, often involving quality-of-life-issues. When prosecutors become involved as partners in community policing, they attend neighborhood meetings, ride with officers on their beats and get a completely different view of the issues and incidents that devastate communities and breed more crime and disorder.

As Jansen and Dague (2006, p.40) explain: "Community prosecution is a grassroots approach to justice that involves citizens, law enforcement and other government agencies in problem-solving efforts to address the safety concerns of the local jurisdiction. . . . Forging a partnership with a community prosecutor can strengthen enforcement value and the services law enforcement provides."

Many local district attorneys' offices report having adopted a "community prosecution" approach to crime control. According to the Bureau of Justice

Statistics, during 2005, two-thirds of all prosecutors' offices used tools other than traditional criminal prosecution to address community problems (Perry, 2006, p.9). City attorneys' offices are also beginning to recognize the value of working with law enforcement and the community to develop creative solutions to livability issues. At the state level: "In 2005 nearly 40 percent of the prosecutors considered their office a community prosecution site actively involving law enforcement and the community to improve public safety" (Perry, 2006, p.1).

Building partnerships is a "crucial feature" of any community prosecution program, especially smaller jurisdictions with limited resources: "Pooling a community's strengths—its agencies, civic groups and citizen volunteers—gives prosecutors essential resources for carrying out new initiatives" (Campbell and Wolf, p.9). Mike Kuykendall, former manager of the Community Prosecution Program, American Prosecutors Research Institute (APRI), Alexandria, Virginia, and current Vice President of Central City/Downtown Services for the Portland (Oregon) Business Alliance, contends:

> [Community prosecution is] a grassroots effort by the local elected prosecutor to get their assistant prosecutors, citizens, local government resources, police and other stakeholders in the community involved in identifying low-level criminal offenses and neighborhood livability issues and engaging in long-term solutions to those offenses. The emphasis is not on arrest and prosecution, but on learning new ways to prevent crime from occurring. . . . That's the vision the federal government has embraced as have the majority of jurisdictions now practicing community prosecution. . . . We do on occasion see prosecutors who claim they're embracing community prosecution by putting lawyers in the field to do just drug prosecutions or other traditional prosecution, but that's not really community prosecution because that's not involving the community in solving problems that affect their neighborhood (Wolf, "Interview with Mike Kuykendall").

Jelahn Stewart, an assistant U.S. attorney, gives an example of how being connected to the community can make a difference. When she was working in the homicide section, she handled a case that had little chance of being prosecuted because there were no witnesses to the crime. One day Stewart was interviewing a woman for a different case and she realized that the woman lived on the same block as the homicide victim in the "deadend" case. Stewart asked the woman, "Do you know a person named Larry (the decedent)?" And when the woman said, "Yeah, I know Larry," Stewart asked, "Do you know where he is, how he's doing?" The woman replied, "Well, he's dead." Next Stewart said, "Really? What happened to him?" When the woman answered that Larry had been shot, Stewart asked, "Who killed him?" The woman responded simply, "Pierre shot him." Stewart's next question, as to how the woman knew who shot Larry, received the answer, "Pierre told me, and he told me what he did with the gun." The interviewee also gave Stewart the names of a number of witnesses. By knowing the community in which the homicide victim had lived, Stewart was able to successfully prosecute the homicide case and get a conviction (Shapiro, 2009).

The similarities of community prosecution to community policing are many, and, as the project profile in Table 7.4 illustrates, community prosecution works well in conjunction with community policing.

Table 7.4	Key Dimensions of Community Prosecution Strategies
Key Dimensions	**Examples from the Sites**
1. Target Problems/Goals	Quality-of-life offenses
	Drug crime
	Gang violence
	Violent crime
	Juvenile crime
	Truancy
	Prostitution
	Housing and environmental issues
	Landlord/tenant issues
	Failure of the justice system to address community needs
	Community alienation from prosecutor and other justice agencies
	Improved cooperation of victims/witnesses
	Improved intelligence gathering for prosecution of serious cases
2. Target Area	Urban/inner city
	Rural/suburban
	Business districts
	Residential neighborhoods
3. Role of the Community	Recipient of prosecutor services
	Advisory
	Core participants in problem solving
	Core participants in implementation
	Community justice panels
	Sanctioning panels
	Ad hoc
	Targeted
4. Content of Response to Community Problems	Facilitating community self-help
	Crime prevention efforts
	Prosecuting cases of interest to the community
	Receiving noncriminal as well as complaints
5. Organizational Adaptations/ Emphasis	Field offices staffed by attorneys
	Field offices staffed by non-attorneys
	Attorneys assigned to neighborhoods
	Special unit or units
	Office-wide organization around community prosecution model
6. Case Processing Adaptations	Vertical prosecution
	Horizontal prosecution
	Community prosecutors do not prosecute cases
7. Interagency Collaboration/ Partnerships	Police
	City attorney
	Housing authority
	Community court/other court
	Other justice agencies (probation, pretrial services)
	Other social services agencies
	Other regulatory agencies

Source: John S. Goldkamp, Cheryl Irons-Gaynn and Doris Weiland. "Community Prosecution Strategies: Measuring Impact." Washington, DC: Bureau of Justice Assistance Bulletin, November 2002, pp.2–3.

Community Prosecution in Austin, Texas *Offenders Re-entering the Austin Community* (2006) describes how downtown Austin dealt with its significant homeless population, many of whom were convicted drug offenders. Community prosecutor Eric McDonald analyzed the problem and discovered that the homeless population included a number of former state jail inmates who had been recently released. The prosecutor was told by the Salvation Army, which runs the largest homeless shelter in the area, that law enforcement vans from neighboring counties were dropping off people at the shelter. When McDonald investigated, he confirmed that the state jail was dropping approximately 60 people a month on the street in front of the shelter, a location the jail had chosen because it was close to a halfway house and many of the city's other social service providers. Unfortunately, many of the offenders had been arrested on drug charges, and the area around the Salvation Army was a hot spot for crack. McDonald realized that, to address the vagrancy and crack cocaine problem, something had to be done about this endless supply of addicts being funneled into the area.

He approached the state jail administrators and found them to be willing partners. One problem, it seemed, was that the jail simply did not have the resources to make sure every inmate had a discharge plan or to ensure that those who did have plans actually carried them out. According to McDonald: "Once [former inmates are] on the street, they can score crack in 5 minutes, so the chances of making it to the halfway house on their own were pretty slim."

McDonald contacted as many potential partners as possible, including the warden, halfway houses, drug rehabilitation facilities, AIDS service providers, homeless shelters and organizations that work with ex-offenders. He also obtained permission to meet with each inmate before his or her release and talked about services available, emphasizing the consequences of reoffending. McDonald then arranged for postrelease housing, and the Austin Police Department provided donated clothes and drove each person to temporary housing.

From September 2003, when the program began, to January 2004, McDonald met with 59 soon-to-be-former inmates who collectively had hundreds of criminal convictions. Fifty-three agreed to go to a halfway house outside of the downtown area. Of the six who refused to participate, five were rearrested, some within days of their release, and one was rearrested four times. Of the 53 in the program, only 10 were rearrested.

The Growth of Community Prosecution Community prosecution builds on the 1980s' innovations of community policing and has spread steadily (Wolf, 2006b, p.1). By 2004 the American Prosecutors Research Institute estimated that 55 percent of prosecutors' officers participated in initiatives that fit the community prosecution model. The nontraditional tools prosecutors are now aggressively using include nuisance abatement; drug-free and prostitute-free zones; landlord–tenant laws; truancy abatement; graffiti cleanup; and community courts, including several types of specialized courts (Wolf and Worrall, 2004, p.xi).

Community Courts

A recent alternative to the traditional courtroom is the community court, also called problem-solving court, a neighborhood-focused court that accepts serious quality-of-life offenses, taking the approach that the court offers an immediate, visible response to these offenses disruptive to the community and a convenient way to process the most frequent types of complaints. For police officers, issuing summonses makes processing offenders much easier than completing the paperwork for an arrest that would be adjudicated in the traditional court, where nothing may happen to the offender.

"Community courts aim to improve efficiency in judicial proceedings, match sanctions and services to offenders and build bridges between public and private agencies that serve offenders. Community courts focus on quality-of-life crimes and on cleaning up neighborhoods that are deteriorating from crime and neglect (California Courts: Collaborative Justice Web site). Figure 7.3 illustrates case flow and interventions at a typical community court.

Since the early 1990s, more than 30 community courts have opened in jurisdictions across the country (Doniger, 2009). Bridging the gap between the justice system and the neighborhoods they serve, community courts apply problem-solving strategies to the complex issues facing state and local courts. Although taking many forms, all community courts address neighborhood public safety issues through community collaboration, creative partnerships and innovative programs: "They build new relationships, engaging residents, schools, churches and other stakeholders as advisors and volunteers to address problems like prostitution, graffiti, vandalism and drugs. They combine punishment and help, requiring low-level offenders to pay back the community while at the same time addressing the issues that often underlie criminal behavior, like drug addiction and unemployment. And they work toward tangible goals like decreased crime, improved neighborhood safety, greater accountability for low-level offenders and increased public confidence in justice" (Doniger).

Although community courts share common principles, their operations are as diverse as the communities they serve. Since the launch of the nation's first community court, the Midtown Community Court in Manhattan in 1993, community courts have been established across the country, in business districts and urban and suburban neighborhoods, implementing a wide range of goals and strategies (Doniger). The Seattle community court focuses on chronic offenders, providing them with necessary help in return for each offender performing community service around the city. The New York City Harlem Community Justice Center has a reentry court that helps juvenile and adult parolees returning from institutions to become productive, law-abiding citizens. And in Dallas, a court housed in a community center explores new low-cost ways to link defendants to community services. According to Doniger: "The spread of these projects across the United States has been matched by increased international interest in community justice. South Africa, Australia, Canada, England and Wales have established community courts, while plans are under way in Scotland and New Zealand."

The community court model has its origins in community policing and problem-oriented policing. Like these two policing innovations, community courts have a problem-solving orientation, focusing on bringing new resources from both inside and outside the justice system to bear on local public safety issues. Community courts have adopted community policing implementation methods by systematically assessing identified problems, engaging diverse stakeholders and evaluating outcomes. Both focus on community engagement: they develop relationships with residents, business owners, religious officials

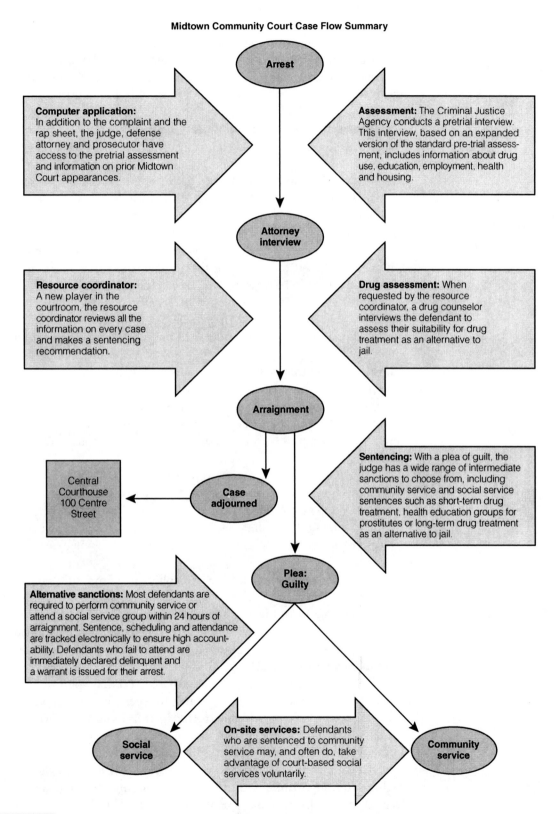

Figure 7.3 Summary of Case Flow and Interventions at the Midtown Community Court
Source: Eric Lee. *How It Works: Summary of Case Flow and Interventions at the Midtown Community Court.*
New York: Center for Court Innovation, 1997, p.4.

and other leaders, and involve these stakeholders in identifying local problems, setting priorities for problem-solving efforts and helping to shape and sustain solutions. This common philosophical and practical approach fosters natural partnerships between community courts and local policing efforts. Leaders in both fields are likely to find fertile ground for collaboration in the following areas:

Communication: Both community court and community policing models place a premium on information. They use data from a wide range of sources to analyze local problems and identify solutions. They also communicate regularly about their work, allowing them to better monitor its impact. For example, the Philadelphia Community Court has an on-site police liaison who updates the ten police districts served by the court on case outcomes and also provides training to new officers about how the community court operates.

Community outreach: Both community policing and community court initiatives are based on the belief that citizens and neighborhood groups play an important role in helping the justice system identify, prioritize and solve local problems. Actively engaging citizens helps improve public trust in the justice system. Greater trust, in turn, helps people feel safer, fosters law-abiding behavior and makes citizens more willing to cooperate in the pursuit of justice (as witnesses or jurors, for example). Police representatives and staff from the Hartford Community Court attend community meetings, listen to community problems and report on how they are working to resolve them. At Bronx Community Solutions in New York, which serves an entire county, the staff meets monthly with community affairs officers from the county's thirteen police precincts to collect police recommendations for community service projects from throughout the Bronx.

Education: Both police and community courts seek to educate the public about the law and the justice system. At the Harlem Community Justice Center, court staff and police officers work together to create workshops for local youth, helping them better understand how the police and courts work. Included are role plays on topics such as what a person should do when he or she is stopped by the police.

Collaboration: By working together, police and community courts can address difficult problems more effectively. Local police officers work side by side with case managers from the Midtown Community Court in New York to identify homeless hot spots and offer services to homeless individuals. The police officer provides both security and authority to the case worker, while the case worker provides expertise in working with this difficult population. Since the program was launched more than a decade ago, these teams have persuaded thousands of clients to visit the courthouse voluntarily to receive help with entitlements, housing, job training, drug treatment, mental health counseling and other services. In Indianapolis, police officers participate in court-run panels that bring together offenders and community members to discuss the impact of low-level crime on local neighborhoods. The panels have proven to be an effective tool for dealing with everything from prostitution to panhandling. At a typical session, police participants help explain the strategies they apply to handle these vexing problems and answer questions from both community members and offenders.

For more information about community courts, see www.courtinnovation. org or write to the Center for Court Innovation at info@courtinnovation.org.

Specialized Courts The Atlanta Community Court is one of the most comprehensive community courts in the country and has the following components: restorative justice, drug court, mental health court, homeless court, reentry court initiatives, family reunification and family court. The Atlanta Municipal Court is planning a merger/consolidation with the City of Atlanta Traffic Court in the near future (Atlanta Community Court Web site).

Other specialized courts include domestic violence court and gun courts.

Shared Principles The Center for Court Innovation lists several shared principles distinguishing what they call problem-solving courts from the conventional approach to case processing and case outcomes in state courts.

Case Outcome: Problem-solving courts seek to achieve tangible outcomes for victims, for offenders and for society, including reductions in recidivism, reduced stays in foster care for children, increased sobriety for addicts and healthier communities.

Judicial Monitoring: Problem-solving courts rely on the active use of judicial authority to solve problems and to change the behavior of litigants. Instead of passing off cases to other judges, to probation departments or to community-based treatment programs, judges at problem-solving courts stay involved with each case throughout the postadjudication process. Drug court judges, for example, closely supervise the performance of offenders in drug treatment, requiring them to return to court frequently for urine testing and courtroom progress reports.

Informed Decision Making: Problem-solving courts seek to improve the quality and quantity of information available in the courtroom through, among other things, innovative computer technology, frequent court appearances and on-site professional staff. With better information, judges can respond more swiftly and effectively to problems and hold defendants, as well as partner agencies, to a higher level of accountability. In community courts, for instance, case workers conduct comprehensive evaluations of defendants to determine their exact social service needs, and many problem-solving courts use computer software linked to off-site partners to alert judges immediately about violations of court orders.

Collaboration: Problem-solving courts employ a collaborative approach, relying on both government and nonprofit partners (criminal justice agencies, social service providers, community groups and others) to help achieve their goals. For example, many domestic violence courts have developed partnerships with batterers' programs and probation departments to help improve the monitoring of defendants.

Nontraditional Roles: Some problem-solving courts have altered the dynamics of the courtroom, including, at times, certain features of the adversarial process. For example, at many drug courts, judges and attorneys (on both sides of the aisle) work together to craft systems of sanctions and rewards for offenders in drug treatment. And by using the institution's authority and prestige to coordinate the work of other agencies, problem-solving courts may engage judges in unfamiliar roles as conveners and brokers.

System Change: Problem-solving courts promote reform outside of the courthouse as well as within it. For example, family treatment courts that handle cases of child neglect have encouraged local child welfare agencies to adopt new staffing patterns and to improve case management practices.

The third component of the criminal justice system, corrections, also is an often overlooked partner in the community policing effort.

Community Corrections

The movement toward community-based corrections has been growing steadily since the 1970s, when states, facing overcrowded correctional facilities strained beyond their intended capacities, began passing community corrections acts as ways to divert nonviolent, first-time offenders from the traditional path of incarceration. Community corrections, also called intermediate sanctions, usually has included a range of correctional alternatives existing along a continuum of increasing control—from day fines to forfeiture, restitution, community service, intensive supervision programs, house arrest, day reporting centers and residential community centers—which are tougher than conventional probation but less restrictive and costly than imprisonment. Traditionally, the task of administering these correctional alternatives has fallen almost exclusively on those internal stakeholders within corrections—probation and parole officers.

Whereas it is one thing to conduct correctional activities outside the confines of barred institutions, it is quite another to actively draw the community and other external stakeholders into the corrections process. As with the overall movement of community justice, this has become the new paradigm in community corrections: "Community corrections includes any activities in the community aimed at helping offenders become law-abiding citizens and request a complicated interplay among judicial and correctional personnel from related public and private agencies, citizen volunteers and civic groups" (Hess and Orthmann, 2009, p.526).

Probation is, by far, the most commonly imposed form of community corrections. Thus, partnerships between police and probation officers hold great potential to affect a large number of offenders within the criminal justice system and, ultimately, significantly affect public safety levels within a community. One type of partnership that has proved successful is that between individual patrol officers and probation officers in the same neighborhood. Probation officers who ride along with patrol officers can often spot probationers violating a condition of their probation, and the officer can make an immediate arrest. Or the probation officer can talk with the offending probationer, letting him or her know that the illegal activities will no longer go unnoticed.

For communities embattled in the gang–drug–gun issue, partnerships between police and corrections officers can prove beneficial. One effort to reduce gun crime across the country has been the Project Safe Neighborhoods (PSN) initiative, a task force idea based on the successful Operation Ceasefire implemented in Boston during the mid-1990s. Under Operation Ceasefire, police and probation and parole officers partnered to proactively search for individuals thought to be at high risk of illegal possession of firearms, jointly conducted nighttime home visits of these individuals and gathered and shared intelligence to vigorously enforce the conditions of probation to ensure offender compliance. It is worth noting that the Supreme Court ruling in *United States v. Knights* (2001) upheld the constitutionality of warrantless searches of probationers' or parolees' homes based on "reasonable suspicion" or "reasonable grounds" by either probation or parole officers or the police. Police–probation partnerships may also include sharing probation or parole data for use in law enforcement Geographic Information Systems (GIS) or CompStat databases to build criminal cases targeting serious offenders.

Philadelphia has forged a partnership between its Adult Probation and Parole Department and local police to address the growing violence in the city and attempt to gain control over increasing numbers of weapons violations. A unique feature of this effort is involving a research partner through the University of Pennsylvania's Department of Criminology: "A statistical model began to emerge from Penn's preliminary analysis of our data and from their mapping of the variables determined to be of interest. We named this model PROBE-Stat, articulating a mission statement to unite community supervision agencies and academic criminology in a data-driven partnership to prevent crime, especially serious violence, committed by and against offenders under court supervision in the community" (Malvestuto and Snyder, 2006).

Other Government Agencies

Criminal justice agencies are not the only local government agencies responsible for responding to community problems. Partnering with other city and county departments and agencies is important to problem-solving success. Sometimes described as **working in "silos,"** local government agencies and departments have traditionally worked quite independently of each other. Under community policing, appropriate government departments and agencies are called on and recognized for their abilities to respond to and address crime and social disorder issues. Fire departments, building inspections agencies, health departments, street departments, parks and recreation departments and child welfare agencies frequently are appropriate and necessary stakeholders in problem-solving initiatives.

working in "silos"
Agencies with common interests work independently with no collaboration.

Chapman and Scheider (2006, p.4) note: "Elected officials have an important role to play in close coordination with their law enforcement executive, to make the community policing philosophy and the strategies it encourages work best and potentially expand beyond law enforcement."

Consolidation of Services Fahim reports: "Increasingly communities are looking to the consolidation mechanism as a way of achieving efficiencies of scale in response to citizen demands for services. However, voters are more often than not reluctant to approve mergers between neighboring communities." She explains: "Consolidation is the mechanism used to achieve economies of scale by reducing numbers of local government units."

Consolidation is not new in the United States. In the 1800s several of our larger cities were established through consolidation of services, including New York, Philadelphia, New Orleans, Boston, St. Louis and San Francisco. According to Fahim: "The vast majority of consolidation efforts fail, either during the process of drafting a charter or once they reach the ballot. Fewer than 10 have been passed since 1990 and fewer than 40 have been successfully implemented since the first one, when the city of New Orleans merged with Orleans Parish in 1805."

Outsourcing Policing Many smaller towns whose police departments consist of only a handful of officers hope to cut costs by eliminating their police department and contracting for services with county sheriff's departments.

Residents often resist this move, citing loss of local control, delayed response times and impersonal police–community relationships, the result of having officers from distant jurisdictions, who are strangers to local residents, respond to several small towns with which they are not familiar. Objectors fear that sheriff's deputies will drive to their town on a call for service and leave when the call is completed. Most contract agencies seem to focus on emergency response and not on forming relationships, holding meetings or engaging in problem-solving partnerships with local residents. In addition, contracting for services does not always cut costs and, in some cases, is actually more expensive.

Kelling and Bratton (2006, p.4) point out that the radically decentralized law enforcement presence in the United States (i.e., more than 17,000 separate police departments) can be seen as both a strength and a weakness: "It is a great strength because the police are better attuned to their local communities and are directly accountable to their concerns. But it is also a terrible weakness in the post September 11 world where information sharing is key."

State and Federal Agencies State and federal agencies may also be of assistance, including the Federal Bureau of Investigation (FBI), the Drug Enforcement Administration (DEA), the U.S. attorney in the region, the state attorney, the state criminal investigative agency and the state highway department.

COPS and Homeland Security describes a partnership between the COPS Office, the FBI and the Bureau of Justice Assistance (BJA) of the U.S. Department of Justice to enhance counterterrorism training and technical assistance to state, local and tribal law enforcement. The FBI and COPS are delivering the BJA-funded State and Local Anti-terrorism Training (SLATT) through the COPS network of local Regional Community Policing Institutes.

COPS has expanded its partnership with the FBI and BJA by developing counterterrorism roll call training programs for line officers, in which short segments on various aspects of counterterrorism are presented to officers during their roll calls.

Private Security Providers

The *Policy Paper: Private Security/Public Policing Partners* (2004, p.1) reports that since September 11, 2001, law enforcement and private security organizations have been under pressure to not only provide traditional services but also to contribute to the national effort to protect the homeland from internal and external threats:

> Despite their similar interests in protecting the people of the United States, the two fields have rarely collaborated. In fact, through the practice of community policing, law enforcement agencies have collaborated extensively with practically every group but private security. By some estimates, 85 percent of the country's critical infrastructure is protected by private security. The need for complex coordination, extra staffing and special resources after a terror attack, coupled with the significant demands of crime prevention and response, absolutely requires boosting the level of partnership between public policing and private security.

Recognizing a need for collaboration between private policing and public policing, the International Association of Chiefs of Police held a summit in early 2004 to discuss possible collaborations between public and private police around the issue of terrorism. Their goal is to develop a national strategy to build such partnerships between federal, state, tribal and local public sector police agencies and private security agencies. The focus of such partnerships will be terrorism prevention and response. The summit was supported by the COPS Office. The summit also looked at the differences in such collaborations, and some are significant, including differences in the screening, hiring, training and responsibilities of private security and public police officers.

Some areas of cooperation are investigating internal theft and economic crimes, responding to burglar alarms, examining evidence from law enforcement in private crime labs, conducting background checks, protecting VIPs and executives, protecting crime scenes, transporting prisoners, moving hazardous materials and controlling crowds and traffic at public events.

According to Dodge (2006, p.84): "The proliferation of cybercrime and the need for specialized knowledge for crime investigation is driving the trend toward increased use of private policing." The expanding responsibilities of private security include surveillance, investigation, crowd control, prison escorts, court security, guarding and patrolling, proactive crime prevention, risk management and insurance assessment, weapons training, crime scene examination and forensic evidence gathering.

Volunteers

Volunteer Programs (n.d., p.1) notes that demands on law enforcement have greatly increased, especially since September 11, while budgets have shrunk and resources have become more limited. Volunteer programs can help leverage existing resources while simultaneously enhancing public safety. Volunteer programs not only allow agencies and officers to focus on policing and enforcement functions by providing supplemental and/or support services, they also create valuable ties between law enforcement and the community. The "Volunteers in Police Service" brochure (n.d.) explains:

> Law enforcement volunteer programs are not designed to replace sworn or civilian personnel. Rather, volunteers are used to supplement and enhance existing or envisioned functions to allow law enforcement professionals to do their job in the most effective manner. Volunteers can provide innumerable benefits to a law enforcement agency. They can help enhance public safety and services, maximize existing resources, and create valuable ties between law enforcement and members of the community. Investing in a volunteer program can help sworn and civilian employees fulfill their primary functions and provide services that may not otherwise be offered.

 Benefits to a police department that uses volunteers may include improved service delivery, increased cost effectiveness, relief of sworn personnel for other duties, improved public image, enhanced understanding of police functions, provision of new program opportunities, increased political support, restored community responsibility, reduced crime and increased property values.

In addition, volunteers may benefit from reduced fear of crime, use of their skills and expertise, the opportunity to help others, enrichment of their daily lives and a greater sense of belonging and worth. These benefits, compiled by the American Association of Retired Persons (AARP), are by no means exhaustive. Police-sponsored programs that use elderly volunteers have, however, raised some concerns.

Profiles of Law Enforcement Volunteer Programs Countless volunteer programs in partnership with law enforcement agencies flourish across the country. For example, the Sacramento County (California) Sheriff's Department, working with the Sacramento Regional Citizen Corps Council, trained 125 volunteers to provide neighborhood emergency training (NEP). NEP workers then held workshops to teach residents disaster preparation and help residents develop personal emergency plans.

In Riverside, California, the police department operates a program called You Are Not Alone. Thirteen volunteers make regular phone calls to older and physically challenged residents to check on them. In the event a volunteer is unable to reach a resident, an emergency contact or a uniformed police officer visits the residence.

The Denver Police Department has trained 40 volunteers to serve on crime scene investigation teams. These volunteers investigate automobile thefts, burglaries and other property crimes that officers may not be able to respond to and are trained in evidence collection and crime scene photography. Volunteers must pass a background investigation, a polygraph test, an interview and a physical agility test before they receive 106 hours of training for the position.

The preceding examples are from *Volunteer Program*, "Part Two" (n.d., pp.50–53).

Concerns about Using Volunteers One frequently expressed concern is that volunteers may do police officers' duties, thereby affecting future departmental hiring decisions. Other concerns are that volunteers need to be supervised while working in the department or they may come into contact with sensitive or confidential material.

Volunteer programs can be tailored to address most objections. Volunteers rarely perform actual police functions. They frequently work in programs the department could not otherwise afford to provide, such as fingerprinting children, distributing literature, maintaining equipment, entering computer data, organizing block groups, conducting department tours and translating. Volunteers do, however, need supervision and recognition, and volunteer programs need a coordinator to handle those tasks. In some cases, a staff member can act as coordinator, or, when an extensive volunteer program is anticipated, a department may enlist a volunteer coordinator.

Older Volunteers with Law Enforcement Older persons make excellent volunteers. The Administration on Aging notes: "Older Americans represent a great reservoir of talent, experience and knowledge which can and is being used to better their communities and the Nation." Older people tend to be dependable, experienced, stable, available, trainable, committed, skilled, conscientious and service oriented. In addition, older volunteers have fewer accidents, are more careful of equipment than younger volunteers, use good judgment, follow directions, like to avoid trouble, have good attendance records and tend to be team players.

Police departments across the country staff innovative programs with elderly citizens. Older volunteers are involved in neighborhood-watch clubs and anonymous reporting and court-watch programs and provide extensive benefits to both the police department and the community.

A joint resolution was adopted by the AARP, the International Association of Chiefs of Police (IACP) and the National Sheriffs' Association (NSA) to address criminal victimization of older people. The three organizations agreed to work together to design interjurisdictional approaches and partnerships to reduce victimization of older persons, assist those who have been victimized and generally enhance law enforcement services to older adults and the community.

This three-way partnership, called **TRIAD**, provides specific information such as crime prevention materials (brochures, program guides and audiovisual presentations on crime prevention and the elderly), policies, exemplary projects relating to the law enforcement response to the older community and successful projects involving the formation of senior advisory councils to advise departments on the needs of seniors. TRIAD also trains police about aging, communication techniques with elderly citizens, victimization of the elderly and management programs using older volunteers. TRIAD has been identified as a concrete example of community policing. Leadership is provided by an advisory group of older persons and those providing services to the elderly called Seniors and Law Enforcement Together (SALT).

TRIAD
A three-way partnership among the American Association of Retired Persons (AARP), the International Association of Chiefs of Police (IACP) and the National Sheriffs' Association (NSA) to address criminal victimization of older people.

Building Partnerships in a Variety of Neighborhoods

The effective mobilization of community support requires different approaches in different communities. Establishing trust and obtaining cooperation are often easier in middle-class and affluent communities than in poorer communities, where mistrust of police may have a long history.

Building partnerships in lower-income neighborhoods may be more difficult because often there are fewer resources and less trust between the citizens and law enforcement.

Building bonds in some neighborhoods may involve supporting basic social institutions (e.g., families, churches, schools) that have been weakened by pervasive crime or disorder. The creation of viable communities is necessary if lasting alliances that nurture cooperative efforts are to be sustained. Under community policing, the police become both catalysts and facilitators in the development of these communities.

Ideas in Practice

VANDALISM TASK FORCE

The sight of a speeding subway train emblazoned with a mélange of spray-painted words and pictures brings to mind a time of disorder and crime in New York City, when taking public transportation was synonymous with taking your life in your own hands. Graffiti-adorned trains and tunnels, buildings, blocks and cars all communicated a message of chaos to New Yorkers and tourists alike. Whether or not the statistics supported these assumptions was irrelevant. The mere impression of disorder was enough.

Today, the city looks much different, due in large part to the efforts and success of the New York Police Department (NYPD), which has successfully driven the crime rate to historic lows, routing out and eradicating criminals of every stripe. Specifically, a small unit of dedicated officers has been working tirelessly to keep the city's vistas graffiti free. Based in Brooklyn, with a satellite command in the Bronx, the Citywide Vandals Taskforce is an amalgamation of the old Special Operations Division Anti-Graffiti/Vandalism Unit, the Transit Bureau Vandal Squad and the Homeless Outreach Unit, placed under the command of Lieutenant Steve Mona, who has been battling graffiti for over 20 years. He is one of the most knowledgeable people in the department when it comes to the graffiti subculture and knows more than most young vandals currently smearing their "tags" across the city.

Mona always refers to them as vandals: "Make no mistake; they are not artists." On this point he is adamant.

Before any discussion of how to combat graffiti vandalism can commence, one must understand exactly what is being fought. Some may look on graffiti as a type of avant-garde art that has a place as an expression of social worth. But that view is not only puerile, it is mistaken:

> Vandals are not interested in artistic expression or social commentary. All they care about is getting their "ups" all over the city. It is not for you or me to see; it is for those who exist in this world, where the more your "tag" is seen, the bigger a celebrity you are. On the one hand, you have the vandals who only care about getting their "tag" all-city, and then there are people who shrug off the severity of graffiti and criticize the department for investing energy in stopping it; they say it is art. Well, I am not an art critic; I am a cop. Deface someone else's property and you are a criminal, not an artist, and you are going to get arrested (Mona).

Mona and his unit are dispatched in plainclothes across the city to target the areas hardest hit by vandals. They keep tabs on what is happening on the street and parlay this information into arrests and more comprehensive investigations.

A small handful of officers are assigned to the GHOST unit, the Graffiti Habitual Offender Suppression Team, and these GHOST cops live up to their name. Tracking and nabbing the city's most industrious and destructive offenders is what they do, and they do it well. Using conventional investigative techniques as well as a newly created graffiti offender databank, these officers can put together cases that would appall even the most tolerant citizen. The databank allows officers from across the city to contribute to the effort. Offenders arrested for graffiti are brought to the attention of the task force, and their arrest information is entered, along with a photo of the damage caused. But an arrest need not be made for the databank to be used. If a complaint is made about graffiti, that information is entered as well, allowing officers to match a number of identical "tags" to compile stronger cases on the offenders when there are arrests.

A "tag" is like a signature, with the vandal writing it the same every time. This information can be critical to identifying offenders and arresting them. Along with the databank, the task force has put together a "worst of the worst" book, a list of the 100 or so graffiti vandals identified as the top menaces. The tome is packed with information on each offender, detailing their area of operation, "tags," pedigree information and more. The graffiti coordinators in each patrol precinct have a copy and use it as a tool to keep this crime in check.

Part of the battle is educating people by explaining how graffiti hurts a community and by disabusing them of the idea that tagging is a victimless crime. Members of the task force regularly speak at community board meetings, schools and other venues about how the task of keeping parks, streets and subways clear of graffiti goes a long way toward cleaning up or outright preventing more serious and dangerous problems. Because vandalism extends the appearance of disorder, it invites other criminal activity by sending the message that the neighborhood is beyond the control of the law.

The task force is intent on furthering the crime decline in the city and is, by far, one of the best weapons for doing this. Their efforts have helped transform New York's reputation back to that of a city that is a preeminent travel destination in the world.

Source: New York City Police Department: http://www.nyc.gov/html/nypd/html/transportation/vandals.html

Successful Partnerships in Action

The following examples of successful partnerships range from very simple to award-winning programs.

Partnerships to Accommodate the Homeless

To address the challenges presented by homelessness, the police need to partner with many organizations, from detoxification facilities to children's shelters, from hospital crisis units to county social services. Police also need to move beyond the arrest-and-detain mentality and take on the role of educator and facilitator, making the homeless aware of available services and encouraging them to seek appropriate assistance.

Until recently, many Oregon police officers regularly swept encampments of homeless people after giving occupants a 24-hour notice. Now, through collaboration with JOIN: A Center for Involvement and the Oregon Department of Transportation, two Portland officers and two JOIN outreach workers identify low-profile encampment areas. The police allow the homeless to remain in these encampments while the outreach workers find them shelters, housing and services as a smooth transition.

This project has improved relations between the city's police and its homeless residents, who now view the officers as helpful friends who are not harassing them. The plan is so successful that it has been guaranteed funding in future years ("Feds Push Efforts to House the Homeless," 2006).

Another exemplary partnership aimed at addressing homelessness exists in South Florida. In 2003 the Taskforce for Ending Homelessness, Inc., a non-profit agency that provides outreach, education and advocacy services for Broward County's homeless population, partnered with the Fort Lauderdale Police Department to form the Homeless Outreach Team (*A Dream Denied,* 2006, p.20). In 2005 the team was comprised of two full-time Fort Lauderdale police officers, two part-time officers and a civilian partner who was previously homeless:

> The team informs chronically homeless individuals of social services available in the community and encourages them to access those services. Repeated visits are often necessary to build rapport, trust and confidence between the workers and homeless individuals.

> In addition, the outreach team has partnered with local shelters to ensure access to beds and services. Those accepting shelter assistance receive priority, entering the program if a bed is open. They are also provided with dinner, breakfast, a hot shower, laundry facilities and a safe night's sleep. In its five years of operation, the Homeless Outreach Team has had over 23,000 contacts with homeless individuals and has placed 11,384 people in shelters. Estimates suggest that there are at least 2,400 fewer arrests each year as a result of the Homeless Outreach Team.

Another achievement of the task force was developing a 2-hour course entitled "Homelessness 101," designed as a sensitivity training clinic to raise police officers' awareness of the reality of homelessness and its causes and the ways in which law enforcement can most effectively address this social problem. The task force also has successfully lobbied the state for a detoxification program specifically for homeless individuals (*A Dream Denied,* p.20).

A Partnership to Prevent Stalking

According to the Bureau of Justice Statistics, during a 12-month period an estimated 14 in every 1,000 persons age 18 or older were victims of stalking. About half (46 percent) of stalking victims experienced at least one unwanted contact per week, and 11 percent of victims said they had been stalked for 5 years or more. Approximately one in four stalking victims reported some form of cyberstalking, such as e-mail (83 percent) or instant messaging, and 46 percent of stalking victims felt fear of not knowing what would happen next (Baum et al., 2009, p.1). However, many incidents of stalking are not reported to law enforcement because victims feel it is a private or personal matter or they report it to another official (40.3 percent). The next most frequent reason for nonreporting is that the victim feels it is not important enough to report or that no crime has occurred (38.4 percent) (Baum et al., p.14).

Stalking is a complex and unique crime, making it more difficult to recognize, investigate and prosecute. The things that make stalking unique are twofold. First, the crime is committed repeatedly against the same victim. Second, these victims suffer extreme fear, and with good reason. Stalking victims are frequently severely injured, some fatally, by their stalkers.

Stalkers, as a group, are highly motivated offenders, are especially determined to commit these crimes and are difficult to deter. Protection orders, conviction and even incarceration may not be sufficient to stop them, as some offenders are able to continue stalking, in some form, even from prison.

Like most police agencies in the United States, the Philadelphia Police Department (PPD) had no protocols or procedures for handling stalking cases. Acknowledging the need to increase officers' ability to recognize and respond to stalking crimes, the PPD agreed to pilot test the National Center for Victims of Crime's Model Stalking Protocol (Valezquez et al., 2009, pp.30–37). With the goals of training the officers and developing a specific protocol on stalking, the PPD took a community policing approach to form key partnerships, beginning with a survey of the department's 7000 officers. The survey found that officers were not knowledgeable about stalking, had not been trained in stalking, did not perceive it as a problem and consequently were not providing the service victims deserved.

The department decided to process all stalking cases through one division during the pilot program. They first coordinated their efforts internally, and then they invited several community victim service agencies and the district attorney's office to serve as partners. All partners had representatives at the planning meetings.

The first step was training. The PPD developed a day-long training program and trained about 75 domestic violence detectives, victim assistance officers, victim assistance organizations and the district attorney's office on stalking. All officers in the division attended a one-hour training session on how to recognize and respond to stalking. An invitation to attend was extended to all interested officers in the entire department, to signal how important the department viewed stalking offenses.

Project leaders then developed a stalking policy for the department, and in preparation for taking the project department-wide, they conducted train-the-trainer training. With funding from the U.S. Department of Justice, Office on Violence against Women, the PPD trained 700 first-line supervisors, who, in turn, trained the officers they supervised. The training covered the interrelated crimes of domestic violence, sexual assault and stalking. It also covered the new protocol in detail, including patrol procedures and individual officer responsibilities.

Although a formal program evaluation has not been done yet, the initiative has had positive effects, according to department leaders, who cite significant increases in the number of stalking and stalking-related investigations and in the quality of affidavits and arrest warrants. Training has eliminated many misconceptions officers held about the law, the process and the willingness of prosecutors to pursue felony charges. All partners in the initiative are now able to provide accurate and consistent information about stalking. The department provides officers with stalking tip cards to carry. In addition, the PPD has started a 24-hour hotline that is answered 7 days a week by partner agencies. With operators fluent in both English and Spanish, the hotline is able to assist victims of stalking, domestic assault and sexual assault. A new partnership with the probation department has also been developed. Police officers and probation officers make unscheduled visits to people who are on probation for domestic-related offenses. These unannounced visits are designed to check that offenders are not in violation of their probation and, in the case of those who have an order of protection against them, the visits provide an additional layer of security to victims.

The training has resulted in the department being added to a judge's study group that reviews domestic violence–related cases and shares information that helps protect victims.

The PPD, the fourth largest in the United States, with 7000 officers, is a big ship to turn. Not every officer is on board yet with the idea that stalking is important or that the new protocol is useful, but department leaders believe that such buy-in will come as they continue to demonstrate their own steady, visible support of the importance of stalking and the protocol and procedures now in place.

The COPS Office published *Creating an Effective Stalking Protocol*, developed by the National Center in 2002 and available online at www.cops.

SUMMARY

Partnerships usually result in a more effective solution to a problem because there are shared responsibilities, resources and goals. A partnership will only be successful, however, if trust exists between and among partners. Four dimensions of trust are shared: priorities, competency, dependability and respect.

Traditional shift and beat rotation works to the detriment of building partnerships. The community (beat) for which a patrol officer is given responsibility should be a small, well-defined geographic area. Officers who have permanent assignments become experts about their beat.

Demands on police from one community of interest can sometimes clash with the rights of another community of interest. Such conflicting interests may impede establishing a common vision and shared goals. When forming partnerships, it is as important to recognize conflicts within a community as it is to recognize commonalities. Criticism of the partnerships in community policing usually centers on time and money.

Departments might free up time for partnerships without expense through effective call management or call reduction. Large cities have begun to implement 311 lines to divert non-emergency calls from the 911 system.

Departments might also enhance partnerships by providing CPAs. A CPA educates the public about the nature of police work and encourages involvement in crime prevention and problem-solving efforts. In addition, key collaborators who might be overlooked include prosecutors, courts, corrections, other government agencies, private security providers, victims, the elderly and even such groups as taxi drivers. Benefits to a police department that uses senior volunteers may include improved service delivery, increased cost effectiveness, relief of sworn personnel for other duties, improved public image, enhanced understanding of police functions, provision of new program opportunities, increased political support, restored community responsibility, reduced crime and increased property values.

Building partnerships in lower-income neighborhoods may be more difficult because often there are fewer resources and less trust between the citizens and law enforcement.

DISCUSSION QUESTIONS

1. What are the most important factors that lead you to trust another person? To distrust someone?

2. Discuss the pros and cons of using volunteers in a law enforcement agency.

3. Select a campus problem you feel is important and describe the partners who might collaborate to address the problem.

4. Why are permanent shift and area assignments for officers important in community policing?

5. Why is trust an issue between police and residents of low-income neighborhoods?

6. What are the main criticisms or arguments against having police involved in community policing partnerships?

7. What strategies can help free up time for officers' involvement in partnerships?

8. Explain the difference between community courts and traditional courts.

GALE EMERGENCY SERVICES DATABASE ASSIGNMENTS   ONLINE Database

- Use the Gale Emergency Services Database to answer the Discussion Questions as appropriate.

- Select and research one of the following topics: Outline your findings and be prepared to discuss them with the class.

  ○ Citizen police academies

  ○ Future of private policing

  ○ Criminalizing homelessness

REFERENCES

Baum, Katrina; Catalano, Shannan; Rand, Michael; and Rose, Kristina. *Stalking Victimization in the United States.* Washington, DC: Bureau of Justice Statistics Special Report, January 2009. (NCJ 224527)

Bonello, Elizabeth M. and Schafer, Joseph A. "Citizen Police Academies: Do They Just Entertain?" *FBI Law Enforcement Bulletin,* November 2002, p.19.

Campbell, Nicole and Wolf, Robert V. *Beyond Big Cities: The Problem-Solving Innovations of Community Prosecutors in Smaller Jurisdictions.* New York: Center for Court Innovation, 2004.

Center for Court Innovation Web site: www.courtinnovation.org.

Chalmers, Steven W. and Tiffin, Charles. "Hispanic Outreach and Intervention Strategy Team." *The Police Chief,* June 2005, pp.58–61.

Chapman, Robert and Scheider, Matthew. *Community Policing for Mayors: A Municipal Service Model for Policing and Beyond.* Washington, DC: Office of Community Oriented Policing Services, 2006.

Community Policing Consortium. www.communitypolicing.org/chap4fw.html, p.13.

COPS and Homeland Security. COPS Fact Sheet. Washington, DC: Office of Community Oriented Policing Services.

Cunningham, William Scott; Renauer, Brian C.; and Khalifa, Christy. "Sharing the Keys to the Courthouse: Adoption of Community Prosecution by State Court Prosecutors." *Journal of Contemporary Criminal Justice,* August 2006, pp.202–219.

Dodge, Mary. "The State of Research on Policing and Crime Prevention: Expanding Roles and Responses." *Criminal Justice Research Reports,* July/August 2006, pp.84–85.

Doniger, Kate. "Inspiring the Judiciary: Community Courts Adapt Community Policing Principles." *Community Policing Dispatch*, February 2009.

A Dream Denied: The Criminalization of Homelessness in U.S. Cities. A Report by the National Coalition for the Homeless and the National Law Center on Homelessness and Poverty, January 2006.

Fahim, Mayraj. "Local Voters Are Not Convinced That Big Is Better." City Mayor Government Web site:www.citymayors.com/government/mergers_locgov.html.

"Feds Push Efforts to House the Homeless." *American City & County*, August 2, 2006.

Hayes, Heather. "How 311 Works." *Federal Computer Week*, February 1, 2008.

Hess, Kären M. and Orthmann, Christine Hess. *Introduction to Law Enforcement and Criminal Justice*, 9th ed. Clifton Park, NY: Delmar, 2009.

Jansen, Steven and Dague, Ellen. "Working with a Neighborhood Community Prosecutor." *The Police Chief*, July 2006, pp.40–44.

Kelling, George L. and Bratton, William J. "Policing Terrorism." *Civic Bulletin*, September 2006.

Malvestuto, Robert J. and Snyder, Frank M. "Office of the Chief Probation Officers." In *2005 Annual Report*. Online: http://courts.phila.gov/pdf/report/2005appd.pdf, accessed September 27, 2006.

Mazerolle, Lorraine; Rogan, Dennis; Frank, James; Famega, Christine; and Eck, John E. *Managing Calls to the Police with 911/311 Systems*. Washington, DC: National Institute of Justice, February 2005. (NCJ 206256)

Moulder, Evelina. "311 Survey: Customer Service Systems Spread to Smaller Cities and Counties." Washington, DC: International City/County Management Association (ICMA), May 13, 2008.

Offenders Re-entering the Austin Community. New York: Center for Court Innovation. Online: www.courtinnovation.org, accessed September 22, 2006.

Office of Community Oriented Policing Services Web site: http://www.cops.usdoj.gov/default.asp?Item=478, accessed October 14, 2009.

Perry, Steven W. *Prosecutors in State Courts, 2005.* Washington, DC: Bureau of Justice Statistics, July 2006. (NCJ 213799)

Policy Paper: Private Security/Public Policing Partnerships. Washington, DC: Community Oriented Policing Services, 2004.

Pope, Jacqueline; Jones, Tena; Cook, Shannon; and Waltrip, Bill. "Citizen's Police Academies: Beliefs and Perceptions Regarding the Program." *Applied Psychology in Criminal Justice*, 2007, pp.42–53.

Shapiro, Ari. "Holder's Prosecution Program a Model for Justice?" National Public Radio, April 8, 2009.

Understanding Community Policing: A Framework for Action. Monograph. Washington, DC: Bureau of Justice Assistance, August 1994. Available online: http://www.ncjrs.gov/txtfiles/commp.txt.

Velazquez, Sonia E.; Garcia, Michelle; Joyce, Elizabeth. "Mobilizing a Community Response to Stalking: The Philadelphia Story." *The Police Chief*, January 2009, pp.30–37.

Volunteer Programs: Enhancing Public Safety by Leveraging Resources. Washington, DC: Volunteers in Police Service and the Bureau of Justice Assistance, no date.

Volunteers in Police Service (VIPS). Online: www.policevolunteers.org.

Wolf, Robert V. "Community Justice around the Globe: An International Overview." *Crime & Justice International*, July/August 2006a, Vol.22, No.93, Special Issue.

Wolf, Robert V. *How Do We Pay for That? Sustaining Community Prosecution on a Tight Budget.* New York: Center for Court Innovation, 2006b.

Wolf, Robert V. "Interview with Mike Kuykendall, Vice President of Central City/Downtown Services, Portland Business Alliance." New York: Center for Court Innovation. Online: www.courtinnovation.org/index.cfm?fuseaction5Document.viewDocument&documentID5572&documentTopicID526&documentTypeID58, accessed September 22, 2006.

Wolf, Robert V. and Worrall, John J. *Lessons from the Field: Ten Community Prosecution Leadership Profiles.* Alexandria, VA: American Prosecutors Research Institute, November 2004.

CHAPTER 9

Early Experiments in Crime Prevention and the Evolution of Community Policing Strategies

DO YOU KNOW . . .

○ What the most commonly implemented crime prevention programs have traditionally been?

○ What types of special crime watches have been used?

○ What organizations have concentrated their efforts on community crime prevention?

○ How volunteers have been used in crime prevention?

○ What traditional programs for youths have promoted positive police-community relations and enhanced crime prevention efforts?

○ What a police–school liaison program is? What its dual goals are?

○ What the most common strategies used in community policing have traditionally been?

○ What was demonstrated in studies of community policing in Flint? Newark? Oakland? San Diego? Houston? Boston? Baltimore County?

○ What was demonstrated in studies of community crime prevention programs in Seattle, Portland and Hartford?

○ What the CPTED Commercial Demonstration Project in Portland found?

○ What components of the criminal justice system can help reduce the crime problem?

○ What court-based approaches have proved effective?

○ How successful the McGruff national campaign was?

○ What characteristics of several exemplary police-community strategies are?

○ What impediments might hinder implementing community policing?

> **Don't be afraid to take a big step if one is indicated. You can't cross a chasm in two small jumps.**
>
> —*David Lloyd George, former prime minister of England*

CAN YOU DEFINE . . .

CPTED	Guardian Angels	PSAs
DARE	PAL	qualitative
empirical study	police–school liaison program	evaluations

Introduction

Community involvement with and assistance in accomplishing the mission of law enforcement is becoming widely accepted. The change toward community involvement is illustrated in a change in the Portland Police Department's mission statement. The old mission statement proclaimed:

> The Bureau of Police is responsible for the preservation of the public peace, protection of the rights of persons and property, the prevention of crime, and the enforcement of all Federal laws, Oregon state statutes and city ordinances within the boundaries of the City of Portland.

The new mission, in contrast, is:

> To work with all citizens to preserve life, maintain human rights, protect property and promote individual responsibility and community commitment.

The change from traditional policing to community involvement does require many chiefs of police and their officers to take risks. Are the results of the shift toward community policing worth the risks? This chapter reviews experiments conducted across the country to answer this question.

Although this chapter may appear somewhat dated, it is a necessary addition to document efforts during the past decades to improve crime prevention strategies and to involve citizens in such efforts. Many lessons were learned from the experiments of this time period.

The chapter begins with a look at traditional approaches to crime prevention and other effective initiatives, including traditional programs for youths. Next is a description of empirical studies in crime prevention conducted in the 1970s and 1980s, followed by a discussion of how community policing efforts may be enhanced through partnerships with the other elements of the criminal

Police officers, state police and city officials meet on the Massachusettes Avenue Bridge to kick off National Night Out with a "Hands Across the River" event in Boston. Officers visiting all 11 police districts in the Boston area to give Community Service Awards to residents who have helped fight crime in their neighborboods.
© AP Images/Olivia Nisbet

justice system—namely, the courts and corrections. Use of the media in crime prevention is discussed as are lessons learned from previous decades. The chapter concludes with a discussion of qualitative evaluations and salient program features, impediments to community policing and the important distinction of programs versus community policing.

Traditional Approaches to Crime Prevention

When crime prevention became popular in the late 1960s and early 1970s, many communities undertook similar types of programs. These programs have continued into the twenty-first century.

 Among the most commonly implemented crime prevention programs have been street lighting projects; property marking projects; security survey projects; citizen patrol projects; and crime reporting, neighborhood-watch or block projects.

Claims of success should be carefully examined. Critics often say that the evaluations are flawed. Indeed, research within communities is extremely difficult because:

○ Measuring what did not happen is nearly impossible.

○ Crime is usually underreported.

○ A reduction in reported crime could be the result of the crime prevention program or because the responsible criminal or criminals left town, went to jail on some other charge, died and so on.

○ Crime can be influenced by everything from seasonal and weather changes, school truancy rates and the flu, to road construction or even a change in a bus stop location. A drop in the crime rate does not necessarily mean a crime prevention program is working.

In addition, many of these programs are evaluated by people who have no training or experience in appropriate research methods; consequently, they sometimes produce flawed results.

Some also argue that crime is not prevented by programs like Neighborhood Watch; instead, they argue, crime is displaced to neighborhoods where the residents are not as likely to report suspicious activity to the police. Even if this is true, such programs do raise community awareness and have a "chilling effect" on criminals who are inhibited by those who watch and call the police.

Use of crime data to evaluate crime prevention projects poses special problems. Crime data, obviously, are limited to reported crimes. Practitioners are aware of the dark side of crime—that is, the huge amount of crime that is unreported. When projects are instituted to enlist the community in preventing crime, the citizens' heightened awareness and involvement often results in an *increase* in reported crime, but this does not necessarily mean that crime itself has actually increased.

As you read this chapter, consider the difficulties in evaluating crime prevention projects or, indeed, any project involving many diverse individuals and problems.

Street Lighting Projects

Since ancient times, lighting has been one means to deter and detect crime. Street lighting projects aimed at crime prevention through environmental design (CPTED) are important elements in a community's crime suppression efforts. Most street lighting projects seek to not only improve the likelihood of deterring and detecting crime but also to improve the safety of law-abiding citizens. Available research indicates that street lighting does not decrease the incidence of crime in participating target areas but that it is useful to reduce citizens' fear of crime and increase their feelings of security.

Property Identification Projects

Often referred to as "Operation Identification" or "O-I" projects, property identification is aimed at deterring burglary and at returning property that is stolen when deterrence fails. Most property identification projects provide citizens with instructions, a marking tool and a unique number to be applied to all valuable items within a household. Stickers are provided to homeowners to display on windows and doors warning possible burglars that the residents have marked their valuables and they are on record with the police. In addition to its deterrent effect, the property identification program also helps police track the source of stolen goods and return stolen property to its rightful owners.

It is sometimes difficult to get people to participate in the program. In addition, although the burglary rate may drop for those enrolled in the program, it may not drop citywide. There is no evidence available to suggest a difference in the number of apprehended or convicted burglars in communities that do or do not participate in the program.

Crime Prevention Security Surveys

Crime prevention user and security surveys are also usually an integral part of projects that focus on the environmental design of facilities and on "target hardening" as a means to deter or prevent crime. Such surveys can reveal opportunities for improvement or that people are afraid to use a particular place because of high levels of victimization due to low lighting or because such locations are isolated, confining or deserted. Surveys used to determine the effectiveness of the existing environmental design are usually conducted by police officers specially trained in this area. They do comprehensive on-site inspection of homes, apartments and businesses. Of particular interest are doors, windows, locks, lighting and shrubbery that might be used to a burglar's advantage. The officer suggests specific ways to make a location more secure. Zahm (2007) explains the approach typically taken in CPTED:

> Crime prevention through environmental design (**CPTED**) is an approach to problem solving that asks what is it about this location that places people at risk, or that results in opportunities for crime? In other words, *why here*? Three case examples will illustrate this point:
>
> **Case #1:** Custodial workers routinely find evidence of smoking, drinking and vandalism in a high school lavatory.

CPTED

Crime Prevention through Environmental Design—altering the physical environment to enhance safety, reduce the incidence and fear of crime and improve the quality of life.

Why here? The lavatory is in an isolated area of the building, adjacent to a ticket booth and concession stand that are active only during athletic events. The school's open lunch policy allows students to eat anywhere on campus, while monitors are assigned only to the cafeteria.

CPTED response: A lock is installed on the lavatory door, and it remains locked unless there is an athletic event. The open lunch policy has been revised: students are still allowed to leave the cafeteria but must eat in designated areas, and a faculty member is charged with patrolling these areas during lunch periods.

Case #2: The back wall of a building in an office center is repeatedly tagged with graffiti.

Why here? The taggers have selected an area that is out of the view of passers-by: a rear corner location where two buildings come together at the end of a poorly lit service lane. Visibility is further reduced by hedges at the site's perimeter. Businesses in the office center are open from 9 AM to 5 PM during the week; however, the tagged building is next to a roller skating rink where activity peaks at night and on weekends.

CPTED response: Hedges are trimmed and wall-mounted light fixtures installed along the service lane, with motion detection lighting in the problem area. The skating rink agrees to change to a "no re-admission" policy to keep skaters inside the building and away from the office property.

Case #3: ATM patrons at a bank are being robbed after dark.

Why here? The bank is situated along a commercial strip in a neighborhood with vacant properties and abandoned businesses. The ATM is in the front corner of the bank building, and the drive-through teller windows are at the side of the building, around the corner from the ATM. Robbers hide in the darkened drive-through teller area and attack unsuspecting ATM users after they complete a transaction.

CPTED response: The bank installs a fence at the corner of the building, creating a barrier between the ATM and the drive-through teller area.

In each of these case examples, asking *why here?* reveals that opportunities for crime and other problems arise out of a variety of environmental conditions related to the building, the site and the location and how the place is used. Solving a problem thus requires a detailed understanding of both crime and place, and the response should consider one of the three objectives of crime prevention through environmental design: control access, provide opportunities to see and be seen, or define ownership and encourage the maintenance of territory. ... Crime Prevention Through Environmental Design is an approach to problem-solving that considers environmental conditions and the opportunities they offer for crime or other unintended and undesirable behaviors. CPTED attempts to reduce or eliminate those opportunities by using elements of the environment to (1) control access; (2) provide opportunities to see and be seen; and (3) define ownership and encourage the maintenance of territory. ...

CPTED emerged out of research on the relationship between crime and place, theories known variously as environmental criminology, situational prevention, rational choice theory, or routine activities theory, among others. Each theoretical approach focuses on the crime event and how a criminal offender understands and uses the environment to commit a crime.

CPTED is unusual when compared with some police activities because it encourages prevention and considers design and place, while policing has traditionally valued an efficient and effective response to incidents, and identifying and arresting offenders.

Citizen Patrol Projects

Many variations of citizen patrol exist in the United States. Some are directed at a specific problem such as crack houses and the sale of drugs in a neighborhood. Others are aimed at general crime prevention and enhanced citizen safety. Citizen patrols may operate throughout a community or may be located within a specific building or complex of buildings such as tenement houses. The most successful patrols are affiliated with a larger community or neighborhood organization, sustain a working relationship with law enforcement and are flexible enough to engage in non–crime prevention activities when patrolling is patently unnecessary.

One hazard of citizen patrols is the possibility of vigilantism, which has a long, often proud, history in the United States and, indeed, in the history of law enforcement and criminal justice. Now this hazard is quite serious because of the increase of readily available handguns in our country.

guardian angels
Private citizen patrols who seek to deter crime and to provide a positive role model for young children.

Probably the best-known citizen patrol is the **Guardian Angels**, a group of private citizens who seek to deter crime and to provide a positive role model for young children. A modern expansion of the Angels is the all-volunteer Internet Safety organization. Membership in this group unites more than 1,000 users from 32 countries who police the Internet through what they call Cyberspace Neighborhood Watch. Calling themselves CyberAngels, they focus on protecting children from online abuse by fighting child pornography and advising online victims about hate mail.

The largest online safety group is WiredSafety (www.wiredsafety.org), a nonprofit organization with more than 9,000 volunteers worldwide. Calling themselves a cyber-neighborhood watch, WiredSafety provides help for online victims of cybercrime and harassment and assists law enforcement anywhere in the world in preventing and investigating cybercrimes through their affiliate, www.wiredcops.org. Volunteers are trained how to patrol the Internet in search of child pornography, child molesters and cyberstalkers.

Citizen Crime Reporting, Neighborhood or Block Programs

Citizen crime reporting programs (CCRPs) help to organize neighborhoods as mutual aid societies and as the eyes and ears of the police. Thousands of neighborhood-watch programs exist in the United States, and many describe them as the backbone of the nation's community crime prevention effort. Usually local residents hold meetings of such programs in their homes or apartments. During the meetings, neighbors get to know each other and what is normal activity for their neighborhood. They receive educational information about crime prevention from the local police department and are told how to contact the police if they see something suspicious. Signs are posted throughout the neighborhood warning possible offenders of the program. Often the programs provide safe houses for children to use if they encounter danger on their way to or from school.

Some programs work to enhance citizens' reporting capability. Whistle Stop programs, for example, provide citizens with whistles, which they can blow if they are threatened or see something requiring police intervention. Anyone hearing the whistle is to immediately call the police. Whistle Stop programs are the modern-day version of the "hue and cry." Other programs have implemented special hotlines whereby citizens can call a specific number with crime information and perhaps receive a monetary reward.

Table 9.1 illustrates the types of activities engaged in by neighborhood-watch programs and the relative popularity of each. Very few of the programs concentrate on only the "neighborhood watch." Project Operation Identification and home security surveys are by far the most common activities of neighborhood-watch programs. Street lighting programs, crime tip hotlines and physical environmental concerns are also quite common.

Table 9.1 Activities Engaged in by Neighborhood Watch Programs (Based on Program Survey Responses from over 500 Programs)

Activity	Number*	Percent
Neighborhood-watch only	49	8.9
Crime Prevention		
Specific Project Operation Identification	425	80.6
Home security surveys	357	67.9
Street lighting improvement	183	34.7
Block parenting	144	27.3
Organized surveillance	66	12.0
Traffic alteration	37	7.0
Emergency telephones	24	4.6
Project Whistle Stop	18	3.4
Specialized informal surveillance	18	3.4
Escort service	12	2.3
Hired guards	11	2.1
Environmental design	7	1.3
Lock provision/installation	4	0.7
Self-defense/rape prevention	3	0.5
Crime Related		
Crime tip hotline	197	37.5
Victim witness assistance	101	19.2
Court watch	17	3.2
Telephone chain	7	1.3
Child fingerprinting	2	0.4
Community Oriented		
Physical environmental concerns	201	38.1
Insurance premium deduction survey	20	3.6
Quality of life	9	1.6
Medical emergency	4	0.7

*Number of surveyed programs that include the activity

Source: James Garofalo and Maureen McLeod. *Improving the Use and Effectiveness of Neighborhood Watch Programs.* Washington, DC: U.S. Department of Justice, National Institute of Justice Research in Action Series, April 1988, p.2.

Ideas in Practice

FIGHTING FORECLOSURE PROBLEMS

Manhattan, Illinois

Following is an example of how police in one community tackled the problem of foreclosed properties. By encouraging frequent collaboration between stakeholders, engaging in problem-solving policing and building trust with the community, local police were able to effectively monitor foreclosed properties with the goals of preserving property values and preventing the foreclosure-related crime that had affected nearby cities, thus preserving quality of life for their citizens.

Fighting Foreclosure Problems in Manhattan, Illinois

Problem properties create more than just an eyesore. They act as a drain on police resources, create hazardous environments and lessen the quality of life for neighbors and community residents.

The Village of Manhattan, Illinois, is a residential community of about 6,897 people south of Chicago. It has more than doubled in size since 2000. With larger nearby towns facing serious foreclosure problems, Manhattan's police department and village administrators decided to take preventive action before their problem grew too large to control.

The village created a database, updated weekly, of all properties in the various stages of foreclosure. Using the database as a guide, the police department, code compliance office, public works department and finance department are responsible for a four-point approach to tracking and securing foreclosed structures: monitoring and securing the buildings; enforcing city codes; shutting off water service; and placing liens, if necessary, on delinquent accounts. Law enforcement officers regularly monitor the vacant houses, check for signs of vandalism and conduct outreach to neighbors in adjacent properties through a Neighborhood Watch program.

Village officials and the Manhattan Police Department have considered these efforts a success. After checking all vacant structures, Manhattan police found that 27 percent of the area's vacant houses were not locked. They secured the houses and, using their monitoring system, identified additional potential problem properties. Since the initiative was put into place, one concerned neighbor alerted the authorities about a distressed homeowner who was illegally stripping his house and selling all valuable construction material and appliances on Craigslist.

Source: Zoe Mentel. "Shutting the Door on Foreclosure and Drug-Related Problem Properties: Two Communities Respond to Neighborhood Disorder." *Community Policing Dispatch*, the e-Newsletter of the COPS Office. July 2009. Vol. 2, Issue 7. Online: http://www.cops.usdoj.gov/html/dispatch/July_2009/communities_respond.htm.

Special Crime Watch Programs

In addition to the traditional types of crime watch programs commonly implemented throughout the country, some communities have developed more specialized types of crime watch programs.

 Specialized crime watch programs include mobile crime watch, youth crime watch, business crime watch, apartment watch, realtor watch and carrier alert.

Honolulu's mobile crime watch enlists the aid of motorists who have CBs, car phones or cell phones. Volunteers attend a short orientation that trains them to observe and report suspicious activity. Participants also receive Mobile Watch decals for their vehicles. They are advised to call 911 if they hear screaming, gunshots, breaking glass or loud explosive noises or if they see someone breaking into a house or car, a car driven dangerously or erratically, a person on the ground apparently unconscious, anyone brandishing a gun or knife or an individual staggering or threatening others.

They are also trained to recognize and report other unusual behaviors such as children appearing lost; anyone being forced into a vehicle; cars cruising erratically and repetitively near schools, parks and playgrounds; a person running and carrying something valuable; parked, occupied vehicles at unusual hours near potential robbery sites; heavier than normal traffic in and out of a house or commercial establishment; someone going door-to-door or passing through backyards; and persons loitering around schools, parks or secluded areas or in the neighborhood.

Most successful community-based programs that focus on crime prevention or safety issues have a close partnership with law enforcement. The community and law enforcement have vital components to offer each other, making cooperation between the two highly desirable. It is difficult to imagine, for instance, an effective community-based crime watch program without input or cooperation from the local police agency. Crime watch programs are built on the premise of mutual aid—citizens and police working together.

Other Efforts to Enhance Crime Prevention

Continuing the community crime prevention momentum generated during the 1960s and 1970s, new programs were initiated during the 1980s and 1990s to encourage citizens to play an active role in reducing crime in their own neighborhoods. These initiatives have included National Night Out; the creation of organizations focused on crime prevention, such as Crime Stoppers and Mothers Against Drunk Driving (MADD); and the expanded use of volunteers.

National Night Out

National Night Out (NNO) is a program that originated in 1984 in Tempe, Arizona. Held annually on the first Tuesday of August, this nationwide program encourages residents to turn on their porch lights, go outside and meet their neighbors. Neighborhood-watch programs are encouraged to plan a party or event during National Night Out.

Since 1984, when 2.5 million people in 23 states gathered for the first NNO, the event has grown significantly. In 2008 over 37 million people in over 15,000 communities located in all 50 states and a large number of U.S. territories, Canadian cities and U.S. military bases around the world gathered with police officers and administrators to celebrate the event with block parties, safety fairs, youth events, cookouts and parades (National Association of Town Watch). Some neighborhoods also use NNO as an opportunity to collect food for the local food shelf or "gently worn" clothing for a local shelter for homeless people or battered women.

Organizations Focused on Crime Prevention

Among the most visible organizations focused on crime are citizen crime prevention associations, Crime Stoppers and MADD.

Citizen Crime Prevention Associations The many activities undertaken by citizen crime prevention associations include paying for crime tips; funding for police–crime prevention programs; supporting police canine programs; raising community awareness through crime prevention seminars, newsletters, cable TV shows and booths; providing teddy bears for kids; raising money through sources such as business contributions, membership fees, charitable gambling and sales of alarms, mace and "Call Police" signs (usually sold as a service to a community, not to raise any substantial money); and funding specific programs such as rewards to community members who call the hotline with crime information.

Crime Stoppers Crime Stoppers is a nonprofit program involving citizens, the media and the police. Local programs offer anonymity and cash rewards to people who furnish police information that leads to the arrest and indictment of felony offenders. Each program is governed by a local board of directors made up of citizens from a cross section of the community, the businesses of the community and law enforcement. The reward money comes from tax-deductible donations and grants from local businesses, foundations and individuals.

When a crime-related call is received by Crime Stoppers, it is logged in with the date, time and a summary of the information given by the caller. Callers are given code numbers to be used on all subsequent calls by the same person regarding that particular case. Each week, one unsolved crime is selected for special treatment by the media. Over 850 programs throughout the United States, Canada, Australia, England and West Africa are members of Crime Stoppers International.

Mothers Against Drunk Driving MADD is a nonprofit, grassroots organization with more than 400 chapters nationwide and, in 2005, approximately two million members and supporters ("25 Years of Saving Lives," 2005, p.17). Its membership is open to anyone: victims, concerned citizens, law enforcement officers, safety workers and health professionals. As noted in their literature: "The mission of Mothers Against Drunk Driving is to stop drunk driving and to support victims of this violent crime."

MADD was founded in California in 1980 after Candy Lightner's 13-year-old daughter was killed by a hit-and-run driver. The driver had been out of jail on bail for only 2 days for another hit-and-run drunk driving crash. He had three previous drunk driving arrests and two convictions; but he was allowed to plea bargain to vehicular manslaughter. His 2-year prison sentence was spent not in prison but in a work camp and later a halfway house. MADD differentiates between accidents and crashes:

> Those injured and killed in drunk driving collisions are not "accident victims." The crash caused by an impaired driver is a violent crime. Drunk driving involves two choices: to drink AND to drive. The thousands of deaths and injuries caused each year by impaired driving can be prevented ... they are not "accidental" ("Help Keep Families Together," n.d., p.2).

MADD seeks to raise public awareness through community programs such as Operation Prom/Graduation, their poster/essay contest, their "Tie One on for Safety" Project Red Ribbon campaign and a Designated Driver program. Their national newsletter, "MADD in Action," is sent to members and supporters. MADD also promotes legislation to strengthen existing laws and adopt new ones. In addition, MADD provides victim services. Annual candlelight vigils are held nationwide to allow victims to share their grief with others who have suffered loss resulting from drunk driving.

According to the Centers for Disease Control and Prevention, 13,470 people were killed in alcohol-impaired driving crashes in 2006 ("Impaired Driving," n.d.). That is nearly one-third of all traffic-related deaths in the United States. When MADD was formed in 1980, approximately 30,000 people a year were killed by drunk drivers ("MADD Reports DUI Deaths Up").

Using Volunteers

Many police departments make extensive use of volunteers.

 Volunteers may serve as reserve officers, auxiliary patrol or community service officers or on an as-needed basis.

Reserve officers, auxiliary patrol or community service officers (CSOs) usually wear uniforms and badges but are unarmed. However, in some departments, reserve officers are armed and receive the same training as sworn officers. They are trained to perform specific functions that assist the uniformed patrol officers. They may be used to patrol watching for suspicious activity; to direct traffic; to conduct interviews with victims of and witnesses to crimes; and to provide crime prevention education at neighborhood watch meetings, civic groups, churches and schools.

CSOs may work with youths to prevent delinquency, refer citizen complaints to the appropriate agency and investigate minor thefts. They are usually heavily involved in public relations activities as well. Some CSOs are paid, but it is much less than police officers. Many departments ask professionals such as physicians, teachers and ministers to volunteer their services, sometimes as expert witnesses.

Often, volunteers perform office functions in police departments, such as conducting tours or answering telephone messages. They might also provide assistance to police at crime prevention programs and neighborhood-watch meetings. Many departments use the American Association of Retired People (AARP) volunteer program, capitalizing on the experience and free time of the elderly citizens of the community.

Volunteers provide a communication link between the citizens and the police department. They can help establish the credibility of the department's public relations and educational efforts. Volunteers provide additional sources of information and perspectives.

Using volunteers may, however, cause certain problems. In fact, some police officers feel volunteers are more trouble than they are worth. Among the reasons commonly given for not using volunteers are that they sometimes lack sensitivity to minorities; some citizens seek profit and gain for themselves and develop programs that are mere window dressing; some citizens lack qualifications and training; because volunteers receive no pay, they cannot be docked or penalized for poor performance; citizens lack awareness of the criminal justice system in general and specific agencies in particular; and the use of volunteers by some departments has led to the failure of the local communities and politicians to take responsibility for solving the larger social problem and/or the refusal to hire adequate numbers of personnel or pay better wages.

In addition, some police unions have reacted negatively to volunteers, who are sometimes viewed as competitors for police jobs. Reserve officers, in particular, tend to cause patrol officers to feel their jobs are threatened by those willing to do police jobs for free or at greatly reduced pay. Officers should know that programs using volunteers are those that could not otherwise exist because of lack of personnel and funding.

ON THE BEAT

Many effective crime prevention programs are used by police departments across the United States. In our department, we have everything from the Neighborhood Watch program to Police Explorer and Reserve Officer programs. School liaison officers are placed in schools to develop positive police–youth relationships, and officers also go out into the community and help youth with their homework or play kickball or basketball with them. All of these components are important in reducing the incidence of crime and connecting with the community we serve.

Without engaging community members in police initiatives it can be next to impos-

sible to have success with a program. For example, without *community* block captains to facilitate neighborhood watches, there would be no Neighborhood Watch program. Without *community* volunteers to be police reserve officers, there would not be a volunteer Police Reserve program. Without *citizen* interest in the daily efforts of police officers, there would not be a successful Citizen's Academy program. Volunteers from the community are an important asset to any police department, and crime prevention programs are much more effective when partnerships and collaborative efforts occur.

—Kim Czapar

Traditional Programs for Youths

Youths have traditionally been included in police–community relations efforts and crime prevention initiatives in several ways.

Common programs aimed at youths include the McGruff "Take a Bite Out of Crime" campaign, police athletic leagues (PALs), Officer Friendly, police explorers, police-school liaison programs and the DARE program.

Other efforts have included school safety programs, bicycle safety programs and programs to fingerprint young children. In different localities, police have developed variations of many of these programs. (Chapter 12 is devoted entirely to projects and programs aimed at youths.)

The McGruff "Take a Bite Out of Crime" Program

The traditional McGruff as a crime prevention spokesperson program, for example, has expanded in some areas to include McGruff Houses, which are safe havens for young children. Another expansion is the McGruff crime dog robot developed by Robotronics. Operated by remote control, the robot winks, blinks, moves his hands and arms, tips and turns his head and has a two-way wireless voice system allowing the operator to talk and listen. The McGruff media campaign is discussed in greater detail later in this chapter.

Police Athletic Leagues

Police departments have also expanded on the National Police Athletic League **(PAL)** program. PAL, now more than 50 years old, was developed to provide opportunities for youths to interact with police officers in gyms or ballparks instead of in a juvenile detention hall.

Each PAL program is unique. For example, officers of the Portland (Oregon) Police Bureau joined with community members and civic leaders to start a PAL dedicated to providing recreational, athletic and educational programs for at-risk youths (www.portlandonline.com).

To accomplish their goals of reducing gang membership and youth violence in the community, reducing the street sale of drugs and providing youth with prosocial opportunities, the department undertook several activities, including a weeklong Sport Quickness Day Camp for 600 at-risk youths. The camp kept the youths productively occupied for 8 hours a day in boxing, wrestling, football, soccer, martial arts, basketball, racquetball, track and field, volleyball and speed and quickness training. The department also organized events in which officers could participate with PAL youths, including a 1-day fishing excursion and trips to Seattle Sea Hawks football games, and provided scholarships to summer camps.

> **PAL (Police Athletic League)**
> Developed to provide opportunities for youths to interact with police officers in gyms or ballparks instead of in a juvenile detention hall.

Officer Friendly

Officer Friendly programs are designed for elementary school children and generally include a police officer who goes into classes to discuss good citizenship, responsibility and general safety. The program uses coloring books and a special activity book that teachers can use with their regular social studies curriculum.

Police Explorers

The traditional police explorer program is affiliated with the Boy Scouts of America, but participants do not have to work their way up through the scouting program. Exploring is for teens (both males and females) to provide them an opportunity to "explore" a possible future career. Explorers usually are trained in various aspects of police work such as fingerprinting, identification techniques, first aid and firearms safety. The minimum age for most programs is 15. Explorers usually have a 3- to 6-month probation, with full membership contingent on completing training and meeting proficiency standards as well as acceptable personal conduct.

Explorer programs have two purposes: positive community relations and early recruitment for police departments. Some departments, in fact, make even greater use of their explorer programs. The Chandler (Arizona) Police Department, for example, used two 18-year-old explorers in a sting operation involving a bar and liquor store's employees who sold alcohol to minors.

Many programs for juveniles involve the schools, which have historically been charged with instilling discipline in the students who attend.

Police–School Liaison Programs

In 1958 Flint, Michigan, developed a highly publicized delinquency prevention program involving joint efforts of school authorities, parents, businesses, social agencies, the juvenile court and the police department. Known as a school liaison program, it became widely replicated across the country.

police–school liaison program

Places an officer in a school to work with school authorities, parents and students to prevent crime and antisocial behavior and to improve police-youth relationships.

 A **police–school liaison program** places an officer in a school to work with school authorities, parents and students to prevent crime and anti-social behavior and to improve police-youth relationships.

The goals of most police–school liaison programs are to reduce crime incidents involving school-age youths, to suppress by enforcement of the law any illegal threats that endanger the children's educational environment and to improve the attitudes of school-age youths and the police toward one another.

Police–school liaison officers do not get involved in school politics or in enforcing school regulations. The school administrators are involved in these matters.

 The joint goals of most police-school liaison programs are to prevent juvenile delinquency and to improve police-youth relations.

The police–school liaison programs can also do much to promote better relations among the police, school administrators and teachers. A number of organizations can focus attention on school–police relations and provide supportive programs both on the local and national levels—for example, the International Association of Chiefs of Police, the National Association of Secondary School Principals and the National Association of School Boards.

Drug use is often a target of police educational programs. Frequently, officers work with schools to develop and promote programs aimed at preventing drug and alcohol abuse, one of the most popular of which is DARE.

The DARE Program

DARE

Drug Abuse Resistance Education—a program aimed at elementary-age school children, seeking to teach them to "say no to drugs."

The Drug Abuse Resistance Education **(DARE)** program was developed jointly by the Los Angeles Police Department and the Los Angeles Unified School District. This controversial program is aimed at elementary school children and seeks to teach them to "say no to drugs," to resist peer pressure and to find alternatives to drug use. The program uses a "self-esteem repair" approach.

The founder and president of DARE America concedes the program is not a "magic bullet" but believes it is a valuable part of the big picture and is confident it helps reduce drug use. Based on research findings, the program has been completely revised. The current program is discussed in Chapter 11.

In recent years, schools across the country have dropped DARE programs, although they still remain popular with parents, teachers and some police officers.

Teachers liked DARE because they felt uncomfortable tackling the topic themselves and because they got a break. Parents liked it because they felt their children would listen to police officers. Unfortunately, they did not. A string of academic studies labeled DARE pointless at best. Some academics—and former drug-takers—argue that efforts to scare young children about drugs that they may not have heard of are actually counterproductive. The federal government opted not to pay for the program. It survives (DARE claims it is still used in 72 percent of America's school districts), but in an altered form. It has even been dropped by the Los Angeles school district, where it began ("In America, Lessons Learned," 2009).

During the 1980s many of these early strategies and programs were adopted by departments moving toward community policing. Also during this time, many departments began experimenting with a variety of community policing strategies.

As evidenced by numerous studies, some strategies were successful; others were not.

Reducing Fear of Crime with Video Surveillance of Public Places

Many studies have tried to determine if closed-circuit television (CCTV) in public places reduces the fear of crime in those who use the areas. These studies looked at whether consumer buying increases in areas with CCTV systems; the basis was the belief that an area benefits from a positive economic impact when people feel safer. Although the findings are mixed, they generally show a somewhat reduced level of fear of crime among people in CCTV areas but *only* if those surveyed were aware they were in an area under surveillance. Most of the studies found that less than half of the interviewees were aware that they were in a CCTV area. Reduced fear of crime may increase the number of people using an area, and this, in turn, may increase the level of natural surveillance. It may also encourage people to be more security conscious (Ratcliffe, 2006, pp.3–4). Because of this, relying on CCTV to reduce fear of crime may require a significant and ongoing publicity campaign (p.9).

One unintended consequence of using CCTV is the possibility of a negative public response to the cameras' existence (pp.5–6):

> In one survey, one-third of respondents felt that one purpose of CCTV was "to spy on people." In other surveys, some city managers were reluctant to advertise the cameras or have overt CCTV systems for fear they would make shoppers and consumers more fearful. In other words, it is hoped that most citizens will feel safer under the watchful eye of the cameras, but CCTV may have the reverse effect on some people.

> Remember that the primary crime prevention mechanism appears to work by increasing a perception of risk in the offender. With their reluctance to advertise the system, some city managers may be inadvertently reducing the cameras' effectiveness. By failing to advertise the cameras' presence, fewer offenders will be aware of the system and so will not perceive an increase in risk. On the whole, however, the public appears to be strongly in favor of a properly managed surveillance system for public areas.

Appendix A presents the results of a large UK Home Office study on the effect of CCTV use implemented in 14 separate systems in a variety of ways, including at a public car park, in town centers, in residential areas and housing estates and in hospital areas.

Empirical Studies of Community Policing

empirical study

Research based on observation or practical experience.

An **empirical study** is based on observation or practical experience. Greene and Taylor (1991, pp.206–221) describe studies of community policing in major cities throughout the country, including Flint, Newark, Oakland, San Diego, Houston, Boston and Baltimore County.

> The most common strategies traditionally used in community policing were foot patrol, newsletters and community organizing.

Flint, Michigan, Neighborhood Foot Patrol Program

The classic Neighborhood Foot Patrol Program of Flint, Michigan, was conducted from January 1979 to January 1982. It focused on 14 experimental neighborhoods to which 22 police officers and 3 supervisors were assigned. The officers were given great discretion in what they could do while on foot patrol, but communication with citizens was a primary objective.

> The Flint Neighborhood Foot Patrol Program appeared to decrease crime, increase general citizen satisfaction with the foot patrol program, reduce citizens' fear of crime and create a positive perception of the foot patrol officers.

The Flint study tried to document what police did on foot patrol and how that differed from motorized patrol (Mastrofski, 1992, p.24):

> Looking at the department's daily report forms, the researchers found that foot officers reported many more self-initiated activities—such as home and business visits and security checks—than police in cars. Officers on foot averaged much higher levels of productivity across most of the standard performance measures: arrests, investigations, stopping of suspicious persons, parking citations and value of recovered property. The only category in which motor patrol officers clearly outproduced their foot patrol counterparts was in providing miscellaneous services to citizens.

According to citizen surveys (Trojanowicz, 1986, pp.165–167), 64 percent were satisfied with the project and 68 percent felt safer. When asked to compare foot patrol and motorized patrol officers, citizens rated the foot patrol officers higher by large margins in four of the six areas: preventing crime, encouraging citizen self-protection, working with juveniles and following up on complaints. Motorized patrol officers were rated superior only in responding to complaints. In addition, in the foot patrol neighborhoods, crime rates were down markedly and calls for service were down more than 40 percent.

No statistical tests were done, however, and results across the 14 neighborhoods varied greatly. Therefore, the results should be interpreted with caution. In addition, problems were encountered in the Flint Foot Patrol Program. For example, because the program was loosely structured, some officers were not accountable, and their job performance was poor. Nonetheless, according to Skolnick and Bayley (1986, p.216):

> Foot patrol ... appears from our observations and other studies to generate four meritorious effects. (1) Since there is a concerned human presence on the street, foot patrol is more adaptable to street happenings, and thus may prevent crime before it begins. (2) Foot patrol officers may make arrests, but they are also around to give warnings either directly or indirectly, merely through their presence. (3) Properly carried out, foot patrol generates goodwill in the neighborhood, which has the derivative consequence of making other crime prevention tactics more effective. This effectiveness in turn tends to raise citizen morale and reduce their fear of crime. (4) Foot patrol seems to raise officer morale.

First Newark, New Jersey, Foot Patrol Experiment

The original Newark Foot Patrol Experiment was done between 1978 and 1979 and addressed the issues of untended property and untended behavior. This experiment used 12 patrol beats. Eight of the beats, identified as using foot patrol, were divided into pairs, matched by the number of residential and nonresidential units in each. One beat in each pair dropped foot patrol. An additional four beats that had not previously used foot patrol added foot patrol officers. As in the Flint experiment, officers had great flexibility in their job responsibilities while on foot patrol.

 In the first Newark Foot Patrol Experiment, residents reported positive results, whereas business owners reported negative results.

In areas where foot patrol was added, residents reported a decrease in the severity of crime and evaluated police performance more positively. Business owners, however, believed that street disorder and publicly visible crime increased and reported that the neighborhood had become worse. Pate (1986, p.155) summarizes the results of the first experiment.

> The addition of intensive foot patrol coverage to relatively short (8- to 16-block) commercial/residential strips during five evenings per week over a one-year period can have considerable effects on the perceptions of residents concerning disorder problems, crime problems, the likelihood of crime, safety and police service. Such additional patrol, however, appears to have no significant effect on victimization, recorded crime or the likelihood of reporting a crime.

> The elimination of foot patrol after years of maintenance, however, appears to produce few notable negative effects. Similarly, the retention of foot patrol does not prove to have notable beneficial effects.

Second Newark, New Jersey, Foot Patrol Experiment

A second foot patrol experiment was conducted in Newark in 1983 and 1984. This experiment used three neighborhoods and a control group (which received no "treatment").

The second Newark Foot Patrol Experiment included a coordinated foot patrol, a cleanup campaign and distribution of a newsletter. Only the coordinated foot patrol was perceived to reduce the perception of property crime and improve assessments of the police.

The cleanup effort and newsletter programs did not affect any of the outcome measures studied, nor did they reduce crime rates.

Oakland, California, Foot Patrol Program

In 1983, Oakland assigned 28 officers to foot patrol in its central business district. In addition, a Report Incidents Directly program was established whereby local businesspeople could talk directly to the patrol officers about any matters that concerned them. Mounted patrols and small vehicle patrols were also used.

The Oakland program, using foot patrol, mounted patrol, small vehicle patrol and a Report Incidents Directly program, resulted in a substantial drop in the rate of crime against individuals and their property.

The crime rate dropped in the Oakland treatment area more than citywide declines, but again, no statistical tests were reported for this experiment.

San Diego, California, Community Profile Project

San Diego conducted a community profile project from 1973 to 1974 designed to improve police–community interactions. Twenty-four patrol officers and three supervisors were given 60 hours of community orientation training. The performance of these officers was compared with 24 other patrol officers who did not receive the training.

The San Diego Community Profile Project provided patrol officers with extensive community-orientation training. These officers became more service oriented, increased their non-law enforcement contacts with citizens and had a more positive attitude toward police–community relations.

The project did not consider the effect of community profiling on crime or on citizens' fear of crime.

Houston, Texas, Fear-Reduction Project

Like the second Newark experiment, Houston conducted a fear-reduction experiment between 1983 and 1984, testing five strategies: a victim recontact program following victimization, a community newsletter, a citizen contact patrol program, a police storefront office and a program aimed to organize the community's interest in crime prevention.

The victim recontact program and the newsletter of the Houston Fear-Reduction Project did not have positive results. In fact, the victim recontact program backfired, with Hispanics and Asians experiencing an increase in fear. Contact was primarily with white homeowners rather than minority renters. The citizen contact patrol and the police storefront office did, however, result in decreases in perceptions of social disorder, fear of personal victimization and the level of personal and property crime.

The police storefront officers developed several programs, including monthly meetings, school programs, a fingerprinting program, a blood pressure program, a ride-along program, a park program and an anticrime newsletter (Skogan and Wycoff, 1986, pp.182–183).

Boston Foot Patrol Project

In 1983 Boston changed from predominantly two-officer motorized patrol to foot patrol and shifted the responsibilities of the foot patrol and motorized one-officer patrol to less serious crimes and noncrime service calls. The experiment studied 105 beats to determine whether high, medium, low, unstaffed or no change in foot patrol affected calls for service by priority.

The Boston Foot Patrol Project found no statistically significant relationship between changes in the level of foot patrol provided and the number of calls for service or the seriousness of the calls.

Violent crimes were not affected by increased or decreased foot patrol staffing. After the department shifted to foot patrol, the number of street robberies decreased but the number of commercial robberies increased.

Baltimore County Citizen Oriented Police Enforcement Project

The Baltimore Citizen Oriented Police Enforcement (COPE) Project, started in 1981, focused on the reduction of citizens' fear of crime. This problem-oriented project focused on solving the community problems of fear and disorder that lead to crime: "'Citizen Oriented Police Enforcement' officers would engage in intensive patrol, develop close contacts with citizens, conduct 'fear surveys' (door-to-door canvassing to identify concerns) and use any means within their power to quell fear" (Taft, 1986, p.10).

Baltimore County's COPE Project reduced fear of crime by 10 percent and crime itself by 12 percent in target neighborhoods. It also reduced calls for service; increased citizen awareness of and satisfaction with the police; and improved police officer attitudes.

A study conducted in 1985 indicated that the COPE Project "passed its first statistical test with flying colors" (Taft, p.20). The results of the study are summarized in Figure 9.1.

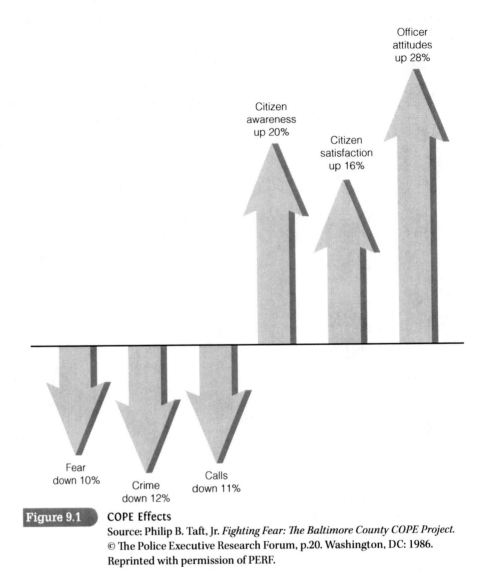

Figure 9.1 COPE Effects

Source: Philip B. Taft, Jr. *Fighting Fear: The Baltimore County COPE Project.*
© The Police Executive Research Forum, p.20. Washington, DC: 1986.
Reprinted with permission of PERF.

Summary and Implications of the Experiments

There is considerable inconsistency in findings across these studies (Greene and Taylor, p.215). Regarding fear of crime, the first Newark project observed a reduction and the second Newark project showed a reduction in the panel analysis (where the data were analyzed by individuals responding) but did not show a reduction in the cross-sectional analysis (where the data were analyzed by area rather than by individuals responding). The Houston study had the opposite results: a reduction in fear in the cross-sectional analysis but not in the panel analysis. In the Flint study, citizen perceptions of the seriousness of crime problems increased. In Baltimore County, fear of crime declined slightly. The San Diego, Oakland and Boston programs did not consider fear of crime. Greene and Taylor (p.216) conclude: "Based on the problems associated with the evaluation of each of these programs, there is at present no consistent evidence that foot patrol reduces fear of crime."

Greene and Taylor also note inconsistent findings regarding crime rates. The Oakland study was the only one to demonstrate a reduction, but no statistical treatment was done. Again they (p.216) conclude: "Clearly, these studies do not point to decreases in crime or disorder as a consequence of community policing or foot patrol."

Greene and Taylor discuss several problems with the research designs of the eight studies of community policing and suggest ways to improve the designs. This is not the view taken by Wycoff (1991, p.103), however, who states that the fear-reduction studies conducted in Houston and Newark "provide evidence of the efficacy of what the authors referred to as 'community-oriented' policing strategies for reducing citizen fear, improving citizens' attitudes toward their neighborhoods and toward the police and reducing crime."

Fear-Reduction Strategies Experiments Compared

Wycoff (pp.107–108) summarizes the seven strategies tested in the Newark and Houston experiments as follows:

Newsletters (Houston and Newark). These were tested with and without crime statistics. They were police produced and provided residents of the test area with information about crime prevention steps they could take, the police department and police programs in their area.

Victim recontact (Houston). Patrol officers made telephone contact with victims to inform them of the status of their case, inquire whether they needed assistance, offer to send crime prevention information, and ask whether victims could provide additional information.

Police community station (Houston). A neighborhood storefront operation was conducted by patrol officers. The station provided a variety of services for the area.

Citizen contact patrol (Houston). Officers concentrated their patrol time within the target area where they made door-to-door contacts, introducing themselves to residents and businesspeople and asking whether there were any neighborhood problems citizens wished brought to the attention of the police.

Community organizing (Houston). Officers from the Community Services Division worked to organize block meetings attended by area patrol officers. They organized a neighborhood committee that met monthly with the district captain and developed special projects ("safe" houses for children, identifying property and a cleanup campaign) for the area.

Signs of crime (Newark). This program focused on social disorder and conducted "random intensified enforcement and order maintenance operations" (e.g., foot patrol to enforce laws and maintain order on sidewalks and street corners, radar checks, bus checks to enforce ordinances and order, enforcement of disorderly conduct laws to move groups off the street corners and road checks for DWI, improper licenses or stolen vehicles). Addressing physical deterioration involved an intensification of city services and the use of juvenile offenders to conduct cleanup work in the target areas.

Coordinated community policing (Newark). This was the "kitchen sink" project that included a neighborhood community police center, a directed police–citizen contact program, a neighborhood police newsletter, intensified law enforcement and order maintenance and a neighborhood cleanup.

Other Crime Prevention Program Studies in the 1980s

Several communities conducted crime prevention studies in the 1980s. Studies in Seattle, Portland and Hartford focused on citizen efforts to prevent residential crime; the study in Portland also focused on preventing crime in and around commercial establishments. Two studies examined the media and crime prevention: the McGruff national media campaign and the effectiveness of anticrime newsletters.

According to Heinzelmann (1986, p.7): "In general, the results of these evaluations are favorable, indicating that community crime prevention programs can serve to reduce crime and fear, and at the same time improve the quality of life and the economic viability of urban neighborhoods and commercial settings."

The Seattle Program

The Citywide Crime Prevention Program (CCPP) of Seattle, described by Lindsay and McGillis (1986, pp.46–67), focused on residential burglaries and included three primary police services: property identification, home security checks and organizing neighborhood block watch programs.

 The Seattle Citywide Crime Prevention Program used property identification, home security checks and neighborhood block watches to significantly reduce the residential burglary rate as well as the number of burglary-in-progress calls.

Fleissner and colleagues (1992, p.9) note: "When citizens and police in South Seattle banded together to fight crime, quarterly crime statistics showed dramatic improvements in the quality of life. Citizen activity spread in the city's other three police precincts; now community policing is a going concern throughout Seattle—a citywide success."

Not only did the burglary rate drop significantly, "burglary-in-progress calls as a proportion of all burglary calls to police increased significantly in treated areas, and their quality was relatively high as measured by presentation of suspect information and the occurrence of subsequent arrests" (Lindsay and McGillis, p.65).

The Portland Program

Portland also instituted a burglary prevention program, which included providing citizens with information about locks, alarms, outside lighting around entrances, removal or trimming of hedges and precautions to take while on vacation (Schneider, 1986, pp.68–86). The program also encouraged citizens to mark property with identification numbers. Door-to-door canvassing and a heavy emphasis on neighborhood rather than individual protection were important components of the program.

The Portland antiburglary program succeeded in reducing the burglary rate for those who participated.

As Schneider (p.84) notes: "In the high crime areas of Portland more than 20 percent of the homes could expect to be burglarized at least once a year. This was reduced to about 8 percent for participating households in those areas." Schneider (p.85) also points out a class bias in this study: "Those attending meetings, engraving their property and displaying the decals tended to be in the higher socioeconomic groups."

The Hartford Experiment

The Hartford Experiment used a three-pronged approach to reduce crime and the fear of crime: changing the physical environment, changing the delivery of police services and organizing the citizens to improve their neighborhoods. This experiment centered on the interdependence of citizens, the police and the environment: "The approach focuses on the interaction between human behavior and the (physically) built environment. It was hypothesized that the proper design and effective use of the built environment can lead to a reduction in crime and fear" (Fowler and Mangione, 1986, p.80).

The program was based on four previous research efforts. First was that of Jacobs (1961), which found that neighborhoods that were relatively crime free had a mix of commercial and residential properties, resulting in many people on the streets and a great opportunity for police surveillance. In addition, a community with such mixed-use property tended to have residents who cared about the neighborhood and watched out for each other.

Angel (1968) described similar findings in his concept of "critical density," which states that if quite a few people are present on the most frequently used streets, they will serve as deterrents to burglary. In addition, Newman's classic work (1972) suggests that crime can be reduced by redesigning buildings to increase the number of doorways and other spaces that could be easily observed. Finally, Repetto (1974), like Newman, found that opportunities for surveillance could reduce crime and, like Jacobs, that neighborhood cohesiveness could have the same result.

Based on this research, the Hartford Experiment focused on Asylum Hill, a residential area a few blocks from the central business district of Hartford that was rapidly deteriorating. It was found that because of the high rate of vehicle traffic, residents did not use their yards and felt no ties to the neighborhood. The physical design of the neighborhood was changed to restrict through traffic and visually define the boundaries of the neighborhood. Cul-de-sacs were built at a few critical intersections, and some streets were made one way.

A second change in the neighborhood involved patrol officer assignments. Instead of rotating assignments within a centralized department, Hartford began using a decentralized team of officers assigned permanently to the Asylum Hill area.

Finally, the Hartford Experiment helped organize the neighborhood, including the establishment of block watch programs, recreational programs for youths and improvements for a large neighborhood park.

As a result of these changes: "Residents used their neighborhood more, walked more often both during the day and evening hours, used the nearby park more often and spent more days per week outside in front of their homes" (Fowler and Mangione, p.96).

The Hartford Experiment restructured the neighborhood's physical environment, changed the way patrol officers were assigned and organized the neighborhood in an effort to reduce crime and the fear of crime.

Fowler and Mangione (p.106) caution: "A crime control program such as this must be custom fit to a particular set of circumstances. What one would want to derive from the Hartford Project is not a program design, but rather an approach to problem analysis and strategies to affect them."

San Francisco Police Department Foot Patrol Program

A more recent study of foot patrol was conducted at the San Francisco (California) Police Department (SFPD) and is reported by Rosenfeld (2008). Among the key findings were:

○ The SFPD committed significant resources to foot beat staffing. The number of hours dedicated to foot beats during the first 6 months of 2007 totaled 83,475, representing an 86 percent increase when compared to the same time period in 2006.

○ Foot patrols increase the community's perception of safety. Eighty-two percent of those responding to the telephone survey and 73 percent of those responding to the written survey felt safer as a result of foot patrols.

○ Both police staff and the community widely accept foot patrols. Seventy-nine percent of the SFPD respondents believe foot patrols are an effective tool for the department. Correspondingly, 90 percent of the community member respondents believe foot patrols are a necessary tool for the SFPD to use in addressing crime and quality of life issues.

Community Policing and the Criminal Justice System

The criminal justice system includes law enforcement, the courts and corrections. What happens in each component of the criminal justice system directly affects the other two components, and many of the trends that affect the criminal justice system as a whole directly affect the type of programs police departments should implement to improve community relations. Consequently, partnerships among the various entities within the criminal justice system are vital to achieving the community policing mission.

A coordinated effort among law enforcement, courts and corrections is required to effectively deal with the crime problem and to elicit the support of the community in doing so.

Effective efforts are those that partner various community institutions to address issues of housing, unemployment, illiteracy, lack of recreational opportunities for youths and other social problems.

Community Policing and the Courts

The way courts address the accused has a direct impact on the crime problem and on community policing efforts. The National Symposium identified two model court programs: the Albany (New York) Community Dispute Resolution Centers and the Madison (Wisconsin) Deferred Prosecution/First Offenders Unit.

 Model court programs also involving the police include community dispute resolution centers and a deferred prosecution/first offenders unit.

Community Dispute Resolution Centers (Albany) The 32 dispute resolution centers were independent, community-based, nonprofit organizations contracted by the Unified Court System of the State of New York, Albany, to (1) provide dispute resolution resources for local communities, (2) prevent escalation of disputes, (3) relieve the courts of matters not requiring judicial intervention and (4) teach individuals to resolve their problems through mediation.

Police officers, probation officers, judges, district attorneys and legal aid offices could refer cases to a local dispute resolution center, or individuals could be self-referred. The mediation, conciliation or arbitration services were provided free. Mediation rather than law enforcement or court intervention was effective.

The Deferred Prosecution/First Offenders Unit (Madison) This program sought to prevent offenders' further involvements in crime by deferring prosecution on the condition that they satisfactorily complete appropriate treatment and rehabilitation programs. The program recognized the hazards of labeling individuals and the potential of treatment for first offenders who accept responsibility for their actions.

An offender's suitability for the program was based on several criteria: the nature of the offense, prior criminal record, admission of guilt, attitude, whether the offender was dangerous to self or community, likelihood of repeating the crime and whether the offender would benefit from the treatment process.

The program used a large network of social service agencies and public and private organizations. Because a "substantial portion" of program participants were shoplifters, the staff conducted a 1-day Saturday workshop on retail theft. Another integral part of the program was voluntary community service, not as a means of punishment but as a way to repay the community for the crime committed and to change the offender's behavior patterns. The program conserved police, prosecutorial, judicial and correctional resources. In addition, offenders' lives were minimally disrupted because they could continue to pursue their occupations and fulfill family obligations.

Community Policing and Corrections

Community-based corrections gained popularity in the 1990s but are still resisted by many neighborhoods. Sometimes referred to as intermediate sanctions, community corrections may take many forms, including halfway houses, prerelease centers, transition centers, work furlough and community work centers, community treatment centers, restitution centers and a host of other innovative approaches to involving the community in efforts to reintegrate offenders into the community *without* danger to the citizens.

Residents may live either part time or full time at such centers, depending on the other conditions set forth by the court.

Sharrock and associates (2008, p.61) describe the grim corrections statistics in Kansas where, in 2006, two-thirds of the offenders entering Kansas prisons were guilty of parole violations, 90 percent of which were for technicalities such as missing meetings. A third of all parole violations involved substance abuse, but fewer than half of the offenders got treatment in prison. Only 18 percent of offenders had completed job training. From 1985 to 2005 the state's spending on corrections increased fourfold. Werholtz, Kansas' secretary of correction, was familiar with the "nothing works" theory based on a seminal study by sociologist Martinson, which concluded: "With few and isolated exceptions, the rehabilitative efforts that have been reported so far have had no appreciable effect on recidivism." But Werholtz hoped that a frequently overlooked caveat in the study noted that perhaps nothing worked because the programs so far had been poorly designed. Perhaps the latest "buzz" at corrections conferences about reentry and reinvestment initiatives might be one solution to the problem. Targeting limited resources at helping the highest-risk offenders with job training, treatment and counseling launched inside prison and continued on the outside might work on the reentry end. The reinvestment part was to channel the money saved by keeping offenders out of prison to the communities to which the offenders returned. Kansas was a prime candidate to test out the theory.

Starting in 2004, prisoners were given job training, treatment and classes in life skills, including money management, parenting and decision making. The year before they were to be released, efforts were made to get each prisoner a job, an apartment and a connection to the right programs to stay within the law.

Although parole officers and social service workers were skeptical, by 2006, 401 fewer people were in prison in Kansas for violating parole than expected, saving $13.8 million in operating costs. Kansas used $2 million of that for community programs, including job training and drug treatment.

Obregon, once a skeptical world-weary parole officer, lamented: "You see the same people over and over. You see these kids and their children's children. Show me that it works and then I will believe in it." Sharrock and colleagues. (p.63) describe her reaction after the program was implemented.

> Today, Obregon is a convert to the reentry method. "It isn't a cookie-cutter program," she says. "We get to understand that person and where they are coming from. But the biggest difference is you give people a running start." Now a "reentry case manager," she spends her days talking to potential landlords and employers, substance abuse counselors, parole officers, police and community leaders on behalf of her 50 prisoners and parolees—including Jeannette Brown.

Brown enrolled in the reentry program in 2005 ... When Brown sat down with her "release team," consisting of substance abuse and corrections counselors; police and parole officers; the reentry program director; mental health, housing and job specialists; a business developer; a volunteer mentor; and Obregon, she brought a notebook filled with her goals: regaining custody of her children, keeping a job, getting her driver's license, no more abusive relationships. When she finally walked out of prison in June 2007, she was greeted at the gates by four reentry staffers, who took her to her new apartment. A couple of parole officers helped her unpack. Obregon took her to a food bank, arranged a doctor's appointment and helped her get an ID. ...

Now when she sees the local cop around, they chat. Instead of dreading her parole meetings, Brown stops by Obregon's office after work to say hello. "Parole officers used to try to put me back in prison; now I feel like they are trying to keep me out."

Early Efforts Using the Media in Crime Prevention

Two different approaches to using the media have also been extensively studied: the "McGruff" media campaign and police–community anticrime newsletters.

The "McGruff" National Media Campaign

McGruff, the crime dog, is to law enforcement what Smokey the Bear is to the National Forest Service. A press release from the National Crime Prevention Council describes the creation of McGruff and the campaign.

The concept of a national public education campaign to teach Americans that they could prevent crime (and how to do so) was first conceived in 1978. The Department of Justice supported the plan, as did distinguished civic leaders and such organizations as the AFL-CIO, the International Association of Chiefs of Police, and the National Sheriffs' Association. The Advertising Council, Inc., agreed to support the campaign. Research and program development advisory groups helped formulate a strategy. ... The first McGruff public service ads were developed in 1979 and premiered in February 1980. ... The campaign's objectives were clear: (1) to change unwarranted feelings and attitudes about crime and the criminal justice system, (2) to generate an individual sense of responsibility for crime prevention, (3) to initiate individual action toward preventing crime, (4) to mobilize additional resources for crime prevention efforts and (5) to enhance existing crime prevention programs and projects conducted by national, state and local organizations.

This campaign, also known as the "Take a Bite Out of Crime" campaign, was aimed at promoting citizen involvement in crime prevention activities through public service announcements (**PSAs**).

PSAs
Public service announcements.

The public favorably received the "McGruff" format and content, and the campaign had a sizable impact on what people know and do about crime prevention.

McGruff, the crime dog, helps teach citizens how to "take a bite out of crime."
© National Crime Prevention Council

Police–Community Anti-Crime Newsletters and Brochures

Barthe (2006, pp.30–31) describes how printed materials can help in crime prevention efforts:

> Ease of production and low distribution costs make fliers and leaflets favorites of police departments and other crime prevention agencies. Using readily available desktop publishing software, an agency can create a cost-effective publicity campaign. Police officers can deliver the material door-to-door or place it on car windshields.

> Mailings can also be an effective way to reach people with crime prevention messages. Some studies have shown newsletters and brochures to be effective ways to spread crime prevention information, but such media do not always produce the intended result. In the early 1980s, the Houston Police Department failed to reduce residents' fear of crime by distributing newsletters containing local crime rates and prevention tips. In Newark, New Jersey, the police department used a similar strategy. While people liked receiving the newsletters, they rarely read them.

General publicity campaigns aimed at victims have had limited effectiveness. A 4-month national press and poster campaign tried to educate people about the importance of locking their parked cars, but it failed to change people's behavior.

Another campaign used posters and television spots to remind people to lock their car doors, but it also proved ineffective. These studies demonstrate that people often pay little attention to crime prevention messages. A common reason given is that potential victims do not feel that it concerns them. For instance, domestic violence awareness campaigns have to compete with the possibility that women do not want to see themselves as victims.

Qualitative Evaluations and Salient Program Features

Qualitative evaluations are more descriptive and less statistical. One large-scale qualitative evaluation, undertaken by the National Symposium on Community Institutions and Inner-City Crime Project, sought to identify model programs for reduction of inner-city crime. According to Sulton (1990, p.8), almost 3,500 national organizations; criminal justice scholars; and federal, state and local government agencies were asked to recommend outstanding local programs. This resulted in the identification of approximately 1,300 programs. Each was sent a request for detailed information, and 350 (27 percent) responded. From these, 18 were selected for site visits.

qualitative evaluations

Assessments that are more descriptive and less statistical; the opposite of quantitative evaluation.

Sulton (p.10) notes that although each program was unique, they shared some common characteristics.

Eighteen model programs shared the following characteristics. The programs:

- Focused on causes of crime.
- Built on community strengths.
- Incorporated natural support systems.
- Had an identifiable group of clients.
- Targeted those who were less affluent.
- Had clearly stated goals and well-defined procedures.
- Had sufficient resources.
- Had a strong leader.

Sulton (p.10) observes that many of the programs focus on specific social problems of inner-city residents "identified as correlates with, if not causes of, inner-city crime, such as emotional or family instability, lack of education, absence of vocational skills, unemployment, drug and alcohol abuse, juvenile gangs and sexual abuse and exploitation." The programs have a clear focus, a clear audience and a clear idea of how to proceed.

On a much smaller scale, but equally instructive, is the Newport News Police Department's reliance on data to identify a problem and to evaluate a solution (adapted from Guyot, 1992, p.321):

Local hunters and other gun owners held target practice at an excavation pit. Officer Hendrickson found that between April and September one year, the department had been called 45 times to chase away shooters and that the problem had existed for at least 15 years. Most of the calls had come from a couple whose nearby home was bullet-riddled and who thought the police were doing a good job because each time they chased away the shooters.

Officer Hendrickson interviewed shooters and learned that most were soldiers from nearby Fort Eustis; many others were sent to the pit by gun shop owners. The officer also determined the pit was close enough to a highway to make any firearms discharge there illegal. Deciding to use education backed by legal sanctions, he first photographed the damage and other evidence, which he used to persuade a judge to give anyone convicted once of illegal shooting a suspended sentence and a small fine; a second offense would result in confiscation of the weapon and a jail sentence. The officer obtained from the property owners permission to arrest on their property and the same from the C & O Railroad for shooters crossing the tracks to reach the pit. He also wrote a pamphlet defining the problem and the department's intended enforcement action, and distributed it to the military base and all area gun shops. Finally, he had "no parking—tow zone" signs erected on the shoulder where most shooters parked.

The results were simple. Officers issued 35 summonses to shooters in September, 15 in October, and the last on November 12. The pit soon became so overgrown that it was uninviting for target practice.

Success in the preceding incident and others might indicate that community policing and problem-solving policing would be readily accepted by law enforcement officials and the communities they serve. Such acceptance is not, however, always the case because of several impediments (Skogan, 2004, pp.162–167):

○ Making community policing an overtime program
○ Making it a special unit
○ Shortchanging the infrastructure
○ Resistance in the ranks
○ Resistance by police managers
○ Resistance by police unions
○ Resistance by special units
○ Competing demands and expectations
○ Lack of interagency cooperation
○ Problems evaluating performance
○ Unresponsive public
○ Nasty misconduct
○ Leadership transitions

Impediments to Community Policing Revisited

Recall from Chapter 5 the challenges facing implementation of community policing:

○ Resistance by police officers
○ Difficulty involving other agencies and organizing the community
○ Reluctance of average citizens to participate, either because of fear or cynicism

Resistance to change is common, especially in a tradition-oriented profession such as law enforcement. Sadd and Grinc (1996, p.8) suggest: "Community policing is a fight for 'hearts and minds' of patrol officers and the public ... involving a shift in the culture of policing." Skolnick and Bayley (pp.225–226) describe six impediments to implementing innovative community-oriented policing.

 Impediments to implementing innovative community-oriented policing include:

○ The powerful pull of tradition.
○ Substantial segments of the public not wanting the police to change.
○ Unions that continue to be skeptical of innovation.
○ The high cost of innovation.
○ Lack of vision on the part of police executives.
○ Police departments' inability to evaluate their own effectiveness.

One challenge is that projects were usually established as special units that some saw as elite: "The perception of elitism is ironic because community policing is meant to close the gap between patrol and special units and to empower and value the rank-and-file patrol officer as the most important agent for police work" (Sadd and Grinc).

Another substantial impediment is how to respond to calls for service. A potential conflict exists between responding to calls for service and community policing efforts because calls for service use much of the time needed for problem identification and resolution efforts. The unpredictability of calls for service presents management problems for agencies wanting to implement community policing strategies. Departments must set their priorities and determine how to balance calls for service (reactive) with a problem-oriented approach (proactive). As stressed throughout this text, the one-on-one interaction between police officers and the citizens they serve is critical.

Cost versus Benefit

Some simple services that police departments might provide for the community cost little and require limited personnel. For example, relatively inexpensive efforts to enhance community safety through crime prevention might include conducting monthly meetings, meeting with school administrators, conducting fingerprinting programs and blood pressure programs, participating in athletic contests, publishing newsletters and providing ride-alongs. Other services, however, may be relatively expensive and require many officers.

Whatever the cost to implement, community policing appears to offer a realistic approach to reducing violence, crime and the drug problem. The remaining chapters discuss several approaches to community policing and problem solving to address these issues.

A Final Note: The Important Distinction between Programs and Community Policing

It must be stressed that programs identified throughout this chapter are not community policing, although community policing may incorporate the use of these and other strategies. Too many police officials think that because they have a neighborhood-watch program or a ride-along program they are doing community policing. In fact, some police chiefs and sheriffs state with pride that they are deeply involved in community policing because they have a DARE program. Community policing is an overriding philosophy that affects every aspect of police operations; it is not a single program or even a hundred programs. Such programs, particularly in isolation, are more community relations or even public relations, not community policing.

SUMMARY

Crime prevention became popular in the late 1960s and early 1970s, with many communities taking an active role. Among the most commonly implemented crime prevention programs have been street lighting projects, property marking projects, security survey projects, citizen patrol projects and crime reporting and neighborhood-watch or block projects. Specialized crime watch programs include mobile crime watch, youth crime watch, business crime watch, realtor watch and carrier alert.

Continuing the community crime prevention momentum generated during the 1960s and 1970s, new programs and organizations were initiated during the 1980s and 1990s to encourage citizens to play an active role in reducing crime in their own neighborhoods. Among the most visible organizations focused on crime are citizen crime prevention associations, Crime Stoppers and MADD. Many police departments also expanded their use of volunteers, who may serve as reserve officers, auxiliary patrol or community service officers or on an as-needed basis.

Youths, who had traditionally been included in police–community relations efforts and crime prevention initiatives, were also addressed through programs including the McGruff "Take a Bite Out of Crime" campaign, PALs, Officer Friendly, police explorers, police–school liaison programs and the DARE program. Many programs for juveniles involve the schools, which historically have been charged with instilling discipline in their students. For example, police–school liaison programs place an officer in a school to work with school authorities, parents and students; to prevent crime and antisocial behavior; and to improve police–youth relationships. The joint goals of most police–school liaison programs are to prevent juvenile delinquency and to improve police–youth relations.

The most common components of community policing experiments have been foot patrol, newsletters and community organizing. Several empirical studies in the 1980s assessed the effectiveness of community policing efforts. The Flint Neighborhood Foot Patrol Program appeared to produce a decrease in crime, an increase in general citizen satisfaction with the foot patrol program, a decline in the public's fear of crime and a positive perception of the foot patrol officers.

In the first Newark Foot Patrol Experiment, residents reported positive results, whereas business owners reported negative results. The second Newark Foot Patrol Experiment used coordinated foot patrol, a cleanup campaign and distribution of a newsletter. Only the coordinated foot patrol reduced the perception of property crime and improved assessments of the police.

The Oakland program, using foot patrol, mounted patrol, small vehicle patrol and a Report Incidents Directly program, resulted in a substantial drop in the rate of crime against persons and their property. The San Diego Community Profile Project provided patrol officers with extensive community orientation training. These officers became more service oriented, increased their non–law enforcement contacts with citizens and had a more positive attitude toward police–community relations.

The Houston Fear-Reduction Project did not achieve desired results from the victim recontact program or the newsletter. Citizen contact patrol and the police storefront operation did, however, result in decreases in the public's perception of social disorder, fear of personal victimization and the level of personal and property crime.

The Boston Foot Patrol Project found no statistically significant relationship between changes in the level of foot patrol provided and the number of calls for service or the seriousness of the calls. Baltimore County's COPE Project reduced fear of crime by 10 percent and crime itself by 12 percent in target neighborhoods. It also reduced calls for service; increased citizen awareness of and satisfaction with the police; and improved police officer attitudes.

Other studies have reviewed the effectiveness of community crime prevention efforts. The Seattle Citywide Crime Prevention Program, using property identification, home security checks and neighborhood block watches, significantly reduced the residential burglary rate as well as the number of burglary-in-progress calls. The Portland antiburglary program also succeeded in reducing the burglary rate for the participants. The Hartford Experiment restructured the physical environment, changed how patrol officers were assigned and organized the neighborhood in an effort to reduce crime and the fear of crime.

The criminal justice system includes law enforcement, the courts and corrections. What happens in each component of the criminal justice system directly affects the other two components. Consequently, a coordinated effort among law enforcement, courts and corrections is required to effectively deal with the crime problem and to elicit the support of the community in doing so. Model court programs include a community dispute resolution center and a deferred prosecution/first offenders unit.

The effectiveness of the media in assisting crime prevention efforts is another evaluation focus. The public has favorably received the "McGruff" format and content. The "McGruff" campaign has had a sizable impact on what the public knows and does about crime prevention.

Eighteen model programs identified by the National Symposium on Community Institutions and Inner-City Crime Project shared the following characteristics: The programs (1) were focused on causes of crime, (2) built on community strengths, (3) incorporated natural support systems, (4) had an identifiable group of clients, (5) targeted those who were less affluent, (6) had clearly stated goals and well-defined procedures, (7) had sufficient resources and (8) had a strong leader.

The implementation of community policing must be weighed against several impediments, including the powerful pull of tradition, substantial segments of the public who do not want the police to change, the skepticism of unions with regard to innovation, the cost of innovation, lack of vision on the part of police executives and the incapacity of police departments to evaluate their own effectiveness.

DISCUSSION QUESTIONS

1. Why is it difficult to conduct research on the effectiveness of community policing?

2. Which studies do you think have the most value for policing in the next few years? Which studies have the most promise?

3. Why would a police department want to reduce fear of crime rather than crime itself?

4. Which of the fear-reduction strategies do you believe holds the most promise?

5. What do you think are the most reasonable aspects of the crime prevention through environmental design (CPTED) approach?

6. Do you think that victims who ignored the CPTED approach to crime prevention are culpable?

7. Has your police department conducted any research on community policing or crime prevention efforts? If so, what were the results?

8. Does your police department have its own McGruff costume or robot? If so, how does the department use him?

9. What do you think are the most important questions regarding police–community relations that should be researched in the next few years?

10. How much of a police department's budget should be devoted to research? Which areas should be of highest priority?

GALE EMERGENCY SERVICES DATABASE ASSIGNMENTS `ONLINE Database`

- Use the Gale Emergency Services Database to help answer the Discussion Questions as appropriate. Be prepared to share and discuss your outline with the class.

- Research and outline at least one of the following subjects: citizen crime reporting, CPTED, National Night Out, police athletic leagues.

REFERENCES

Angel, S. *Discouraging Crime through City Planning.* Berkeley: University of California Press, 1968.

Barthe, Emmanuel. *Crime Prevention Publicity Campaigns.* Washington, DC: U.S. Department of Justice, Office of Community Oriented Policing Services, Problem-Oriented Guides for Police, Response Guides Series, Guide No.5, June 2006.

Fleissner, Dan; Fedan, Nicholas; and Klinger, David. "Community Policing in Seattle: A Model Partnership between Citizens and Police." *National Institute of Justice Journal,* August 1992, pp.9–18.

Fowler, Floyd J., Jr. and Mangione, Thomas W. "A Three-Pronged Effort to Reduce Crime and Fear of Crime: The Hartford Experiment." In *Community Crime Prevention: Does It Work?* edited by Dennis P. Rosenbaum. Beverly Hills: Sage Publications, 1986, pp.87–108.

Greene, Jack R. and Taylor, Ralph B. "Community-Based Policing and Foot Patrol: Issues of Theory and Evaluation." In *Community Policing: Rhetoric or Reality,* edited by Jack R. Greene and Stephen D. Mastrofski. New York: Praeger Publishers, 1991, pp.195–223.

Guyot, Dorothy. "Problem-Oriented Policing Shines in the Stats." In *Source Book: Community-Oriented Policing: An Alternative Strategy,* edited by Bernard L. Garmire. Washington, DC: ICMA, May 1992, pp.317–321.

Heinzelmann, Fred. "Foreword." *Community Crime Prevention: Does It Work?* edited by Dennis P. Rosenbaum. Newbury Park: Sage Publications, 1986, pp.7–8.

"Help Keep Families Together." Irving, TX: MADD, no date.

"Impaired Driving." Atlanta, GA: Centers for Disease Control, no date.

"In America, Lessons Learned; Drug Education." *The Economist,* March 7, 2009, p.34.

Jacobs, J. *The Death and Life of Great American Cities.* New York: Vintage, 1961.

Lindsay, Betsy and McGillis, Daniel. "Citywide Community Crime Prevention: An Assessment of the Seattle Program." In *Community Crime Prevention: Does It Work?* edited by Dennis P. Rosenbaum. Beverly Hills: Sage Publications, 1986, pp.46–67.

"MADD Reports DUI Deaths Up." DUI Library, July 1, 2004. http://www.dui.com/dui-library/fatalities accidents;statistics/madd-dui-deaths.

Mastrofski, Stephen D. "What Does Community Policing Mean for Daily Police Work?" *National Institute of Justice Journal,* August 1992, pp.23–27.

Newman, O. *Defensible Space: Crime Prevention through Urban Design.* New York: Macmillan, 1972.

Pate, Anthony M. "Experimenting with Foot Patrol: The Newark Experience." In *Community Crime Prevention: Does It Work?* edited by Dennis P. Rosenbaum. Beverly Hills: Sage Publications, 1986, pp.137–156.

Police Foundation. *The Newark Foot Patrol Experiment.* Washington, DC: The Police Foundation, 1981.

Ratcliffe, Jerry. *Video Surveillance of Public Places.* Washington, DC: Center for Problem Oriented Policing, 2006.

Repetto, T. A. *Residential Crime.* Cambridge: Ballinger, 1974.

Rosenfeld, Ben. City and County of San Francisco: Office of the Controller, April 8, 2008.

Sadd, Susan and Grinc, Randolph M. *Implementation Challenges in Community Policing.* Washington, DC: National Institute of Justice Research in Brief, February 1996.

Schneider, Anne L. "Neighborhood-Based Antiburglary Strategies: An Analysis of Public and Private Benefits from the Portland Program." In *Community Crime Prevention: Does It Work?* edited by Dennis P. Rosenbaum. Beverly Hills: Sage Publications, 1986, pp.68–86.

Sharrock, Justine; Perry, Celia; and Phillips, Jen. "The Shawnee Redemption." *Mother Jones,* July/August 2008, pp.61–63.

Skogan, Wesley G. "Community Policing: Common Impediments to Success." In *Community Policing: The Past, Present, and Future,* edited by Lorie Fridell and Mary Ann Wycoff. Washington, DC: The Annie E. Casey Foundation and Police Executive Research Forum, 2004, pp.159–168.

Skogan, Wesley G. and Wycoff, Mary Ann. "Storefront Police Offices: The Houston Field Test." In *Community Crime Prevention: Does It Work?* edited by Dennis P. Rosenbaum. Beverly Hills: Sage Publications, 1986, pp.179–199.

Skolnick, Jerome H. and Bayley, David H. *The New Blue Line: Innovation in Six American Cities.* New York: The Free Press, 1986.

Sulton, Anne Thomas. *Inner-City Crime Control: Can Community Institutions Contribute?* Washington, DC: The Police Foundation, 1990.

Taft, Philip B., Jr. *Fighting Fear: The Baltimore County C.O.P.E. Project.* Washington, DC: Police Executive Research Forum, 1986.

Trojanowicz, Robert C. "Evaluating a Neighborhood Foot Patrol Program: The Flint, Michigan, Project." In *Community Crime Prevention: Does It Work?* edited by Dennis P. Rosenbaum. Beverly Hills: Sage Publications, 1986, pp.157–178.

"Twenty-Five Years of Saving Lives." *Driven*, Fall 2005, pp.9–17.

Wycoff, Mary Ann. "The Benefits of Community Policing: Evidence and Conjecture." In *Community Policing: Rhetoric or Reality,* edited by Jack R. Greene and Stephen D. Mastrofski. New York: Praeger Publishers, 1991, pp.103–120.

Zahm, Diane. *Using Crime Prevention through Environmental Design in Problem Solving.* Washington, DC: Center for Problem-Oriented Policing, 2007.

ADDITIONAL RESOURCES

Every interest organization has a Web page on the Internet, including several federal agencies. A search using the words *community policing* or *crime prevention* will yield a tremendous amount of current information. Many organizations offer expertise in building partnerships and provide a variety of publications, training and services that can strengthen local efforts. A sampling follows.

Bureau of Justice Assistance Clearinghouse, Box 6000, Rockville, MD 20850; (800) 688–4252.

Center for Community Change, 1000 Wisconsin Ave. NW, Washington, DC 20007; (202) 342–0519.

Citizens Committee for New York City, 305 7th Ave., 15th Floor, New York, NY 10001; (212) 989–0909.

Community Policing Consortium, 1726 M St. NW, Suite 801, Washington, DC 20006; (202) 833–3305 or (800) 833–3085.

National Center for Community Policing, School of Criminal Justice, Michigan State University, East Lansing, MI 48824; (517) 355–2322.

National Crime Prevention Council, 1700 K St. NW, 2nd Floor, Washington, DC 20006-3817; (202) 466–6272.

National Training and Information Center, 810 North Milwaukee Ave., Chicago, IL 60622–4103; (312) 243–3035.

Police Executive Research Forum, 2300 M St. NW, Suite 910, Washington, DC 20006; (202) 466–7820.

CHAPTER 10

Safe Neighborhoods and Communities: From Traffic Problems to Crime

DO YOU KNOW . . .

- What role crime prevention plays in community policing?
- What is usually at the top of the list of neighborhood concerns and what behaviors are involved?
- What engineering and enforcement responses can address the problem of speeding in residential areas?
- How community policing has addressed citizen fear of crime?
- What the three primary components of CPTED are?
- How CPTED directly supports community policing?
- What two side effects of place-focused opportunity blocking may be?
- What the risk factor prevention paradigm is?
- What three federal initiatives can assist communities in implementing community policing?
- What the Weed and Seed program does?
- What partnerships have been implemented to prevent or reduce crime and disorder?

CAN YOU DEFINE . . .

cocoon neighborhood watch	opportunity blocking	synergism
contagion	place	target hardening
diffusion	risk factor prevention paradigm	traffic calming

> In the last analysis, the most promising and so the most important method of dealing with crime is by preventing it—by ameliorating the conditions of life that drive people to commit crime and that undermine the restraining rules and institutions erected by society against anti-social conduct.
>
> —*President's Commission on Law Enforcement and Administration of Justice, 1967*

Introduction

Community policing stresses using partnerships and problem solving to address making neighborhoods and communities safer, including looking at concerns related to traffic, at neighborhood disorder, at crime and at the fear of crime. Many Americans, including many police, believe traffic problems and crime prevention are solely the responsibility of law enforcement. When crime surges in a community, the usual public response is to demand the hiring of more officers. Citizens often believe that a visible police presence will deter and reduce crime, even though most studies indicate this is not the case. For example, the classic study *Kansas City Preventive Patrol Experiment* found overwhelming evidence that decreasing or increasing routine preventive patrol within the range tested had no effect on crime, citizen fear of crime, community attitudes toward the police on the delivery of police services, police response time or traffic accidents. In 1975 the FBI's Uniform Crime Report noted:

> Criminal justice professionals readily and repeatedly admit that, in the absence of citizen assistance, neither more manpower, nor improved technology, nor additional money will enable law enforcement to shoulder the monumental burden of combating crime in America.

The advent of community policing and partnerships is often credited with the dramatic decrease in crime witnessed in the late 1990s (Rosen (2006, p.1). Despite predictions that a significant crime wave would occur in the 1990s as a result of the increase in the population of youth and young adults (a "boom" that never materialized), the United States experienced the longest and deepest decline in crime since World War II. According to Franklin Zimring of the University of California, Berkeley, School of Law, these drops in the crime rate may have resulted from modest improvements in policing ("New Research Reveals," 2007). The New York Police Department (NYPD), for example, increased its workforce by 35 percent (13,000 people), changed its management style and engaged in more aggressive police work, particularly in public-order offenses.

Other variables that are may have contributed to a decrease in the crime rate are the booming economy, a drop in the high-risk (teens to young adult) population and an increase in the number of people in prison. Research, however, has been unable to consistently demonstrate a clear correlation between these variables and the crime rate, as it is noted that the drop in the youth population and an increase in the incarceration rate also occurred in the 1980s when crime across the country soared.

Furthermore, and in contrast to what was happening in the United States, Canada experienced a 30 percent drop in violent crime during the 1990s at a time when the country's prison population was declining; there were fewer officers on the street; and the economic gains were moderate. Therefore, from these contrasting scenarios and societal variables, the difficulty in determining the causes of fluctuating crime rates becomes apparent.

In 2005 and 2006, it appeared that the downward trend in violent crime rates of the 1990s was over. Violent crime was growing at an alarming rate. The FBI reported the largest single-year-percentage increase in violent crime in 14 years.

At the Police Executive Research Forum (PERF) National Violent Crime Summit in August 2006, 170 representatives—mayors, police chiefs and public officials—from more than 50 cities met to discuss the gathering storm of violent crime sweeping across our nation's communities. The information they shared was sobering. Murder was up 27.5 percent in the first 6 months in Boston, 27 percent in Memphis and 25 percent in Cincinnati. Robbery was up in even more startling numbers. Even communities with relatively low crime rates saw significant increases in 2005 and early 2006.

Police chiefs pointed to gangs, violent criminals returning from prisons, drug trafficking and juveniles with easy access to guns as the forces behind the uptick in violent crime. Others, such as Trenton, New Jersey's Mayor Douglas Palmer, suggested that the focus on fighting terrorism had taken resources away from preventing crime and enforcing the law: "We are sacrificing hometown security for homeland security" (Rosen, p.12). Additional factors identified by PERF summit participants as contributing to the increasing violent crime trend included a decrease in police department staffing levels; decreased federal involvement in crime prevention and community policing; a strained social service community, educational system and criminal justice system, particularly courts and corrections; the glamorization of violence and the "thug" pop culture; and the phenomenon of crime becoming "a sport" (Rosen, p.9).

In discussing ways to stem the potential tide of increasing violent crime, participants in the summit were reminded of the crime wave that gripped the country during the late 1980s and early 1990s and how that situation was turned around. Los Angeles Police Chief William Bratton recalled the Omnibus Crime Bill of 1994, with its emphasis on community policing and problem solving, and how efforts then were focused on the holistic treatment of a community, an approach that, by all accounts, significantly helped reduce crime in the late 1990s (Rosen, p.14).

The release of violent crime rate data for 2007, however, shows a drop in violent crime across the country, so it seems probable that the rising rates of 2005 and 2006 were only minor fluctuations (Schwartz, 2008). The biggest declines were observed in the largest cities. And while it may be hypothesized that big cities are doing better because they have more resources and more advanced policing methods, criminologists do not know for sure what factors have accounted for the differing rates. In all, violent crime rates in 2007 fell 1.4 percent and property crime rates fell 2.1 percent. There were significant differences regionally however. The overall drop in homicides was 2.7 percent but most of that was in cities with populations over a million. The homicide rate in New York City was down 20 percent and in Los Angeles, 19 percent. Mid-size cities with populations of 100,000 to 249,000 had a 1.9 percent rise in murder rates. In small cities with 50,000 to 99,000 residents, murder rates increased 3.7 percent. Most of the decline in violent crime was in the Northeastern cities. Violent crime increased in the South, especially in large cites such as Atlanta (murder rates went up 17 percent) and New Orleans (up 29 percent). Although crime rates are difficult to predict, preliminary analysis of 2008 data indicates that economic conditions are having an effect on people's behavior. Crime, especially property crime, is rising again.

Whether the violent crime rate truly is trending upward or whether recent statistics are merely a "blip" in an overall downward trend, the importance of getting the community involved in staving off local crime and disorder is clear. The broad nature of policing in the 1990s highlighted the critical contributions that citizens and community agencies and organizations can make to combat crime. For communities to thrive, citizens need to have a sense of neighborhood and work together as a team. The resulting synergism can accomplish much more than isolated individual efforts. **Synergism** occurs when individuals channel their energies toward a common purpose and accomplish together what they could not accomplish alone.

synergism
Occurs when individuals channel their energies toward a common purpose and accomplish what they could not accomplish alone.

The technical definition of synergism is "the simultaneous actions of separate entities which together have greater total effect than the sum of their individual efforts." A precision marching band and a national basketball championship team are examples of synergism. Although there may be some outstanding solos and a few spectacular individual "dunks," it is the total team effort that produces the results.

The police and the citizens they serve must realize that their combined efforts are greater than the sum of their individual efforts on behalf of the community. When police take a problem-solving approach to community concerns and include the community, what they are doing often falls under "crime prevention."

 Crime prevention is a large part, in fact a cornerstone, of community policing.

Community policing and crime prevention are, however, distinct entities. Further, crime is usually not the greatest concern of a neighborhood—traffic-related problems are of greater concern because they affect all citizens daily.

This chapter begins with a discussion of the traffic concerns of neighborhoods and how community policing partnerships have addressed these concerns. This is followed by a look at how community policing addresses disorder concerns and citizen fear of crime. Next is a discussion of how advances in technology are used to fight crime and a brief return to the topic of CPTED (crime prevention through environmental design), introduced in Chapter 9. The discussion then turns to the national focus on community policing and crime prevention and the assistance offered by Community Oriented Policing Services (COPS), the Community Policing Consortium and the Weed and Seed program. This is followed by descriptions of partnerships and strategies to prevent or reduce crime and disorder in general and a look at specific strategies to prevent burglaries in public housing, burglaries at single-family construction sites, thefts of and from vehicles, robberies at automated teller machines (ATMs), witness intimidation, identity theft, robbery of taxi drivers, street prostitution, human trafficking, assaults in and around bars, violent confrontations with individuals who are mentally ill and crimes against businesses. The chapter concludes with examples of partnerships to prevent crime.

Conspicuously absent from this chapter are discussions of domestic violence. Domestic violence is most certainly a crime, but the discussion of community policing and domestic violence is placed later in the text (Chapter 14), where violence is discussed in depth.

Traffic Enforcement and Safety

 Traffic problems top the list of concerns of most neighborhoods and communities. Concerns include speeding in residential areas, street racing, red light running, impaired drivers and nonuse of seat belts.

Speeding in Residential Areas

Sweeney (2006, p.62) reports a speeding "storm" brewing on our streets and highways and that worldwide, speeding is a contributing factor in about 31 percent of all fatal crashes, equating to nearly 14,000 lives per year lost in the United

States. The National Highway Traffic Safety Administration (NHTSA) estimates the economic cost to society for speeding-related crashes is $40.4 billion a year, $78,865 per minute or $1,281 every second (*Traffic Safety Facts*, 2006).

Engineering responses to speeding include using traffic calming, posting warning signs and signals, conducting anti-speeding public awareness campaigns, informing complainants about actual speeds and providing realistic driver training.

In many cities, "traffic calming" has been the response. **Traffic calming** devices, such as speed bumps and traffic circles (roundabouts), are intended to slow traffic in residential areas and are popular in communities where residents believe the measures make children safer and neighborhoods quieter.

Not everyone agrees that traffic calming is a good tactic. For example, Sacramento, California, had recently completed several traffic calming projects, including conversions of once-flowing one-way streets to two-way streets and lane reductions from two lanes to one lane. In a field survey, Grimes (2008) asked Sacramento residents: "Are you calm while you sit in city traffic, or are you agitated, angry and charged up? Do you imagine that while you sit in one lane of traffic that used to be two lanes, while cars around you are idling and spewing fumes in the air for neighbors, pedestrians and cyclists to breathe, that you are somehow helping the environment?" According to Grimes: "Traffic congestion increases fuel consumption and the release of harmful emissions. Numerous traffic-engineering studies in cities across the United States show that arbitrarily interrupting traffic with 'nuisance' or 'speed-breaker' stop signs, speed bumps and roundabouts increases intentional violation and can actually increase the overall speed on the road where they are used." She calls traffic calming a euphemism for traffic obstruction and diversion.

traffic calming
Describes a wide range of road and environmental design changes that either make it more difficult for a vehicle to speed or make drivers believe they should slow down for safety.

Enforcement responses to reduce speeding include (1) enforcing speeding laws, (2) enforcing speeding laws with speed cameras or photo radar, (3) using speed display boards, (4) arresting the worst offenders and (5) having citizen volunteers monitor speeding (Scott, 2001b, pp.15–19).

Such aggressive enforcement of speed limits may seem to run counter to community policing efforts to establish rapport with citizens.

The highway safety community, which includes the police, courts, municipal engineering departments and the public, needs a new "action plan" to address the problem of speeding (Sweeney, p.63), a plan that should include:

○ Increasing public perception of the hazards of speeding.
○ Using new paradigms in highway design.
○ Setting self-enforcing and realistic speed limits.
○ Convincing officers of the need to enforce the speed laws.
○ Using metrics to target and evaluate efforts.

Closely related to the challenge of preventing speeding is the challenge of preventing street racing.

Street Racing

Street racing of automobiles has been an American tradition since the early 1950s, and probably many years before. Today's street racers are very much like their grandparents who were racing in the 1960s: "Contemporary street racing is just as exciting for its devotees as it was for the ducktail and leather jacket generation. It's all about the speed, the flash, the guts, the adrenaline and the danger" (Domash, 2006, p.30). According to Vargas (2006): "Law enforcement officials say street-racing crashes have increased since the release of such movies as *The Fast and the Furious*."

According to Domash (p.31): "Cops nationwide are working to deter drivers and spectators, while providing safer alternatives to illegal racing." In 2003 the Boise, Idaho, Police Athletic League stated its own racing program with two donated cars, a Chevelle painted like a police car that reaches speeds of 138 mph and a Corvette that reaches approximately 100 mph in a quarter-mile run. The cars are fixtures at the local high school drag races put on at Firebird Raceway. The races are backed by donations that enable the officers to give out T-shirts and encourage youngsters to come to the track to race. Most of the street racing interdiction programs are affiliated with "Beat the Heat," an organization that began in 1984 in Jacksonville, Florida (Domash).

In Ontario, Canada, 33 people lost their lives due to street racing incidents from 2001 to 2007. In October, 2007 a new law took effect and 60 seconds later the first violator was stopped. In the first 24 hours after the law took effect, 24 people had their cars towed and licenses suspended. The law includes an automatic 7-day impound for the car; driver's licenses are suspended for a week; and a minimum fine of $2,000 is imposed for anyone caught driving 50 km over the posted speed limit (McFarlane, 2007).

Red Light Running

The Federal Highway Administration (FHWA) and Insurance Institute for Highway Safety (IIHS) estimate that red light running causes as many as 218,000 crashes that result in about 880 deaths and 181,000 injuries. Automated red light cameras are being used in many jurisdictions to address the problem of red light running.

In Phoenix, Arizona, parents formed a group named the Red Means Stop Coalition after their sons and daughters were hit by red light runners. The group works alongside local police departments, the governor's highway safety office and local corporations to elevate the issue of red light running prevention in the press and among elected and public officials. Similar traffic safety groups across the United States complement the efforts of law enforcement officials by informing the public of the red light running problem and focusing on driver behavior changes.

Civil liberties groups have expressed concern that the cameras could be used to spy on people and that privacy issues must be addressed (Samuels, 2006).

Nonuse of Seat Belts

Recent statistics show that 82 percent of Americans are wearing their safety belts, with 34 states reporting increased numbers of seat belt users over the previous year (Bolton, 2006, p.70). Hawaii led the list with belt use reported at

95.3 percent. Several other states and territories reported usage rates higher than 90 percent. The NHTSA estimates that safety belt use at rates higher than the 90 percent level prevents 15,700 fatalities and 350,000 serious injuries each year. The country also saves about $67 billion in economic costs of fatalities and injuries from motor vehicle crashes.

Strategies used to encourage seat belt use vary from incentives for safe driving to mandatory use policies and fines for failure to buckle up. Click It or Ticket, an annual nationwide, high-visibility seat belt enforcement program, is an example of the latter. Officers in participating agencies are asked to focus on seat belt compliance and ticketing of violators. At the same time, federal funding pays for advertising that highlights the program and seat belt safety. The enforcement includes surveys that measure "before and after" seat belt use, seat belt checkpoints, saturation patrols, fixed patrols and extensive media coverage. Agencies are encouraged to create partnerships with the media and other community organizations. These partners have conducted child/family vehicle check-up clinics, assisted at child seat checkpoints, attended the department's Click It or Ticket news conference and assisted with public education. NHTSA points out that since the campaign began, seat belt use has climbed to its highest level ever and that child fatalities from traffic crashes have dropped 20 percent.

Impaired Drivers

"Simply put, drunk driving is a police concern because alcohol increases the risk that drivers will get in traffic crashes and kill or injure themselves or others. Alcohol impairment is the primary factor in traffic fatalities" (Scott et al., 2006, p.1) Among the most serious problems related to impaired drivers is the repeat offender because data show that those who drink and drive at least twice a month account for about 90 percent of all drunk driving trips (Scott et al.).

Responses to address the drunk driving problem include legislation (lowering the legal limit for per se violations), strict enforcement by police, curtailing driving privileges, sanctioning convicted drunk drivers (requiring installation of electronic ignition locks that prevent intoxicated drivers from operating their vehicles), monitoring drunk drivers, providing public education, providing alternative transportation and environmental design, and locating licensed establishments in areas that reduce the need for patrons to drive (Scott et al., pp.40–46).

As of August 2005, laws setting a legal blood alcohol content (BAC) of .08 have taken effect in all 50 states, the District of Columbia and Puerto Rico, an effort that took nearly 20 years of work by proponents. It goes without saying that a driver younger than the legal drinking age of 21 years who has *any* amount of alcohol in his or her body is guilty of driving under the influence of alcohol. Some of the most promising and potentially effective approaches to eliminating drunk driving have come through improvements in technology for monitoring a driver's BAC, such as ignition interlocks, passive alcohol sensors and Secure Continuous Remote Alcohol Monitor (SCRAM) devices (Dewey-Kollen, 2006a, p.103). Passive alcohol sensors (PASs) help agencies to work more effectively in enforcing driving while intoxicated (DWI) restrictions: "Research shows the use of passive alcohol sensors can increase detection of DWI by about 50 percent at checkpoints and about 10 percent on routine patrols" (Dewey-Kollen, 2006b, pp.10–11). If all police officers used PAS technology, DWI arrests in the United States could increase by an estimated 140,000 to 700,000 (Dewey-Kollen).

Emerging technologies include infrared sensing that enforcement officers can use to help determine an offender's alcohol content level, devices that can detect subdural blood alcohol concentrations through a driver's hand placed on the steering wheel, and algorithms to detect a vehicle's weaving so an officer can determine if the driver is impaired. Chuck Hurley, CEO of Mothers Against Drunk Driving (MADD), predicts that, given the steady development of such technologies: "Within 10 years it is possible that cars won't be operable if a driver is impaired" (Dewey-Kollen, 2006a).

Safe Communities

Nine agencies within the U.S. Department of Transportation (DOT) are working together to promote and implement a safer national transportation system by combining the best injury prevention practices into the Safe Communities approach to serve as a national model.

A *safe community* is defined as "a community that promotes injury prevention activities at the local level to solve local highway and traffic safety and other injury problems. It uses a 'bottom up' approach involving its citizens in addressing key injury problems." According to the Safe Communities Web site, safe communities have six elements. The community:

○ Uses an integrated and comprehensive injury control system with prevention, acute care and rehabilitation partners as active and essential participants in addressing community injury problems.

A patrol officer helps a girl through a bike safety course designed to teach children how to control their bikes, avoid obstacles and properly use their brakes. Bicycle safety classes can significantly reduce incidents of child injury.
© AP Images/John Lovretta

○ Has a comprehensive, community-based coalition/task force with representation from citizens; law enforcement; public health, medical, injury prevention, education, business, civic and service groups; public works offices; and traffic safety advocates that provides program input, direction and involvement in the Safe Community program.

○ Conducts comprehensive problem identification and uses estimating techniques that determine the economic costs associated with traffic-related fatalities and injuries within the context of the total injury problem.

○ Conducts program assessments from a "best practices" and a prevention perspective to determine gaps in highway and traffic safety and other injury activity.

○ Implements a plan with specific strategies that addresses the problems and program deficiencies through prevention countermeasures and activities.

○ Evaluates the program to determine the impact and cost benefit where possible.

In addition to traffic concerns, citizens are often more concerned about minor offenses (disorders) than they are about crime and violence in their communities.

Addressing Disorder Concerns

Neighborhood and business district improvements such as cleaning up trash, landscaping and planting flowers can serve as a focus for community organizing and help residents take pride in their neighborhoods. Key partnerships in beautification projects include police departments, the public works staff, the business community and residents. These partnerships can also be expanded to help fight crime and to reduce the fear of crime.

Addressing disorder goes far beyond beautification. Allowing neighborhood disorder to go unchecked creates "broken windows," an advertisement that no one in the area cares what happens. This condition attracts more disorder, crime, criminals and other destructive elements. When communities begin to clean up the neighborhood, report crime, improve security, look out for each other and work cooperatively, crime and disorder problems begin to disappear. Many of the topics in this chapter describe how *broken windows* get fixed and, as a result, how neighborhoods improve.

Reducing the Fear of Crime

A major goal of community policing is to reduce the fear of crime in communities so that citizens will be willing to join together to prevent crime.

 Various community policing efforts to reduce citizens' fear of crime have included enhanced foot and vehicle patrol in high-crime neighborhoods, citizen patrols, neighborhood cleanup campaigns, community education and awareness programs, the placement of police substations in troubled neighborhoods, and the installation of closed-circuit video surveillance cameras.

An increasingly popular approach to reduce the fear of crime is video surveillance of public places.

Video Surveillance of Public Places

Video cameras connected to closed-circuit television (CCTV), can be used as a tool for "place management," for providing medical assistance or for gathering information. Strategically placed cameras can be used to monitor traffic flow, public meetings or demonstrations that may require additional police resources. The devices can also be a community safety feature, allowing camera operators to contact medical services if they see someone suffering from illness or injury as a result of criminal activity or noncrime medical emergencies. In addition, cameras can be used to gather intelligence and monitor known offenders' behavior in public places—for example, shoplifters in public retail areas (Ratcliffe, 2006).

According to the Center for Problem Oriented Policing, use of CCTV can prevent crime by creating a deterrent to potential offenders who are aware of the cameras' presence (Ratcliffe). A key element in such prevention through deterrence, however, rests on adequate signage and recognition by the public that they are under surveillance. If offenders are unaware they are being watched, or if they are under the influence of drugs or alcohol and, thus, "altered" to the point where they do not care that they are being monitored, the deterrent value of CCTV is significantly diminished (Ratcliffe).

CCTV can also impact crime by helping police detect crimes in-progress and provide visual identification of offenders for later arrest and prosecution. The value of this tool in this capacity is dependent, however, on how rapidly police can respond to incidents identified by camera operators: "Although there may be some initial crime reduction due to the installation and publicity of a new system, offenders may soon learn what types of incidents elicit a police response and the speed of that response. The availability of local resources is therefore a factor in the success of this mechanism" (Ratcliffe, 2006, p.9).

Fake, or decoy, cameras are also used to create the illusion that people are being monitored. For example, the public transportation systems in some communities have installed both active and dummy cameras on board their bus fleet to enhance the public's perception of widespread surveillance capabilities. Augmenting the deterrent impact and crime prevention value through the use of such tactics is a concept referred to as a diffusion of benefits (Ratcliffe). Despite these numerous benefits, video surveillance can have unintended consequences.

Unintended Consequences of Video Surveillance
Among the unintended consequences of video surveillance are displacement, increased suspicion or fear of crime and increased reported crime.

Displacement occurs when offenders, aware of the surveillance cameras, simply move their activity to another area out of camera sight. However, general crime prevention literature suggests that the amount of crime displaced rarely matches the amount of crime reduced. Video surveillance may also force offenders to be more imaginative and diversify operations.

Another concern is that the public may respond negatively to the cameras. Ratcliffe reports on one survey in which one-third of respondents felt one purpose of the cameras was to spy on people. Other surveys showed some city managers were reluctant to advertise the cameras or have the cameras very visible for fear they would make shoppers and consumers more fearful. Ironically, although it is hoped that most citizens would feel safer under the watchful eye of the cameras, the surveillance may have the reverse effect on some people.

A third concern is that reported crime rates will increase for some offenses with low reporting rates such as minor acts of violence, graffiti tagging and drug offenses. The public needs to be prepared for the fact that the increase in recorded crime does not reflect an increase in actual crime. In addition to concerns about these potential unintended consequences, the public may be concerned about privacy issues.

Public Concerns Regarding Video Surveillance
As noted in the discussion of using cameras to detect red light runners, civil liberties unions often object to video surveillance, claiming it is an invasion of privacy and citing the Fourth Amendment's prohibition against unreasonable search and seizure. However, the Fourth Amendment protects *people*, **not** *places*. The Fourth Amendment does not protect people in clearly public places where there is no expectation of privacy. However, as Ratcliffe, points out: "The public is unlikely to support CCTV if there is a risk that video of them shopping on a public street when they should be at work will appear on the nightly news." He suggests that a policy be established covering when recorded images are to be released to the police, media or other agencies in the criminal justice system. He further recommends that video footage not be released for any reason other than to enhance the criminal justice system.

Evaluation of Video Surveillance
Establishing whether video surveillance reduces crime is difficult because this problem-oriented solution is seldom implemented without incident or without other crime prevention measures being initiated simultaneously. In addition, as noted, use of video surveillance may inadvertently increase the crime rate, especially for offenses with low reporting rates.

Research results are mixed, with some studies finding video surveillance to be effective against property crime and less effective against personal crime and public order offenses. Other studies report mixed results regarding reducing fear of crime. Several studies produced inconclusive results. Ratcliffe reports the following general findings:

○ CCTV is more effective at combating property offenses than violent or public order crime (though there have been successes in this area).
○ CCTV appears to work best in small, well-defined areas (such as public car parks).
○ The individual context of each area and the way the system is used appear to be important.
○ Achieving *statistically significant* reductions in crime can be difficult (i.e., crime reductions that clearly go beyond the level that might occur as a result of the normal fluctuations in the crime rate are difficult to prove).
○ A close relationship with the police appears important in determining a successful system.
○ There is an investigative benefit to CCTV once an offense has been committed.
○ CCTV appears to be somewhat effective in reducing fear of crime but only among a subset of the population.

In addition to using video surveillance in public places, other advances in technology are also being used to fight and, in some instances, prevent crime.

Using Advancing Technology to Fight Crime

Numerous types of technology, including cell phones, fax machines, e-mail and computer applications, can be used effectively in crime fighting and prevention efforts.

Although it is not new, crime mapping technology is the very first step in proactive policing to identify hot spots; this is especially important with the event-driven, rapid-feedback CompStat systems (Sanow, 2006, p.6). Biometric identification systems are also becoming more sophisticated and can use one or more of several different physical and/or behavioral characteristics such as iris, retinal and facial recognition; hand and finger geometry; fingerprint and voice identification; and dynamic signature (Cohn, 2006). For example, the Los Angeles Police Department is now using ultra–high-tech face recognition devices to fight crime ("LAPD Uses Face Recognition Technology to Fight Crime," 2006). The department's old-fashioned mug shot book has been replaced by digital photos in a mobile identifier. An officer can enter a photo of an individual and then compare skin texture against database photos. The next stage will be to use information in the iris pattern, combining iris, skin and face recognition in a single high-resolution image shot.

Recognizing the need for investigators to keep up with technology, the National Institute of Justice has funded an Electronic Crimes Partnership Initiative (ECPI) to teach police officers how to retrieve digital evidence from computers or cell phones (Ritter, 2006). Such evidence proved critical in recent high-profile homicide cases. For example, the "BTK" serial murderer, Dennis Rader, who terrorized Wichita, Kansas, for 30 years, was found when evidence on a computer disk led police to the former church council president and Cub Scout leader. Evidence retrieved from the computer of convicted murderer Scott Peterson included a map of the island where his wife's body was found and also revealed he had shopped online for a boat and had studied local water currents.

BBC News has reported on a research project that could lead to the first major breakthrough in fingerprint technology in more than 20 years. The technology involves use of microscopic (nano) particles that can bind to fingerprints and make them glow, the end result being that police find more fingerprints and detect more crimes ("Glowing Fingerprints Plan Backed," 2006).

Researchers in the United Kingdom are working to make shoe prints found at crime scenes as useful as fingerprints and DNA; an automated system is being developed that will be able to search through records of patterns on shoe soles to identify the footwear worn by a criminal (Ward, 2006). The pilot system can already identify 85 percent of samples. It has yet to be tried with partial footprints.

Although new technologies continue to be developed and applied to policing, other crime prevention methods rely on more conventional, low-tech measures such as locks, lights and community links—all common elements in CPTED.

ON THE BEAT

A big piece in the crime prevention puzzle centers around systems used by the police department for tracking crimes and neighborhood concerns. Geographic Information System (GIS) crime mapping is a tool many departments use to map patterns of crime incidents; our department uses a mapping system to help determine where our greatest needs exist. Neighborhood concerns are entered into a system designed to track these issues and document officers' efforts.

Consider this example: John Doe, a local resident, calls the police department to report that people are constantly running a stop sign in the neighborhood. This stop sign is next to a city park frequently used by children and adults. Several other residents are reporting similar concerns. An officer takes the complaint and enters the information into the tracking system. From that point on, the information is passed along to a district officer to follow up on and track any police efforts at that location. The officer logs the date, time and any action that was taken. The next time John Doe calls the police department and asks what is being done about the stop sign, the person taking the phone call can pull up the information on the computer and explain in detail what has been done. This system is great for tracking complaints and also police actions made in each particular case. It can be used for everything from traffic complaints to reports of suspicious drug activity. This is one example of a community policing strategy that seems to really work for both the police department and the community.

—Kim Czapar

Crime Prevention through Environmental Design

CPTED has been a strategy for dealing with crime for decades and has had some proven successes.

CPTED has three major components: target hardening, changes to the physical environment and community building.

Target hardening refers to making potential objectives of criminals more difficult to obtain. The three main devices used for target hardening are improved locks, alarm systems and security cameras. Most people do not object to locks and alarm systems properly used, but some have "Big Brother" concerns about surveillance cameras.

Changes to the physical environment often include increased lighting, which has been a means of increasing security for centuries. Phillips (p.10) contends: "Although there is a strong indication that increased lighting decreases the fear of crime, there is no statistically significant evidence that street lighting affects the actual level of crime." Other changes usually involve removing items that give potential offenders the ability to hide—for example dense vegetation, high shrubs, walls and fences.

Community building, the third element of CPTED, can have the greatest impact on how individuals perceive the livability of their neighborhood. Community

target hardening
Refers to making potential objectives of criminals more difficult to obtain through the use of improved locks, alarm systems and security cameras.

Glass doors or doors with windows right next to them present an easy access opportunity for burglars.
© Flying Colours Ltd/ Getty Images

building seeks to increase residents' sense of ownership of the neighborhood and of who does and does not belong there. Community building techniques can include social events such as fairs or neighborhood beautification projects.

In addition to the trio of major components, CPTED is defined by five underlying principles: territoriality, natural surveillance, access management, physical maintenance and order maintenance ("Using Environmental Design to Prevent School Violence," 2008). *Territoriality* establishes ownership and sends a clear message of who does and does not belong in a neighborhood. *Natural surveillance* allows potential victims a clear view of surroundings and inhibits crime. *Access control* delineates boundaries and areas where people do and do not belong (e.g., signs, clearly marked entrances and exits, limited access to certain areas). *Physical maintenance* includes timely repairs and upkeep of the physical space and removal of trash and graffiti. *Order maintenance* includes paying attention to unacceptable behavior and encouraging activities that are clearly acceptable. It may also include the presence of uniformed authority figures.

By emphasizing the systematic analysis of crime in a particular location, CPTED directly supports community policing by providing crime prevention strategies tailored to solve specific problems.

The Importance of Place

place

A very small area reserved for a narrow range of functions, often controlled by a single owner and separated from the surrounding area.

Eck (n.d.) contends: "Most places have no crimes and most crime is highly concentrated in and around a relatively small number of places. If we can prevent crime at these high crime places, then we might be able to reduce total crime." His definition of **place** is specific: "A place is a very small area reserved for a narrow range of functions, often controlled by a single owner and separated from the surrounding area." This concept of place is similar to the hot spots discussed in Chapter 4.

Eck suggests that **opportunity blocking**, changes to make crime more difficult, riskier, less rewarding or less excusable, is one of the oldest forms of crime prevention. Opportunity blocking at places may have a greater direct effect on offenders than other crime prevention strategies, he contends. Eck notes two side effects from place-focused opportunity blocking efforts.

Two side effects of place-focused opportunity blocking efforts are displacement of crime and diffusion of prevention benefits.

Displacement, in which offenders simply change the location of their crimes, has been discussed as a potential negative of prevention efforts. However, concern about displacement may cause a benefit of prevention efforts to be overlooked—that is, diffusion. **Diffusion** of prevention benefits occurs when criminals believe that the opportunity blocking of one type of criminal activity is also aimed at other types of criminal activity. For example, when magnetic tags were put in books in a university library, book theft declined, as did the theft of audiotapes and videotapes, which were not tagged. According to Eck: "Diffusion is the flip side of the coin of crime contagion. **Contagion** [emphasis added] suggests that when offenders notice one criminal opportunity they often detect similar opportunities they have previously overlooked. Crime then spreads. The broken window theory is an example of a contagion theory. Thus under some circumstances offenders may be uncertain about the scope of prevention efforts and avoid both the blocked opportunities and similar unblocked opportunities. When this occurs, prevention may spread."

The Risk Factor Prevention Paradigm

The **risk factor prevention paradigm** seeks to identify key risk factors for offending and then implement prevention methods designed to counteract them.

Risk factors have been broadly defined as "those characteristics, variables, or hazards that, if present for a given individual, make it more likely that this individual, rather than someone selected from the general population, will develop a disorder" (Mrazek and Haggerty, 1994, p.127). As Shader (n.d., p.1) explains:

In recent years, the juvenile justice field has adopted an approach from the public health arena in an attempt to understand the causes of delinquency and work toward its prevention (Farrington, 2000). For example, the medical community's efforts to prevent cancer and heart disease have successfully targeted risk factors (Farrington). To evaluate a patient's risk of suffering a heart attack, a doctor commonly asks for the patient's medical history, family history, diet, weight, and exercise level because each of these variables has an effect on the patient's cardiac health. After this risk assessment, the doctor may suggest ways for the patient to reduce his or her risk factors. Similarly, if a youth possesses certain risk factors, research indicates that these factors will increase his or her chance of becoming a delinquent. A risk assessment may aid in determining the type of intervention that will best suit the youth's needs and decrease his or her risk of offending. Farrington (2000) calls this recent movement toward the public health model the "risk factor paradigm," the basic idea of which is to "identify the key

opportunity blocking
Changes to make crime more difficult, risky, less rewarding or less excusable; one of the oldest forms of crime prevention.

diffusion
Occurs when criminals believe that the opportunity blocking of one type of criminal activity is also aimed at other types of criminal activity.

contagion
Suggests that when offenders notice one criminal opportunity they often detect similar opportunities they have previously overlooked; crime then spreads; the broken window theory is an example.

risk factor prevention paradigm
Seeks to identify key risk factors for offending and then implement prevention methods designed to counteract them.

risk factors for offending and tool prevention methods designed to counteract them" (Farrington, 2000).

Although community policing occurs on the local level, it often takes funding from the federal level to get programs off the ground and flying or to keep them going after they have become established. To encourage jurisdictions across the country to make the paradigm shift to community policing, several national organizations have been created that offer financial support, training opportunities and other types of resources.

National Emphasis on Community Policing and Crime Prevention

 Three federal initiatives to assist communities in implementing community policing are the COPS Office, the Community Policing Consortium and the Weed and Seed program.

The Office of Community Oriented Policing Services

The Violent Crime Control and Law Enforcement Act of 1994 authorized $8.8 billion over 6 years for grants to local police agencies to add 100,000 officers and promote community policing. To implement this law, Attorney General Janet Reno created the Office of Community Oriented Policing Services (or COPS) in the Department of Justice.

Although originally the COPS Office was destined to go out of business after 6 years, its success at increasing the numbers of police officers across the country and in raising awareness of community policing has resulted in Congress extending the life of the agency for several more years. According to the COPS Web site:

> The COPS Office was created as a result of the Violent Crime Control and Law Enforcement Act of 1994. As a component of the Justice Department, the mission of the COPS Office is to advance community policing in jurisdictions of all sizes across the country. Community policing represents a shift from more traditional law enforcement in that it focuses on prevention of crime and the fear of crime on a very local basis. Community policing puts law enforcement professionals on the streets and assigns them a beat, so they can build mutually beneficial relationships with the people they serve. By earning the trust of the members of their communities and making those individuals stakeholders in their own safety, community policing makes law enforcement safer and more efficient, and makes America safer.

COPS provides grants to tribal, state and local law enforcement agencies to hire and train community policing professionals, acquire and deploy cutting-edge crime-fighting technologies, and develop and test innovative policing strategies. COPS-funded training helps advance community policing at all levels of law enforcement—from line officers to law enforcement executives—as well as others in the criminal justice field. COPS has invested $11.3 billion to add community policing officers to the nation's streets and schools, enhance crime-fighting technology, support crime prevention initiatives and provide training and technical assistance to advance community policing. As of the end of fiscal year 2004, COPS had funded more than 118,768 community policing officers and deputies.

Because community policing is by definition inclusive, COPS training also reaches state and local government leaders and the citizens they serve. This broad range of programs helps COPS offer agencies support in virtually every aspect of law enforcement.

The Community Policing Consortium

Another organization that provides assistance is the Community Policing Consortium, a partnership of five police organizations: the International Association of Chiefs of Police (IACP), the National Organization of Black Law Enforcement Executives (NOBLE), the National Sheriffs' Association (NSA), the Police Executive Research Forum (PERF) and the Police Foundation (PF). The consortium, funded and administered by COPS within the Department of Justice, provides training throughout the United States, particularly to agencies that receive COPS grants. The training materials emphasize community policing from a local perspective, community partnerships, problem solving, strategic planning and assessment. Their quick-read periodicals, *The Community Policing Exchange, Sheriff Times* and the *Information Access Guide,* relate real-life experiences of community policing practitioners across the country.

The Weed and Seed Program

A third federal initiative is the Weed and Seed program. Launched in 1991 with three sites, it has since grown to include 300 sites nationwide, ranging in size from several neighborhood blocks to several square miles, with populations ranging from 3,000 to 50,000. The program strategically links concentrated, enhanced law enforcement efforts to identify, arrest and prosecute violent offenders, drug traffickers and other criminals operating in the target areas and community policing (weeding) with human services—including after-school, weekend and summer youth activities; adult literacy classes; and parental counseling—and neighborhood revitalization efforts to prevent and deter further crime (seeding).

The Weed and Seed program seeks to identify, arrest and prosecute offenders (weed) while simultaneously working with citizens to improve quality of life (seed).

The Weed and Seed Data Center notes that four fundamental principles underlie the Weed and Seed strategy: collaboration, coordination, community participation and leveraging of resources.

Partnerships to Prevent or Reduce Crime and Disorder

Partnerships to prevent or reduce crime and disorder include business anticrime groups, local government–community crime prevention coalitions, community coalitions, grassroots organizations and landlords and residents in public housing using advances in technology and celebrating community successes.

The specific needs of communities across the country, and the crime and disorder problems that plague them, are as diverse as the communities themselves. One strength of community policing is being able to adapt to these specific community needs and find creative solutions to each area's unique problems. The discussion now turns to examine various partnerships that have been formed to address specific crime and disorder problems experienced by jurisdictions throughout the United States.

Addressing Specific Problems

As has been stressed throughout this text, problem solving is a key component of community policing. An invaluable resource for communities engaged in problem solving is the Center for Problem Oriented Policing, a nonprofit organization comprising affiliated police practitioners, researchers and universities dedicated to the advancement of problem-oriented policing. Its mission is to advance the concept and practice of problem-oriented policing in open and democratic societies. It does so by making readily accessible information about ways in which police can more effectively address specific crime and disorder problems.

Another invaluable resource is the COPS Office, introduced earlier. This office has published a series of Problem-Oriented Guides, which focus on understanding and preventing specific community problems. Several of the most recent guides are cited in the following discussion. The COPS Office also provides funding for community policing initiatives and hiring and provides training through its regional community policing institutes.

Preventing Burglary in Public Housing

Eck notes: "Public housing complexes have become notorious for high crime rates in the United States." He suggests that restricting pedestrian access and movement is key to reducing burglary in such places. A second strategy is target hardening by providing locks and improved security to access points. A third approach is to make burglary targets unattractive to offenders. Eck suggests that focusing on residences with previous burglaries is effective, as is focusing on residences surrounding burgled dwellings. Focusing only on those living around at-risk places rather than an entire neighborhood is called **cocoon neighborhood watch**.

cocoon neighborhood watch

Focusing on only those living around at-risk places rather than an entire neighborhood.

Preventing Acquaintance Rape of College Students

Rape is one of the most common violent crimes on American college campuses today. Prevention has focused almost entirely on building security, escorts for students after dark and workshops focusing on protection from dangerous strangers on campus. Unfortunately, these techniques are not very successful, because almost all sexual assaults occur between people who know each other and are part of the "legitimate" campus environment. The COPS Office has a problem-solving guide that can help police and campus public safety officers effectively prevent the problem (Sampson, 2003). The guide describes the problem and its scope, causes and contributing factors; methods for analyzing the problem on a particular campus; tested responses; and measures for assessing response effectiveness.

Preventing Burglary at Single-Family House Construction Sites

Construction site burglary has been recognized as a significant problem in the United States and elsewhere in the world, with an estimated $1 billion to $4 billion worth of materials, tools and construction equipment stolen every year in the United States alone (Boba and Santos, 2006). Boba and Santos recommend that police establish cooperative working relationships with builders and that builders, in turn, share information about burglary problems and patterns, local building practices and loss prevention efforts. If it can be established that certain houses are at high risk for victimization, response measures can be concentrated at those locations.

Specific responses to reduce construction site burglary include improving builder practices: limiting the number of construction sites supervised, coordinating delivery and installation, screening and training workers and subcontractors, limiting the hiring of subcontractors, having a tracking system for tools, encouraging hiring loss prevention personnel, hiring on-site private security patrols and establishing an employee hotline to report crime.

Target hardening measures are also recommended, including improving lighting, installing and monitoring closed-circuit television, installing alarm systems, using portable storage units, installing fencing, marking property, installing global positioning satellite locater chips and displaying crime prevention signage.

Preventing Theft of and from Vehicles

Thefts of and from vehicles might be prevented by hiring parking attendants, improving surveillance at deck and lot entrances and exits, hiring dedicated security patrols, installing and monitoring CCTV systems, improving the lighting, securing the perimeter, installing entrance barriers and electronic access and arresting and prosecuting persistent offenders.

Many police departments furnish citizens with information on how to prevent auto theft. Information may be provided in the form of pamphlets, newspaper stories, public service announcements on television or speeches to civic organizations. The two main messages of anti–car theft programs are to not leave the keys in the car ignition and to lock the car.

These messages are conveyed in a variety of ways, from stickers on dashboards to posters warning that leaving keys in the ignition is a violation of the law if the car is parked on public property. In addition, leaving one's keys in the ignition is an invitation to theft, could become a contributing cause of some innocent person's injury or death and could raise the owner's insurance rates.

New York City has developed a voluntary anti–auto theft program that enlists the aid of motorists. The Combat Auto Theft (CAT) program allows the police to stop any car marked with a special decal between 1 A.M. and 5 A.M. Car owners sign a consent form affirming that they do not normally drive between 1 A.M. and 5 A.M., the peak auto theft hours. Those who participate in the program waive their rights to search and seizure protection.

Preventing Robberies at Automated Teller Machines

Automated teller machines, or ATMs, were first introduced in the late 1960s in the United States and now can be found almost everywhere. However, bank customers sometimes trade safety for convenience because the most recently available data show the overall rate of ATM-related crime is between one per 1 million and one per 3.5 million transactions (Scott, 2001a, p.2). Scott (p.4) presents the following general conclusions about ATM robbery. Most are committed by a lone offender, using some type of weapon, against a lone victim. Most occur at night, with the highest risk between midnight and 4 A.M. Most involve robbing people of cash after they have made a withdrawal. Robberies are somewhat more likely to occur at walk-up ATMs than at drive-through ATMs. About 15 percent of victims are injured. The average loss is between $100 and $200.

Specific responses to reduce ATM robberies include altering lighting, landscaping and location; installing mirrors on ATMs; installing ATMs in police stations; providing ATM users with safety tips; installing CCTV; installing devices to allow victims to summon police during a robbery; and setting daily cash withdrawal limits (Scott, pp.15–24).

Preventing Witness Intimidation

People who are witnesses to or victims of crime are sometimes reluctant to report criminal offenses or to assist in their investigation. This reluctance may be in response to a perceived or actual threat of retaliation by the offender(s) or their associates. Dedel (2006) points out that historically witness intimidation is most closely associated with organized crime and domestic violence, but recently it has occurred in investigations of drug offenses, gang violence and other types of crime.

An effective strategy to prevent witness intimidation usually requires multiagency partnerships including the police; prosecutors; and other agencies such as public housing, public benefits and social service agencies. The strategy should also consider how to limit liability should the witness actually be harmed. Dedel suggests liability can be limited in several ways:

○ Taking reports of intimidation seriously and engaging in the defined process for protecting witnesses

○ Promising only those security services that can reasonably be provided

○ Documenting all offers of assistance and all efforts to protect witnesses, along with the acceptance or refusal of such assurance

○ Making sure witnesses understand the circumstances under which protections will be withdrawn and documenting all decisions to withdraw security

Specific responses to reducing intimidation by protecting witnesses include minimizing the risk of identification witnesses face when reporting crime or offering statements; protecting the anonymity of witnesses; using alarms and other crime prevention devices; reducing the likelihood of contact between witnesses and offenders; transporting witnesses to and from work and school; supporting witnesses; keeping witnesses and defendants separated at the courthouse; and relocating witnesses, either temporarily, for a short term or permanently through the Federal Witness Security Program (Dedel).

Strategies to deter intimidators include admonishing them and explaining the laws concerning intimidation, requesting high bail and no-contact orders, increasing penalties for intimidation and prosecuting intimidators. Increasing patrols in a targeted area or compelling witnesses to testify is usually ineffective. Most states have material witness laws that allow the arrest and detention of a person who refuses to provide information in court. Dedel recommends: "Because of concerns for the rights of victims and the lack of proof that compelling witnesses to testify is effective, this should be the option of last resort."

Domestic Violence

Domestic disputes are some of the most common calls for police service. Many domestic disputes do not involve violence, but the COPS Office has a guide discussing those that do (Sampson, 2007). The guide helps police analyze and respond to their local problem.

In the United States, domestic violence accounts for about 20 percent of the nonfatal violent crime women experience. Through the community policing philosophy and its practices, some law enforcement agencies are seeking to improve their effectiveness in dealing with the problem of domestic violence by forming police–community partnerships to enhance their response options. PERF, with funding from the COPS Office, explored the nature, function and impact of such police–community partnerships. The research shows that partnerships between the police and community residents and agencies have improved the way agencies communicate with each other and the way they focus their energies on improving the safety of victims of domestic violence. This publication highlights such initiatives around the country that can be replicated to better address domestic violence.

Preventing Identity Theft

"Identity theft occurs when any person willfully obtains the personal identifying information of another and uses it for any illegal purposes" (Lawrence 2006, p.62). According to the *Federal Trade Commission—2006 Identity Theft Survey Report*, approximately 8.3 million U.S. adults discovered that they were victims of some form of identity theft in 2005. Four commonly recognized types of identity theft are described in Figure 10.1.

According to Newman (2004, p.2), congressional hearings on identity theft in the 1990s found that police generally did not regard identity theft victims as "true victims" because the credit card companies that absorbed the financial loss typically did not report the loss to local police. Studies also showed that victims seldom reported the loss or theft of a credit card to police, because they believed the card company would cover the loss: "However, because the repeated use of a victim's identity caused serious disruption and emotional damage, more victims began to report the offense. ... Credit-reporting

	Financial Gain	**Concealment**
High Commitment (lots of planning)	*Organized:* A fraud ring systematically steals personal information and uses it to generate bank accounts, obtain credit cards, etc. *Individual:* The offender sets up a look-alike Internet Web site for a major company; spams consumers, luring them to the site by saying their account information is needed to clear up a serious problem; steals the personal/ financial information the consumer provides; and uses it to commit identity theft.	*Organized:* Terrorists obtain false visas and passports to avoid being traced after committing terrorist acts.* *Individual:* The offender assumes another's name to cover up past crimes or avoid capture over many years.
Opportunistic (low commitment)	An apartment manager uses personal information from rental applications to open credit card accounts.	The offender uses another's name and ID when stopped or arrested by police.

Figure 10.1   The Four Types of Identity Theft

*An Algerian national facing U.S. charges of identity theft allegedly stole the identities of 21 members of a Cambridge, Massachusetts, health club and transferred the identities to one of the people convicted in the failed 1999 plot to bomb the Los Angeles International Airport.

Source: Graeme Newman. *Identity Theft.* Washington, DC: Community Oriented Policing Services Office, 2004.

agencies now require that victims do so as part of an 'identity theft affidavit'" (Newman).

Until recently, victims had great difficulty in getting reports of identity theft from the police. However, in response to growing media coverage and congressional testimony concerning identity theft, the IACP adopted a resolution in 2000 urging all police departments to provide incident reports and other assistance to identity theft victims.

In 2005, 6.4 million households, representing 5.5 percent of all households in the United States, discovered that at least one member had experienced one or more types of identity theft. This is the first time that data for a full year on identity theft have been available from the National Crime Victimization Survey (NCVS): "

Unauthorized use of an existing credit card account, the most prevalent type of identity theft, was experienced by about 3 million households. About 1.6 million households experienced theft of existing accounts other than a credit card (such as a banking account), and 1.1 million households discovered misuse of personal information (such as a social security number). An estimated 790,000 households experienced more than one type of identity theft during the same episode" (Baum, 2007, p.1).

○ Ten percent of households with incomes of $75,000 or higher experienced identity theft; that was about twice the percentage of households earning less than $50,000.

○ Across all types of identity theft, the average amount lost per household was $1,620.

Majoras (2005, p.14), chairperson of the FTC, contends: "The magnitude of the problem alone makes the case for partnerships among law enforcement agencies."

Preventing Street Prostitution

Street prostitution is a sign of neighborhood disorder and attracts strangers, drug dealers, pimps and other criminals into a neighborhood. Prostitutes, often addicted to drugs and/or infected with the human immunodeficiency virus (HIV), wait on street corners for customers from more orderly and affluent neighborhoods, who cruise the streets and frequently assume any females they see to be prostitutes. Women residents of the neighborhood become afraid to wait for a bus or walk to a store. Parents do not want their children exposed to the problem and worry about the dangerous trash (used condoms and needles) left on public and private property. Whereas prostitution has often been a low priority for police, it is a high-priority issue for affected neighborhoods (Scott and Dedel, 2006b).

Traditional responses have been largely ineffective. Basically consisting of arrest and prosecution, they include neighborhood "sweeps," in which as many prostitutes as possible are arrested and sporadic arrests of "johns" are conducted. Community policing has spawned a multitude of other responses, many of which have proved more effective. Some responses include establishing a very visible police presence; holding public protests against prostitution; educating and warning prostitute and clients; targeting the worst offenders; obtaining restraining orders against prostitutes; suspending government aid to prostitutes; imposing curfews on prostitutes; exposing clients to humiliating publicity; notifying those with influence over a client's conduct (employers, spouses, etc); restricting a client's ability to drive by vehicle confiscation or drivers license revocation; helping prostitutes to quit; encouraging prostitutes to report serious crime; providing prostitutes with information about known dangerous clients; diverting traffic by closing alleys, streets and parking lots; providing enhanced lighting; securing abandoned buildings; and holding property owners responsible when their property is being used for prostitution (Scott, 2001c).

As more and more police departments develop their own Web sites, many are posting online photos of johns and others involved in the prostitution trade. For example, the Canton (Ohio) Police Department's Web site posts numerous photos, preceded by this statement:

> The following individuals were arrested by the Canton Police Department and convicted in Canton Municipal Court for either soliciting for prostitution or patronizing prostitution. This service is provided as a deterrent to prostitution in Canton, Ohio. Our citizens deserve an environment that promotes health, safety and stability.

A related problem often involving prostitution is that of human trafficking.

Preventing Human Trafficking

"It's a thriving international business in our increasingly interconnected global economy generating some $9 billion in profits each year ... It's called 'human trafficking'—and it involves buying, selling and smuggling people—often women and children—and forcing them into what amounts to modern-day slavery" (Human Trafficking, 2006). Clawson and colleagues (2006) describe the background and scope of the problem:

The United States is widely regarded as a destination country for trafficking in persons, yet the exact number of human trafficking victims within the United States has remained largely undetermined since passage of the Trafficking Victims Protection Act (TVPA) in 2000. Initial estimates cited in the TVPA suggested that approximately 50,000 individuals are trafficked into the United States each year. This number was reduced to 18,000 to 20,000 in the U.S. Department of State's June 2003 *Trafficking in Persons Report.* In its 2005 report, the Department of State's Office to Monitor and Combat Trafficking in Persons cites 14,500 to 17,500 individuals annually. These shifting figures call into question the reliability of estimates and have potential consequences for the availability of resources to prevent human trafficking, prosecute traffickers and protect and serve victims of this crime.

Due to the covert nature of the crime, accurate statistics on the nature, prevalence and geography of human trafficking are difficult to calculate. Trafficking victims are closely guarded by their captors; many victims lack accurate immigration documentation; trafficked domestic servants remain "invisible" in private homes; and private businesses often act as a "front" for a back-end trafficking operation, which make human trafficking a particularly difficult crime to identify and count. A method to obtain valid and reliable estimates of this inherently hidden problem is critical for planning and assessing national and international interdiction and prevention initiatives. Estimates on the number of persons being trafficked often only include data on women and children who are being sexually exploited. Data on men, boys, persons who are trafficked for other work (e.g., agriculture, sweat shops, domestic work, servile marriage), and those who are trafficked within borders are excluded.

Most victims speak no English. In addition, most are fearful of strangers and the police. Research by Wilson and associates (2006) found that unfortunately, most police departments do not consider human trafficking a high priority. Although local law enforcement agencies are aware of the nature and seriousness of the crime, few have engaged in proactive endeavors to address the problem.

Police officers and citizens alike must be made more aware of suspicious activities to watch for, such as avoiding strangers, never leaving the place of employment and showing fear of authorities.

The U.S. Department of Justice has made grants to Salt Lake City, Utah, and nine other communities to address the problem of human trafficking. The spokesperson for the U.S. Attorney for Utah stated: "One of the big needs is training of basically everyone from law enforcement to first responders to anyone who could be in a position to identify a case of human trafficking" ("Salt Lake and 9 Other Communities Get Grant to Identify and Prosecute Human Traffickers," 2006).

According to the United States State Department, traffickers earn about $9.5 billion annually on sales of people. The International Labor Organization estimates are much higher, at $32 billion a year or about $13,000 for each trafficked person ("About 14,500 People Are Trafficked," 2007).

Another challenge to community policing is preventing assaults in and around bars.

Preventing Assaults in and around Bars

Assaults in and around bars are a frequent problem in large cities as well as small towns. Most of these assaults are alcohol-related, but some are not. The majority occur on weekend nights at a relatively small number of places (Scott and Dedel, 2006a).

In addition to alcohol, factors that contribute to aggression and violence in bars include the type of establishment, the concentration of bars, the closing time, aggressive bouncers, a high proportion of young male strangers, price discounting of drinks, continued service to drunken patrons, crowding and lack of comfort, competitive situations, a low ratio of staff to patrons, lack of good entertainment, unattractive décor and dim lighting, tolerance for disorderly conduct, availability of weapons and low levels of police enforcement and regulation.

An effective strategy to address the problem of violence in and around bars requires a broad-based coalition incorporating the interests of the community, the bars and the government (Scott and Dedel). In addition, any response strategy should address as many identified risk factors as possible, such as the practices of serving and patterns of consumption, the physical comfort of the environment, the overall permissiveness of the environment and the availability of public transportation to disperse crowds after bars have closed. Scott and Dedel recommend combining two groups of responses to address the problem: (1) responses to reduce how much alcohol patrons drink and (2) responses to make the bar safer.

Reducing Alcohol Consumption Alcohol consumption can be reduced by establishing responsible beverage service programs including monitoring drinking to prevent drunkenness, promoting slower drinking rates, prohibiting underage drinking, providing reduced-alcohol or nonalcoholic beverages, requiring or encouraging food services with alcohol services and discouraging alcohol price discounts. Additional measures include establishing and enforcing server liability laws and reducing the concentration and/or number of bars (Scott and Dedel).

Making Bars Safer Bars can be made safer by training staff to handle patrons nonviolently; establishing adequate transportation; relaxing or staggering bar closing times; controlling bar entrances, exits and immediate surroundings; maintaining an attractive, comfortable, entertaining atmosphere; establishing and enforcing clear rules of conduct for bar patrons; reducing potential weapons and other sources of injury; communicating about incidents as they occur; and banning known troublemakers from bars.

Preventing Robbery of Taxi Drivers

A barrier to understanding the problem of taxi driver robbery is a lack of data collected on the crime. Much of what is known about taxi robbery is included in records on assaults and homicides by occupation. These data consistently show that taxi drivers have the highest or one of the highest risks of job-related homicides and nonfatal assaults (Smith, 2005). Several risk factors increase taxi drivers' chances of becoming robbery victims: They have contact with a large number of strangers; they often work in high-crime areas; they usually carry cash in an unsecured manner and handle money as payment; they usually work alone, often to (or through) isolated locations; and they often work late at night or early in the morning (Smith).

Among the strategies used to prevent taxi driver robberies are separating drivers from passengers, recording activity with security cameras, having a radio or alarm to call for help, keeping track of taxi locations with automatic vehicle location (AVL) systems, putting trunk latches on the inside of vehicle trunks and near drivers and disabling vehicles (Smith).

Other strategies focus on limiting the availability of cash, including eliminating cash payments, dropping cash off, keeping cash locked up or out of sight and minimizing expectations about the amount of money present (Smith).

Some strategies focus on other driver practices such as controlling who gets into the taxi, directing passengers to particular seats in the cab, finding out the destination before moving, sharing destination information with others, putting additional people in the cab, setting rules and asking those who do not meet them to get out, trying not to provoke passengers, knowing where to go for help late at night, allowing others to see inside the cab, limiting where the cab will make a drop off, staying in the cab unless it is safe to get out and limiting injury when a robbery occurs by simply handing over the money and not fighting back (Smith).

Police practices might also help to prevent taxi driver robberies, including targeting repeat offenders and authorizing police stops without reasonable suspicion or probable cause if the drivers have signed an authorization to do so.

Finally, industry rules, regulations and practices might include controlling the environment around taxi stands, eliminating passenger and driver conflict over money, setting driver competency standards, running driver safety training programs, screening passengers by the dispatching company and exempting drivers from seat belt use.

Preventing Violent Confrontations with People with Mental Illness

The importance of communicating effectively with individuals who are mentally ill and partnering with mental health professionals was discussed in Chapter 6. Among the most important partners in working with violent individuals who are mentally ill is the mental health community, including emergency hospitals to which police may take those in crisis.

Cordner (2006, pp.21–28) describes how the police response to incidents might be improved. He points out that problem solving is usually focused on underlying problems and conditions that give rise to incidents rather than the specific incidents themselves. However, it is widely recognized that traditional police responses to violent individuals are often not effective with those who are mentally ill. Among the responses suggested are training generalist police officers; providing more information to patrol officers; using less-lethal weapons; deploying specialized police officers as members of a crisis intervention team (CIT); or deploying specialized nonpolice responders.

A partnership approach to dealing effectively with violent individuals who are mentally ill should involve stakeholders—for example, initiating assisted outpatient treatment, establishing crisis response sites, establishing jail-based diversion and establishing mental health courts.

Preventing Crimes against Businesses

The annual cost of crime against business is in the billions of dollars. Such victimization hurts business owners, employees, neighbors, customers and the general public (Chamard, 2006). One way to address the problem of crimes against businesses is to develop police–business partnerships. Such partnerships can take a variety of forms, ranging from an individual business working with the police to address a specific problem to an area wide partnership including businesses from a particular geographic location. The partnerships can also be issue specific or business specific. One of the most common police–individual business partnerships involves police assisting retailers in preventing shoplifting.

Police–Individual Business Partnerships to Prevent Shoplifting
Shoplifting might be prevented by improving store layout and displays, upgrading security, establishing early warning systems (to notify other stores about shoplifters), banning known shoplifters, installing and monitoring CCTV systems, using electronic article surveillance (EAS) and attaching ink tags to merchandise.

With EAS a tag is attached to each piece of merchandise. When a person pays for an article, the tag is deactivated and removed by a checkout clerk. Tags that have not been removed or deactivated are detected at store exit gates, and an alarm is sounded. Ink tags, rather than setting off an alarm if not removed, ruin the merchandise to which they are attached when the offender tries to remove them.

Area-Specific Police Business Partnerships
One approach to area-specific police–business partnerships is the business improvement district (BID), a consortium of property and business owners who voluntarily pay a special assessment in addition to their regular taxes. The funds from the special assessment are spent on beautification, security, marketing or whatever the membership decides is needed to enhance the viability of the area. Goals usually include raising the standards of public spaces; reducing crime, social disorder and the fear of victimization; improving public transportation; generating sales and revenues for area businesses; and increasing the number of local jobs. The United States has an estimated 2,000 BIDs (Chamard). Although no solid research has been conducted, anecdotal evidence suggests this approach holds promise.

Issue-Specific Police–Business Partnerships
Issue-specific partnerships focus on a certain type of crime or a particular situation, often a public order problem such as public drinking or panhandling that has reached the point where intervention is required (Chamard). Such partnerships need not last after the specific problem has been solved.

Business-Specific Police–Business Partnerships
Business-specific partnerships are often formed in response to an outbreak of crimes targeting a particular type of business such as robberies of banks or convenience stores (Chamard). Others are formed to address specific chronic problems such as safety in public parking lots and garages.

Ideas in Practice

IDENTITY THEFT AND FRAUD PREVENTION PROGRAM

Beaverton, Oregon, Police Department Wins Webber Seavey Award

The Webber Seavey Award recognizes innovative police programs from around the world and is co-sponsored by the International Association of Chiefs of Police (IACP) and Motorola, Inc.

The Beaverton, Oregon, Police Department began its identity theft and fraud prevention program in 2003, after analyzing the increasing case load they were seeing. Identity theft and fraud cases were up 54 percent over the previous 4 years, similar to what police departments all over the country were experiencing. According to the Bureau of Justice Statistics, an estimated 3.6 million households, or about 3 percent of all households in the nation, were the victim of at least one type of identity theft during a 6-month period in 2004. Forty-eight percent had experienced an unauthorized use of credit cards; 25 percent had other accounts, such as banking accounts, used without permission; 15 percent experienced the misuse of personal information and 12 percent experienced multiple types of theft at the same time (Bureau of Justice Statistics, 2004).

Beaverton police applied for and won a $238,375 federal grant from the Department of Justice to tackle the community's identity theft problem. They formed a planning committee, which decided to direct their efforts toward enhanced investigations, helping victims and educating the public on protecting themselves from these crimes.

"The department formed a Special Enforcement Unit and during its first 2 years, members of the unit made 494 fraud-related arrests, prevented the loss of more than $701,000 from citizens and businesses and recovered $33,170," said Michelle Harrold, a management analyst with the Beaverton police.

Partnerships for this initiative also included a banking industry group to help police solve a case involving more than $126,450, and a marketing firm to assist in outreach.

Careful to make their efforts proactive, the department provided targeted training to officers and volunteers to enable them to assist victims of identity theft and fraud. They also developed identity theft and fraud prevention literature which officers gave out to residents and local businesses, and they posted prevention information and tips on their web site. "The team really hit the streets and worked with our local retailers to try to change habits that put their businesses at risk," Harrold said.

The police department conducted free workshops and educational seminars for the community. Some seminars were designed especially for the business community in an effort to make them more aware of business practices that put them and their customers at risk.

Because thieves often search recycling and garbage for personal identifying information of potential victims, community members were informed that shredding sensitive documents with a cross cut shredder is a good preventative practice. The department recommended shredding paper containing personal information such as credit card statements, financial statements, preapproved credit card offers, old tax documents, checks and household bills.

Going a step further, the police department provided free document shredding events for the public at which a commercial-sized shredding truck was available. Participants were allowed to bring up to three boxes of documents, per vehicle, to be shredded and were encouraged, at the same time, to bring canned food to donate to the Oregon Food Bank.

"We need to compliment the community for working with us. The key to our success is it's an ongoing program" said Beaverton Police Chief David Bishop.

Source: This article was adapted from the following sources: The Bureau of Justice Statistics; the International Association of Chiefs of Police (IACP) Web site (http://www.theiacp.org/awards/webber/2006WebberSeaveyAwards.htm); Christina Lent, The Beaverton Valley Times, October 26, 2006; and Ant Hill Marketing (http://www.anthillmarketing.com/pdf/beaverton_police_06_08_04.pdf)

Partnerships in Action against Crime and Disorder

Partnerships across the country are working on reducing crime and disorder, some focusing on one specific area, and others taking more comprehensive approaches.

Norfolk, Virginia, cut homicides by more than 10 percent and has reduced overall crime rates citywide by 26 percent and in some neighborhoods by as much as 40 percent. A good share of the credit goes to Police Assisted Community Enforcement (PACE), a crime prevention initiative that works neighborhood by neighborhood in conjunction with teams of social, health and family services agencies (the Family Assistance Services Team, or FAST) and public works and environmental agencies (Neighborhood Environmental Assistance Teams, or NEAT) to cut through red tape and help residents reclaim their neighborhoods (*350 Tested Strategies to Prevent Crime*, 1995).

The Minnesota Crime Prevention Association enlisted the support of families, public officials and 45 statewide and local organizations, including schools and churches, to wage a campaign against youth violence. Actions ranged from encouraging children and parents to turn off violent television shows to providing classroom training in violence prevention (*350 Tested Strategies to Prevent Crime*).

In Trenton, New Jersey, a partnership of schools, parents, city leaders and others led to a Safe Haven program in which the schools in the neighborhood became multipurpose centers after school hours for youth activities including sports, crafts and tutoring. Children have flocked to the centers as a positive alternative to being at home alone after school or being at risk on the streets (*350 Tested Strategies to Prevent Crime*).

Crime near a college campus in Columbus, Ohio, became an opportunity for a partnership formed by the City of Columbus, the State of Ohio, Ohio State University, the Franklin County Sheriff and the Columbus Police. The Community Crime Patrol puts two-person, radio-equipped teams of observers into the neighborhoods near the campus during potential high-crime hours. A number of these paid, part-time observers are college students interested in careers in law enforcement (*350 Tested Strategies to Prevent Crime*).

In Danville, Virginia, a partnership approach to working with public housing residents resulted in a 53 percent reduction in calls about fights, a 50 percent reduction in domestic violence calls and a 9 percent reduction in disturbance calls. The Virginia Crime Prevention Association worked with the Danville Housing Authority to bring public housing residents, local law enforcement, social services and other public agencies together into an effective, problem-solving group. Residents were at the heart of the group, identifying problems that were causing high rates of aggravated assault in the community and working to provide remedies such as positive alternatives for youths and social services and counseling for adults and children. Residents developed a code of conduct for the community, spelling out expectations for the behavior of those who live there (*350 Tested Strategies to Prevent Crime*).

Boston's Neighborhood Justice Network, in partnership with the Council of Elders, the Jewish Memorial Hospital, the Boston Police Department, the Department of Public Health and the Commission on Affairs of the Elderly, created a program to help reduce violence and other crimes against older people. It provides basic personal and home crime prevention education, assistance in dealing with city agencies, training in nonconfrontational tactics to avert street crime and other helpful services that reduce both victimization and fear among the city's older residents (*350 Tested Strategies to Prevent Crime*).

These are just a few of a wide range of programs designed by community groups that are changing the quality of life in small towns and large cities, in neighborhoods and housing complexes, in schools and on playgrounds. These groups have proved that there is strength in numbers and that partnerships can provide the community basis for correcting the problems and conditions that can lead to crime. They achieved success because the people involved developed the skills to work together effectively.

SUMMARY

Synergism occurs when individuals channel their energies toward a common purpose and accomplish together what they could not accomplish alone. It can greatly enhance community policing efforts to prevent or reduce crime and disorder. Crime prevention is a large part, and in fact a cornerstone, of community policing.

Traffic problems top the list of concerns of most neighborhoods and communities. Concerns include corridor safety, speeding in residential areas, street racing, red light running, impaired drivers and nonuse of seat belts. Engineering responses to speeding include using traffic calming, posting warning signs and signals, conducting anti-speeding public awareness campaigns, informing complainants about actual speeds and providing realistic driver training. Enforcement responses to speeding include (1) enforcing speeding laws, (2) enforcing speeding laws with speed cameras or photo radar, (3) using speed display boards, (4) arresting the worst offenders and (5) having citizen volunteers monitor speeding.

Various community policing efforts to reduce citizens' fear of crime have included enhanced foot and vehicle patrol in high-crime neighborhoods, citizen patrols, neighborhood cleanup campaigns, community education and awareness programs, the placement of police substations in troubled neighborhoods and the installation of closed circuit video surveillance cameras.

One frequently used strategy is crime prevention through environmental design. CPTED has three major components: target hardening, changes to the physical environment and community building. By emphasizing the systematic analysis of crime in a particular location, CPTED directly supports community policing by providing crime prevention strategies tailored to solve specific problems. Another approach to crime prevention is focusing on place. Two side effects of place-focused opportunity blocking efforts are displacement of crime and diffusion of prevention benefits.

The risk factor prevention paradigm seeks to identify key risk factors for offending and then implement prevention methods designed to counteract them. It is useful in identifying strategies that might be effective for a specific community.

Three federal initiatives to assist communities in implementing community policing are the Community Oriented Policing Services Office, the Community Policing Consortium and the Weed and Seed program. The Weed and Seed program seeks to identify, arrest and prosecute offenders (weed) while simultaneously working with citizens to improve quality of life (seed).

Partnerships to prevent or reduce crime and disorder include business anti-crime groups, local government–community crime prevention coalitions, community coalitions, cooperation with grassroots organizations and working with landlords and residents of public housing.

DISCUSSION QUESTIONS

1. What examples of synergy have you been a part of or witnessed?

2. What crime prevention programs are in your community? Have you participated in any of them?

3. Traffic calming techniques have gained wide support from some drivers but, at the same time, the anger of other drivers. What accounts for the differing perspectives?

4. How does CCTV work to prevent crime and reduce fear?

5. What could be the explanation for some CCTV applications not having the desired effect?

6. Name and explain the five principles underlying CPTED.

7. Because taxes pay for police to combat crime, why should citizens get involved?

8. Why is it so difficult to know the reason for rises and declines in crime?

9. What is it about human trafficking that makes it difficult to detect or even understand the scope of the problem?

10. Which do you feel merits the most attention from community policing: concerns about disorder, fear of crime or crime itself?

GALE EMERGENCY SERVICES DATABASE ASSIGNMENTS
ONLINE Database

- Use the Gale Emergency Services Database to help answer the Discussion Questions as appropriate.

  - One of the most effective and least expensive security initiatives is to design and build safety from crime and fear of crime into a structure. Research CPTED and discuss how the following can affect crime and/or fear of crime: smell and sound, parking garages, maintenance, color, mix of activities, restrooms, signage, vehicle–pedestrian conflicts, loitering and "hanging out."

REFERENCES

"About 14,500 People Are Trafficked into the United States Each Year." Washington, DC: Producer Price Index (PPI) of U.S. Labor Statistics, June 27, 2007.

Baum, Katrina. *Identity Theft, 2007.* Washington, DC: Bureau of Justice Statistics Bulletin, November 2007. (NCJ 219411)

Boba, Rachel and Santos, Roberto. *Burglary at Single-Family House Construction Sites.* Washington, DC: Office of Community Oriented Policing Services, Problem-Oriented Guides for Police, Problem-Specific Guides Series, No. 43, August 2006.

Bolton, Joel. "Police Help Safety Belt Use Hit Record Mark." *The Police Chief,* March 2006, p.70.

Chamard, Sharon. *Partnering with Businesses to Address Public Safety Problems.* Washington, DC: Office of Community Oriented Policing Services, Problem-Oriented Guides for Police, Problem-Specific Guides Series, No. 5, April, 2006.

Clawson, Heather J.; Layne, Mary; and Small, Kevonne. *Estimating Human Trafficking into the United States: Development of a Methodology.* Washington, DC: U.S. Department of Justice, September 2006.

Cohn, Jeffrey. "Keeping an Eye on School Security: The Iris Recognition Project in New Jersey Schools." *NIJ Journal,* July 2006.

Cordner, Gary. *People with Mental Illness.* Washington, DC: Office of Community Oriented Policing Services, Problem-Oriented Guides for Police, Problem-Specific Guides Series, No. 40, May 2006.

Dedel, Kelly. *Witness Intimidation.* Washington, DC: Office of Community Oriented Policing Services, Problem-Oriented Guides for Police, Problem-Specific Guides Series, No. 42, July 2006.

Dewey-Kollen, Janet. "Improving Drunk Driving Enforcement, Part One. *Law and Order,* May 2006a, pp.100–103.

Dewey-Kollen, Janet. "10 Ways to Improve DUI Enforcement." *Law and Order,* September 2006b, pp.10–17.

Domash, Shelly Feuer. "How to Crack Down on Street Racing." *Police,* June 2006, pp.30–35.

Eck, John E. "Preventing Crime at Places." In *Preventing Crime: What Works, What Doesn't, What's Promising: A Report to the United States Congress,* edited by Lawrence W. Sherman, Denise Gottfredson, Doris MacKenzie, John Eck, Peter Reuter and Shawn Bushway. www.ncjrs.org/works/index.htm.

Farrington, David P. "Explaining and Preventing Crime: The Globalization of Knowledge—The American Society of Criminology 1999 Presidential Address." *Criminology,* February 2000, pp.1–24.

Federal Trade Commission—2006 Identity Theft Survey Report. Washington, DC: Federal Trade Commission, November 2007.

"Glowing Fingerprints Plan Backed." BBC News, February 14, 2006.

Grimes, Katy. "The Deceit of Sacramento's 'Traffic Calming.'" *The Sacramento Union,* May 8, 2008.

"Human Trafficking." Washington DC: Federal Bureau of Investigation, June 12, 2006.

Lawrence, Randy. "Identity Theft: Info and Tactics for Fighting the Latest Crime of Choice." *Law Officer Magazine,* September 2006, pp.62–65.

"LAPD Uses Face Recognition Technology to Fight Crime." *Law Enforcement News,* July 26, 2006.

Majoras, Deborah Platt. "Combating Identity Theft: Partnerships Are Powerful." *The Police Chief,* February 2005, pp.14–15.

McFarlane, Diane. "Ontario's Tough New Street Racing Law." www.newsflavor.com

Mrazek, P.J. and Haggerty, R.J. editors. *Reducing Risks for Mental Disorders: Frontiers for Preventative Intervention Research.* Washington, DC: National Academy Press, 1994.

"New Research Reveals Historic 1990s US Crime Decline." EurekaAlert, operated by the American Association for the Advancement of Science (AAAS), February 16, 2007.

Newman, Graeme R. *Identity Theft.* Washington, DC: Office of Community Oriented Policing Services, Problem-Oriented Guides for Police, Problem-Specific Guides Series, No. 25, June 2004.

Phillips, Eric. *Crime Prevention through Environmental Design in the Bancroft Neighborhood.* http://freenet.msp.mn.us/org/npcr/reports/npcr1034/npcr1034.html.

Ratcliffe, Jerry. *Video Surveillance of Public Places.* Washington, DC: Office of Community Oriented Policing Services, Problem-Oriented Guides for Police, Problem-Specific Guides Series, No. 4, February 2006.

Ritter, Nancy. "Digital Evidence: How Law Enforcement Can Level the Playing Field with Criminals." *NIJ Journal,* July 2006.

Rosen, Marie Simonetti. *Chief Concerns: A Gathering Storm—Violent Crime in America.* Draft version. Washington, DC: Police Executive Research Forum, October 2006.

"Salt Lake and 9 Other Communities Get Grant to Identify and Prosecute Human Traffickers." *Desert News Publishing Company,* October 5, 2006.

Sampson, Rana. *Acquaintance Rape of College Students.* Washington, DC: Office of Community Oriented Policing Services, Problem-Oriented Guides for Police, Problem-Specific Guides Series, No. 17, August 2003.

Sampson, Rana. *Domestic Violence.* Washington, DC: Office of Community Oriented Policing Services, Problem-Oriented Guides for Police, Problem-Specific Guides Series, No. 45, January 2007.

Samuels, Adrienne. "It Could Be a Snap to Catch Red-Light Runners but Camera Idea Raises Privacy Issue." *The Boston Globe,* October 4, 2006.

Sanow, Ed. "Crime Hot Spots." *Law and Order,* September 2006, p.6.

Schwartz, Emma. "Crime Rates Shown to Be Falling. *U.S. News and World Report,* June 11, 2008

Scott, Michael S. *Robbery at Automated Teller Machines.* Washington, DC: Office of Community Oriented Policing Services, Problem-Oriented Guides for Police, Problem-Specific Guides Series, No. 8, September 14, 2001a.

Scott, Michael S. *Speeding in Residential Areas.* Washington, DC: Office of Community Oriented Policing Services, Problem-Oriented Guides for Police, Problem-Specific Guides Series, No. 3, August 14, 2001b.

Scott, Michael S. and Dedel, Kelly. *Assaults in and around Bars,* 2nd ed. Washington, DC: Office of Community Oriented Policing Services, Problem-Oriented Guides for Police, Problem-Specific Guides Series, No. 1, August 2006a.

Scott, Michael S. and Dedel, Kelly. *Street Prostitution.* 2nd ed. Washington, DC: Office of Community Oriented Policing Services, Problem-Oriented Guide for Police, Problem-Specific Guides Series, No. 2, August 6, 2006b.

Scott, Michael S. with Emerson, Nina J.; Antonacci, Louis B.; and Plant, Joel B. *Drunk Driving.* Washington, DC: Office of Community Oriented Policing Services, Problem-Oriented Guides for Police, Problem-Specific Guides Series, No. 36, February 2006.

Shader, Michael. *Risk Factors for Delinquency: An Overview.* Washington, DC: Office of Juvenile and Delinquency Prevention, no date.

Smith, Martha J. *Robbery of Taxi Drivers.* Washington, DC: Office of Community Oriented Policing Services, Problem-Oriented Guides for Police, Problem-Specific Guides Series, No. 34, March 2005.

Sweeney, Earl M. "Excessive Speed Causing Upward Trend in Traffic Fatalities." *The Police Chief,* September 2006, pp.62–64.

350 Tested Strategies to Prevent Crime: A Resource for Municipal Agencies and Community Groups. Washington, DC: National Crime Prevention Council, 1995.

Traffic Safety Facts 2006. Washington, DC: National Highway Traffic Safety Administration, 2006.

"Using Environmental Design to Prevent School Violence." Atlanta, GA: Centers for Disease Control, June 23, 2008.

Vargas, Theresa. "Street-Racing Deaths Hit Families, Communities." *Washington Post,* October 5, 2006.

Ward, Mark "Shoeprint Analysis to Fight Crime." BBC News, March 31, 2006.

Wilson, Deborah G.; Walsh, William F. and Kleuber, Sherilyn. "Trafficking in Human Beings: Training and Services among U.S. Law Enforcement Agencies." *Police Practice and Research,* Vol. 7, No. 2, 2006, p.149.

GLOSSARY

Number in parentheses indicates the chapter in which the term is introduced.

A

acculturation—A society takes in or assimilates other cultures. Also called *assimilation*. (6)

action research—Emphasizes full participation in the research by everyone directly affected by the process and results. (16)

ADA—The Americans with Disabilities Act of 1990. (6)

Alzheimer's disease (AD)—A progressive, irreversible and incurable brain disease with no known cause that affects four million elderly Americans; the classic symptom is memory loss. (6)

analysis (in SARA)—Examines the identified problem's causes, scope and effects; includes determining how often the problem occurs and how long it has been occurring, as well as conditions that appear to create the problem. (4)

assessment (in SARA)—Refers to evaluating how effective the intervention was; was the problem solved? (4)

assimilation—A society takes in or assimilates various other cultures to become a "melting pot." Also called *acculturation*. (6)

asymmetric warfare—Combat in which a weaker group attacks a superior group by not attacking the stronger adversary head on but rather attacking areas where the adversary least expects to be hit, causing great psychological shock and giving power to the powerless by destroying the stronger adversary's ability to use its conventional weapons. (15)

attention deficit hyperactivity disorder (ADHD)—A common disruptive behavior disorder characterized by heightened motor activity (fidgeting and squirming), short attention span, distractibility, impulsiveness and lack of self-control. (6)

B

bias—A prejudice that inhibits objectivity; can evolve into hate. (6)

bias crime—A criminal offense committed against a person, property or society that is motivated, in whole or in part, by an offender's bias against an individual's or group's race, religion, ethnic/national origin, gender, age, disability or sexual orientation. Also called *hate crime*. (14)

bias incident—Use of bigoted and prejudiced language; does not in itself violate hate crime laws. (14)

bifurcated society—The widening of the gap between those with wealth (the "haves") and those living in poverty (the "have nots"), with a shrinking middle class. (3)

binge drinking—Five or more drinks in a row during the previous 2 weeks. (11)

bowling alone—A metaphor referring to a striking decline in social, capital and civic engagement in the United States. (3)

broken window phenomenon—Suggests that if it appears no one cares about the community, as indicated by broken windows not being repaired, then disorder and crime will thrive. (3)

bullying—Name calling, fistfights, purposeful ostracism, extortion, character assassination, repeated physical attacks and sexual harassment. Also called *peer child abuse*. (12)

C

call management—Calls are prioritized based on the department's judgment about the emergency nature of the call (e.g., imminent harm to a person or a crime in progress), response time, need for backup and other local factors. Also called *call reduction*. (7)

call reduction—Calls are prioritized based on the department's judgment about the emergency nature of the call (e.g., imminent harm to a person or a crime in progress), response time, need for backup and other local factors. Also called *call management*. (7)

call stacking—A process a computer-aided dispatch system performs in which nonemergency, lower-priority calls are ranked and held or "stacked" so the higher priorities are continually dispatched first. (7)

change management—The development of an overall strategy to review the present state of an organization, envision the future state of the organization and devise a means of moving from one to the other. (5)

closed drug market—Dealers sell only to people they know or who are vouched for by other buyers. (11)

cocoon neighborhood watch—Focusing on only those living around at-risk places rather than an entire neighborhood. (10)

coercive isomorphism—Occurs when organizations adopt something due to pressure either from the state or other organizations. (16)

collaboration—Occurs when a number of agencies and individuals make a commitment to work together and contribute resources to obtain a common, long-term goal. (7)

communication process—Involves a sender, a message, a channel, a receiver and sometimes feedback. (6)

community—The specific geographic area served by a police department or law enforcement agency and the individuals, organizations and agencies within that area. (3)

community justice—An ethic that transforms the aim of the justice system into enhancing community life or sustaining communities. (3)

community mobilization—Includes improved communication and joint policy and program development among justice, community-based and grassroots organizations. (13)

community policing—A philosophy or orientation that emphasizes working proactively with citizens to reduce fear, solve crime-related problems and prevent crime. (1)

community relations—Efforts to interact and communicate with the community—team policing, community resource officers and school liaison officers. See also *public relations*. (1)

conditional threat—The type of threat often seen in extortion cases; warns that a violent act will happen unless certain demands or terms are met. (12)

conservative crime control—Comes down hard on crime; wages "war" on crime and drugs. (11)

contagion—Suggests that when offenders notice one criminal opportunity they often detect similar opportunities they have previously overlooked; crime then spreads; the broken window theory is an example. (10)

contagion effect—The media coverage of terrorism inspires more terrorism. (15)

CPTED—Crime Prevention through Environmental Design—altering the physical environment to enhance safety, reduce the incidence and fear of crime and improve the quality of life. (9)

crack children—Children who were exposed to cocaine while in the womb. (6)

crime-specific planning—Uses the principles of problem solving to focus on identified crime problems. (4)

crisis behavior—Results when a person has a temporary breakdown in coping skills; not the same as mental illness. (6)

critical mass—The smallest number of citizens and organizations needed to support and sustain the community policing initiative. (5)

D

DARE—Drug Abuse Resistance Education—a program aimed at elementary-age school children, seeking to teach them to "say no to drugs." (9)

decentralization—An operating principle that encourages flattening of the organization and places decision-making authority and autonomy at the level where information is plentiful, usually at the level of the patrol officer. (5)

deconfliction—Protocol or guidelines to avoid conflict. (15)

demographics—The characteristics of a human population or community. (3)

developmental assets—Forty ideals, experiences and qualities established by the Search Institute to "help young people make wise decisions, choose positive paths, and grow up competent, caring and responsible." (12)

diffusion—Occurs when criminals believe that the opportunity blocking of one type of criminal activity is also aimed at other types of criminal activity. (10)

direct threat—Identifies a specific act against a specific target and is delivered in a straightforward, clear and explicit manner. (12)

discretion—Freedom to make choices among possible courses of action or inaction, for example, to arrest or not arrest. (2)

displacement—The theory that successful implementation of a crime-reduction initiative does not really prevent crime; instead it just moves the crime to the next block. (3, 4)

diversion—Turning youths away from the criminal justice system, rerouting them to another agency or program. (3)

DOC model—Dilemmas-Options-Consequences— Challenges officers to carefully consider their decisions and the short- and long-term consequences of those decisions, with the goal of fusing problem solving and morality. (4)

E

EBD—Emotionally/behaviorally disturbed. (6)

effectiveness—Producing the desired result or goal; doing the right things. (4)

efficiency—Minimizing waste, expense or unnecessary effort; results in a high ratio of output to input; doing things right. (4)

empirical study—Research based on observation or practical experience. (9)

empowered—Granting authority and decision making to lower-level officers. (5)

ethnocentrism—The preference for one's own way of life over all others. (6)

experimental design—Research method involving the random assignment of individuals to experimental (treatment) and control (no treatment) conditions. (16)

F

fetal alcohol syndrome (FAS)—The leading known cause of mental retardation in the Western world; effects include impulsivity, inability to predict consequences or to use appropriate judgment in daily life, poor communication skills, high levels of activity, distractibility in small children and frustration and depression in adolescents. (6)

flat organization—Typical pyramid organization charts have the top pushed down and the sides expanded at the base. In a police department, it means fewer lieutenants and captains, fewer staff departments and fewer staff assistants but more sergeants and more patrol officers. (5)

formal power structure—Includes divisions of society with wealth and political influence: federal, state and local agencies and governments, commissions and regulatory agencies. (3)

frankpledge system—The Norman system requiring all freemen to swear loyalty to the king's law and to take responsibility for maintaining the local peace. (1)

G

gang—An organized group of people existing for some time with a special interest in using violence to achieve status. See also *street gang* and *youth gang*. (13)

gateway theory—Teaches that milder illicit drugs—such as marijuana—lead directly to experimentation with and an addiction to hard drugs such as crack cocaine and heroin. (11)

geographic profiling—A crime-mapping technique that takes the locations of past crimes and, using a complex mathematical algorithm, calculates probabilities of a suspect's residence. (4)

ghetto—An area of a city usually inhabited by individuals of the same race or ethnic background who live in poverty and apparent social disorganization. (3)

graffiti—Painting or writing on buildings, walls, bridges, bus stops and other available public surfaces; used by gangs to mark their turf. (13)

Guardian Angels—Private citizen patrols who seek to deter crime and to provide a positive role model for young children. (9)

gun interdiction—Local police direct intensive patrols to specific geographic areas with high rates of gun-related incidents of violence. (14)

H

hate crime—A criminal offense committed against a person, property or society that is motivated, in whole or in part, by an offender's bias against an individual's or group's race, religion, ethnic/national origin, gender, age, disability or sexual orientation. Also called *bias crime*. (14)

heterogeneous—Involving things (including people) that are unlike, dissimilar, different; the opposite of homogeneous. (3)

homogeneous—Involving things (including people) that are basically similar, alike; the opposite of heterogeneous. (3)

hot spots—Locations where most crimes occur. (4)

hue and cry—The summoning of all citizens within earshot to join in pursuing and capturing a wrongdoer. (1)

human relations—Efforts to relate to and understand other individuals or groups. (1)

I

impact evaluation—Determines if the problem declined. (4)

incident—An isolated event that requires a police response; the primary work unit in the professional model. (4)

incivilities—Occur when social control mechanisms have eroded and include unmowed lawns, piles of accumulated trash, graffiti, public drunkenness, fighting, prostitution, abandoned buildings and broken windows. (3)

indirect threat—Tends to be vague, unclear and ambiguous; the plan, the intended victim, the motivation and other aspects of the threat are masked or equivocal. (12)

informal power structure—Includes religious groups, wealthy subgroups, ethnic groups, political groups and public interest groups. (3)

interoperability—The compatibility of communication systems such as EMS, fire and rescue, and police and across levels of government. (15)

isomorphism—Similar in structural characteristics. Isomorphism results in a one-size-fits-all approach to community policing; in contrast to refraction. (16)

J

jargon—The technical language of a profession. (6)

jihad—Holy war. (15)

K

kinesics—The study of body movement or body language. (6)

L

leakage—Occurs when a student intentionally or unintentionally reveals clues to feelings, thoughts, fantasies, attitudes or intentions that may signal an impending violent act. (12)

least-effort principle—Concept proposing that criminals tend to commit acts of crimes within a comfort zone located near but not too close to their residence. (4)

liberal crime control—Emphasizes correctional policies and broader social reforms intended to expand opportunities for those "locked out" of the American dream; wages "war" on poverty and inequality of opportunity. (11)

Lucifer effect—the transformation of good people into evil ones. (2)

M

magnet phenomenon—Occurs when a phone number or address is associated with a crime simply because it was a convenient number or address to use. (4)

mediation—The intervention of a third party into an interpersonal dispute, where the third party helps disputants reach a resolution; often termed alternative dispute resolution (ADR). (4)

mimetic isomorphism—Occurs when an organization copies or imitates another. (16)

mission statement—A written declaration of purpose. (2)

moniker—A nickname, often of a gang member. (13)

N

negative contacts—Unpleasant interactions between the police and the public; may or may not relate to criminal activity. (2)

news media echo effect—The theory that the media have the power, through their coverage of isolated, high-profile cases, to influence the operations of the criminal justice system and even the disposition of individual cases. (8)

NIMBY syndrome—"Not in my backyard"; the idea that it is fine to have a halfway house—across town, not in my backyard. (3)

911 policing—Incident-driven, reactive policing. (2)

nonverbal communication—Includes everything other than the actual words spoken in a message, such as tone, pitch and pacing. (6)

normative isomorphism—Results from professionalism, with influences coming from other organizations involved in the same profession. (16)

O

open drug market—Dealers sell to all potential customers, eliminating only those suspected of being police or some other threat. (11)

opportunity blocking—Changes to make crime more difficult, risky, less rewarding or less excusable; one of the oldest forms of crime prevention. (10)

organizational development—A law enforcement strategy to address the gang problem, that includes special police units and special youth agency crisis programs. (13)

P

Pager Information Network (PIN)—A system to simultaneously notify all the media. (8)

PAL (Police Athletic League)—Developed to provide opportunities for youths to interact with police officers in gyms or ballparks instead of in a juvenile detention hall. (9)

paradigm—A model or a way of viewing a specific aspect of life such as politics, medicine, education and the criminal justice system. (1)

paradigm shift—A new way of thinking about a specific subject. (1)

participatory leadership—A management style in which each individual has a voice in decisions, but top management still has the ultimate decision-making authority. (5)

patronage system—Politicians rewarded those who voted for them with jobs or special privileges; prevalent during the political era. Also called the *spoils system.* (1)

peer child abuse—Another term for *bullying*— name calling, fistfights, purposeful ostracism, extortion, character assassination, repeated physical attacks and sexual harassment. (12)

perp walks—The police practice of parading suspects before the media, often simply for the publicity provided by news media coverage. (8)

place—A very small area reserved for a narrow range of functions, often controlled by a single owner and separated from the surrounding area. (10)

plea bargaining—A practice in which prosecutors charge a defendant with a less serious crime in exchange for a guilty plea, thus eliminating the time and expense of a trial. (3)

police culture—The informal values, beliefs and expectations passed on to newcomers in the department; may be at odds with the formal rules, regulations, procedures and role authority of managers. (2)

police–school liaison program—Places an officer in a school to work with school authorities, parents and students to prevent crime and antisocial behavior and to improve police–youth relationships. (9)

political era—Extended into the first quarter of the twentieth century and witnessed the formation of police departments. (1)

posttraumatic stress disorder (PTSD)—A persistent reexperiencing of a traumatic event through intrusive memories, dreams and a variety of anxiety-related symptoms. (6)

poverty syndrome—Includes inadequate housing, education and jobs and a resentment of those who control the social system. (6)

privatization—Using private security officers or agencies to provide services typically considered to be law enforcement functions. (3)

proactive—Anticipating problems and seeking solutions to those problems, as in community policing. The opposite of reactive. (1)

problem-oriented policing (POP)—A department-wide strategy aimed at solving persistent community problems by grouping incidents to identify problems and to determine possible underlying causes. (4)

problem-solving approach—Involves proactively identifying problems and making decisions about how best to deal with them. (4)

process evaluation—Determines if the response was implemented as planned. (4)

process mapping—A method of internal analysis that takes a horizontal view of a system, in contrast to the traditional vertical view; involves personnel at all levels and uses flowcharts to visually depict how information, materials and activities flow in an organization; how work is handed off from one unit or department to another; and how processes work currently and what changes should be made to attain a more ideal process flow. (14)

professional model—Emphasized crime control by preventive automobile patrol coupled with rapid response to calls. The predominant policing model used during the reform era (1970s and 1980s). (1)

progressive era—Emphasized preventive automobile patrol and rapid response to calls for service. Also called the *reform era.* (1)

PSAs—Public service announcements. (9)

psychopath—A category of violent individuals who tend to be socially inept loners, such as the "Trench Coat Mafia" kids. In contrast to a sociopath. (12)

public information officer (PIO)—An officer trained in public relations and assigned to disseminate information to the media, thereby providing accurate, consistent information while controlling leaks of confidential or inaccurate information and managing controversial or negative situations to the department's benefit. (8)

public relations—Efforts to enhance the police image. (1)

pulling levers—Refers to a multiagency law enforcement team imposing all available sanctions on gang members who violate established standards for behavior. (13)

Q

qualitative data—Examines the excellence (quality) of the response, that is, how satisfied were the officers and the citizens; most frequently determined by surveys, focus groups or tracking complaints and compliments. (4)

qualitative evaluations—Assessments that are more descriptive and less statistical; the opposite of quantitative evaluation. (9)

quantitative data—Examine the amount of change (quantity) as a result of the response; most frequently measured by before-and-after data. (4)

R

racial profiling—A form of discrimination that singles out people of racial or ethnic groups because of a belief that these groups are more likely than others to commit certain types of crimes. Race-based enforcement is illegal. (6)

random assignment—Dependence on a random number table or machine-generated random number that indicates the particular group to which an individual or entity will be assigned. Whether a person is a member of the treatment group or the control (no treatment) group is purely by chance. (16)

rave—A dance party with fast-paced electronic music, light shows and use of a wide variety of drugs and alcohol. (11)

reactive—Responding after the fact; responding to calls for service. The opposite of proactive. (1)

reform era—Emphasized preventive automobile patrol and rapid response to calls for service. Also called the *progressive era*. (1)

representing—A manner of dress to show allegiance or opposition to a gang; uses an imaginary line drawn vertically through the body. (13)

response (in SARA)—Acting to alleviate the problem, that is, selecting the alternative solution or solutions. (4)

restorative justice—Advocates a balanced approach to sentencing that involves offenders, victims, local communities and government to alleviate crime and violence and obtain peaceful communities. (3)

risk factor prevention paradigm—Seeks to identify key risk factors for offending and then implement prevention methods designed to counteract them. (10)

S

scanning (in SARA)—Refers to identifying recurring problems and prioritizing them to select one problem to address. (4)

selective enforcement—The use of police discretion, deciding to concentrate on specific crimes such as drug dealing and to downplay other crimes such as white-collar crime. (2)

social capital—Refers to the strength of a community's social fabric and includes the elements of trustworthiness (citizens' trust of each other and their public institutions) and obligations (expectation that service to each other will be reciprocated). Two levels of social capital are local (found among family members and citizens and their immediate, informal groups) and public (found in networks tying individuals to broader community institutions such as schools, civic organizations, churches and various levels of government, including the police). (3)

social contract—A legal theory that suggests that for everyone to receive justice, each person must relinquish some individual freedom. (3)

social intervention—Includes crisis intervention, treatment for youths and their families, outreach and referral to social services. (13)

social opportunities—Include providing basic or remedial education, training, work incentives and jobs for gang members. (13)

sociopath—A category of violent individuals usually characterized as bullies—outgoing and manipulative, instigating fights; a type of violent leader. In contrast to a psychopath. (12)

soundbites—Good, solid information stated briefly, that is, within 7 to 12 seconds. (8)

spoils system—Politicians rewarded those who voted for them with jobs or special privileges. Prevalent during the political era. Also called the *patronage system*. (1)

stakeholders—Those people who have an interest in what happens in a particular situation. (7)

stepping stone theory—Teaches that milder illicit drugs—such as marijuana—lead directly to experimentation with and an addiction to hard drugs such as crack cocaine and heroin. (11)

stereotyping—Assuming all people within a specific group are the same, lacking individuality. (6)

strategic planning—Long-term, large-scale, futuristic planning. (5)

straw purchasers—Weapons buyers fronting for people linked to illegal gun trafficking. (14)

street gang—A group of people whose allegiance is based on social needs and who engage in acts injurious to the public; the preferred term of most local law enforcement agencies. (13)

suppression—Includes tactics such as prevention, arrest, imprisonment, supervision and surveillance. (13)

symbiotic—Describes a relationship of mutual dependence upon each other. (8)

syndrome of crime—A group of signs, causes and symptoms that occur together to foster specific crimes. (3)

synergism—Occurs when individuals channel their energies toward a common purpose and accomplish what they could not accomplish alone. (10)

T

target hardening—Refers to making potential objectives of criminals more difficult to obtain through the use of improved locks, alarm systems and security cameras. (10)

tattling—Something done to get someone in trouble, in contrast to telling or reporting to keep someone safe. (12)

terrorism—The unlawful use of force or violence against persons or property to intimidate or coerce a government, the civilian population or any segment thereof, in furtherance of political or social objectives (FBI). (15)

thin blue line—The distancing of the police from the public they serve. (1)

tipping point—That point at which an ordinary, stable phenomenon can turn into a crisis. (3)

tithing—A group of 10 families. (1)

tithing system—The Anglo-Saxon principle establishing the principle of collective responsibility for maintaining local law and order. (1)

traffic calming—Describes a wide range of road and environmental design changes that either make it more difficult for a vehicle to speed or make drivers believe they should slow down for safety. (10)

transition management—Overseeing, controlling and leading the change from an organization's present state to its future state. (5)

TRIAD—A three-way partnership among the American Association of Retired Persons (AARP), the International Association of Chiefs of Police (IACP) and the National Sheriffs' Association (NSA) to address criminal victimization of older people. (7)

turf—Territory occupied by a gang, often marked by graffiti. (13)

two-wave survey—Study method where the first wave consists of a pretest before a strategy is implemented, and the second wave consists of a posttest after the strategy has been implemented for a given amount of time. (16)

V

veiled threat—One that strongly implies but does not explicitly threaten violence. (12)

vision—Intelligent foresight; starts with a mental image that gradually evolves from abstract musings to a concrete series of mission statements, goals and objectives. (5)

W

white flight—The departure of white families from neighborhoods experiencing racial integration or from cities experiencing school desegregation. (3)

working in "silos"—Agencies with common interests work independently with no collaboration. (7)

Y

youth gang—A subgroup of a street gang; may refer to a juvenile clique within a gang. (13)

Z

zeitgeist—The general intellectual, moral and cultural "spirit" of the times. (16)

zero tolerance—A policy of punishing all offenses severely, no matter how minor an offense may be. (12)

CPSIA information can be obtained
at www.ICGtesting.com
Printed in the USA
FFOW04n1241250318
46052481-46965FF

9 781111 524494